Frommer's

Philadelphia & the Amish Country

13th Edition

by Amy Donohue

Here's what the critics say about Frommer's:

"Amazingly easy to use. Very portable, very complete."

—Booklist

"Detailed, accurate, and easy-to-read information for all price ranges."
—Glamour Magazine

"Hotel information is close to encyclopedic."

—Des Moines Sunday Register

"Frommer's Guides have a way of giving you a real feel for a place."
—Knight Ridder Newspapers

WILEY

Wiley Publishing, Inc.

About the Author

Amy Donohue was born and raised in and around Philadelphia and has thus eaten her fair share of cheesesteaks and Amish pretzels. She is senior editor at *Philadelphia* magazine, where she edits and writes travel and lifestyle features and compiles the yearly "Best Of Philly" cover story every August. She has also written for *Town & Country*, *Time Out New York*, *Men's Health*, and *House Beautiful*, and recently wrote a guide to Philadelphia's suburban Main Line for *Four Seasons Hotel* magazine. She enjoys horseback riding in the gorgeous Chester and Bucks counties and is a proud season ticket holder at Citizens Bank Park.

Published by:

Wiley Publishing, Inc.

111 River St.
Hoboken, NJ 07030-5774

ISBN 0-7645-7561-9

Editor: Stephen Bassman
Production Editor: M. Faunette Johnston
Cartographer: Nick Trotter
Photo Editor: Richard Fox
Production by Wiley Indianapolis Composition Services

Front cover photo: Liberty Bell
Back cover photo: Amish buggy

For information on our other products and services or to obtain technical support, please contact our Customer Care Department within the U.S. at 800/762-2974, outside the U.S. at 317/572-3993 or fax 317/572-4002.

Wiley also publishes its books in a variety of electronic formats. Some content that appears in print may not be available in electronic formats.

Manufactured in the United States of America

5   4   3   2   1

Contents

List of Maps

An Invitation to the Reader

In researching this book, we discovered many wonderful places—hotels, restaurants, shops, and more. We're sure you'll find others. Please tell us about them, so we can share the information with your fellow travelers in upcoming editions. If you were disappointed with a recommendation, we'd love to know that, too. Please write to:

Frommer's Philadelphia & the Amish Country, 13th Edition
Wiley Publishing, Inc. • 111 River St. • Hoboken, NJ 07030-5774

An Additional Note

Please be advised that travel information is subject to change at any time—and this is especially true of prices. We therefore suggest that you write or call ahead for confirmation when making your travel plans. The authors, editors, and publisher cannot be held responsible for the experiences of readers while traveling. Your safety is important to us, however, so we encourage you to stay alert and be aware of your surroundings. Keep a close eye on cameras, purses, and wallets, all favorite targets of thieves and pickpockets.

Other Great Guides for Your Trip:

Frommer's Maryland & Delaware

Frommer's USA

Frommer's New England

Frommer's Exploring America by RV

Frommer's Unofficial Guide to the Best RV & Tent Campgrounds in the USA

Frommer's Star Ratings, Icons & Abbreviations

Every hotel, restaurant, and attraction listing in this guide has been ranked for quality, value, service, amenities, and special features using a **star-rating system.** In country, state, and regional guides, we also rate towns and regions to help you narrow down your choices and budget your time accordingly. Hotels and restaurants are rated on a scale of zero (recommended) to three stars (exceptional). Attractions, shopping, nightlife, towns, and regions are rated according to the following scale: zero stars (recommended), one star (highly recommended), two stars (very highly recommended), and three stars (must-see).

In addition to the star-rating system, we also use **seven feature icons** that point you to the great deals, in-the-know advice, and unique experiences that separate travelers from tourists. Throughout the book, look for:

Finds	Special finds—those places only insiders know about
Fun Fact	Fun facts—details that make travelers more informed and their trips more fun
Kids	Best bets for kids and advice for the whole family
Moments	Special moments—those experiences that memories are made of
Overrated	Places or experiences not worth your time or money
Tips	Insider tips—great ways to save time and money
Value	Great values—where to get the best deals

The following **abbreviations** are used for credit cards:

AE	American Express	DISC	Discover	V	Visa
DC	Diners Club	MC	MasterCard		

Frommers.com

Now that you have the guidebook to a great trip, visit our website at **www.frommers.com** for travel information on more than 3,000 destinations. With features updated regularly, we give you instant access to the most current trip-planning information available. At Frommers.com, you'll also find the best prices on airfares, accommodations, and car rentals—and you can even book travel online through our travel booking partners. At Frommers.com, you'll also find the following:

- Online updates to our most popular guidebooks
- Vacation sweepstakes and contest giveaways
- Newsletter highlighting the hottest travel trends
- Online travel message boards with featured travel discussions

What's New in Philadelphia

Founding father William Penn—who still hovers proudly above Center City Philadelphia in the form of a statue atop City Hall—would be astonished at the wealth of new restaurants, shops, and additions and renovations in Society Hill's historic district over the past few years. He'd love South Philly's two new sports stadiums, also. Here are some of the city's newest highlights:

PLANNING YOUR TRIP The Philadelphia International Airport has a new terminal: The sleek, glass-and-steel, ultramodern **Terminal A West** has 13 new wide-body international gates, 60 ticket counters, and 11 new restaurants.

ACCOMMODATIONS Philly's hotel-building boom of the 1990s has slowed, but the result is some 30,000 beds in the region, many of them being sold at deep discounts these days; even luxury properties offer incredibly affordable weekend deals. The most recently built hotel is the **Hyatt Regency Philadelphia at Penn's Landing,** 201 S. Columbus Blvd. (© 215/928-1234), on the Delaware waterfront, with Keating's Restaurant on the riverbank terrace and immediate access to I-95. See p. 73. The most spectacular rehab in the city is the **Ritz-Carlton Philadelphia,** 10 Avenue of the Arts (S. Broad St.; © 215/523-8000), in a historic bank with a 140-foot-high, grand domed lobby. See p. 81.

DINING Philadelphia is a wonderful dining city—it merits several mentions in *Gourmet's* America's Top Restaurants—and things have gotten even more fabulous over the past 5 years, with a crop of new glamour spots to lounge and nibble, as well as earthy, affordable BYOBs opening in many neighborhoods. Stephen Starr is the restaurateur behind many of the sexiest spots (see "Stephen Starr: Restaurateur Extraordinaire," p. 99), with 11 cool spots, including brand-new **Barclay Prime,** 237 S. 18th St. (© 215/732-7560), a mod steakhouse in a circa 1919 building on Rittenhouse Square, and **Washington Square,** 210 Washington Sq. (© 215/592-7787), the hipster hangout with the LA-style garden in warm months and the dark, intimate dining rooms and bar in the winter.

Lovers of modern French cuisine incorporating local Pennsylvania ingredients already know chef Jean-Marie Lacroix from his 2 decades at the Four Seasons Hotel Philadelphia. Now he has a gorgeous new haute-eatery, **Lacroix,** 210 W. Rittenhouse Sq. (© 215/790-2533), a few blocks away, inside the Rittenhouse Hotel. **Fork,** 306 Market St. (© 215/625-9425), the beloved Old City bistro, has expanded and added a light take-out menu in a gourmet shop next door. For a quick bite, with or without the kids, in a futuristic setting with a chic roof bar, **Continental Midtown,** 1801 Chestnut St. (© 215/567-1800), offers blue Naugahyde booths and glittery '70s inspired lighting, and great burgers and pad Thai. **Tria,** at 18th and Sansom (© 215/972-8742), is a pretty, small wine bar with modernist decor, inventive snacks, and an impressive selection of quirky wines, beers, and cheeses.

SIGHTSEEING The old is new again. The National Park Service has implemented a $130-million renovation plan, including the gleaming new interactive **Liberty Bell Pavilion,** Chestnut Street between 5th and 6th streets (© **215/965-2305**), where even at night the bell is visible through lofty glass walls, surrounded by beautiful walkways and landscaping. Within a block, the new glass-and-steel **National Constitution Center,** 525 Arch St. (© **215/409-6600**), provides an entertaining exploration of this amazing document, the root of America's achievements. The stretch of Broad Street south of City Hall has been renamed the **Avenue of the Arts,** and its crowning glory is the majestic glass-enclosed **Kimmel Center for the Performing Arts,** opened at Broad and Spruce streets in 2001 and joining the Academy of Music a block north as one of the nation's leading performing arts complexes (© **215/893-1999** for tickets). The **Philadelphia Museum of Art,** 26th Street and the Ben Franklin Parkway (© **215/763-8100**), has added a wonderful outdoor martini bar above the "Rocky Steps" for its popular Friday evening gallery hours.

For fans who make the journey to South Philadelphia for professional sports, the 66,000-seat **Lincoln Financial Field,** One Lincoln Financial Field Way (© **215/463-5500**), opened in the fall of 2003. See p. 158. The Phillies are justifiably proud of their intimate, modern **Citizens Bank Park** ball field, Broad Street at Pattison Avenue (© **215/463-1000**), seating 43,000, which opened in 2004 with wonderful local food vendors such as Tony Luke's steaks and Peace-a-Pizza, plus the rollicking McFadden's Pub. There are great views from every seat, plus city skyline views from many tiers. See p. 159.

SHOPPING The lack of tax on clothing here attracts shoppers, and the top news is yet more expansion in size and increased quality at the **King of Prussia Court and Plaza** (© **610/ 265-5727**), a 450-store behemoth near the junction of suburban routes 202 and I-276. It's got top national chain restaurants, movie theaters, and even simulated rock climbing for the kids. See p. 180. The **Old City** neighborhood, just north and east of Independence Hall, has become a mecca for contemporary and 20th-century crafts, art, and specialty services, and **Pine Street,** long known for antiques, now has some trendy new home stores, also. **Rittenhouse Row,** especially the stretch of Walnut Street just east of Rittenhouse Square, has an exciting new **Coach** store, **Zara** for European clothing at affordable prices, and a new location of **Jack Kellmer Jewelers** (p. 189).

AFTER DARK Look to the **Avenue of the Arts** as the local capital of classic performances. You'll find The Philadelphia Orchestra in the cello-shaped **Verizon Hall** of the **Kimmel Center** (© **215/893-1999**), p. 196, and great theater at the restored movie palace now known as the **Prince Music Theater,** 1412 Chestnut St. (© **215/972-1000**), p. 197. The blocks of **Old City** have cool lounges such as **32 Degrees,** 16 S. 2nd St. (© 215/627-3132), p. 207, where 2004's *Real World Philadelphia* cast hung out, or head uptown to the mod, Delano-hotel-style **Denim Lounge,** 1712 Walnut St. (© **215/ 735-6700**), p. 207.

1

The Best of Philadelphia

Here's a homework assignment before your visit to Philadelphia. Rent two quintessentially Philly movies: 1940's *The Philadelphia Story*, about a conservative, but lovable, upper-crust WASP family, and 1976's *Rocky*, with its affecting tale of a South Philly underdog-makes-good.

Yes, the city has changed since these were made—more nightlife, more sophistication, more lobster-wasabi spring rolls, more political scandals—but *not all that much*. Both movies are beloved by Philadelphians, because they're Hollywood-ized but accurate reflections of our glamour and our grit. And we wouldn't have it any other way.

You can see the contrasts if you walk Center City for just one long afternoon: You'll pass beneath manicured trees and impeccable brownstones near Rittenhouse Square, and then find yourself 30 minutes later, ordering dim sum at a tiny, noisy Chinatown lunch counter. Philly is the wide, graceful sweep of the Benjamin Franklin Parkway, punctuated by the massive, neoclassical Philadelphia Museum of Art at one end, and ornate, French-inspired City Hall at the other; it's also the gritty streets of South Philly's Italian Market, where live chickens squawk (in terror!), and fresh sausages sizzle on a corner grill wafting aromas that would convert a PETA-registered vegan.

Philadelphians might take historical attractions a bit for granted, but we're secretly very proud of them. The new Liberty Bell Pavilion in Independence National Historical Park, with its glass walls and exquisite lighting that glows around the bell at night? We love it. The National Constitution Center, modern, in steel and limestone? We think it's cool, and visited as soon as it opened. The surrounding hills of Bucks County and the Amish Country? We can't wait for summer, when we tube down the rivers, browse for antiques, and watch our children milk a cow.

Once known as a town of nightlife extremes—either stuffy piano bars or shot-and-a-beer joints—Philly now offers a full range of hip after-dark options, and even has the imprimatur of cool as the site of last year's *Real World* on MTV. We now sip "hypnotinis" at Old City lounges, pose at Stephen Starr's gorgeous Striped Bass bar, and dance at the cool gay lounge Bump. Philly's favorite new place to spend a summer night, though, is in a seat at the new Citizen's Bank Park, watching the Phils win (or lose), gazing at the skyline spectacularly framed by the bleachers.

One funny thing about Philadelphians: We never leave. Almost everyone you meet was born here, got married here, might have lived in Los Angeles for one sunny year—but came back to our city, which is so familiar and beautiful, whether draped in snow or glowing with cherry blossoms. You should also know that we do eat cheesesteaks; we fight the urge as much as possible, but there's nothing to beat down an incipient hangover like one of these foot-long, grease-dripping, Cheez Whiz–smothered babies. They're best eaten at 3am, and that's why Pat's and Geno's Steaks both stay open 24 hours a day.

The Eastern Seaboard

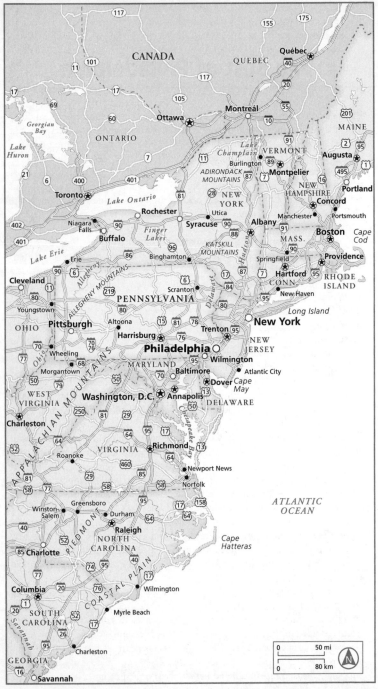

1 Frommer's Favorite Philadelphia Experiences

- **Taking Afternoon Tea at the Swann Lounge:** The quintessential luxury tea is found at the Four Seasons, overlooking Alexander Calder's Swann Fountain, one of the city's most beautiful works of art, and the wide, stately Benjamin Franklin Parkway. See p. 79.

- **Visiting the Barnes Foundation:** The Barnes Foundation Gallery in Merion houses the most important private collection of Impressionist and early French modern paintings in the world, displaying more Cézannes than all the museums of France put together. The museum is in the midst of litigation over whether to relocate to downtown Philadelphia (against the wishes of the foundation's deceased founder), so you must schedule a visit several months in advance around its open hours from Friday to Sunday (or Wed–Fri in the summertime). See p. 128.

- **Wandering Through Fairmount Park:** It would take dozens of outings to fully explore the 100 miles of trails in this 8,900-acre giant of an urban park—some of them are virtually unchanged since Revolutionary times. We'll settle for gazing at the hundreds of flame azaleas that bloom behind the Art Museum in spring, and the dozen Georgian country mansions, kept in immaculate condition, that pepper the park. See p. 149.

- **Shopping on First Friday:** On the first Friday of every month, the galleries, stores, and studios of Old City—just north of Independence National Historical Park—remain open with refreshments and artists on hand until 9pm. Wander along the cobblestone streets, stopping into one of the many coffee bars or bistros. See p. 181.

- **Stepping Back in Time in Historic Philadelphia:** Everyone knows about the miraculous reclamation of this country's Colonial capital, from work on the Liberty Bell to renovation on hundreds of row houses with their distinctive brickwork and 18th-century formal gardens (and welcoming benches). But the new tours (especially the nighttime "Lights of Liberty" show, p. 127), the costumed town criers with free maps, and the Revolutionary War–era street theater bring the experience even closer. Just wander; they'll find you. See "Independence National Historical Park: America's Most Historic Square Mile," in chapter 7.

- **Snacking on Pretzels, Hoagies, and Philly's Famous Cheesesteaks:** Philadelphia has a rich tradition of cuisine from haute (as in the shad roe from fish caught in the Delaware River each Apr) to hot (the warm, soft, salty pretzels served slathered with mustard at stands all over town). The hoagie is something else—cold cuts, lettuce, and onions layered with oil and vinegar—along with its cousin the cheesesteak, also served on an enormous elongated bun. See "Local Favorites: Cheesesteaks, Hoagies & More," in chapter 6.

- **Strolling Around Independence Square at Night:** The combination of history, elegance, and proportion among the three main buildings that contained America's first government always induces a sense of wonder at this country's good fortune in its founding citizens. You might even feel the urge to jump aboard one of the horse-drawn carriages lined up nearby. See "Independence National Historical Park: America's Most Historic Square Mile," p. 120.

- **Enjoying the Lights at Night:** The William Penn statue atop City Hall, the Ben Franklin Bridge, and

> **Fun Fact A Central City**
>
> Thirty-eight percent of the nation's population lives within a 4½-hour drive from Philadelphia.

seven Schuylkill River bridges are permanently lighted, joining the beautiful white pin lights that outline the boathouses along the Schuylkill River.

- **Touring an Open House:** If you're in the city at the right time, don't miss the tours of restored mansions in Society Hill, Rittenhouse Square, or Fairmount Park for a delightful lesson in Colonial-era interior design and Americana. The open houses are scattered throughout the year, but during the pre-Christmas season, with their period decorations, they are especially lovely. See the "Philadelphia Calendar of Events," in chapter 2.

- **Breathing Deeply at the Philadelphia Flower Show:** In early March, the Flower Show—the largest and most prestigious indoor exhibition of its kind in the world—descends on the Pennsylvania Convention Center, with acres of orchids and traditional and exotic displays. See p. 135.

- **Exploring the Philadelphia Museum of Art:** It has a stupendous collection of masterpieces, period rooms, and crafts, and is becoming one of the hottest museums in the country for special exhibitions. Look for more blockbusters like the recent van Gogh and the mid-1990s Cézanne exhibitions. Wednesday and Friday evening hours have become convivial social scenes, with cocktails and live music. See p. 129.

- **Cheering the Regattas Along the Schuylkill:** On any spring weekend, stand along Boathouse Row just north of the Philadelphia Museum of Art, and get ready to cheer. Crews race each other every 5 minutes or so, with friends along the riverbanks rooting them on. See p. 150.

- **Stocking Up at the Reading Terminal Market:** From Bassett's ice cream to the food of the 12th Street Cantina, this is a century-old mother lode of unpackaged, fresh, honest-to-goodness provisions. Amish farmers come every Thursday through Saturday to sell their custards and scrapple (a breakfast meat of herbed pork blended with cornmeal and fried before serving). And what could be more convenient than the market's location right underneath the Convention Center? See p. 104.

- **Exploring South Philly:** Exuberant attitude punctuates every interchange you'll have, whether on a stroll (with ample tastings) through the Italian Market or wandering farther south to seek out the area's great pizzas, cannoli, or famed cheesesteaks. See "South Street: The Hippest Street in Town (Sort Of)," p. 205.

- **Dining on Walnut Street:** Walnut Street near Rittenhouse Square has a confluence of world-class restaurants within mere feet of each other, including **Le Bec-Fin** (p. 99), **Pasion!** (p. 102), **Striped Bass** (p. 102), **Brasserie Perrier** (p. 101), **Susanna Foo** (p. 104), and **Alma de Cuba** (p. 100). Whatever your taste or price range, you should try one of them.

- **Catching a Phillies Game at the New Ball Park:** A summer night at the new Citizens Bank Park means great views from every seat in this old-fashioned-style stadium, with its amazing local foods such as Tony Luke's cheesesteaks. If you sit on the third level, you'll also see a perfectly framed view of the Center City skyline. See p. 158.

- **Taking in the Mummer's Parade:** Grown men dancing in feathers, sequins, and spandex mark the annual New Year's Day Mummers Parade (**www.mummers.com**), in which thousands strut their way up Broad Street. The music is loud and antiquated, but the experience is festive and fun, with live music at the Convention Center. See p. 135.

2 Best Hotel Bets

- **Best Historic Hotel:** Well, it's only the "lite" version of what it used to be, when Thomas Edison designed the fixtures and the ballroom defined swank. But the top floor of the **Park Hyatt Philadelphia at the Bellevue,** Broad and Walnut streets, or 1415 Chancellor Court, between Walnut and Locust streets (© **800/223-1234**), with its Library Lounge bar and pastel-painted, domed Barrymore tea room, carries traces of a century's worth of history. See p. 79.
- **Best for Business Travelers: Hotel Sofitel,** 120 S. 17th St. (© **800/SOFITEL**), is one of the upscale chain with a French accent. Philly Sofitel's location is incredibly convenient, and the rooms are large and elegant, with easy access to plugs and modem jacks at a handsome desk. You'll find personal voice mail, also. The service staff is efficient and courteous. See p. 79.
- **Best for a Romantic Getaway:** The **Penn's View Hotel,** Front and Market streets (© **800/331-7634**), feels like an exquisite club, with views over the Delaware River. And how could you not like what the *New York Times* hails as "the mother of all wine bars" downstairs? See p. 77.
- **Best Hotel Lobby for Pretending You're Rich:** There's no place like the cool, plush **Four Seasons Hotel,** 1 Logan Sq. (© **800/332-3442**), for rubbing elbows with the moneyed elite (it's also a great place to stay if you *are* the moneyed elite). The Swann Lounge overlooking Logan Circle is a constant stream of chic outfits, custom suits, and the frequent black tie. See p. 78.
- **Best for Families: The Hilton Inn at Penn,** in West Philadelphia at 3600 Sansom St. (© **800/445-8667**), is a cross-town ride from the historical sights, but offers the whole family space to roam among spacious corridors, ever-present fruit to munch on and tea to sip in a comfortable library lounge, plus TV for children to watch while parents exercise. Also, the campus of U. Penn across the street is perfect for throwing a Frisbee or playing tag. See p. 87. Slightly tattered but more moderately priced is the **Embassy Suites Center City,** 1776 Benjamin Franklin Pkwy. at Logan Square (© **800/362-2779**), with cute little open-air balconies (yes, the railings are sturdy), and an opulent buffet breakfast at the TGI Friday's at street level. It's 5 minutes to the premier children's museums and Logan Circle. And all the rooms are suites, so parents can have their privacy. See p. 82.
- **Best Moderately Priced Hotel:** The **Hotel Windsor,** 1700 Benjamin Franklin Pkwy. near Rittenhouse Square and City Hall (© **877/784-8379**), is the best

choice in its price range. A one-room suite with two double beds and full kitchen goes for $139. A generous continental breakfast is included in the rate. See p. 83.

- **Best B&B:** Many, many more B&Bs are listed through **A Bed & Breakfast Connection/Bed & Breakfast of Philadelphia** (p. 73) than are listed independently. A favorite among the latter is **Shippen Way Inn,** 418 Bainbridge St. (© **800/245-4873** or 215/627-7266), which has nine rooms in two Queen Village row houses built around 1750 and lovingly maintained. You might also try **Ten Eleven Clinton,** 1011 Clinton St. (© **215/923-8144**), an elegant 1836 Federal town house on a quiet tree-lined street. See the "Historic Bed & Breakfasts" box on p. 78 for more on both.

- **Best Service:** The training process for every employee of the **Ritz-Carlton** hotels is legendary, and the staff at the hotel at 10 Avenue of the Arts (© **800/241-3333**) is no exception. Guests pay top prices (though weekend packages are actually quite affordable) to be pampered. It's a fantasyland of amenities; service attendants earn points for thinking of extras like both foam and down pillows in the closets and bookmarks in the *TV Guide*s. See p. 81.

- **Best Hotel for Historic District Hopping:** If you're here to see Independence Park, why not wake up looking at it through the floral chintz curtains at the **Omni Hotel at Independence Park,** 4th and Chestnut streets (© **800/843-6664**)? All 150 guest rooms have views of the Greek Revival Second Bank of the U.S. and a half-dozen of America's Georgian jewels. And the clip-clopping of horses and carriages below maintains the sense of history. See p. 76.

- **Best Hotel Health Club:** The **Wyndham Philadelphia at Franklin Plaza,** 17th and Race streets (© **800/996-3426**), with 758 rooms—second only in quantity to the Convention Center Marriott—has the best facilities for hotel guests, including a 45-foot indoor pool, a track, three racquetball courts, three squash courts, outdoor handball, and two tennis courts—all on the third-floor lobby roof. Weights and Nautilus machines round out the picture inside. See p. 85.

- **Best Hotel Pool:** Above the garage complex of the **Park Hyatt Philadelphia at the Bellevue** (see "Best Historic Hotel," above) is the Sporting Club, with its four-lane, junior Olympic pool. Hotel guests and local members can use the pool and the other 2 acres of health facilities, or you can pay $20 for a 1-day pass to the club. See p. 79. The **Four Seasons Hotel**'s indoor pool at 1 Logan Sq. (© **800/332-3442**) is smaller, but is absolutely spectacular for laps or lounging. See p. 78.

- **Best Views:** Many of the hotel listings in chapter 5 specify one side or another as preferable. In Center City, rooms at the **Rittenhouse Hotel,** 210 W. Rittenhouse Sq. (© **800/635-1042**), all have wonderful views of the Philly landscape, from the leafy park below on the east to the western view of the Schuylkill and the Parkway. See p. 80. The new **Hyatt Regency Philadelphia at Penn's Landing,** on the Delaware River waterfront at 201 S. Columbus Blvd. (© **800/228-1234**), commands spectacular views of Center City to the west and Camden to the east. See p. 73.

- **Best Hotel Restaurants:** The Zagat guide to local restaurants has listed the **Fountain Restaurant** in the **Four Seasons** (see "Best Hotel Lobby for Pretending You're Rich," above) as one of the country's top 50 dining spots. Recently refurbished, it is virtually flawless, with high prices to match the high quality. It now has a worthy rival in the **Rittenhouse Hotel**'s restaurant **Lacroix,** opened in 2003 by Jean-Marie Lacroix, for 2 decades the chef at the Fountain. This haute-meets-modern French restaurant is soothing and sleek, with park views, limestone accents, and elegant green-velvet seating; it has received great acclaim from *Esquire*'s John Mariani, among others. See p. 99.

- **Best Splurge Hotel: The Ritz-Carlton Philadelphia,** 10 Avenue of the Arts (© **215/523-8000**), is an overwhelming dose of luxury, with its massive domed lobby,

lavish furnishings, and clubby bars. Upgrade to the Club Level for less than $50 and experience a lounge spread of champagne and endless hors d'oeuvres. See p. 81.
- **Best Trendy Hotel:** Philly's luxuriously hip **Hotel Sofitel,** 120 S. 17th St. (© **800/SOFITEL**), has modern decor, a groovy long bar, and lots of French people swanning in and out frequently, plus Deco-contemporary furniture and a great location for shopping near Walnut Street. See p. 79.
- **Best Hostel:** Centrally located near all the historical and nightlife attractions, the **Bank Street Hostel,** 32 S. Bank St. (© **800/392-4678** or 215/922-0222), is smack in the Old City/Society Hill nexus; it's perfect for budget or adventurous travelers. See p. 90.

3 Best Restaurant Bets

- **Best Spot for a Romantic Dinner:** The appropriately named **Pasion!,** 211 S. 15th St. (© **215/875-9895**), recently doubled in size but kept its intimate, glowing ambience, along with its terrific South American fusion cuisine. Warm and exotic. See p. 102.
- **Best Spot for a Business Lunch: Lacroix** at the Rittenhouse Hotel, 210 W. Rittenhouse Sq. (© **215/546-9000**), offers a three-course, $26 prix-fixe lunch that is stunningly good in its ethereal but unstuffy dining room. Your dining partners will be the city's power brokers, and the menu of the day might include ragout of lobster and white asparagus or a delightful spring lamb shank with parsley and lemon. See p. 99.
- **Best Spot for a Celebration:** If you have a special occasion to celebrate—even if it's just being in Philadelphia—the newly redecorated **Le Bec-Fin,** 1523 Walnut

St. (© **215/567-1000**), is the proper choice if you crave a lavish setting. Georges Perrier's prix-fixe menu has an international reputation, and those dessert carts are unforgettable. Advance reservations are a must. See p. 99.
- **Best Decor:** Chic, elegant and modern, there is no more beautiful dining space in Philly than **Striped Bass** at 1500 Walnut St. (© **215/732-4444**), the new American restaurant in a turn-of-the-20th-century brokerage house. Its triple-height ceiling, marble columns, velvet banquettes, retro-glittery light fixtures, and intimate bar define good style in Philadelphia. See p. 102.
- **Best View:** Sitting on the deck of the **Moshulu,** 411 S. Columbus Blvd. (© **215/923-2500**), a 1904 "tall ship" that's been converted into a roomy, luxe French-Asian restaurant, might sound touristy, but in reality, it's utterly delightful.

Even in the winter, the ship's indoor dining rooms offer lovely Delaware River and Society Hill views. And in summer, the breeze is as cooling as one of its 20 wines by the glass.

- **Best Wine List:** Two restaurants owned by the Sena family offer impressive wine selections: **La Famiglia,** 8 S. Front St. (© 215/922-2803), p. 93, has one of the finest cellars in the world according to *Wine Spectator* magazine. One block north, the **Ristorante Panorama** (© 215/922-7800), p. 97, in the Penn's View Inn at Front and Market streets (© 215/922-7800), p. 77, is a charming Italian trattoria that has the largest single wine-dispensing and -preserving machine in the world, with 120 different bottles available by the glass, or as a 3-oz. "taste." Order a "flight"—five glasses grouped around a theme. Flights fall in the $14 to $50 range.

- **Best Value:** Dining at the mod-Deco bar at **Brasserie Perrier** at 1619 Walnut St. (© 215/568-3000), with its $16 steak frites or incomparable roasted chicken (also $16), means you're savoring cuisine overseen by the city's most famous chef, Georges Perrier of Le Bec-Fin. The restaurant behind this colorful lounge offers haute-bistro food at higher prices, with entrees in the $35 range. See p. 101.

- **Best Value, Fixed-Price Meal:** There's nothing like **Le Bec-Fin**'s $45 lunch at 1523 Walnut St. (© 215/567-1000), for classic French. See p. 99.

- **Best for Kids:** Kids love the burgers, grilled cheeses, soups, and other classic American fare at **Marathon Grill,** 1839 Spruce St. (© 215/731-0800), a former diner turned into a stylish modern space that serves breakfast, lunch, and dinner (plus snacks all afternoon). Parents also love the casual, romping-permitted vibe of the place, plus the full bar and upscale side of the menu, with its grilled fish and savory pastas. See p. 108.

- **Best Date Restaurant:** For a classy bistro with contemporary fare in Old City, reserve a deuce at **Fork,** 306 Market St. (© 215/625-9425). See p. 97. **Friday Saturday Sunday,** 261 S. 21st St. (© 215/546-4232), has been a classic, intimate date spot since the 1970s, and boasts consistent fare, glowing lighting, and great value. See p. 101.

- **Best American Cuisine:** Using local ingredients from Amish and Bucks Country boutique farmers, incorporating elements of new American cuisine without the annoying flourishes, **Fork** at 306 Market St. (© 215/625-9425) is as popular for brunch as it is for a late-night snack. In this warm, sophisticated dining room in a former warehouse, dine on pan-seared salmon or spicy hanger steak. See p. 97.

- **Best Chinese Cuisine:** A reserved former librarian, born in inner Mongolia and raised in northern China and Taiwan, Susanna Foo quietly built up a national reputation with her eponymous **Susanna Foo,** 1512 Walnut St. (© 215/545-2666). Her innovative mix of East and West relies on reductions rather than on dashes of soy sauce and ginger, and skillets and saucepans rather than a wok. The dim sum—appetizer-size portions—is a city favorite. See p. 104.

- **Best Continental Cuisine:** The **Fountain Restaurant** at the Four Seasons Hotel, 1 Logan Sq., between 18th Street and Franklin Parkway (© 215/963-1500), is consistently rated best in town for understated, complex versions of classic Continental dishes. Since the food is so uniformly excellent, my advice is to go with the chef's choices on the fixed-price menu. See p. 98.

- **Best French Cuisine:** Right now, it's the serene **Lacroix** in the Rittenhouse Hotel, where the exquisite menu is rooted in classical French cooking, but benefits from Chef Jean-Marie Lacroix's modern technique. See p. 99.
- **Best Italian Cuisine:** Philadelphia must have 1,000 Italian restaurants, but the **Saloon,** 750 S. 7th St. (© 215/627-1811), is a dignified, elegant place for fine pasta and steak that draws everyone in town sooner or later. See p. 108.
- **Best Seafood:** The best in town is **Striped Bass,** 1500 Walnut St. (© 215/732-4444), located on the most chic dining block in the city. The dinner scene in *The Sixth Sense* was filmed here. See p. 102. For those on a budget, Philly's **McCormick & Schmick's,** 1 S. Broad St. (© 215/568-6888), part of a chain of seafood restaurants, serves fresh fish at affordable prices, in a clubby environment. See p. 102.
- **Best Steakhouse:** With a half-dozen great choices, including the Capital Grille and the Palm, the top choice is the **Prime Rib,** 1701 Locust St. (© 215/772-1701), offering great porterhouse served with fresh shredded horseradish. The ambience is a timeless 1940s-style place—jazz combos and formally clad waiters included. See p. 102.
- **Best Burgers and Beer:** In this case, bigger is better. The **Independence Brew Pub,** at 1150 Filbert St., right under Reading Terminal Headhouse (© 215/922-4292), has hundreds of seats, all happily occupied with diners chowing on delicious thin-crust pizzas and

spectacular sundaes. An on-site brewery produces five different ales, porters, and lagers fresh each day. No reservations for parties under six. See p. 107.

- **Best Pizza: Marra's,** 1734 E. Passyunk Ave., between Morris and Moore streets (© 215/463-9249), in South Philadelphia, has pies with thin crusts and delicious, spicy traditional toppings, baked in brick ovens; enjoy them in old wooden booths. See p. 109.
- **Best Cheesesteak:** A great cheesesteak achieves a certain balance between cheese, meat, onion, and roll, and **Jim's Steaks,** 400 South St. (© 215/928-1911), cooks up a mighty, meaty combo. Line up with the masses on South Street and be sure to specify "with" or "without" onions. See listing on p. 114 and the "Ultimate Cheesesteak Taste Test" box on p. 116.
- **Best Hoagies:** Also known as submarines, grinders, or torpedoes, hoagies are what you want on hand as you cheer on the Eagles' latest Super Bowl bid. South Philly's **Primo Hoagies,** 2043 Chestnut St. (© 215/564-1264), have the perfect ratio of dense, chewy roll, spicy meat, wonderful oregano, and oil.
- **Best Desserts:** Weekends, the **Ritz-Carlton Hotel,** 10 Avenue of the Arts (© 215/523-8000), offers a dessert buffet in its grand lobby, and this wonderfully excessive spread of 40 desserts has become a popular way to end a Friday or Saturday evening downtown (8pm–midnight). Priced at $19 per person, you may want to skip dinner altogether and save stomach space for tarte Tatin and chocolate gâteau. See p. 81.
- **Best Breakfast:** The **Down Home Diner** at Reading Terminal Market (© 215/627-1955), open from 7am, has wonderful blueberry

pancakes, fresh eggs with garlic grits, and a breakfast "pizza" with sausage biscuits, smoked cheddar, and tomato. All ingredients are fanatically organic, from small-scale producers wherever possible. Lunch has its charms, too, with meatloaf, black-eyed pea and ham-hock soup, and pecan pie. The vintage jukebox plays great old American tunes.

- **Best Brunch:** Nearly every restaurant offers Sunday brunch, ranging from standard bagels with spreads to a full brunch menu. The **White Dog Café,** 3420 Sansom St. (© **215/386-9224**), in West Philadelphia, swings both ways, offering everything from simple breakfast dishes to elaborate late-morning feasts in a completely comfortable, unpretentious environment. See p. 109.

- **Best People-Watching:** Beautiful types head to **Washington Square,** 210 W. Washington Sq. (© **215/592-7787**), the sophisticated American restaurant and bar in an Art Deco landmark building, with an outdoor area of tables and banquettes next to a leafy park. **Rouge,** at 205 S. 18th St. (© **215/732-6622**), is a bistro with alfresco cafe tables that become the city's most sought-after real estate from May through September. If you want to spot a celebrity (Cameron Diaz and Mel Gibson both dined here), head for another of the Stephen Starr–owned operations such as **Buddakan,** 325 Chestnut St. (© **215/574-9440**), where a huge gilded Buddha presides over a trendy crowd. See p. 93.

- **Best Afternoon Tea:** The advent of true luxury hotels in Philadelphia has brought with it exquisite afternoon teas served all over town. The Cassatt Lounge at the **Rittenhouse Hotel,** 210 W. Rittenhouse

Sq. (© **215/546-9000**), has muted, lovely decor, a tucked-in garden, and Mary Cassatt's drawings commemorating her brother's house, which once stood on the site. See p. 80.

- **Best for Pretheater Dinner:** At sleek **Bliss,** 220 S. Broad St. (© **215/731-1100**), the eclectic menu features pastas, Asian-inspired dishes, and grilled fare; it is next door to the Kimmel Center and the Merriam. **Ernesto's 1521 Café,** 1521 Spruce St. (© **215/546-1521**), is an affordable, modern Italian trattoria with handmade pasta. See p. 106 and 106 respectively.

- **Best Outdoor Dining:** In Center City, head for 18th Street along Rittenhouse Square, between Walnut and Locust streets: Anywhere you park among **Devon Seafood Grill, Rouge** (p. 103), or **Potcheen** and **Bleu** (both at the Sheraton Rittenhouse Square, p. 85) on that block is great, with Bleu serving the best cuisine.

- **Best Late-Night Dining:** When it's after midnight, I head for Chinatown. **Shiao Lan Kung,** 930 Race St. (© **215/928-0282**), while not very impressive in its decor, has wonderful hot pot dishes, and you can order fresh sea bass from the tank.

- **Best Ice Cream: Bassett's Ice Cream** (© **215/925-4315**), an original 1892 tenant of Reading Terminal Market, has long claimed supremacy for its rich, smooth flavors. Plus they make a terrific milkshake. New **Capogira Gelateria** at 109 S. 13th St. (© **215/351-0900**) hand-makes irresistibly rich Italian gelato in exotic flavors such as Mexican chocolate with chipotle peppers. See p. 104 for a description of Reading Terminal Market.

2

Planning Your Trip to Philadelphia

This chapter tackles the hows of your trip to Philadelphia—those issues required to get your trip together and get on the road, whether you're a frequent traveler or a first-timer.

1 Visitor Information

TOURIST OFFICE The Independence Visitor Center, 6th and Market streets, Philadelphia, PA 19107 (© 800/537-7676, 215/965-7676, or 215/636-1666), opened in late 2001 as a collaboration between public and private sectors, is a great one-stop introductory destination. It offers a wealth of publications, from seasonal calendars of events to maps for the city and region, along with a cafe, book and gift shop, and a first-class exhibition on Philadelphia's place in history.

Knowledgeable volunteers staff the phones and counters. Definitely ask for the "Official Visitors Guide," a seasonal compendium of exhibitions, events, and the like. The Center also offers an increasing number of package tours combining special museum exhibitions, concerts, or sporting events with discount hotel prices, free city transit passes, and Amtrak discounts. Once you're in town, note that many bus tours, historic trolley rides, and walking tours start from here.

Tips **Destination: Philadelphia—Red Alert Checklist**

- Did you book in advance? If you're planning on going to a popular restaurant or theatrical event you'll need to reserve in advance. Many attractions in the historic district have increased security and also require that you book a time slot, and museums such as the **Barnes Foundation** (p. 128) have limited attendance, so call ahead.
- Did you confirm the hours of operation? Many scheduled tours, festivals, and special events change regularly, so call ahead for opening and closing hours.
- Did you bring your ID cards that could entitle you to discounts (AAA and AARP cards, student IDs, and so on)?
- Did you bring emergency drug prescriptions and extra glasses and/or contact lenses?
- Do you have your credit card PINs?
- If you have an e-ticket, do you have documentation?
- Did you leave a copy of your itinerary with someone at home?

WEBSITES For the growing number of visitors who have access to the Internet, there are a number of websites that you'll find helpful. The Independence Visitor Center site is at www.independencevisitorcenter.com. Other sites include: www.digitalcity.com/philadelphia, which contains a great deal of user feedback and opinions along with excellent and pithy summaries of events, sights, and restaurants; www.gophila.com, run by the city's tourism marketing bureau and very up-to-date; the private www.phillyvisitor.com, driven by paid advertisers and hotlinks; www.cityspin.com/Philadelphia; and http://philadelphia.citysearch.com. For the latest in city events and hot topics, visit www.phillymag.com, the website of the city's most upscale and informed publication, *Philadelphia* magazine. (Full disclosure: I'm a senior editor at *Philadelphia*.)

2 Money

Except for truly deluxe experiences, you will find moderate prices in Philadelphia—less than those in New York and on a par with those in Washington, D.C.

Minimal cash is required, since credit cards are accepted universally and ATMs linked to national networks are strewn around the airport, tourist destinations, and increasingly within hotels. It's a good idea to exchange at least some money—just enough to cover airport incidentals and transportation to your hotel—before you leave home, so you can avoid the less-favorable rates you'll get at airport currency exchange desks. Check with your local American Express or Thomas Cook office or your bank. American Express cardholders can order foreign currency over the phone at © 800/807-6233.

It's best to exchange currency or traveler's checks at a bank, not a currency exchange, hotel, or shop.

ATMS

ATMs are linked to a network that most likely includes your bank at home. **MasterCard** (which includes Maestro and Cirrus) (© 800/424-7787; www.mastercard.com) and Visa's **PLUS** (© 800/843-7587; www.visa.com) are the two most popular networks in the U.S.; call or check online for ATM locations at your destination. Be sure you know your four-digit PIN before you leave home and be sure to find out your daily withdrawal limit before you depart. You can also get cash advances on your credit card at an ATM. Keep in mind that credit card companies try to protect themselves from theft by limiting the funds

---

Tips **What Things Can Cost**

- The best hamburger in town, at **Rouge,** a stylish bistro on Rittenhouse Square: $12. See p. 103.
- A room at the **Sofitel** hotel, near shopping destinations and City Hall: From $179. See p. 79.
- Coffee at the Parisian-style cafe **La Colombe,** at 19th and Walnut streets: $1. See p. 115.
- A cab ride from **Fork** restaurant in Old City to the Radisson Plaza Warwick Hotel: $6. See p. 97.
- Admission to the **Philadelphia Museum of Art** for one adult: $10 Tuesday to Saturday, or pay what you wish on Sunday. See p. 129.

someone can withdraw away from home. It's therefore best to call your credit card company before you leave and let them know where you're going and how much you plan to spend. You'll get the best exchange rate if you withdraw money from an ATM, but keep in mind that many banks impose a fee every time a card is used at an ATM in a different city or bank. On top of this, the bank from which you withdraw cash may charge its own fee.

For tips and telephone numbers to call if your wallet is stolen or lost, see "Lost & Found," in the "Fast Facts" section, p. 69.

3 When to Go

Philadelphia is great to visit any time, although given the city's seasonal popularity and the constant flow of conventions, you'll find the best deals in the fall and winter. Concert and museum seasons run from early October to early June, and July 4th is obviously a huge crowd scene at Independence Hall.

The city has four distinct seasons with temperatures ranging from the 90s (30s Celsius) in summer to the 30s (around 0 Celsius) in winter. (Below-zero temperatures normally hit only one out of every four winters.) Summers, the height of tourist season, can get swelteringly humid. In the fall, the weather becomes drier. Spring temperatures are variable; count on comfortable breezes.

Average Temperatures & Precipitation in Philadelphia

	Jan	Feb	Mar	Apr	May	June	July	Aug	Sept	Oct	Nov	Dec
High °F/C	40/4	41/5	50/10	62/17	73/23	81/27	85/29	83/28	77/25	66/19	54/12	43/6
Low °F/C	26/-3	26/-3	33/1	43/6	53/12	63/17	68/20	66/19	60/16	49/9	39/4	29/-2
Precip. in days	11	9	11	11	11	10	9	9	8	8	10	10

PHILADELPHIA CALENDAR OF EVENTS

For more details and up-to-the-minute information, contact the **Independence Visitor Center**, 6th and Market streets, Philadelphia, PA 19107 (② **800/537-7676**), or see the calendar at www.gophila.com.

January

Mummer's Parade. Starting at 8am and lasting most of the day, this parade of 30,000 spangled strutters march with feathers and banjos in a celebration that must have been pagan in origin. (The word "mummer" comes from the French *momer*, meaning "to go masked.") The strange but very entertaining parade of string bands and comics takes place on Broad Street, starting at Oregon Avenue in South Philly and finishing at City Hall. There is also an indoor competition at the Convention Center on New Year's Day by the "Fancy Brigade" Mummers. If you have visited the Mummer's Museum beforehand, the gaudiness and elaborateness of the costumes won't amaze you quite so much, but the music (everyone ends up humming "Oh, Dem Golden Slippers") and festivity will have you entranced. Call ② **215/336-3050** for details. January 1 (or the following Sat in case of bad weather).

Benjamin Franklin's Birthday. The Franklin Institute Science Museum (p. 132) celebrates its namesake's birthday with scientific demonstrations and a big birthday cake. Call ② **215/448-1200** for details. Second or third Sunday of the month.

February

Black History Month. The African-American Museum in Philadelphia, 7th and Arch streets, offers a full complement of exhibitions, lectures, and music. Call ✆ **215/574-0380** for details. All month.

Chinese New Year. You can enjoy dragons and fireworks at 11th and Arch streets, traditional 10-course banquets at Chinese restaurants, or a visit to the Chinese Cultural Center at 125 N. 10th St. Call ✆ **215/923-6767** for details on the festivities. Mid- to late February.

March

Philadelphia Flower Show. Now held in the Convention Center, this is the largest indoor flower show in the world, with acres of gardens and rustic settings. With the citywide institution of Flower Show Week, the show and surrounding festivities are even bigger and better than before. You can usually get tickets at the door, but the Pennsylvania Horticultural Society at 325 Walnut St. sells them in advance. Call ✆ **800/611-5960** or 215/988-8800 for information or for tour packages. Early March.

The Book and the Cook Festival. For the past decade, Philadelphia has combined its love for reading and eating into this festival. For 5 days, eminent food critics, cookbook authors, and restaurateurs are invited to plan dream meals with participating city restaurants. If you're a foodie, you know that the chance to stroll through Reading Terminal Market with Alice Waters, or to dine on what she cooks, is an experience you'll remember for a long time. The festival has recently expanded into food samplings and wine and beer tastings all over town. The list of participating restaurants is published in January, and many get booked quickly. Call ✆ **215/686-3662** for a schedule and to make a reservation. Usually the third week of the month.

St. Patrick's Day Parade. The parade starts at noon on 20th Street and the Parkway, turns on 17th Street to Chestnut Street, then goes down Chestnut Street to Independence Mall. The Parkway is the most spacious vantage point, and the Irish Pub at 2007 Walnut St. will be packed. Call the Independence Visitor Center for details (✆ **215/636-1666**). Sunday closest to March 17.

April

Philadelphia Antiques Show. Started in 1961, this antiques show is one of the finest in the nation, with 50-odd major English and American exhibitors. It's held at the 103rd Engineers Armory, 33rd and Market streets. Call ✆ **215/387-3500** for information. First weekend of the month.

Easter Sunday. This day brings fashion shows and music to Rittenhouse Square. The Easter Bunny usually makes an appearance at Lord & Taylor's and the Gallery. Call ✆ **215/686-2876** for details.

Penn Relays. Nearly 50,000 spectators gather for the finale of this weekend event at the University of Pennsylvania's Franklin Field. Elite college and high school runners compete over 3 days, and there are more than 20,000 participants. Call ✆ **215/898-6145** for information.

Spring Tour of Fairmount Park. The dogwood and cherry trees along both sides of the Schuylkill are in blossom. Trolley buses make a special run along Wissahickon Creek, a lovely woodland minutes away from Center City. Call ✆ **215/636-1666** for details. Last Sunday of the month (or first Sun in May).

May

Philadelphia Open House. These tours give you a rare chance to see Germantown, Society Hill, and University City mansions. Call ✆ 215/928-1188 for information, or check www.friendsofindependence.org/openhouse. Late April to early May.

PrideFest America. This diverse set of panels, programs, and parties for the world's GLBT communities is held throughout the city. Call ✆ 215/732-FEST for information. First week in May.

Philadelphia International Children's Festival. This festival, featuring excellent kid-oriented performances, plus craft-making and food, takes place on or near the University of Pennsylvania campus, based at 3680 Walnut St. Call ✆ 215/898-3900 for programs and prices. First week of the month.

Dad Vail Regatta. This is one of the largest collegiate rowing events in the country. You can picnic on East River Drive near Strawberry Mansion. Call ✆ 215/542-1443 for details, or visit www.dadvail.org. Second Saturday of the month.

Rittenhouse Square Flower Market. This market has been an annual event since 1914. Plants, flowers, and baked goods are some of the irresistibles for sale. Call ✆ 215/636-1666 for details. Third Thursday of the month.

Jam on the River. This event was cooked up as Philadelphia's homage to New Orleans and has expanded to include blues as well as jazz. It's based at the expanded Festival Pier, now with a video wall, at Penn's Landing. In recent years, Little Feat and the Preservation Hall Jazz Band have been in attendance. Call ✆ 215/636-1666 for particulars. Late May.

Devon Horse Show, Route 30, Devon. This event, held outside of Philadelphia in the suburbs known as the Main Line, includes jumping competitions, carriage races, and a great country fair with plenty of food stalls—burgers as well as watercress sandwiches—under cheerful awnings. Call ✆ 610/964-0550 for details. End of the month into early June.

June

Mellon Jazz Festival. A top-drawer collection of jazz artists is featured at the Mann Music Center, jazz clubs like Zanzibar Blue, and the Kimmel Center. Call the Independence Visitor Center for details, and for Kimmel events call ✆ 215/893-1955. June through August

Head House Square. Local craftspeople, food vendors, and street artists set up shop on Saturday from noon to midnight and Sunday from noon to 6pm. Call the Visitor Center (✆ 215/965-7676 or 800/537-7676) for details. Throughout the summer.

Elfreth's Alley Days. Row-house dwellers, many in Colonial costumes, open up their homes for inspection and admiration. There are demonstrations of Colonial crafts. Call ✆ 215/574-0560 for details. First weekend of the month.

Wachovia USPro Cycling Championships. The 156-mile course of this country's premier 1-day cycling event starts and finishes on the Parkway, following the incredible climb up the cliffs at Manayunk. See **http://procyclingtour.com**. First weekend of the month.

Rittenhouse Square Fine Arts Annual. Philadelphia moves outdoors with this event, in which hundreds of professional and student works of art go on sale. Call ✆ 215/685-0000 for details. First 2 weeks of June.

Betsy Ross House. Flag Day festivities, invented here in 1891, are held at 12:30pm, usually with a National Guard band and a speech. Call ℂ **215/686-1252** for details. June 14.

Bloomsday. The Rosenbach Museum and the Irish Pub at 2007 Walnut St. both celebrate the 24-hour time span of James Joyce's novel *Ulysses*. Call ℂ **215/732-1600** for details. June 16.

July

Sunoco Welcome America! The whole town turns out for this week-long festival to celebrate America's birthday with theater, free entertainment, and assorted pageantry. The Fourth of July brings special ceremonies to Independence Square, including a reading of the Declaration of Independence, a presentation of the prestigious Liberty Medal (past winners include Colin Powell), and an evening parade up the Parkway. Principal locations are the terrace by the Philadelphia Museum of Art, City Hall (where the world's largest hoagie is assembled), and Penn's Landing. Call ℂ **215/636-1666** or log onto www.americasbirthday.com for information. The week before July 4th, with fireworks at Penn's Landing July 3 and on the Ben Franklin Parkway July 4.

Mann Music Center Summer Concerts. This outdoor venue in Fairmount Park offers selected free concerts through August, and cheap lawn seats for pop performers and the Philadelphia Orchestra. See p. 197 for more information about the concerts, or call ℂ **215/546-7900** for a schedule.

August

Pennsylvania Dutch Festival. Reading Terminal Market (p. 104) is the venue for this weeklong festival featuring quilts, music, food, crafts, and the like. Call ℂ **215/922-2317** for more information. First week of August.

Philadelphia Folk Festival. Suburban Poole Farm, Schwenksville. This festival offers bluegrass, Irish, Cajun, klezmer, and cowboy music, as well as dancing, juggling, puppetry, and crafts. It has a national reputation and draws major crowds. Call ℂ **215/247-1300** for details. Usually late in the month.

September

Philadelphia Fringe Festival. Inaugurated in 1997, this festival brings up to 500 cutting-edge performances, experimental films, and art installations to the nooks and crannies of the Old City. Call ℂ **215/413-9006** for details. Throughout the first half of the month.

Fairmount Park Festival. This festival, which runs through November, includes the Harvest Show at Memorial Hall and parades of varying themes down the Parkway. Call ℂ **215/685-0052** for details. Most weekends in September, October, and November.

Philadelphia Distance Run. One of the nation's premier races, this is a half marathon through Center City and Fairmount Park. In town, it's bigger than the November marathon and gets plenty of national running figures. Call ℂ **215/564-6499** or visit www.philadistancerun.org if you wish to join the ranks of 7,500 runners. Usually the third Sunday of the month.

October

Columbus Day Parade. There's a parade along the Parkway; also look for South Philadelphia fairs. Call **215/686-2085** for details. Second Monday of the month at noon.

November

Philadelphia Marathon. The marathon starts and finishes at the

---

⌐Tips **Quick ID**

Tie a colorful ribbon or piece of yarn around your luggage handle, or slap a distinctive sticker on the side of your bag. This makes it less likely that someone will mistakenly appropriate it. And if your luggage gets lost, it will be easier to find.

Art Museum, looping through Center City and then Fairmount Park. Call ✆ **215/685-0054** or visit www.philadelphiamarathon. com for more information. Usually the Sunday before Thanksgiving.

Philadelphia Museum of Art Craft Show. This preeminent exhibition and retail sale of the finest American contemporary crafts involves works in clay, glass, fiber, jewelry, metal, wearables, and wool. Tickets are $12 (2 days for $18). At the Convention Center. Call ✆ **215/684-7930.** Usually the second weekend of the month.

Thanksgiving Day Parade. This parade features cartoon characters, bands, floats, and Santa Claus. Thanksgiving Day.

December

Holiday Activities Around Town. Christmas sees many activities in Center City, beginning with tree lightings in City Hall courtyard and on Rittenhouse Square. The festivities at the Gallery at Market East and Strawbridge and Clothier include organs and choirs, as does the famous, beloved light show at Lord & Taylor (formerly Wanamaker's). Society Hill and Germantown Christmas walking tours are lovely, with the same leafy decorations as Fairmount Park. Throughout the month. Ask about specific events at the Independence Visitor Center (p. 121).

Nutcracker **Ballet.** The Pennsylvania Ballet performs Tchaikovsky's classic at the Academy of Music (p. 195), Broad and Locust streets. Call ✆ **215/551-7014** for details. Throughout the month.

Private Lights. For an unusual Christmas experience, visit the 2700 block of South Colorado Street, south of Oregon Avenue, between 17th and 18th streets. The sight of some 40 houses bathed in interconnected strands of holiday lights is spectacular. The lights usually go up right after Thanksgiving.

Lucia Fest, American Swedish Historical Museum (p. 144), 1900 Pattison Ave. in South Philadelphia. It sounds Italian, but the Lucia Fest is a Swedish pageant held by candlelight. Call ✆ **215/389-1776** for information. First weekend of the month.

Christmas Tours of Fairmount Park and Germantown. Colonial mansions sparkle with wreaths, holly, and fruit arrangements donated by local garden clubs. Call ✆ **215/684-7922** or 215/848-1777 for details. Tours begin mid-month.

New Year's Eve. Fireworks are held at the Great Plaza of Penn's Landing on December 31.

---

4 Travel Insurance

Check your existing insurance policies and credit card coverage before you buy travel insurance. You may already be covered for lost luggage, canceled tickets, or medical expenses.

The cost of travel insurance varies widely, depending on the cost and length of your trip, your age and health, and the type of trip you're taking, but expect to pay between 5% and 8% of the cost of the vacation itself.

TRIP-CANCELLATION INSURANCE Trip-cancellation insurance helps you get your money back if you have to back out of a trip, if you have to go home early, or if your travel supplier goes bankrupt. Allowed reasons for cancellation can range from sickness to natural disasters to the State Department declaring your destination unsafe for travel. (Insurers usually won't cover vague fears, though, as many travelers discovered who tried to cancel their trips in October 2001 because they were wary of flying.) In this unstable world, trip-cancellation insurance is a good buy if you're getting tickets well in advance—who knows what the state of the world, or of your airline, will be in 9 months? Insurance policy details vary, so read the fine print—and make sure that your airline or cruise line is on the list of carriers covered in case of bankruptcy. A good resource is **"Travel Guard Alerts,"** a list of companies considered high-risk by Travel Guard International (see website below). Protect yourself further by paying for the insurance with a credit card—by law, consumers can get their money back on goods and services not received if they report the loss within 60 days after the charge is listed on their credit card statement.

Note: Many tour operators, particularly those offering trips to remote or high-risk areas, include insurance in the cost of the trip or can arrange insurance policies through a partnering provider, a convenient and often cost-effective way for the traveler to obtain insurance. Make sure the tour company is a reputable one, however: Some experts suggest you avoid buying insurance from the tour or cruise company you're traveling with, saying it's better to buy from a "third party" insurer than to put all your money in one place.

For more information, contact one of the following recommended insurers: **Access America** (© 866/807-3982; www.accessamerica.com); **Travel Guard International** (© 800/826-4919; www.travelguard.com); **Travel Insured International** (© 800/243-3174; www.travelinsured.com); and **Travelex Insurance Services** (© 888/457-4602; www.travelex-insurance.com).

MEDICAL INSURANCE Most health insurance policies cover you if you get sick away from home—but check, particularly if you're insured by an HMO.

LOST-LUGGAGE INSURANCE On domestic flights, checked baggage is covered up to $2,500 per ticketed passenger. On international flights (including U.S. portions of international trips), baggage coverage is limited to approximately $9.07 per pound, up to approximately $635 per checked bag. If you plan to check items more valuable than the standard liability, see if your valuables are covered by your homeowner's policy, get baggage insurance as part of your comprehensive travel-insurance package, or buy Travel Guard's "BagTrak" product. Don't buy insurance at the airport, as it's usually overpriced. Be sure to take any valuables or irreplaceable items with you in your carry-on luggage, as many valuables (including books, money, and electronics) aren't covered by airline policies.

If your luggage is lost, immediately file a lost-luggage claim at the airport, detailing the luggage contents. For most airlines, you must report delayed, damaged, or lost baggage within 4 hours of arrival. The airlines are required to deliver luggage, once found, directly to your house or destination free of charge.

5 Health & Safety

STAYING HEALTHY

The best thing to do if you become sick in Philadelphia is to check with your hotel concierge, and ask if he or she can contact a doctor for you. Or go to an emergency room at Jefferson University Hospital at 11th and Walnut streets, the Hospital of the University of Pennsylvania at 34th and Spruce, or Pennsylvania Hospital at 8th and Spruce streets.

For hospitals and emergency numbers, see "Fast Facts," p. 69.

If you suffer from a chronic illness, consult your doctor before your departure. For conditions like epilepsy, diabetes, or heart problems, wear a **MedicAlert identification tag** (© 888/633-4298; www.medicalert. org), which will immediately alert doctors to your condition and give them access to your records through MedicAlert's 24-hour hotline.

Pack **prescription medications** in your carry-on luggage, and carry prescription medications in their original containers, with pharmacy labels—otherwise they won't make it through airport security. Also bring along copies of your prescriptions in case you lose your pills or run out. Don't forget an extra pair of contact lenses or prescription glasses.

STAYING SAFE

Philadelphia's Center City (bordered by the Delaware and Schuylkill rivers from east to west, and from South Street to Spring Garden Street from south to north) is quite safe, especially in the high-traffic areas of Old City and along Walnut Street and Rittenhouse Square. It is always a good idea to be aware of others around you, especially after dark on quiet streets, and in off-the-beaten-path neighborhoods such as around the college campuses in West Philadelphia.

6 Specialized Travel Resources

TRAVELERS WITH DISABILITIES

Most disabilities shouldn't stop anyone from traveling. There are more options and resources out there than ever before.

For basic Philadelphia information, contact the **Mayor's Commission on People with Disabilities,** Municipal Services Building, Room 900, 1401 JFK Blvd., Philadelphia, PA 19107 (© 215/686-2798), or see the excellent website at **www.phila.gov/aco/ links.html**. SEPTA (the local transit authority) publishes a special "Transit Guide for the Disabled"; you can request it from **SEPTA Special Services,** 1234 Market St., 4th Floor, Philadelphia, PA 19107 (© 215/580-7145). All SEPTA buses are lift-equipped. Market East and University City subway stations are wheelchair

accessible, but most other stops are not. Artreach publishes "Access the Arts: A Guide for People with Disabilities," providing information for more than 75 area facilities; the brochure is $5 and can be ordered at (© 215/ 951-0316). The Philadelphia airport has a variety of services including 15 TDD telephones, elevators and escalators, Braille ATMs, and curb cuts.

Travelers with disabilities will find the tourist areas of Philadelphia accessible. All Center City curbs are cut at intersections, even though some streets in Society Hill and those bordering Independence National Historical Park have uneven brick sidewalks, and Dock Street itself is paved with rough cobblestones.

Parking can be tough, however, as handicapped parking spots are rare. The same is true for Chestnut Street,

Avoiding "Economy-Class Syndrome"

Deep vein thrombosis, or as it's know in the world of flying, "economy-class syndrome," is a blood clot that develops in a deep vein. It's a potentially deadly condition that can be caused by sitting in cramped conditions—such as an airplane cabin—for too long. During a flight (especially a long-haul flight), get up, walk around, and stretch your legs every 60 to 90 minutes to keep your blood flowing. Other preventative measures include frequent flexing of the legs while sitting, drinking lots of water, and avoiding alcohol and sleeping pills. If you have a history of deep vein thrombosis, heart disease, or other condition that puts you at high risk, some experts recommend wearing compression stockings or taking anticoagulants when you fly; always ask your physician about the best course for you. Symptoms of deep vein thrombosis include leg pain or swelling, or even shortness of breath.

the Parkway, and the University of Pennsylvania campus. The Independence Visitor Center has a level entrance and publishes "Accessibilities," a brochure detailing all park sites.

Virtually all theaters and stadiums accommodate wheelchairs. Call ahead to plan routes. To aid people with hearing impairments, the Kimmel Center and Academy of Music provide free infrared headsets for concerts; the Annenberg Center rents them for $2.

The Free Library of Philadelphia runs a **Library for the Blind and Physically Handicapped,** very conveniently located at 919 Walnut St. (© 215/683-3213); it's open Monday through Friday from 9am to 5pm. It adjoins the **Associated Services for the Blind,** which offers transcriptions into Braille for a fee.

If you are handicapped and travel with Amtrak or Greyhound/Trailways, be aware that on the former you can receive a 15% discount and a special seat with advance notification (© 800/USA-RAIL), and on the latter a free seat for a companion (© 800/229-9424; for these special tickets, call 800/752-4841).

Many of the major car-rental companies now offer hand-controlled cars for disabled drivers. **Avis Rent a Car** has an "Avis Access" program that offers such services as a dedicated 24-hour toll-free number (© 888/879-4273) for customers with special travel needs; special car features such as swivel seats, spinner knobs, and hand controls; and accessible bus service. Hertz (© 800/654-3131, or 800/654-2280 for hearing impaired) requires between 24 and 72 hours advance reservation at most of its locations.

The U.S. National Park Service offers a **Golden Access Passport** that gives free lifetime entrance to all properties administered by the National Park Service—national parks, monuments, historic sites, recreation areas, and national wildlife refuges—for persons who are visually impaired or have permanent disabilities, regardless of age. You may pick up a Golden Access Passport at any NPS entrance fee area by showing proof of medically determined disability and eligibility for receiving benefits under federal law. Besides free entry, the Golden Access Passport also offers a 50% discount on federal-use fees charged for such facilities as camping, swimming, parking, boat launching, and tours. For more information, go to www.nps.gov/fees_passes.htm or call © 888/467-2757.

Many travel agencies offer customized tours and itineraries for travelers with disabilities. **Flying Wheels Travel** (© 507/451-5005; www.flyingwheelstravel.com) offers escorted tours and cruises that emphasize sports and private tours in mini-size sports and private tours in mini-vans with lifts. **Access-Able Travel Source** (© 303/232-2979; www.access-able.com) offers extensive access information and advice for traveling around the world with disabilities. **Accessible Journeys** (© 800/846-4537 or 610/521-0339; www.disabilitytravel.com) caters specifically to slow walkers and wheelchair travelers and their families and friends.

Organizations that offer assistance to travelers with disabilities include **MossRehab** (www.mossresourcenet.org), which provides a library of accessible-travel resources online; **SATH (Society for Accessible Travel & Hospitality)** (© 212/447-7284; www.sath.org; annual membership fees: $45 adults, $30 seniors and students), which offers a wealth of travel resources for all types of disabilities and informed recommendations on destinations, access guides, travel agents, tour operators, vehicle rentals, and companion services; and the **American Foundation for the Blind (AFB)** (© 800/232-5463; www.afb.org), a referral resource for the blind or visually impaired that includes information on traveling with Seeing Eye dogs.

For more information specifically targeted to travelers with disabilities, the community website **iCan** (www.icanonline.net/channels/travel/index.cfm) has destination guides and several regular columns on accessible travel. Also check out the quarterly magazine **Emerging Horizons** ($15 per year, $20 outside the U.S.; www.emerginghorizons.com); and *Open World* magazine, published by SATH (see above; subscription: $13 per year, $21 outside the U.S.).

GAY & LESBIAN TRAVELERS

Center City is welcoming to gay and lesbian residents and visitors. Philadelphia has an advertising campaign that specifically markets to gay travelers, and the "Gayborhood," the area bordered by 9th and Juniper streets and Walnut and South streets, is filled with gay restaurants, bookstores, clubs, and social services. See p. 208 for specific clubs and bars. You can also check the weekly *Philadelphia Gay News* (www.epgn.com), which is widely available. The lesbian-oriented *Labyrinth* is available free at Giovanni's Room, a popular gay bookstore at 12th and Pine streets. Outside the city (see chapter 11, "Side Trips from Philadelphia"), the village of New Hope is a popular destination for gay and lesbian travelers.

For meetings, gallery exhibitions, and social events, consult the **William Way Community Center,** 1315 Spruce St. (© 215/735-2220; www.waygay.org), or drop by **Millennium Coffee,** 212 S. 12th St. (© 215/731-9798), a sleek scene open till midnight.

Giovanni's Room, 345 S. 12th St. (© 215/923-2960; www.giovannisroom.com), is a national resource for publications produced by and for gays and lesbians, as well as for feminist and progressive literature.

To report anti-gay violence or discrimination, call the **Philadelphia Lesbian and Gay Task Force Hotline** at © 215/772-2000. ACT UP/Philadelphia meets on Monday; call © 215/731-1844.

The International Gay and Lesbian Travel Association (IGLTA) (© 800/448-8550 or 954/776-2626; www.iglta.org) is the trade association for the gay and lesbian travel industry, and offers an online directory of gay- and lesbian-friendly travel businesses; go to their website and click on "Members."

Many agencies offer tours and travel itineraries specifically for gay and lesbian travelers. **Above and Beyond Tours** (℃ 800/397-2681; www.abovebeyondtours.com) is the exclusive gay and lesbian tour operator for United Airlines. **Now, Voyager** (℃ 800/255-6951; www.nowvoyager. com) is a well-known San Francisco–based gay-owned and operated travel service. **Olivia Cruises & Resorts** (℃ 800/631-6277; www. olivia.com) charters entire resorts and ships for exclusive lesbian vacations and offers smaller group experiences for both gay and lesbian travelers.

The following travel guides are available at most travel bookstores and gay and lesbian bookstores, or you can order them from **Giovanni's Room** bookstore, 1145 Pine St., Philadelphia, PA 19107 (℃ 215/923-2960; www.giovannisroom.com); *Out and About* (℃ 800/929-2268; www.out andabout.com), which offers guidebooks and a newsletter ($20/yr.; 10 issues) packed with solid information on the global gay and lesbian scene; *Spartacus International Gay Guide* (Bruno Gmünder Verlag; www. spartacusworld.com/gayguide) and *Odysseus: The International Gay Travel Planner* (Odysseus Enterprises Ltd.), both good, annual English-language guidebooks focused on gay men; the *Damron* guides (www. damron.com), with separate, annual books for gay men and lesbians; and *Gay Travel A to Z: The World of Gay & Lesbian Travel Options at Your Fingertips* by Marianne Ferrari (Ferrari International; Box 35575, Phoenix, AZ 85069), a very good gay and lesbian guidebook series.

SENIOR TRAVEL

With its compact downtown and widely available senior discounts, Philadelphia is a welcoming city for seniors. Most museums and attractions offer discounts, as do some hotels, and the tourist-friendly Phlash

bus line is always free to seniors. The Independence Visitor Center publishes "Seniors on the Go," which lists dozens of specific senior benefits and discounts around town. Seniors should bring photo ID.

Mention the fact that you're a senior when you make your travel reservations. Although all of the major U.S. airlines except America West have canceled their senior discount and coupon book programs, many hotels still offer discounts for seniors. In Philadelphia, people over the age of 60 qualify for reduced admission to theaters, museums, and other attractions, as well as discounted fares on public transportation.

Members of **AARP** (formerly known as the American Association of Retired Persons), 601 E St. NW, Washington, DC 20049 (℃ 888/ 687-2277; www.aarp.org), get discounts on hotels, airfares, and car rentals. AARP offers members a wide range of benefits, including *AARP The Magazine* and a monthly newsletter. Anyone over 50 can join.

Many reliable agencies and organizations target the 50-plus market. **Elderhostel** (℃ 877/426-8056; www.elderhostel.org) arranges study programs for those 55 and over (and a spouse or companion of any age) in the U.S. and in more than 80 countries around the world. Most courses last 5 to 7 days in the U.S. (2–4 weeks abroad), and many include airfare, accommodations in university dormitories or modest inns, meals, and tuition. **ElderTreks** (℃ 800/741-7956; www.eldertreks.com) offers small-group tours to off-the-beaten-path or adventure-travel locations, restricted to travelers 50 and older. **INTRAV** (℃ 800/456-8100; www. intrav.com) is a high-end tour operator that caters to the mature, discerning traveler, not specifically seniors, with trips around the world that include guided safaris, polar expeditions, private-jet adventures, and small-boat cruises down jungle rivers.

Recommended publications offering travel resources and discounts for seniors include: the quarterly magazine *Travel 50 & Beyond* (www.travel 50andbeyond.com); *Travel Unlimited: Uncommon Adventures for the Mature Traveler* (Avalon); *101 Tips for Mature Travelers,* available from Grand Circle Travel (© **800/221-2610** or 617/350-7500; www.gct.com); and *Unbelievably Good Deals and Great Adventures That You Absolutely Can't Get Unless You're Over 50* (McGraw-Hill), by Joann Rattner Heilman.

FAMILY TRAVEL

Philadelphia is a wonderful destination for families, with its accessible layout, and historical sites that are meaningful to all ages. From the kid-friendly Please Touch Museum to Sesame Place amusement park to the characters dressed in Colonial-era garb who wander Independence National Historical Park, there is a wealth of attractions for children. See "Especially for Kids," p. 153, and visit www.gophila.com/family for some excellent packages and ideas.

Children under 12 (and in many cases, under 18) can stay free with parents in most Philadelphia hotels, and some hotels offer one-bedroom/pull-out-sofa suites geared toward families that can be more affordable than booking two rooms; several hotels offer free breakfasts and even dinners to kids. (See "Family-Friendly Hotels," on p. 86.) Be sure to reserve cribs and playpens in advance.

Many of Philadelphia's finest restaurants, such as Morimoto and Lacroix, are happy to accommodate children, and there are dozens of casual restaurants where kids and parents can both dine well. See p. 107 for "Family-Friendly Restaurants."

A good resource for family travel in Philadelphia is Metrokids, a newspaper which lists cultural attractions geared toward families, along with special issues devoted to factory tours, the Camden Aquarium, and the like. Call © **888/490-4668** with specific questions, or visit www.metrokids.com.

Children will love visiting Valley Forge Park, Hershey, PA, Amish country, and Gettysburg. All these destinations have a wonderful mix of history and pure fun (and chocolate, of course, in Hershey) that conjure up a past or different way of life, and basic American themes such as freedom and independence.

To locate those accommodations, restaurants, and attractions that are particularly kid-friendly, refer to the "Kids" icon throughout this guide.

Familyhostel (© **800/733-9753;** www.learn.unh.edu/familyhostel) takes the whole family, including kids ages 8 to 15, on moderately priced domestic and international learning vacations. Lectures, fields trips, and sightseeing are guided by a team of academics.

Recommended family travel Internet sites include **Family Travel Forum** (www.familytravelforum.com), a comprehensive site that offers customized trip planning; **Family Travel Network** (www.familytravelnetwork.com), an award-winning site that offers travel features, deals, and tips; **Traveling Internationally with Your Kids** (www.travelwithyourkids.com), a comprehensive site offering sound advice for long-distance and international travel with children; and **Family Travel Files** (www.thefamilytravel files.com), which offers an online magazine and a directory of off-the-beaten-path tours and tour operators for families.

Another great resource is *Frommer's Unofficial Guide to the Mid-Atlantic with Kids* (Wiley Publishing, Inc.).

WOMEN TRAVELERS

More and more hotels are ratcheting up security measures for women traveling alone on business or for pleasure. Some are even offering secure "women only" floors, with the added perk of spa services.

Check out the award-winning website **Journeywoman** (www.journey woman.com), a "real life" women's travel information network where you can sign up for a free e-mail newsletter and get advice on everything from etiquette and dress to safety; or the travel guide *Safety and Security for Women Who Travel* by Sheila Swan and Peter Laufer (Travelers' Tales, Inc.), offering common-sense tips on safe travel.

MULTICULTURAL TRAVELERS

Philadelphia is a diverse city that has wonderful ethnic neighborhoods ranging from the booming Vietnamese area in South Philadelphia to the largely African-American West Philly. An excellent way to learn about Philadelphia's multicultural heritage is to take one of the Greater Philadelphia Tourism and Marketing Corporation's "Philadelphia Neighborhood Tours," which are offered some Saturdays from 10am to 1pm, and do more than skim the surface. They are in-depth, well-planned and fun. Popular tours include "Latin Soul, Latin Flavor," "Philadelphia's Civil Rights Struggle," and "Voices of Chinatown." Call © 215/599-2295 or visit www.go phila.com/index-neighborhoodtours. htm to book one.

The Internet offers a number of helpful travel sites for the black traveler. **Black Travel Online** (www.black travelonline.com) posts news on upcoming events and includes links to articles and travel-booking sites. **Soul of America** (www.soulofamerica.com) is a comprehensive website, with travel tips, event and family reunion postings, and sections on historically black beach resorts and active vacations.

Agencies and organizations that provide resources for black travelers include: **Rodgers Travel** (© 800/ 825-1775; www.rodgerstravel.com), a Philadelphia-based travel agency with an extensive menu of tours in destinations worldwide, including heritage and private group tours; the **African American Association of Innkeepers International** (© 877/422-5777; www.africanamericaninns.com), which provides information on member B&Bs in the U.S., Canada, and the Caribbean; and **Henderson Travel & Tours** (© 800/327-2309 or 301/ 650-5700; www.hendersontravel.com), which has specialized in trips to Africa since 1957.

For more information, check out the following collections and guides: *Go Girl: The Black Woman's Guide to Travel & Adventure* (Eighth Mountain Press), a compilation of travel essays by writers including Jill Nelson and Audre Lorde, with some practical information and trip-planning advice; *The African American Travel Guide* by Wayne Robinson (Hunter Publishing; www.hunter publishing.com), with details on 19 North American cities; *Steppin' Out* by Carla Labat (Avalon), with details on 20 cities; *Travel and Enjoy Magazine* (© 866/266-6211; www.travel andenjoy.com; subscription: $38 per year), which focuses on discounts and destination reviews; and the more narrative *Pathfinders Magazine* (© 877/ 977-PATH; www.pathfinderstravel. com; subscription: $15 per year), which includes articles on everything from Rio de Janeiro to Ghana as well as information on upcoming ski, diving, golf, and tennis trips.

STUDENT TRAVEL

There are more colleges and universities in and around Philadelphia than in any other city in the country, so students will find a warm reception from area vendors and sights. A valid student ID will get you discounts on cultural sites, accommodations, car rentals, and more. When in Philadelphia, head for the **University of Pennsylvania,** 34th and Walnut streets (© **215/898-5000**); **Temple University,** N. Broad Street (© **215/ 204-7000**); or **International House,** 3701 Chestnut St. (© **215/387-5125**). All three publish free papers listing lectures, performances, films, and social events.

SINGLE TRAVELERS

Single travelers are often hit with a "single supplement" to the base price of a hotel room. To avoid it, you can agree to room with other single travelers on the trip, or you can find a compatible roommate before you go from one of the many roommate locator agencies.

Travel Buddies Singles Travel Club (© **800/998-9099;** www.travel buddiesworldwide.com), based in Canada, runs small, intimate, single-friendly group trips and will match you with a roommate free of charge. **TravelChums** (© **212/787-2621;** www.travelchums.com) is an Internet-only travel-companion matching service with elements of an online personals-type site, hosted by the respected New York–based Shaw Guides travel service. **The Single Gourmet Club** (www.singlegourmet. com/chapters.php) is an international social, dining, and travel club for singles of all ages, with club chapters in 21 cities in the U.S. and Canada. Annual membership fees vary from city to city.

TRAVELING WITH PETS

We have made a special note in the accommodations listings if pets are allowed in a particular lodging. See chapter 5.

7 Planning Your Trip Online

SURFING FOR AIRFARES

The "big three" online travel agencies, **Expedia.com**, **Travelocity.com**, and **Orbitz.com** sell most of the air tickets bought on the Internet. (Canadian travelers should try expedia.ca and Travelocity.ca; U.K. residents can go for expedia.co.uk and opodo.co.uk.). Each has different business deals with the airlines and may offer different fares on the same flights, so it's wise to shop around. Expedia and Travelocity will also send you **e-mail notification** when a cheap fare becomes available to your favorite destination. Of the smaller travel agency websites, **SideStep** (www.sidestep.com) has gotten the best reviews from Frommer's authors. It's a browser add-on that purports to "search 140 sites at once," but in reality only beats competitors' fares as often as other sites do.

Also remember to check **airline websites,** especially those for low-fare carriers such as Southwest, JetBlue, AirTran, WestJet, or Ryanair, whose fares are often misreported or simply missing from travel agency websites. Even with major airlines, you can often shave a few bucks from a fare by booking directly through the airline and avoiding a travel agency's transaction fee. But you'll get these discounts only by **booking online:** Most airlines now offer online-only fares that even their phone agents know nothing about. For the websites of airlines that fly to and from your destination, see p. 33.

Great **last-minute deals** are available through free weekly e-mail services provided directly by the airlines. Most of these are announced on Tuesday or Wednesday and must be purchased online. Most are only valid for travel that weekend, but some (such as Southwest's) can be booked weeks or months in advance. Sign up for weekly e-mail alerts at airline websites or check mega-sites that compile comprehensive lists of last-minute specials, such as **Smarter Travel** (www.smartertravel.com). For last-minute trips, **site59.com** and **last minutetravel.com** in the U.S. and **lastminute.com** in Europe often have better air-and-hotel package deals than the major-label sites. A website listing numerous bargain sites and airlines around the world is **www. itravelnet.com**.

If you're willing to give up some control over your flight details, use what is called an **"opaque" fare service** like **Priceline** (www.priceline.com; www.priceline.co.uk for Europeans) or its smaller competitor **Hotwire** (www.hotwire.com). Both offer rock-bottom prices in exchange for travel on a "mystery airline" at a mysterious time of day, often with a mysterious change of planes en route. The mystery airlines are all major, well-known carriers—and the possibility of being sent from Philadelphia to Chicago via Tampa is remote; the airlines' routing computers have gotten a lot better than they used to be. But your chances of getting a 6am or 11pm flight are pretty high. Hotwire tells you flight prices before you buy; Priceline usually has better deals than Hotwire, but you have to play their "name our price" game. If you're new at this, the helpful folks at **BiddingForTravel** (www.biddingfortravel.com) do a good job of demystifying Priceline's prices and strategies. Priceline and Hotwire are great for flights within North America and between the U.S. and Europe. But for flights to other parts of the world, consolidators will almost always beat their fares. *Note:* In 2004 Priceline added non-opaque service to its roster. You now have the option to pick exact flights, times, and airlines from a list of offers—or opt to bid on opaque fares as before.

For much more about airfares and savvy air-travel tips and advice, pick up a copy of *Frommer's Fly Safe, Fly Smart* (Wiley Publishing, Inc.).

SURFING FOR HOTELS

Shopping online for hotels is generally done one of two ways: by booking through the hotel's own website or through an independent booking agency (or a fare-service agency like Priceline; see below). These Internet hotel agencies have multiplied in mind-boggling numbers of late, competing for the business of millions of consumers surfing for accommodations around the world. This competitiveness can be a boon to consumers who have the patience and time to shop and compare the online sites for good deals—but shop they must, for prices can vary considerably from site to site. And keep in mind that hotels at the top of a site's listing may be there for no other reason than that they paid money to get the placement.

Of the "big three" sites, **Expedia** offers a long list of special deals and "virtual tours" or photos of available rooms so you can see what you're paying for (a feature that helps counter the claims that the best rooms are often held back from bargain booking websites). **Travelocity** posts unvarnished customer reviews and ranks its properties according to the AAA rating system. Also reliable are **Hotels. com** and **Quikbook.com**. An excellent free program, **TravelAxe** (www. travelaxe.net), can help you search multiple hotel sites at once, even ones you may never have heard of—and conveniently lists the total price of the room, including the taxes and service charges. Another booking site, **Travelweb** (www.travelweb.com), is partly owned by the hotels it represents (including the Hilton, Hyatt, and Starwood chains) and is therefore plugged directly into the hotels' reservations systems—unlike independent online agencies, which have to fax or e-mail reservation requests to the hotel, a good portion of which get misplaced in the shuffle. More than once, travelers have arrived at the

Frommers.com: The Complete Travel Resource

For an excellent travel-planning resource, we highly recommend **Frommers.com** (www.frommers.com), voted Best Travel Site by *PC Magazine*. We're a little biased, of course, but we guarantee that you'll find the travel tips, reviews, monthly vacation giveaways, bookstore, and online-booking capabilities thoroughly indispensable. Among the special features are our popular **Destinations** section, where you'll get expert travel tips, hotel and dining recommendations, and advice on the sights to see for more than 3,500 destinations around the globe; the **Frommers.com Newsletter,** with the latest deals, travel trends, and money-saving secrets; our **Community** area featuring **Message Boards,** where Frommer's readers post queries and share advice (sometimes even our authors show up to answer questions); and our **Photo Center,** where you can post and share vacation tips. When your research is done, the **Online Reservations System** (www.frommers.com/book_a_trip) takes you to Frommer's preferred online partners for booking your vacation at affordable prices.

hotel, only to be told that they have no reservation. To be fair, many of the major sites are undergoing improvements in service and ease of use, and Expedia will soon be able to plug directly into the reservations systems of many hotel chains—none of which can be bad news for consumers. In the meantime, it's a good idea to **get a confirmation number** and **make a printout** of any online booking transaction. An easy way to book directly online at most Philadelphia hotels is to visit the Greater Philadelphia Tourism and Marketing Corporation's links to many lodgings at **www. gophila.com/accommodations**. You can also find discounted booking for some inns and small hotels in Philadelphia at **www. philadelphiasbest.net**, and at **www. bnbphiladelphia.com**.

In the opaque website category, **Priceline** and **Hotwire** are even better for hotels than for airfares; with both, you're allowed to pick the neighborhood and quality level of your hotel before offering up your money. Priceline's hotel product even covers Europe and Asia, though it's much better at getting five-star lodging for three-star prices than at finding anything at the bottom of the scale. On the down side, many hotels stick Priceline guests in their least desirable rooms. Be sure to go to the Bidding-ForTravel website (see above) before bidding on a hotel room on Priceline; it features a fairly up-to-date list of hotels that Priceline uses in major cities. For both Priceline and Hotwire, you pay up front, and the fee is nonrefundable. *Note:* Some hotels do not provide loyalty program credits or points or other frequent-stay amenities when you book a room through opaque online services.

SURFING FOR RENTAL CARS

For booking rental cars online, the best deals are usually found at rental-car company websites, although all the major online travel agencies also offer rental-car reservations services. Priceline and Hotwire work well for rental cars, too; the only "mystery" is which major rental company you get, and for most travelers the difference between Hertz, Avis, and Budget is negligible.

8 The 21st-Century Traveler

INTERNET ACCESS AWAY FROM HOME

Travelers have any number of ways to check their e-mail and access the Internet on the road. Of course, using your own laptop—or even a PDA (personal digital assistant) or electronic organizer with a modem—gives you the most flexibility. But even if you don't have a computer, you can still access your e-mail and even your office computer from cybercafes.

WITHOUT YOUR OWN COMPUTER

It's hard nowadays to find a city that *doesn't* have a few cybercafes. Although there's no definitive directory for cybercafes—these are independent businesses, after all—three places to start looking are at **www.cyber captive.com** and **www.cybercafe. com**.

Aside from formal cybercafes, most **youth hostels** nowadays have at least one computer you can get to the Internet on. And most **public libraries** across the world offer Internet access free or for a small charge. Avoid **hotel business centers** unless you're willing to pay exorbitant rates.

Most major airports now have **Internet kiosks** scattered throughout their gates. These kiosks, which you'll also see in shopping malls, hotel lobbies, and tourist information offices around the world, give you basic Web access for a per-minute fee that's usually higher than cybercafe prices. The kiosks' clunkiness and high price mean they should be avoided whenever possible.

To retrieve your e-mail, ask your **Internet Service Provider (ISP)** if it has a Web-based interface tied to your existing e-mail account. If your ISP doesn't have such an interface, you can use the free **mail2web** service (www. mail2web.com) to view and reply to your home e-mail. For more

flexibility, you may want to open a free, Web-based e-mail account with **Yahoo! Mail** (http://mail.yahoo.com). (Microsoft's Hotmail is another popular option, but Hotmail has severe spam problems.) Your home ISP may be able to forward your e-mail to the Web-based account automatically.

If you need to access files on your office computer, look into a service called **GoToMyPC** (www.gotomypc. com). The service provides a Web-based interface for you to access and manipulate a distant PC from anywhere—even a cybercafe—provided your "target" PC is on and has an always-on connection to the Internet (such as with Road Runner cable). The service offers top-quality security, but if you're worried about hackers, use your own laptop rather than a cybercafe computer to access the GoToMyPC system.

WITH YOUR OWN COMPUTER

Wi-fi (wireless fidelity) is the buzzword in computer access, and more and more hotels, cafes, and retailers are signing on as wireless "hotspots" from where you can get high-speed connection without cable wires, networking hardware, or a phone line (see below). You can get wi-fi connection one of several ways. Many laptops sold in the last year have built-in wi-fi capability (an 802.11b wireless Ethernet connection). Mac owners have their own networking technology, Apple AirPort. For those with older computers, an 802.11b/**Wi-fi card** (around $50) can be plugged into your laptop. You sign up for wireless access service much as you do cellphone service, through a plan offered by one of several commercial companies that have made wireless service available in airports, hotel lobbies, and coffee shops, primarily in the U.S. (followed by the U.K. and Japan).

T-Mobile Hotspot (www.t-mobile. com/hotspot) serves up wireless connections at more than 1,000 Starbucks coffee shops nationwide. **Boingo** (www.boingo.com) and **Wayport** (www.wayport.com) have set up networks in airports and high-class hotel lobbies. IPass providers (see below) also give you access to a few hundred wireless hotel lobby setups. Best of all, you don't need to be staying at the Four Seasons to use the hotel's network; just set yourself up on a nice couch in the lobby. The companies' pricing policies can be byzantine, with a variety of monthly, per-connection, and per-minute plans, but in general you pay around $30 a month for limited access—and as more and more companies jump on the wireless bandwagon, prices are likely to get even more competitive.

There are also places that provide **free wireless networks** in cities around the world. To locate these free hotspots, go to **www.personaltelco. net/index.cgi/WirelessCommunities**.

If wi-fi is not available at your destination, most business-class hotels throughout the world offer dataports for laptop modems, and a few thousand hotels in the U.S. and Europe now offer free high-speed Internet access using an Ethernet network cable. You can bring your own cables, but most hotels rent them for around $10. **Call your hotel in advance** to see what your options are.

In addition, major Internet Service Providers (ISP) have **local access numbers** around the world, allowing you to go online by simply placing a local call. Check your ISP's website or call its toll-free number and ask how you can use your current account away from home, and how much it will cost.

If you're traveling outside the reach of your ISP, the **iPass** network has dial-up numbers in most of the world's countries. You'll have to sign up with an iPass provider, who will then tell you how to set up your computer for your destination(s). For a list of iPass providers, go to www.ipass. com. One solid provider is **i2roam** (www.i2roam.com; ⓒ **866/811-6209** or 920/235-0475).

Wherever you go, bring a **connection kit** of the right power and phone adapters, a spare phone cord, and a spare Ethernet network cable—or find out whether your hotel supplies them to guests.

Digital Photography on the Road

Many travelers are going digital these days when it comes to taking vacation photographs. Not only are digital cameras left relatively unscathed by airport X-rays, but with digital equipment you don't need to lug armloads of film with you as you travel. In fact, nowadays you don't even need to carry your laptop to download the day's images to make room for more. With a **media storage card,** sold by all major camera dealers, you can store hundreds of images in your camera. These "memory" cards come in different configurations—from memory sticks to flash cards to secure digital cards—and different storage capacities (the more megabytes of memory, the more images a card can hold) and range in price from $30 to over $200. (**Note:** Each camera model works with a specific type of card, so you'll need to determine which storage card is compatible with your camera.) When you get home, you can print the images out on your own color printer or take the storage card to a camera store, drugstore, or chain retailer. Or have the images developed online with a service like **Snapfish** (www.snapfish.com) for something like 25¢ a shot.

Online Traveler's Toolbox

Veteran travelers usually carry some essential items to make their trips easier. Following is a selection of handy online tools to bookmark and use.

- **Airplane Seating and Food.** Find out which seats to reserve and which to avoid (and more) on all major domestic airlines at www.seatguru.com. And check out the type of meal (with photos) you'll likely be served on airlines around the world at www.airlinemeals.com.
- **Foreign Languages for Travelers** (www.travlang.com). Learn basic terms in more than 70 languages and click on any underlined phrase to hear what it sounds like.
- **Intellicast** (www.intellicast.com) and **Weather.com** (www.weather.com). Gives weather forecasts for all 50 states and for cities around the world.
- **Mapquest** (www.mapquest.com). This best of the mapping sites lets you choose a specific address or destination, and in seconds, it will return a map and detailed directions.
- **Subway Navigator** (www.subwaynavigator.com). Download subway maps and get savvy advice on using subway systems in dozens of major cities around the world.
- **Time and Date** (www.timeanddate.com). See what time (and day) it is anywhere in the world.
- **Travel Warnings** (http://travel.state.gov/travel_warnings.html, www.fco.gov.uk/travel, www.voyage.gc.ca, www.dfat.gov.au/consular/advice). These sites report on places where health concerns or unrest might threaten American, British, Canadian, and Australian travelers. Generally, U.S. warnings are the most paranoid; Australian warnings are the most relaxed.
- **Universal Currency Converter** (www.xe.com/ucc). See what your dollar or pound is worth in more than 100 other countries.
- **Visa ATM Locator** (www.visa.com), for locations of PLUS ATMs worldwide, or **MasterCard ATM Locator** (www.mastercard.com), for locations of Cirrus ATMs worldwide.

USING A CELLPHONE ACROSS THE U.S.

Just because your cellphone works at home doesn't mean it'll work elsewhere in the country (thanks to our nation's fragmented cellphone system). It's a good bet that your phone will work in major cities. But take a look at your wireless company's coverage map on its website before heading out—T-Mobile, Sprint, and Nextel are particularly weak in rural areas. If you need to stay in touch at a destination where you know your phone won't work, **rent** a phone that does from **InTouch USA** (© **800/872-7626;** www.intouchglobal.com) or a rental car location, but beware that you'll pay $1 a minute or more for airtime.

If you're venturing deep into national parks, you may want to consider renting a **satellite phone ("satphones"),** which are different from cellphones in that they connect to satellites rather than ground-based towers. A satphone is more costly than a cellphone but works where there's no cellular signal and no towers. Unfortunately, you'll pay at least $2 per minute to use the phone, and it only works where you can see the horizon (i.e., usually not indoors). In North America, you can rent Iridium satellite phones from **RoadPost** (www.road post.com; ✆ **888/290-1606** or 905/ 272-5665). InTouch USA (see above) offers a wider range of satphones but at higher rates.

If you're not from the U.S., you'll be appalled at the poor reach of our **GSM (Global System for Mobiles) wireless network,** which is used by much of the rest of the world (see below). Your phone will probably work in most major U.S. cities; it definitely won't work in many rural areas. (To see where GSM phones work in the U.S., check out www.t-mobile. com/coverage/national_popup.asp.) And you may or may not be able to send SMS (text messaging) home— something Americans tend not to do anyway, for various cultural and technological reasons. (International budget travelers like to send text messages home because it's much cheaper than making international calls.) Assume nothing—call your wireless provider and get the full scoop. In a worst-case scenario, you can always rent a phone; InTouch USA delivers to hotels.

9 Getting There

BY PLANE

THE MAJOR AIRLINES By air, Philadelphia is 2½ hours from Miami or Chicago, and 6 hours from the West Coast. Some two dozen carriers fly from more than 100 cities in the U.S. and 16 destinations abroad. Since **US Airways** uses Philadelphia International Airport (PIA) as a hub, this airline has terrific schedules and good fares into town (contact **US Airways** at ✆ 800/428-4322, or www.us airways.com). One reason US Airways is offering low fares is because it has new and zealous competition from **Southwest Airlines,** which began service to Philadelphia in May 2004 and has quickly become a strong competitor. Southwest now offers more than 40 flights a day in and out of Philly, with nonstop service from 16 cities nationwide; call ✆ **800/435-9792,** or visit www.southwest.com. You can also check flight schedules and make reservations on all of the following other domestic airlines:

American Airlines and **American Eagle** (✆ 800/433-7300 or 215/ 365-4000; www.americanair.com); **America West** (✆ 800/235-9292; www.americawest.com); **Continental Airlines** and **Continental Express** (✆ 800/525-0280; www.fly continental.com); **Delta Air Lines** (✆ 800/221-1212 or 215/667-7720; www.delta.com); **Frontier Airlines** (✆ 800/432-1359; www.frontierair lines.com); **Midwest Express** (✆ 800/ 452-2022; www.midwestexpress.com); **National Airlines** (✆ 888/757-5387; www.nationalairlines.com); **Northwest Airlines** (✆ 800/225-2525 domestic, or 800/447-4747 international; www.nwa.com); and **United Airlines** (✆ 800/241-6522 or 215/ 568-2800; www.ual.com).

For international carriers with direct flights, see p. 52.

GETTING THROUGH THE AIRPORT

With the federalization of airport security, security procedures at U.S. airports are more stable and consistent than ever. Generally, you'll be fine if you arrive at the airport **1 hour** before a domestic flight and **2 hours** before an international flight; if you show up late, tell an airline employee and she'll probably whisk you to the front of the line.

Bring a **current, government-issued photo ID** such as a driver's license or passport. Have your ID ready to show at check-in, the security checkpoint, and sometimes even the gate. (Children under 18 do not need government-issued photo IDs for domestic flights, but they do for international flights to most countries.)

In 2003, the TSA phased out **gate check-in** at all U.S. airports. And **e-tickets** have made paper tickets nearly obsolete. Passengers with e-tickets can beat the ticket-counter lines by using airport **electronic kiosks** or even **online check-in** from your home computer. Online check-in involves logging on to your airlines' website, accessing your reservation, and printing out your boarding pass—and the airline may even offer you bonus miles to do so! If you're using a kiosk at the airport, bring the credit card you used to book the ticket or your frequent-flier card. Print out your boarding pass from the kiosk and simply proceed to the security checkpoint with your pass and a photo ID. If you're checking bags or looking to snag an exit-row seat, you will be able to do so using most airline kiosks. Even the smaller airlines are employing the kiosk

system, but always call your airline to make sure these alternatives are available. **Curbside check-in** is also a good way to avoid lines, although a few airlines still ban curbside check-in; call before you go.

Security checkpoint lines are getting shorter than they were during 2001 and 2002, but some doozies remain. If you have trouble standing for long periods of time, tell an airline employee; the airline will provide a wheelchair. Speed up security by **not wearing metal objects** such as big belt buckles. If you've got metallic body parts, a note from your doctor can prevent a long chat with the security screeners. Keep in mind that only **ticketed passengers** are allowed past security, except for folks escorting passengers with disabilities or children.

Federalization has stabilized **what you can carry on** and **what you can't.** The general rule is that sharp things are out, nail clippers are okay, and food and beverages must be passed through the X-ray machine—but that security screeners can't make you drink from your coffee cup. Bring food in your carry-on rather than checking it, as explosive-detection machines used on checked luggage have been known to mistake food (especially chocolate, for some reason) for bombs. Travelers in the U.S. are

---

(Tips Don't Stow It—Ship It

If ease of travel is your main concern and money is no object, you can ship your luggage and sports equipment with one of the growing number of luggage-service companies that pick up, track, and deliver your luggage (often through couriers such as Federal Express) with minimum hassle for you. Traveling luggage-free may be ultra-convenient, but it's not cheap: One-way overnight shipping can cost from $100 to $200, depending on what you're sending. Still, for some people, especially the elderly or the infirm, it's a sensible solution to lugging heavy baggage. Specialists in door-to-door luggage delivery are **Virtual Bellhop** (www.virtualbellhop.com), **SkyCap International** (www.skycapinternational.com), **Luggage Express** (www.usxpluggageexpress.com), and **Sports Express** (www.sportsexpress.com).

allowed one carry-on bag, plus a "personal item" such as a purse, briefcase, or laptop bag. Carry-on hoarders can stuff all sorts of things into a laptop bag; as long as it has a laptop in it, it's still considered a personal item. The Transportation Security Administration (TSA) has issued a list of restricted items; check its website (www.tsa.gov/public/index.jsp) for details.

Airport screeners may decide that your checked luggage needs to be searched by hand. You can now purchase luggage locks that allow screeners to open and re-lock a checked bag if hand-searching is necessary. Look for Travel Sentry certified locks at luggage or travel shops and Brookstone stores (you can buy them online at www.brookstone.com). These locks, approved by the TSA, can be opened by luggage inspectors with a special code or key. For more information on the locks, visit www.travelsentry.org. If you use something other than TSA-approved locks, your lock will be cut off your suitcase if a TSA agent needs to hand-search your luggage.

FLYING FOR LESS: TIPS FOR GETTING THE BEST AIRFARE

Passengers sharing the same airplane cabin rarely pay the same fare. Travelers who need to purchase tickets at the last minute, change their itinerary at a moment's notice, or fly one-way often get stuck paying the premium rate. Here are some ways to keep your airfare costs down.

- Passengers who can book their ticket **long in advance,** who can **stay over Saturday night,** or who **fly midweek** or **at less-trafficked hours** may pay a fraction of the full fare. If your schedule is flexible, say so, and ask if you can secure a cheaper fare by changing your flight plans.

- You can also save on airfares by keeping an eye out in local newspapers for **promotional specials** or **fare wars,** when airlines lower prices on their most popular routes. You rarely see fare wars offered for peak travel times, but if you can travel in the off-months, you may snag a bargain.
- Search **the Internet** for cheap fares (see "Planning Your Trip Online").
- Try to book a ticket **in its country of origin.** For instance, if you're planning a one-way flight from Johannesburg to Bombay, a South Africa–based travel agent will probably have the lowest fares. For multileg trips, book in the country of the first leg; for example, book New York–London–Amsterdam–Rome–New York in the U.S.
- **Consolidators,** also known as bucket shops, are great sources for international tickets, although they usually can't beat the Internet on fares within North America. Start by looking in Sunday newspaper travel sections; U.S. travelers should focus on the *New York Times, Los Angeles Times,* and *Miami Herald.* For less-developed destinations, small travel agents who cater to immigrant communities in large cities often have the best deals. *Beware:* Bucket shop tickets are usually nonrefundable or rigged with stiff cancellation penalties, often as high as 50% to 75% of the ticket price, and some put you on charter airlines, which may leave at inconvenient times and experience delays. Several reliable consolidators are worldwide and available on the Net. **STA Travel** is now the world's leader in student travel, thanks to their purchase of Council Travel. It also offers good fares for travelers of all ages. **ELTExpress (Flights.com)**

Travel in the Age of Bankruptcy

Airlines go bankrupt, so protect yourself by **buying your tickets with a credit card,** as the Fair Credit Billing Act guarantees that you can get your money back from the credit card company if a travel supplier goes under (and if you request the refund within 60 days of the bankruptcy). **Travel insurance** can also help, but make sure it covers against "carrier default" for your specific travel provider. And be aware that if a U.S. airline goes bust mid-trip, a 2001 federal law requires other carriers to take you to your destination (albeit on a space-available basis) for a fee of no more than $25, provided you rebook within 60 days of the cancellation.

(© 800/TRAV-800; www.eltex press.com) started in Europe and has excellent fares worldwide, but particularly to that continent. It also has "local" websites in 12 countries. **FlyCheap** (© **800/FLY-CHEAP;** www.1800flycheap.com) is owned by package-holiday megalith MyTravel and so has especially good access to fares for sunny destinations. **Air Tickets Direct** (© **800/778-3447;** www. airticketsdirect.com) is based in Montreal and leverages the currently weak Canadian dollar for low fares; it'll also book trips to places that U.S. travel agents won't touch, such as Cuba.

- Join **frequent-flier clubs.** Accrue enough miles, and you'll be rewarded with free flights and elite status. It's free, and you'll get the best choice of seats, faster response to phone inquiries, and prompter service if your luggage is stolen, your flight is canceled or delayed, or if you want to change your seat. You don't need to fly to build frequent-flier miles—**frequent-flier credit cards** can provide thousands of miles for doing your everyday shopping.
- For many more tips about air travel, including a rundown of the major frequent-flier credit cards, pick up a copy of *Frommer's Fly Safe, Fly Smart* (Wiley Publishing, Inc.).

LONG-HAUL FLIGHTS: HOW TO STAY COMFORTABLE

Long flights can be trying; stuffy air and cramped seats can make you feel as if you're being sent parcel post in a small box. But with a little advance planning, you can make an otherwise unpleasant experience almost bearable.

- Your choice of airline and airplane will definitely affect your legroom. Find more details at www.seat guru.com, which has extensive details about almost every seat on six major U.S. airlines. For international airlines, research firm Skytrax has posted a list of average seat pitches at www.airlinequality. com.
- Emergency exit seats and bulkhead seats typically have the most legroom. Emergency exit seats are usually held back to be assigned the day of a flight (to ensure that the seat is filled by someone able-bodied); it's worth getting to the ticket counter early to snag one of these spots for a long flight. Many passengers find that bulkhead seating (the row facing the wall at the front of the cabin) offers more legroom, but keep in mind that bulkheads are where airlines often put baby bassinets, so you may be sitting next to an infant.
- To have two seats for yourself in a three-seat row, try for an aisle seat in a center section toward the back of coach. If you're traveling with a

companion, book an aisle and a window seat. Middle seats are usually booked last, so chances are good you'll end up with three seats to yourselves. And in the event that a third passenger is assigned the middle seat, he or she will probably be more than happy to trade for a window or an aisle.

- Ask about entertainment options. Many airlines offer seatback video systems where you get to choose your movies or play video games—but only on some of their planes. (Boeing 777s are your best bet.)
- To sleep, avoid the last row of any section or a row in front of an emergency exit, as these seats are the least likely to recline. Avoid seats near highly trafficked toilet areas. Avoid seats in the back of many jets—these can be narrower than those in the rest of coach class. You also may want to reserve a window seat so that you can rest your head and avoid being bumped in the aisle.
- Get up, walk around, and stretch every 60 to 90 minutes to keep your blood flowing. This helps avoid **deep vein thrombosis,** or "economy-class syndrome," a potentially deadly condition that can be caused by sitting in cramped conditions for too long. Other preventative measures include drinking lots of water and avoiding alcohol (see next bullet). See the "Avoiding 'Economy-Class Syndrome'" box on p. 22.
- Drink water before, during, and after your flight to combat the lack of humidity in airplane cabins—which can be drier than the

---

Tips Coping with Jet Lag

Jet lag is a pitfall of traveling across time zones. If you're flying north-south and you feel sluggish when you touch down, your symptoms will be caused by dehydration and the general stress of air travel. When you travel east to west or vice-versa, however, your body becomes thoroughly confused about what time it is, and everything from your digestion to your brain gets knocked for a loop. Traveling east, say, from Chicago to Paris, is more difficult on your internal clock than traveling west, say from Atlanta to Hawaii, as most peoples' bodies find it more acceptable to stay up late than to fall asleep early.

Here are some tips for combating jet lag:

- **Reset your watch** to your destination time before you board the plane.
- **Drink lots of water** before, during, and after your flight. Avoid alcohol.
- **Exercise and sleep well** for a few days before your trip.
- If you have trouble sleeping on planes, **fly eastward on morning flights.**
- **Daylight** is the key to resetting your body clock. At the website for **Outside In** (www.bodyclock.com), you can get a customized plan of when to seek and avoid light
- If you need help getting to sleep earlier than you usually would, some doctors recommend taking either the hormone melatonin or the sleeping pill Ambien—but not together. Some recommend that you take 2 to 5 milligrams of melatonin about 2 hours before your planned bedtime—but again, always check with your doctor on the best course of action for you.

Flying with Film & Video

Never pack film—developed or undeveloped—in checked bags, as the new, more powerful scanners in U.S. airports can fog film. The film you carry with you can be damaged by scanners as well. X-ray damage is cumulative; the faster the film, and the more times you put it through a scanner, the more likely the damage. Film under 800 ASA is usually safe for up to five scans. If you're taking your film through additional scans, U.S. regulations permit you to demand hand inspections. In international airports, you're at the mercy of airport officials. On international flights, store your film in transparent baggies, so you can remove it easily before you go through scanners. Keep in mind that airports are not the only places where your camera may be scanned: Highly trafficked attractions are X-raying visitors' bags with increasing frequency.

Most photo supply stores sell protective pouches designed to block damaging X-rays. The pouches fit both film and loaded cameras. They should protect your film in checked baggage, but they also may raise alarms and result in a hand inspection.

You'll have little to worry about if you are traveling with **digital cameras.** Unlike film, which is sensitive to light, the digital camera and storage cards are not affected by airport X-rays, according to Nikon. Still, if you plan to travel extensively, you may want to play it safe and hand-carry your digital equipment or ask that it be inspected by hand. See "Digital Photography on the Road," p. 31.

Carry-on scanners will not damage **videotape** in video cameras, but the magnetic fields emitted by the walk-through security gateways and handheld inspection wands will. Always place your loaded camcorder on the screening conveyor belt or have it hand-inspected. Be sure your batteries are charged, as you may be required to turn the device on to ensure that it's what it appears to be.

Sahara. Bring a bottle of water on board. Avoid alcohol, which will dehydrate you.

- If you're flying with kids, don't forget to carry on toys, books, pacifiers, and chewing gum to help them relieve ear pressure buildup during ascent and descent. Let each child pack his or her own backpack with favorite toys.

BY CAR

It's not surprising that two-thirds of all visitors arrive by car—Philadelphia is some 300 miles (6 or so hr.) from Boston, 100 miles (2 hr.) from New

York City, 135 miles (3 hr.) from Washington, D.C., and 450 miles (9 hr.) from Montreal. Tolls between Philadelphia and either New York City or Washington come to about $12.

Philadelphia is easily accessible via a series of interstate highways that circle or pass through the city. Think of Center City as a rectangle. I-95 whizzes by its bottom and right sides. The Pennsylvania Turnpike (I-276) is the top edge, just widened to six lanes with the same E-ZPass electronic toll system that the New Jersey Turnpike and New York City use. I-76 splits off and snakes along the Schuylkill River along the left side into town. I-676 traverses Center City under Vine Street, connecting I-76 to adjacent Camden, New Jersey, via the Ben Franklin Bridge over the Delaware. The "Blue Route" of I-476 forms a left edge for the suburbs, about 15 miles west of town, connecting I-276 and I-76 at its northern end with I-95 to the south.

Here are routes to City Hall, in the very center of town, from various directions:

NEW JERSEY TURNPIKE SOUTHBOUND EXIT 6 Take the Pennsylvania Turnpike westbound to exit 358 and change to U.S. 13 southbound. Follow the signs a short distance to I-95 southbound and enter at exit 22, heading south. Exit for Center City at I-676 (Vine St. Expwy.) westbound to 15th Street, then turn left and travel southbound 2 blocks.

NEW JERSEY TURNPIKE EXIT 4 Take N.J. 73 northbound to N.J. 38 westbound, then change to U.S. 30 westbound (the signage is abominable) and follow it over the Ben Franklin Bridge ($3 this way, but free eastbound; E-ZPass is accepted) to I-676. Go south on 6th Street to Walnut Street (historic district will be on the left), turn right, and travel westbound to 15th Street.

FROM I-95 NORTHBOUND Just past Philadelphia International Airport, take Pa. 291 toward Center City, Philadelphia. Cross the George C. Platt Memorial Bridge and turn left onto 26th Street, then follow 26th Street directly onto I-76 (Schuylkill Expwy.) westbound to exit 39 (30th St. Station). Go 1 block to Market Street and turn right. Go east on Market Street to City Hall, which will be in front of you.

FROM THE PENNSYLVANIA TURNPIKE (I-76) Take exit 326 to I-76 (Schuylkill Expwy.) eastbound to I-676 (Vine St. Expwy.). Take I-676 eastbound to 15th Street, turn right, and proceed southbound 2 blocks.

BY TRAIN

Philadelphia is a major Amtrak stop (© **800/USA-RAIL**; www.amtrak. com). It's on the Boston–Washington, D.C., northeast corridor, which has extensions south to Florida, west to Pittsburgh and Chicago, and east to Atlantic City. The Amtrak terminal is Penn Station (30th St.), about 15 blocks from City Hall. Regular service, called Northeast Direct, takes 85 minutes from New York City; Metroliner service is 77 minutes for the same trip, or 100 minutes from Washington. The new Acela trims the time to New York to 72 minutes, and Philly to Boston on Acela is 5 hours, 9 minutes.

SEPTA commuter trains (© **215/ 580-7800**; www.septa.com) also

---

(Tips) Major Money-Saving Travel Tip

Keep in mind that a trip to Philadelphia can be much cheaper if you take **New Jersey Transit** (© **800/582-5946** or 215/569-3752; www.njtransit.com) commuter trains out of Penn Station in New York City or Newark to Trenton, then switch across the platform to the R7 Philadelphia-bound SEPTA commuter train (© 215/580-7800 or www.septa.com) that makes several convenient Center City stops before heading out to Chestnut Hill. The New Jersey Transit train from New York to Trenton travels every 20 minutes from 5:14am to 1:41am, takes 80 minutes, and costs $10 one-way or $16 round-trip. The SEPTA portion costs another $7 each way, $14 round-trip and takes about 50 minutes. Rates and times are, of course, subject to change.

connect 30th Street Station and several Center City stations to Trenton, New Jersey, to the northeast; to Harrisburg to the west; and directly to airport terminals to the south.

Sample round-trip fares on Amtrak as of press time were: New York City to Philadelphia, $98 peak, $204 on Acela; Washington to Philadelphia, $94 peak, $230 on Acela; one train daily to or from Chicago, around $265. Peak hours are Friday and Sunday, and days surrounding major holidays, from 11am to 11pm.

10 Packages for the Independent Traveler

Before you start your search for the lowest airfare, you may want to consider booking your flight as part of a travel package. Package tours are not the same thing as escorted tours. Package tours are simply a way to buy the airfare, accommodations, and other elements of your trip (such as car rentals, airport transfers, and sometimes even activities) at the same time and often at discounted prices—kind of like one-stop shopping. Packages are sold in bulk to tour operators— who resell them to the public at a cost that usually undercuts standard rates.

One good source of package deals is the airlines themselves. Most major airlines offer air/land packages, including **American Airlines Vacations** (© 800/321-2121; www.aavacations. com), **Delta Vacations** (© 800/221-6666; www.deltavacations.com), **Continental Airlines Vacations** (© 800/301-3800; www.covacations. com), and **United Vacations** (© 888/854-3899; www.unitedvacations. com). Several big **online travel agencies**—Expedia, Travelocity, Orbitz, Site59, and Lastminute.com—also do a brisk business in packages. If you're unsure about the pedigree of a smaller packager, check with the Better Business Bureau in the city where the company is based, or go online at www.bbb.org. If a packager won't tell you where they're based, don't fly with them.

Travel packages are also listed in the travel section of your local Sunday newspaper. Or check ads in the national travel magazines such as *Arthur Frommer's Budget Travel Magazine, Travel & Leisure, National Geographic Traveler,* and *Condé Nast Traveler.*

Package tours can vary by leaps and bounds. Some offer a better class of hotels than others. Some offer the same hotels for lower prices. Some offer flights on scheduled airlines, while others book charters. Some limit your choice of accommodations and travel days. You are often required to make a large payment up front. On the plus side, packages can save you money, offering group prices but allowing for independent travel. Some even let you add on a few guided excursions or escorted day trips (also at prices lower than if you booked them yourself) without booking an entirely escorted tour.

Before you invest in a package tour, get some answers. Ask about the **accommodations choices** and prices for each. Then look up the hotels' reviews in a Frommer's guide and check their rates online for your specific dates of travel. You'll also want to find out what **type of room** you get. If you need a certain type of room, ask for it; don't take whatever is thrown your way. Request a nonsmoking room, a quiet room, a room with a view, or whatever you fancy.

Finally, look for **hidden expenses.** Ask whether airport departure fees and taxes, for example, are included in the total cost.

11 Escorted General-Interest Tours

Escorted tours are structured group tours, with a group leader. The price usually includes everything from airfare to hotels, meals, tours, admission costs, and local transportation.

Many people get comfort and security from escorted trips. Escorted tours—whether by bus, motor coach, train, or boat—let travelers sit back and enjoy their trip without having to spend lots of time behind the wheel or worrying about details. You know your costs up front, and there are few surprises. Escorted tours can take you to the maximum number of sights in the minimum amount of time with the least amount of hassle—you don't have to sweat over the plotting and planning of a vacation schedule. Escorted tours are particularly convenient for people with limited mobility. They can also be a great way to make new friends.

On the downside, an escorted tour often requires a big deposit up front, and lodging and dining choices are predetermined. You'll get little opportunity for serendipitous interactions with locals. The tours can be jam-packed with activities, leaving little room for individual sightseeing, whim, or adventure—plus they also often focus only on the heavily touristed sites, so you miss out on the lesser-known gems.

Before you invest in an escorted tour, ask about the **cancellation policy:** Is a deposit required? Can they cancel the trip if they don't get enough people? Do you get a refund if they cancel? If *you* cancel? How late can you cancel if you are unable to go? When do you pay in full? *Note:* If you choose an escorted tour, think strongly about purchasing trip-cancellation insurance, especially if the tour operator asks you to pay up front. See the section on "Travel Insurance," p. 19.

You'll also want to get a complete **schedule** of the trip to find out how much sightseeing is planned each day and whether enough time has been allotted for relaxing or wandering solo.

The **size** of the group is also important to know up front. Generally, the smaller the group, the more flexible the itinerary, and the less time you'll spend waiting for people to get on and off the bus. Find out the **demographics** of the group as well. What is the age range? What is the gender breakdown? Is this mostly a trip for couples or singles?

Discuss what is included in the **price.** You may have to pay for transportation to and from the airport. A box lunch may be included in an excursion, but drinks might cost extra. Tips may not be included. Find out if you will be charged if you decide to opt out of certain activities or meals.

Before you invest in an escorted tour, get some answers. Ask about the **accommodations choices** and prices for each. Then look up the hotels' reviews in a Frommer's guide and check their rates online for your specific dates of travel. You'll also want to find out what **type of room** you get. If you need a certain type of room, ask for it; don't take whatever is thrown your way. Request a nonsmoking room, a quiet room, a room with a view, or whatever you fancy.

Finally, if you plan to travel alone, you'll need to know if a **single supplement** will be charged and if the company can match you up with a roommate.

SAVING ON YOUR HOTEL ROOM

The **rack rate** is the maximum rate that a hotel charges for a room. Hardly anybody pays this price, however, except in high season or on holidays. To lower the cost of your room:

- **Ask about special rates or other discounts.** Always ask whether a room less expensive than the first one quoted is available, or whether any special rates apply to you. You may qualify for corporate, student, military, senior, or other discounts. Mention membership in AAA, AARP, frequent-flier programs, or trade unions, which may entitle you to special deals as well. Find out the hotel policy on children—do kids stay free in the room or is there a special rate?
- **Dial direct.** When booking a room in a chain hotel, you'll often get a better deal by calling the individual hotel's reservation desk rather than the chain's main number.
- **Book online.** Many hotels offer Internet-only discounts, or supply rooms to Priceline, Hotwire, or Expedia at rates much lower than the ones you can get through the hotel itself. Shop around. And if you have special needs—a quiet room, a room with a view—call the hotel directly and make your needs known after you've booked online.
- **Remember the law of supply and demand.** Resort hotels are most crowded and therefore most expensive on weekends, so discounts are usually available for midweek stays. Business hotels in downtown locations are busiest during the week, so you can expect big discounts over the weekend. Many hotels have high-season and low-season prices, and booking the day after "high season" ends can mean big discounts.
- **Look into group or long-stay discounts.** If you come as part of a large group, you should be able to negotiate a bargain rate, since the hotel can then guarantee occupancy in a number of rooms. Likewise, if you're planning a long stay (at least 5 days), you might qualify for a discount. As a general rule, expect 1 night free after a 7-night stay.
- **Avoid excess charges and hidden costs.** When you book a room, ask whether the hotel charges for parking. Use your own cellphone, pay phones, or prepaid phone cards instead of dialing direct from hotel phones, which usually have exorbitant rates. And don't be tempted by the room's minibar offerings: Most hotels charge through the nose for water, soda, and snacks. Finally, ask about local taxes and service charges, which can increase the cost of a room by 15% or more. If a hotel insists upon tacking on a surprise "energy surcharge" that wasn't mentioned at check-in or a "resort fee" for amenities you didn't use, you can often make a case for getting it removed.
- **Carefully consider your hotel's meal plan.** If you enjoy eating out and sampling the local cuisine, it makes sense to choose a Continental Plan (CP), which includes breakfast only, or a European Plan (EP), which doesn't include any meals and allows you maximum flexibility. If you're more interested in saving money, opt for a Modified American Plan (MAP), which includes breakfast and one meal, or the American Plan (AP), which includes three meals. If you must choose a MAP, see if you can get a free lunch at your hotel if you decide to do dinner out.
- **Book an efficiency.** A room with a kitchenette allows you to shop for groceries and cook your own meals. This is a big money saver, especially for families on long stays.

> **Tips** **House Swapping**
>
> House swaps are a great way to get a local's perspective of Philadelphia. Log onto **www.4homex.com/ushomeexchangeinfo.htm** for more information, or try **www.Philadelphia.craigslist.org**.

LANDING THE BEST ROOM

Somebody has to get the best room in the house. It might as well be you. You can start by joining the hotel's frequent-guest program, which may make you eligible for upgrades. A hotel-branded credit card usually gives its owner "silver" or "gold" status in frequent-guest programs for free. Always ask about a corner room. They're often larger and quieter, with more windows and light, and they often cost the same as standard rooms. When you make your reservation, ask if the hotel is renovating; if it is, request a room away from the construction. Ask about nonsmoking rooms, rooms with views, rooms with twin, queen-, or king-size beds. If you're a light sleeper, request a quiet room away from vending machines, elevators, restaurants, bars, and discos. Ask for a room that has been most recently renovated or redecorated.

If you aren't happy with your room when you arrive, ask for another one. Most lodgings will be willing to accommodate you.

12 Recommended Books

ART & ARCHITECTURE Try *Philadelphia's Architecture* (MIT Press, 1984), which goes into environmental issues as well, or the more coffee-table *An Architectural Guidebook to Philadelphia* (Gibbs Smith, 1999) by Frances Morrone and James Iska. Roslyn Brenner's *Philadelphia's Outdoor Art: A Walking Tour* (Camino Books, 1987) has a makeshift text but contains good photography.

Old Philadelphia in Early Photographs, 1839–1914 (Dover, 1976) by Robert F. Looney is a superb photographic history. Robert Llewellyn has also assembled a sensitive book of more recent photographs in *Philadelphia* (Thomasson-Grant, 1986).

BIOGRAPHY John Lukacs's *Philadelphia: Patricians & Philistines 1900–1950* (Farrar, Straus & Giroux, 1981) is a charming, slightly offbeat collection of profiles of seven colorful figures who flourished during this period and have faded into obscurity since.

The Kelly family—John, Jack, and Grace—receives a hagiographic and slightly dated treatment in John McCallum's *That Kelly Family* (A.S. Barnes, 1957). Another "immigrant made good" story, although more measured, is the biography of former Mayor Frank Rizzo, Joseph Daughen's *The Cop Who Would Be King* (Little, Brown, 1977).

FICTION Try Pete Dexter's *God's Pocket* (Warner Books, 1990) for a gritty contemporary look at the city by a former newspaper reporter turned big-league novelist and scriptwriter. Donald Zochert's *Murder in the Hellfire Club* (Holt, Rinehart & Winston, 1978) is an amusing historical mystery, with Colonists framed for murder in 1770s London and Ben Franklin on hand to solve the case.

HISTORY It is impossible to read about the transformation of the Colonies to the United States, and the first 50 years of independence, without learning about Philadelphia.

Christopher and James Collier, two brothers—one a writer on jazz, the other a history professor—have an intensely novelistic and readable summary of the 1787 Constitutional Convention with *Decision in Philadelphia* (Ballantine, reissued 1987). Carl Bridenbaugh's *Rebels and Gentlemen* (Oxford University Press, 1965) is a good summary of events leading up to independence. Catherine Drinker Bowen's *Miracle at Philadelphia* (Atlantic–Little, Brown, 1960) is a vivid retelling of the 1787 Constitutional Convention.

E. Digby Baltzell's *Puritan Boston and Quaker Philadelphia* (Free Press, 1960) is a thoughtful and amusing comparison between these two preeminent Colonial cities, explaining why their histories turned out so differently. Baltzell's first classic effort here was *Philadelphia Gentlemen: The Making of a National Upper Class* (Free Press, 1958).

The transformation from ideal seaport to ideal manufacturing city is covered in *Civil War Issues in Philadelphia 1956–1965* by William Dusinberre (University of Pennsylvania Press, 1965).

W. E. B. Du Bois's *The Philadelphia Negro* (University of Pennsylvania Press, 1899) is a classic analysis of racism and its social effects in the North since the Civil War. Jean Seder has edited *Voices of Another Time: 3 Memories* (Institute for the Study of Human Issues, 1985), three oral histories of African-American women who were born in the South but who spent their lives in Philadelphia, complete with recipes, cures, and proverbs.

Edwin Wolf II's *Philadelphia: Portrait of an American City* (Stackpole Books, 1975) is one of the more engaging histories, with beautiful and appropriate illustrations. The building of the Benjamin Franklin Parkway, a Champs Elysées in the midst of the Colonial grid, is covered in David Bruce Brownlee's *Building the City Beautiful* (Philadelphia Museum of Art catalog, 1989).

From the moment that the superb 1990s mayor Ed Rendell (now governor of Pennsylvania) took office, he allowed Buzz Bissinger complete behind-the-scenes access to his ideas and meetings. Bissinger's written the best recent history of the city in *A Prayer for the City: The True Story of a Mayor and Five Heroes in a Race Against Time* (Random House, 1998).

For International Visitors

Whether it's your first visit or your tenth, a trip to the United States may require an additional degree of planning. This chapter will provide you with essential information, helpful tips, and advice for the more common problems that some visitors encounter.

The **International Visitors Council** at 1 Parkway, 1515 Arch St., 12th Floor, Philadelphia, PA 19102 (© **215/683-0999;** www.ivc.org) offers special services to international visitors, as does the **Independence Visitor Center,** 6th and Market streets, Philadelphia, PA 19106 (© **800/537-7676;** www.independence visitorcenter.com).

1 Preparing for Your Trip

ENTRY REQUIREMENTS

Check at any U.S. embassy or consulate for current information and requirements. You can also obtain a visa application and other information online at the **U.S. State Department**'s website, at **www.travel.state.gov.**

VISAS The U.S. State Department has a **Visa Waiver Program** allowing citizens of certain countries to enter the United States without a visa for stays of up to 90 days. At press time these included Andorra, Australia, Austria, Belgium, Brunei, Denmark, Finland, France, Germany, Iceland, Ireland, Italy, Japan, Liechtenstein, Luxembourg, Monaco, the Netherlands, New Zealand, Norway, Portugal, San Marino, Singapore, Slovenia, Spain, Sweden, Switzerland, and the United Kingdom. Citizens of these countries need only a valid passport and a round-trip air or cruise ticket in their possession upon arrival. If they first enter the United States, they may also visit Mexico, Canada, Bermuda, and/or the Caribbean islands and return to the United States without a visa. Further information is available from any U.S. embassy or consulate.

Canadian citizens may enter the United States without visas; they need only proof of residence.

Citizens of all other countries must have (1) a valid passport that expires at least 6 months later than the scheduled end of their visit to the United States, and (2) a tourist visa, which may be obtained without charge from any U.S. consulate.

To obtain a visa, the traveler must submit a completed application form (either in person or by mail) with a 1½-inch-square photo, and must demonstrate binding ties to a residence abroad. Usually you can obtain a visa at once or within 24 hours, but it may take longer during the summer rush from June through August. If you cannot go in person, contact the nearest U.S. embassy or consulate for directions on applying by mail. Your travel agent or airline office may also be able to provide you with visa applications and instructions. The U.S. consulate or embassy that issues your visa will determine whether you will be issued a multiple- or single-entry visa and any restrictions regarding the length of your stay.

British subjects can obtain up-to-date visa information by calling the **U.S. Embassy Visa Information Line** (✆ **0891/200-290**) or by visiting the American Embassy London's website at www.usembassy.org.uk.

Irish citizens can obtain up-to-date visa information through the **Embassy of the USA Dublin,** 42 Elgin Rd., Dublin 4, Ireland (✆ **353/1-668-8777**) or by checking www.usembassy.ie.

Australian citizens can obtain up-to-date visa information by contacting the **U.S. Embassy Canberra,** Moonah Place, Yarralumla, ACT 2600 (✆ **02/6214-5600**) or by checking the U.S. Diplomatic Mission's website at http://usembassy-australia.state.gov/consular.

Citizens of **New Zealand** can obtain up-to-date visa information by contacting the **U.S. Embassy New Zealand,** 29 Fitzherbert Terrace, Thorndon, Wellington (✆ **644/472-2068**), or get the information directly from http://usembassy.org.nz.

MEDICAL REQUIREMENTS

Unless you're arriving from an area known to be suffering from an epidemic (particularly cholera or yellow fever), inoculations or vaccinations are not required for entry into the United States. If you have a medical condition that requires **syringe-administered medications,** carry a valid signed prescription from your physician—the Federal Aviation Administration (FAA) no longer allows airline passengers to pack syringes in their carry-on baggage without documented proof of medical need. If you have a disease that requires treatment with **narcotics,** you should also carry documented proof with you—smuggling narcotics aboard a plane is a serious offense that carries severe penalties in the U.S.

For **HIV-positive visitors,** requirements for entering the United States are somewhat vague and change frequently. According to the latest publication of *HIV and Immigrants: A Manual for AIDS Service Providers,* the Immigration and Naturalization Service (INS) doesn't require a medical exam for entry into the United States, but INS officials may stop individuals because they look sick or because they are carrying AIDS/HIV medicine.

If an HIV-positive noncitizen applies for a non-immigrant visa, the question on the application regarding communicable diseases is tricky no matter which way it's answered. If the applicant checks "no," INS may deny the visa on the grounds that the applicant committed fraud. If the applicant checks "yes" or if INS suspects the person is HIV-positive, it will deny the visa unless the applicant asks for a special waiver for visitors. This waiver is for people visiting the United States for a short time, to attend a conference, for instance, to visit close relatives, or to receive medical treatment. For up-to-the-minute information, contact **AIDSinfo** (✆ **800/448-0440,** or 301/519-6616 outside the U.S.; www.aidsinfo.nih.gov) or the **Gay Men's Health Crisis** (✆ **212/367-1000;** www.gmhc.org).

DRIVER'S LICENSES Foreign driver's licenses are mostly recognized in the U.S., although you may want to get an international driver's license if your home license is not written in English.

PASSPORT INFORMATION

Safeguard your passport in an inconspicuous, inaccessible place like a money belt. Make a copy of the critical pages, including the passport number, and store it in a safe place, separate from the passport itself. If you lose your passport, visit the nearest consulate of your native country as soon as possible for a replacement. Passport applications are downloadable from the websites listed below.

Note: The International Civil Aviation Organization has recommended a policy requiring that *every* individual who travels by air have a passport. In response, many countries are now requiring that children must be issued their own passport to travel internationally, where before those under 16 or so may have been allowed to travel on a parent or guardian's passport.

FOR RESIDENTS OF CANADA

You can pick up a passport application at one of 28 regional passport offices or most travel agencies. Canadian children who travel must have their own passport. However, if you hold a valid Canadian passport issued before December 11, 2001, that bears the name of your child, the passport remains valid for you and your child until it expires. Passports cost C$85 for those 16 years and older (valid 5 years), C$35 children 3 to 15 (valid 5 years), and C$20, children under 3 (valid 3 years). Applications, which must be accompanied by two identical passport-size photographs and proof of Canadian citizenship, are available at travel agencies throughout Canada or from the central **Passport Office,** Department of Foreign Affairs and International Trade, Ottawa, ON K1A 0G3 (© **800/567-6868;** www. dfait-maeci.gc.ca/passport). Processing takes 5 to 10 days if you apply in person, or about 3 weeks by mail.

FOR RESIDENTS OF THE UNITED KINGDOM

As a member of the European Union, you need only an identity card, not a passport, to travel to other E.U. countries. However, if you already possess a passport, it's always useful to carry it. To pick up an application for a standard 10-year passport (5-year passport for children under 16), visit the nearest Passport Office, major post office, or travel agency. You can also contact the **United Kingdom Passport Service** at © **0870/571-0410** or visit its website at www.passport.gov.uk. Passports are £33 for adults and £19 for children under 16, with another £30 fee if you apply in person at the Passport Office. Processing takes about 2 weeks (1 week if you apply at the Passport Office).

FOR RESIDENTS OF IRELAND

You can apply for a 10-year passport, costing €57, at the **Passport Office,** Setanta Centre, Molesworth Street, Dublin 2 (© **01/671-1633;** www.irl gov.ie/iveagh). Those under age 18 and over 65 must apply for a €12 3-year passport. You can also apply at 1A South Mall, Cork (© **021/272-525**) or over the counter at most main post offices.

FOR RESIDENTS OF AUSTRALIA

You can get an application from your local post office or any branch of Passports Australia, but you must schedule an interview at the passport office to present your application materials. Call the **Australian Passport Information Service** at © **131-232,** or visit the government website at www. passports.gov.au. Passports for adults are A$144 and for those under 18 are A$72.

FOR RESIDENTS OF NEW ZEALAND

You can pick up a passport application at any New Zealand Passports Office or download it from their website. Contact the **Passports Office** at © **0800/225-050** in New Zealand or 04/474-8100, or log on to www. passports.govt.nz. Passports for adults are NZ$80 and for children under 16 NZ$40.

CUSTOMS
WHAT YOU CAN BRING IN

Every visitor more than 21 years of age may bring in, free of duty, the following: (1) 1 liter of wine or hard liquor;

(2) 200 cigarettes, 100 cigars (but not from Cuba), or 3 pounds of smoking tobacco; and (3) $100 worth of gifts. These exemptions are offered to travelers who spend at least 72 hours in the United States and who have not claimed them within the preceding 6 months. It is altogether forbidden to bring into the country foodstuffs (particularly fruit, cooked meats, and canned goods) and plants (vegetables, seeds, tropical plants, and the like). Foreign tourists may bring in or take out up to $10,000 in U.S. or foreign currency with no formalities; larger sums must be declared to U.S. Customs on entering or leaving, which includes filing form CM 4790. For more specific information regarding U.S. Customs and Border Protection, contact your nearest U.S. embassy or consulate, or the **U.S. Customs** office (© **202/927-1770** or www.customs. ustreas.gov).

WHAT YOU CAN TAKE HOME

U.K. citizens returning from a non-E.U. country have a customs allowance of: 200 cigarettes; 50 cigars; 250g of smoking tobacco; 2 liters of still table wine; 1 liter of spirits or strong liqueurs (over 22% volume); 2 liters of fortified wine, sparkling wine, or other liqueurs; 60cc (ml) perfume; 250cc (ml) of toilet water; and £145 worth of all other goods, including gifts and souvenirs. People under 17 cannot have the tobacco or alcohol allowance. For more information, contact HM Customs & Excise at © **0845/010-9000** (from outside the U.K., 020/8929-0152), or consult their website at www.hmce.gov.uk.

For a clear summary of **Canadian** rules, request the booklet *I Declare,* issued by the **Canada Customs and Revenue Agency** (© **800/461-9999** in Canada, or 204/983-3500; www. ccra-adrc.gc.ca). Canada allows its citizens a C$750 exemption, and you're allowed to bring back duty-free one carton of cigarettes, 1 can of tobacco, 40 imperial ounces of liquor, and 50 cigars. In addition, you're allowed to mail gifts to Canada valued at less than C$60 a day, provided they're unsolicited and don't contain alcohol or tobacco (write on the package "Unsolicited gift, under C$60 value"). All valuables should be declared on the Y-38 form before departure from Canada, including serial numbers of valuables you already own, such as expensive foreign cameras. *Note:* The C$750 exemption can only be used once a year and only after an absence of 7 days.

The duty-free allowance in **Australia** is A$400 or, for those under 18, A$200. Citizens age 18 and over can bring in 250 cigarettes or 250 grams of loose tobacco, and 1,125 milliliters of alcohol. If you're returning with valuables you already own, such as foreign-made cameras, you should file form B263. A helpful brochure available from Australian consulates or Customs offices is *Know Before You Go.* For more information, call the **Australian Customs Service** at © **1300/363-263,** or log on to www. customs.gov.au.

The duty-free allowance for **New Zealand** is NZ$700. Citizens over 17 can bring in 200 cigarettes, 50 cigars, or 250 grams of tobacco (or a mixture of all three if their combined weight doesn't exceed 250g); plus 4.5 liters of wine and beer, or 1.125 liters of liquor. New Zealand currency does not carry import or export restrictions. Fill out a certificate of export, listing the valuables you are taking out of the country; that way, you can bring them back without paying duty. Most questions are answered in a free pamphlet available at New Zealand consulates and Customs offices: *New Zealand Customs Guide for Travellers, Notice no. 4.* For more information, contact **New Zealand Customs,** The Customhouse, 17–21 Whitmore St.,

Box 2218, Wellington (© **0800/428-786** or 04/473-6099; www.customs.govt.nz).

HEALTH INSURANCE

Although it's not required of travelers, health insurance is highly recommended. Unlike many European countries, the United States does not usually offer free or low-cost medical care to its citizens or visitors. Doctors and hospitals are expensive, and in most cases will require advance payment or proof of coverage before they render their services. Policies can cover everything from the loss or theft of your baggage and trip cancellation to the guarantee of bail in case you're arrested. Good policies will also cover the costs of an accident, repatriation, or death. See "Travel Insurance," p. 19, for more information. Packages such as **Europ Assistance's "Worldwide Healthcare Plan"** are sold by European automobile clubs and travel agencies at attractive rates. **Worldwide Assistance Services, Inc.** (© **800/821-2828;** www.worldwideassistance.com) is the agent for Europ Assistance in the United States.

Though lack of health insurance may prevent you from being admitted to a hospital in nonemergencies, don't worry about being left on a street corner to die: The American way is to fix you now and bill the living daylights out of you later.

INSURANCE FOR BRITISH TRAVELERS Most big travel agents offer their own insurance and will probably try to sell you their package when you book a holiday. Think before you sign. **Britain's Consumers' Association** recommends that you insist on seeing the policy and reading the fine print before buying travel insurance. **The Association of British Insurers** (© **020/7600-3333;** www.abi.org.uk) gives advice by phone and publishes *Holiday Insurance,* a free guide to policy provisions and prices. You might also shop around for better deals: Try **Columbus Direct** (© **020/7375-0011;** www.columbusdirect.net).

INSURANCE FOR CANADIAN TRAVELERS Canadians should check with their provincial health plan offices or call **Health Canada** (© **613/957-2991;** www.hc-sc.gc.ca) to find out the extent of their coverage and what documentation and receipts they must take home in case they are treated in the United States.

MONEY

CURRENCY The U.S. monetary system is very simple: The most common **bills** are the $1 (colloquially, a "buck"), $5, $10, and $20 denominations. There are also $2 bills (seldom encountered), $50 bills, and $100 bills (the last two are usually not welcome as payment for small purchases). All the paper money was recently redesigned, making the famous faces adorning them disproportionately large. The old-style bills are still legal tender.

There are seven denominations of coins: 1¢ (1 cent, or a penny); 5¢ (5 cents, or a nickel); 10¢ (10 cents, or a dime); 25¢ (25 cents, or a quarter); 50¢ (50 cents, or a half dollar); the new gold-colored "Sacagawea" coin worth $1; and, prized by collectors, the rare, older silver dollar.

(Tips Small Change

When you change money, ask for some small bills or loose change. Petty cash will come in handy for tipping and public transportation. Consider keeping the change separate from your larger bills, so it's readily accessible and you'll be less of a target for theft.

Tips Dear Visa: I'm Off to Philly!

Some credit card companies recommend that you notify them of any impending trip abroad so that they don't become suspicious when the card is used numerous times in a foreign destination and block your charges. Even if you don't call your credit card company in advance, you can always call the card's toll-free emergency number (see "Credit Cards & ATMs," below) if a charge is refused—a good reason to carry the phone number with you. But perhaps the most important lesson here is to carry more than one card with you on your trip; a card might not work for any number of reasons, so having a backup is the smart way to go.

Note: The "foreign-exchange bureaus" so common in Europe are rare even at airports in the United States, and nonexistent outside major cities. It's best not to change foreign money (or traveler's checks denominated in a currency other than U.S. dollars) at a small-town bank, or even a branch in a big city; in fact, leave any currency other than U.S. dollars at home—it may prove a greater nuisance to you than it's worth.

TRAVELER'S CHECKS Though traveler's checks are widely accepted, make sure that they're denominated in U.S. dollars, as foreign-currency checks are often difficult to exchange. The three traveler's checks that are most widely recognized—and least likely to be denied—are **Visa, American Express,** and **Thomas Cook.** Be sure to record the numbers of the checks, and keep that information in a separate place in case they get lost or stolen. Most businesses are pretty good about taking traveler's checks, but you're better off cashing them in at a bank (in small amounts, of course) and paying in cash. *Remember:* You'll need identification, such as a driver's license or passport, to change a traveler's check.

CREDIT CARDS & ATMS Credit cards are the most widely used form of payment in the United States: **Visa** (Barclaycard in Britain), **MasterCard** (EuroCard in Europe, Access in Britain, Chargex in Canada), **American Express, Diners Club, Discover,** and **Carte Blanche.** There are, however, a handful of stores and restaurants that do not take credit cards, so be sure to ask in advance. Most businesses display a sticker near their entrance to let you know which cards they accept. (*Note:* Businesses may require a minimum purchase, usually around $10, to use a credit card.)

It is strongly recommended that you bring at least one major credit card. You must have a credit or charge card to rent a car. Hotels and airlines usually require a credit card imprint as a deposit against expenses, and in an emergency a credit card can be priceless.

You'll find **automated teller machines (ATMs)** on just about every block—at least in almost every town—across the country. Many blocks in Philadelphia have more than one ATM, in fact, and there are ATMs inside most convenience stores throughout the city. One local chain, the **Wawa stores** (which are deli/convenience stores), offers no-fee ATMS in every one of its many locations.

Some ATMs will allow you to draw U.S. currency against your bank and credit cards. Check with your bank before leaving home, and remember that you will need your personal identification number (PIN) to do so. Most accept Visa, MasterCard, and American Express, as well as ATM cards from other U.S. banks. Expect to be charged up to $3 per transaction, however, if you're not using your own bank's ATM.

One way around these fees is to ask for cash back at grocery stores that accept ATM cards and don't charge usage fees. Of course, you'll have to purchase something first.

ATM cards with major credit card backing, known as "debit cards," are now a commonly acceptable form of payment in most stores and restaurants. Debit cards draw money directly from your checking account. Some stores enable you to receive "cash back" on your debit-card purchases as well.

SAFETY

GENERAL   SUGGESTIONS

Although tourist areas are generally safe, U.S. urban areas tend to be less safe than those in Europe or Japan. You should always stay alert. This is particularly true of large American cities, and in Philadelphia, the areas north and south of Center City and parts of West Philadelphia can be dicey. If you're in doubt about which neighborhoods are safe, don't hesitate to make inquiries with the hotel front desk staff or the local tourist office.

Avoid deserted areas, especially at night, and don't go into public parks after dark unless there's a concert or similar occasion that will attract a crowd. (The more popular parks in Center City Philadelphia such as Rittenhouse Square are filled with people late into the evening, and are well-patrolled by police officers.) Be careful of handbags and other belongings in raucous areas such as South Street,

and late at night around landmarks like Pat's Steaks.

Avoid carrying valuables with you on the street, and keep expensive cameras or electronic equipment bagged up or covered when not in use. If you're using a map, try to consult it inconspicuously—or better yet, study it before you leave your room. Hold onto your pocketbook, and place your billfold in an inside pocket. In theaters, restaurants, and other public places, keep your possessions in sight.

Always lock your room door—don't assume that once you're inside the hotel you are automatically safe and no longer need to be aware of your surroundings. Hotels are open to the public, and in a large hotel, security may not be able to screen everyone who enters.

DRIVING SAFETY Driving safety is important, too, and carjacking is not unprecedented. Question your rental agency about personal safety and ask for a traveler-safety brochure when you pick up your car. Obtain written directions—or a map with the route clearly marked—from the agency showing how to get to your destination. (Many agencies now offer the option of renting a cellphone for the duration of your car rental; check with the rental agent when you pick up the car. Otherwise, contact **InTouch USA** at ☎ **800/872-7626** or www.intouchusa.com for short-term cellphone rental.) And, if possible, arrive and depart during daylight hours.

If you drive off a highway and end up in a dodgy-looking neighborhood, leave the area as quickly as possible. If

Travel Tip

Be sure to keep a copy of all your travel papers separate from your wallet or purse, and leave a copy with someone at home should you need it faxed in an emergency.

SIZE CONVERSION CHART

Women's Clothing

American	4	6	8	10	12	14	16	
French	34	36	38	40	42	44	46	
British	6	8	10	12	14	16	18	

Women's Shoes

American	5	6	7	8	9	10	
French	36	37	38	39	40	41	
British	4	5	6	7	8	9	

Men's Suits

American	34	36	38	40	42	44	46	48
French	44	46	48	50	52	54	56	58
British	34	36	38	40	42	44	46	48

Men's Shirts

American	14½	15	15½	16	16½	17	17½
French	37	38	39	41	42	43	44
British	14½	15	15½	16	16½	17	17½

Men's Shoes

American	7	8	9	10	11	12	13
French	39½	41	42	43	44½	46	47
British	6	7	8	9	10	11	12

you have an accident, even on the highway, stay in your car with the doors locked until you assess the situation or until the police arrive. If you're bumped from behind on the street or are involved in a minor accident with no injuries, and the situation appears to be suspicious, motion to the other driver to follow you. Never get out of your car in such situations. Go directly to the nearest police precinct, well-lit service station, or 24-hour store.

Park in well-lit and well-traveled areas whenever possible. Always keep your car doors locked, whether the vehicle is attended or unattended. Never leave any packages or valuables in sight. If someone attempts to rob you or steal your car, don't try to resist the thief/carjacker. Report the incident to the police department immediately by calling ✆ **911.**

2 Getting to the U.S.

International carriers that fly into **Philadelphia International Airport** (✆ 215/937-6800; www.phl.org) include **Air Canada** (✆ 888/247-2262; ww.aircanada.com); **Air France** (✆ 800/237-2747; www.airfrance. com); **Air Jamaica** (✆ 800/523-5585; www.airjamaica.com); **British**

Airways (✆ 800/247-9297; www. british-airways.com); and **Lufthansa** (✆ 800/645-3880; www.lufthansa. de). **US Airways International** offers nonstop flights between Philadelphia and more than a dozen European cities, including London, Paris, Rome,

---

Tips Prepare to Be Fingerprinted

Since January 2004, many international visitors traveling on visas to the United States have been photographed and fingerprinted at Customs in a new program created by the Department of Homeland Security called **US-VISIT**. Non–U.S. citizens arriving at airports and on cruise ships must undergo an instant background check as part of the government's ongoing efforts to deter terrorism by verifying the identity of incoming and outgoing visitors. Exempt from the extra scrutiny are visitors entering by land or those from 28 countries (mostly in Europe) that don't require a visa for short-term visits. For more information, go to the Homeland Security website at **www.dhs.gov/dhspublic**.

Manchester, and Munich (© 800/ 428-4322; www.usairways.com).

From Ireland, **Aer Lingus** (© 0818/365-000 in Ireland, or 800/ IRISH AIR in the U.S.; www.aer lingus.ie) can fly you to New York City or Boston, and arrange a flight to Philadelphia from there. From Australia and New Zealand, **Qantas** (in Australia, © 131313, or in the U.S. © 800/227-4500; www.qantas.com. au) and **Air New Zealand** (© 0800/ 737 000; www.airnz.co.nz) offer flights to Los Angeles, from which you can connect to Philadelphia. **South African Airways** (in South Africa, © 0861/359 722; www.flysaa.com) connects to Philadelphia via Atlanta.

You can get to Philadelphia from Montreal on **Amtrak** trains (© 800/ USA-RAIL; www.amtrak.com).

AIRLINE   DISCOUNTS The smart traveler can find numerable ways to reduce the price of a plane ticket simply by taking time to shop around. For example, overseas visitors can take advantage of the APEX

(Advance Purchase Excursion) reductions offered by all major U.S. and European carriers. For more money-saving airline advice, see "Getting There," in chapter 2. For the best rates, compare fares and be flexible with the dates and times of travel.

IMMIGRATION AND CUSTOMS CLEARANCE Visitors arriving by air, no matter what the port of entry, should cultivate patience and resignation before setting foot on U.S. soil. Getting through immigration control can take as long as 2 hours on some days, especially on summer weekends, so be sure to carry this guidebook or something else to read. This is especially true in the aftermath of the September 11, 2001, terrorist attacks, when security clearances were considerably beefed up at U.S. airports.

People traveling by air from Canada, Bermuda, and certain countries in the Caribbean can sometimes clear Customs and Immigration at the point of departure, which is much quicker.

3 Getting Around the U.S.

BY PLANE Some large airlines (for example, Northwest and Delta) offer travelers on their transatlantic or transpacific flights special discount tickets under the name **Visit USA,** allowing mostly one-way travel from

one U.S. destination to another at very low prices. These discount tickets are not on sale in the United States and must be purchased abroad in conjunction with your international ticket. This system is the best, easiest, and fastest way to see the United States at low cost. You should obtain information well in advance from your travel agent or the office of the airline concerned, since the conditions attached to these discount tickets can be changed without advance notice.

BY TRAIN International visitors (excluding Canada) can also buy a **USA Rail Pass,** good for 15 or 30 days of unlimited travel on Amtrak (© **800/USA-RAIL;** www.amtrak. com). The pass is available through many overseas travel agents. Prices in 2004 for a 15-day pass were $295 off peak, $440 peak; a 30-day pass costs $385 off peak, $550 peak. With a foreign passport, you can also buy passes at some Amtrak offices in the United States, including locations in San Francisco, Los Angeles, Chicago, New York, Miami, Boston, and Washington, D.C. Reservations are generally required and should be made for each part of your trip as early as possible. Regional rail passes are also available.

BY BUS Although bus travel is often the most economical form of public transit for short hops between U.S. cities, it can also be slow and uncomfortable—certainly not an option for everyone (particularly when Amtrak, which is far more luxurious, is sometimes only slightly more expensive). **Greyhound/Trailways** (© **800/231-2222;** www.greyhound. com), the sole nationwide bus line, offers an **International Ameripass** that must be purchased before coming to the United States, or by phone through the Greyhound International Office at the Port Authority Bus Terminal in New York City (© **212/ 971-0492**). The pass can be obtained from foreign travel agents or through Greyhound's website (order at least 21 days before your departure to the U.S.) and costs less than the domestic version. The 2004 passes cost as follows: 4 days ($160), 7 days ($219), 10 days ($269), 15 days ($329), 21 days ($379), 30 days ($439), 45 days ($489), or 60 days ($599). You can get more info on the pass at the website, or by calling © **402/330-8552.** In addition, special rates are available for seniors and students.

BY CAR Philadelphia is an excellent city for walking, and with the complexities and expense of parking, it's often easier and faster to walk or take a cab around town than to drive yourself. But unless you plan to spend the bulk of your vacation time in Philadelphia, the most cost-effective, convenient, and comfortable way to travel around the United States is by car. The interstate highway system connects cities and towns all over the country; in addition to these high-speed, limited-access roadways, there's an extensive network of federal, state, and local highways and roads. Some of the national car-rental companies include **Alamo** (© 800/462-5266; www. alamo.com), **Avis** (© 800/230-4898; www.avis.com), **Budget** (© 800/527-0700; www.budget.com), **Dollar** (© 800/800-3665; www.dollar.com), **Hertz** (© 800/654-3131; www.hertz. com), **National** (© 800/227-7368; www.nationalcar.com), and **Thrifty** (© 800/847-4389; www.thrifty.com).

If you plan to rent a car in the United States, you probably won't need the services of an additional automobile organization. If you're planning to buy or borrow a car, automobile-association membership is recommended. **AAA, the American Automobile Association** (© **800/ 222-4357**), is the country's largest auto club and supplies its members with maps, insurance, and, most important, emergency road service. The cost of joining runs from $63 for singles to $87 for two members, but if you're a member of a foreign auto club with reciprocal arrangements, you can enjoy free AAA service in America.

FAST FACTS: **For the International Traveler**

Automobile Organizations Auto clubs will supply maps, suggested routes, guidebooks, accident and bail-bond insurance, and emergency road service. The **American Automobile Association (AAA)** is the major auto club in the United States. If you belong to an auto club in your home country, inquire about AAA reciprocity before you leave. You may be able to join AAA even if you're not a member of a reciprocal club; to inquire, call AAA (✆ **800/222-4357**). AAA is actually an organization of regional auto clubs; so look under "AAA Automobile Club" in the White Pages of the telephone directory. AAA has a nationwide emergency road service telephone number (✆ 800/AAA-HELP). In Philadelphia, AAA is at 2040 Market St. (✆ **215/864-5000**); call ✆ **800/222-4357** for emergency service.

Business Hours Offices are usually open weekdays from 9am to 5pm. Banks are open weekdays from 9am to 3pm or later and sometimes Saturday mornings. Stores typically open between 9 and 10am and close between 5 and 6pm from Monday through Saturday; in Philadelphia, many stores stay open until 7 or 8pm on Wednesdays. Stores in shopping complexes or malls tend to stay open late: until about 9pm on weekdays and weekends, and many malls and larger department stores are open on Sundays.

Currency & Currency Exchange See "Money" under "Preparing for Your Trip," above. In Philadelphia, you can exchange money at **Travelex/Thomas Cook** in the Philadelphia Airport in Terminals A, D, and between A and B, from 6:30am to 8pm, and at the corner of 18th Street and JFK Boulevard (✆ **800/287-7362**).

Drinking Laws The legal age for purchase and consumption of alcoholic beverages is 21; proof of age is required and often requested at bars, nightclubs, and restaurants, so it's always a good idea to bring ID when you go out. In Pennsylvania, liquor and wine are sold only in state-run stores such as the one on Chestnut Street at 19th Street (www.lcb.state.pa.us), but you can purchase beer at many delis and at some bars.

Do not carry open containers of alcohol in your car or any public area that isn't zoned for alcohol consumption. The police can fine you on the spot. And nothing will ruin your trip faster than getting a citation for DUI ("driving under the influence"), so don't even think about driving while intoxicated.

Electricity Like Canada, the United States uses 110–120 volts AC (60 cycles), compared to 220–240 volts AC (50 cycles) in most of Europe, Australia, and New Zealand. If your small appliances use 220–240 volts, you'll need a 110-volt transformer and a plug adapter with two flat parallel pins to operate them here. Downward converters that change 220–240 volts to 110–120 volts are difficult to find in the United States, so bring one with you.

Embassies & Consulates All embassies are located in the nation's capital, Washington, D.C. Some consulates are located in major U.S. cities, and most nations have a mission to the United Nations in New York City. If your country isn't listed below, call for directory information in Washington, D.C. (© **202/555-1212**) or log on to **www.embassy.org/embassies**.

The embassy of **Australia** is at 1601 Massachusetts Ave. NW, Washington, DC 20036 (© **202/797-3000;** www.austemb.org). There are consulates in New York, Honolulu, Houston, Los Angeles, and San Francisco.

The embassy of **Canada** is at 501 Pennsylvania Ave. NW, Washington, DC 20001 (© **202/682-1740;** www.canadianembassy.org). Other Canadian consulates are in Buffalo (NY), Detroit, Los Angeles, New York, and Seattle.

The embassy of **Ireland** is at 2234 Massachusetts Ave. NW, Washington, DC 20008 (© **202/462-3939;** www.irelandemb.org). Irish consulates are in Boston, Chicago, New York, and San Francisco.

The embassy of **Japan** is at 2520 Massachusetts Ave. NW, Washington, DC 20008 (© **202/238-6700;** www.embjapan.org). Japanese consulates are located in many cities including Atlanta, Boston, Detroit, New York, San Francisco, and Seattle.

The embassy of **New Zealand** is at 37 Observatory Circle NW, Washington, DC 20008 (© 202/328-4800; www.nzemb.org). New Zealand consulates are in Los Angeles, Salt Lake City, San Francisco, and Seattle.

The embassy of the **United Kingdom** is at 3100 Massachusetts Ave. NW, Washington, DC 20008 (© **202/462-1340;** www.britainusa.com). Other British consulates are in Atlanta, Boston, Chicago, Cleveland, Houston, Los Angeles, New York, San Francisco, and Seattle.

You can find other European embassies by calling © **411** (information) for their phone numbers.

Emergencies Call © **911** to report a fire, call the police, or get an ambulance anywhere in the United States. This is a toll-free call. (No coins are required at public telephones.)

If you encounter serious problems, contact the **Traveler's Aid International** (© **202/546-1127,** or 215/523-7580 in Philadelphia; www.travelers aid.org) to help direct you to a local branch. This nationwide, nonprofit, social-service organization geared to helping travelers in difficult straits offers services that might include reuniting families separated while traveling, providing food and/or shelter to people stranded without cash, or even emotional counseling. If you're in trouble, seek them out.

Gasoline (Petrol) Petrol is known as gasoline (or simply "gas") in the United States, and petrol stations are known as both gas stations and service stations. Gasoline costs about half as much here as it does in Europe (about $2 per gal. at press time), and taxes are already included in the printed price. One U.S. gallon equals 3.8 liters or .85 imperial gallons.

Holidays Banks, government offices, post offices, and many stores, restaurants, and museums are closed on the following legal national holidays: January 1 (New Year's Day), the third Monday in January (Martin Luther King, Jr., Day), the third Monday in February (Presidents' Day, Washington's Birthday), the last Monday in May (Memorial Day), July 4 (Independence Day), the first Monday in September (Labor Day), the second Monday in October (Columbus Day), November 11 (Veterans Day/Armistice Day), the fourth Thursday in November (Thanksgiving

Day), and December 25 (Christmas). Also, the Tuesday following the first Monday in November is Election Day and is a federal government holiday in presidential-election years (held every 4 years, and next in 2008).

Legal Aid If you are "pulled over" for a minor infraction (such as speeding), never attempt to pay the fine directly to a police officer; this could be construed as attempted bribery, a much more serious crime. Pay fines by mail, or directly into the hands of the clerk of the court. If accused of a more serious offense, say and do nothing before consulting a lawyer. Here the burden is on the state to prove a person's guilt beyond a reasonable doubt, and everyone has the right to remain silent, whether he or she is suspected of a crime or actually arrested. Once arrested, a person can make one telephone call to a party of his or her choice. Call your embassy or consulate.

Mail If you aren't sure what your address will be in the United States, mail can be sent to you, in your name, c/o General Delivery at the main post office of the city or region where you expect to be. (Call ✆ **800/275-8777** for information on the nearest post office.) Philadelphia's main post offices are at 9th and Market streets, and on 30th Street, across from 30th Street Station. The addressee must pick up mail in person and must produce proof of identity (driver's license, passport, and so on). Most post offices will hold your mail for up to 1 month, and are open Monday to Friday from 8am to 6pm, and Saturday from 9am to 3pm.

Generally found at intersections, mailboxes are blue with a red-and-white stripe and carry the inscription U.S. Mail. If your mail is addressed to a U.S. destination, don't forget to add the five-digit postal code (or zip code), after the two-letter abbreviation of the state to which the mail is addressed. This is essential for prompt delivery.

At press time, domestic postage rates were 23¢ for a postcard and 37¢ for a letter. For international mail, a first-class letter of up to ½ ounce costs 80¢ (60¢ to Canada and Mexico); a first-class postcard costs 70¢ (50¢ to Canada and Mexico); and a preprinted postal aerogramme costs 70¢.

Measurements See the chart on the inside front cover of this book for details on converting metric measurements to U.S. equivalents.

Taxes The United States has no value-added tax (VAT) or other indirect tax at the national level. Every state, county, and city has the right to levy its own local tax on all purchases, including hotel and restaurant checks, airline tickets, and so on. The hotel tax in Philadelphia is 14%. There is no sales tax on clothing in Pennsylvania, which makes it a popular shopping destination; Franklin Mills Mall, just north of Philadelphia, which includes Saks Fifth Avenue and Neiman Marcus outlet stores, is particularly bargain-oriented. Philadelphia's sales tax on other items is 7%.

Telephone, Telegraph, Telex & Fax The telephone system in the United States is run by private corporations, so rates, especially for long-distance service and operator-assisted calls, can vary widely. Generally, hotel surcharges on long-distance and local calls are astronomical, so you're usually better off using a **public pay telephone,** which you'll find clearly marked in most public buildings and private establishments as well as on the street. Convenience grocery stores and gas stations always have them. Many convenience groceries and packaging services sell **prepaid calling**

cards in denominations up to $50; these can be the least expensive way to call home. Many public phones at airports now accept American Express, MasterCard, and Visa credit cards. **Local calls** made from public pay phones in most locales cost either 25¢ or 35¢. Pay phones do not accept pennies, and few will take anything larger than a quarter.

You may want to look into leasing a cellphone for the duration of your trip.

Most long-distance and international calls can be dialed directly from any phone. **For calls within the United States and to Canada,** dial 1 followed by the area code and the seven-digit number. **For other international calls,** dial 011 followed by the country code, city code, and the telephone number of the person you are calling.

Calls to area codes **800, 888, 877,** and **866** are toll-free. However, calls to numbers in area codes **700** and **900** (chat lines, bulletin boards, "dating" services, and so on) can be very expensive—usually a charge of 95¢ to $3 or more per minute, and they sometimes have minimum charges that can run as high as $15 or more.

For **reversed-charge or collect calls,** and for person-to-person calls, dial 0 (zero, not the letter O) followed by the area code and number you want; an operator will then come on the line, and you should specify that you are calling collect, or person-to-person, or both. If your operator-assisted call is international, ask for the overseas operator.

For **local directory assistance** ("information"), dial 411; for long-distance information, dial 1, then the appropriate area code and 555-1212.

Telegraph and telex services are provided primarily by Western Union. You can bring your telegram into the nearest Western Union office (there are hundreds across the country) or dictate it over the phone (© 800/325-6000). You can also telegraph money, or have it telegraphed to you, very quickly over the Western Union system, but this service can cost as much as 15% to 20% of the amount sent.

Most hotels have **fax machines** available for guest use (be sure to ask about the charge to use it). Many hotel rooms are even wired for guests' fax machines. A less expensive way to send and receive faxes may be at stores such as **The UPS Store** (formerly Mail Boxes Etc.), a national chain of retail packing service shops. (Look in the Yellow Pages directory under "Packing Services.")

There are two kinds of telephone directories in the United States. The so-called **White Pages** list private households and business subscribers in alphabetical order. The inside front cover lists emergency numbers for police, fire, ambulance, the Coast Guard, poison-control center, crime-victims hotline, and so on. The first few pages will tell you how to make long-distance and international calls, complete with country codes and area codes. Government numbers are usually printed on blue paper within the White Pages. Printed on yellow paper, the so-called **Yellow Pages** list all local services, businesses, industries, and houses of worship according to activity with an index at the front or back. (Drugstores/pharmacies and restaurants are also listed by geographic location.) The Yellow Pages also include city plans or detailed area maps, postal zip codes, and public transportation routes.

Time The continental United States is divided into **four time zones:** Eastern Standard Time (EST), Central Standard Time (CST), Mountain Standard Time (MST), and Pacific Standard Time (PST). Alaska and Hawaii have their own zones. For example, noon in New York City (EST) is 11am in Chicago (CST), 10am in Denver (MST), 9am in Los Angeles (PST), 8am in Anchorage (AST), and 7am in Honolulu (HST). Philadelphia is in the Eastern Standard Time zone.

Daylight saving time is in effect from 1am on the first Sunday in April through 1am on the last Sunday in October, except in Arizona, Hawaii, most of Indiana, and Puerto Rico. Daylight saving time moves the clock 1 hour ahead of standard time.

Tipping Tips are a very important part of certain workers' income, and gratuities are the standard way of showing appreciation for services provided. (Tipping is certainly not compulsory if the service is poor!) In hotels, tip **bellhops** at least $1 per bag ($2–$3 if you have a lot of luggage) and tip the **chamber staff** $1 to $2 per day (more if you've left a disaster area for him or her to clean up). Tip the **doorman** or **concierge** only if he or she has provided you with some specific service (for example, calling a cab for you or obtaining difficult-to-get theater tickets). Tip the **valet-parking attendant** $1 every time you get your car.

In restaurants, bars, and nightclubs, tip **service staff** 15% to 20% of the check, tip **bartenders** 10% to 15%, tip **checkroom attendants** $1 per garment, and tip **valet-parking attendants** $1 per vehicle.

As for other service personnel, tip **cab drivers** 15% of the fare; tip **skycaps** at airports at least $1 per bag ($2–$3 if you have a lot of luggage); and tip **hairdressers** and **barbers** 15% to 20%.

Toilets You won't find public toilets or "restrooms" on the streets in most U.S. cities, but they can be found in hotel lobbies, bars, restaurants, museums, department stores, railway and bus stations, and service stations. In Philadelphia, Independence National Historical Park sites have clean, free restrooms. Large hotels around Center City and some fast-food restaurants and Starbucks cafes are a good bet for good, clean facilities. If possible, avoid the toilets at parks and beaches, which tend to be dirty; some may be unsafe. Restaurants and bars in resorts or heavily visited areas may reserve their restrooms for patrons. Some establishments display a notice indicating this. You can ignore this sign or, better yet, avoid arguments by paying for a cup of coffee or a soft drink, which will qualify you as a patron.

4

Getting to Know Philadelphia

This chapter sets out to answer all your travel questions, furnishing you with the practical information that you'll need to handle any and every experience during your stay in Philadelphia—from figuring out the city layout and transportation to knowing business hours.

1 Orientation

ARRIVING

BY PLANE Most flights into and from Philadelphia use **Philadelphia International Airport** (© **215/937-6800;** www.phl.org), at the southwest corner of the city. For up-to-the-minute information on airline arrival and departure times and gate assignments, call © **800/PHL-GATE.** With 26 million passengers in 2004, it's one of the country's fastest growing airports, especially with the advent of service by Southwest and Frontier airlines. There are flights to more than 100 cities in the United States and more than 1,000 arrivals and departures daily.

The airport is laid out with a central corridor connecting the five basic depots. US Airways, the "hub" tenant, has already collaborated on a new Terminal F for commuters, and the airport has added ultramodern Terminal A West, for international service (gates A14 to A26). Terminal B is the place to catch taxis, buses, and hotel limousines. There is an impressive shopping corridor between Terminals B and C, where you can buy gifts such as electronic gadgets, caviar, jewelry, or even browse at the Gap.

Since security concerns increased in 2001, short-term parking is not allowed, so your parking options are garage or economy (long term). Economy parking is available for $7 per day at more distant lots, while garage parking opposite the terminals is $3 for the first 30 minutes, $15 for up to 3 hours, and $17 for 4 to 24 hours.

For medical emergencies at the airport, call © 215/937-3111.

Getting into Town from the Airport A high-speed rail link with direct service between the airport and Center City runs daily every 30 minutes from 5:09am to 12:09am. Trains leave the airport at 9 and 39 minutes past the hour; they follow the loop of a raised pedestrian bridge, stop in front of every terminal and are easy to find. Trains to the airport depart from Market East (a Convention Center connection), Suburban Station at 16th Street, and 30th Street Station. The 30-minute trip costs $5.50 for adults; children's fares are $1.50 weekdays and 75¢ weekends; and the family fare is $17.

A taxi from the airport to Center City takes about 20 minutes and costs a flat rate of $20 plus tip. Taxi dispatch is available 24 hours a day at the airport.

If you're interested in airport limousines or shuttles to garages, hotels, or Center City destinations, fares start at about $10. Try **Deluxe Limo** (© 215/

463-8787) from 6am to 11pm, **Lady Liberty** (© **215/724-8888**) from 5am to midnight, or **Philadelphia Airport Shuttle** (© **215/333-1441**) from 5am to 10pm. Fees start at about $40 to take you from the airport to most suburban destinations, and from $75 to $120 to go to Atlantic City. **Crystal Limousine** (© **610/353-4324**) charges $70 for a sedan from the airport into Center City or the suburbs, and $150 from the airport to Atlantic City.

All major car-rental operations have desks at the airport and Zone 2 pick-up (a section of the parking area). These include **Alamo** (© 800/327-9633); **Avis** (© 800/331-1212); **Budget** (© 800/527-0700); **Dollar** (© 800/800-4000); **Hertz** (© 800/654-3131); and **National** (© 800/227-7368).

BY TRAIN   Trains arrive at Penn (30th St.) Station in West Philadelphia, just on the other side of the Schuylkill River from Center City, and about 15 blocks from City Hall. Take a taxi or SEPTA (see below) from the station to your hotel.

VISITOR INFORMATION

The newly constructed **Independence Visitor Center,** 6th and Market streets, Philadelphia, PA 19106 (© **800/537-7676,** 215/965-7676, or 215/636-1666; **www.independencevisitorcenter.com**), is extremely convenient, with underground parking just off I-95 (enter at 5th St. or 6th St. between Market and Arch sts.), and it has rejuvenated Independence Mall 1 block north of the Liberty Bell. The $38-million facility has a great offering of customer services through volunteers and automated kiosks, five exhibition nooks, a film theater, a cafe, and a gift shop and bookstore. The second-floor balconies are great for photo-ops of Independence National Historical Park highlights.

The center parcels out free tickets to the major landmarks of Independence National Historical Park such as Independence Hall and the Liberty Bell Pavilion. This service is vital since security concerns have clamped down on who gets in and when. They sell other tickets such as the SEPTA (an extensive network of trolleys, buses, commuter trains, and subways) DayPass ($5.50). Plus, you

---

Tips   **Four Conversation-Starters to Avoid in Philadelphia**

1. "Philadelphians are consistently rated by magazine's such as *Men's Fitness* as some of the fattest people in the country. Maybe if you people didn't eat so many cheesesteaks, you wouldn't be so huge!"
2. "I heard that the producers of MTV's *Real World* decided Philadelphia's unions were so difficult that they yanked plans to film in Philly's Old City until city officials begged them to reconsider. Phew, close call at losing a great opportunity to burnish your city's image!"
3. "Speaking of unions, isn't it true that it takes three unions to put down a tablecloth at your $520-million, state-of-the-art Convention Center?"
4. "I hear the FBI has acknowledged that they're investigating your mayor and several of his associates and have even bugged offices in City Hall. Say, have you been awarded any city contracts lately?"

can make any kind of reservations—hotel, restaurant, event—here. Many bus tours, trolley rides, and walking tours conveniently begin at the visitor center.

The center is open daily from 8:30am to 5pm, and until 7pm during the summer. If you're planning in advance, call ② **800/537-7676** to get material on all the special seasonal promotions and ② **800/967-2283** to preorder timed tickets to sites such as Independence Hall.

CITY LAYOUT

MAIN ARTERIES & STREETS   Unlike Boston, Philadelphia has no Colonial cow paths that were turned into streets. If you can count and remember the names of trees (many of the east-west streets sport tree names, such as Walnut, Locust, and Spruce), you'll know exactly where you are in the Center City grid. For the overview, go to (or pretend you're at) the top of **City Hall,** the ornate, just renovated French Second Empire–style structure in the very center of things, at the intersection of Broad and Market streets. **Broad Street** runs 4 miles south, where the Delaware and Schuylkill flow together, and 8 miles north—all perfectly straight. (Broad has been renamed Avenue of the Arts for 8 blocks just south of City Hall, to highlight the concentration of performance halls.) The other major north-south streets are numbered. Except for a few two-way exceptions, traffic on even-numbered streets heads south and on odd-numbered streets, north. **Front Street** (which would be 1st St.), near the Delaware's edge off to the right, and neighboring **2nd Street** were the major thoroughfares in Colonial times. Smaller streets between the numbered streets are named. The major east-west streets in Philadelphia's Center City run from Spring Garden Street in the north down to South Street. You'll spend much of your time between Arch and Pine streets, especially south of Chestnut Street, both for the historical attractions and for the current restaurant and nightlife vibrancy.

The Colonial city, now **Independence National Historical Park,** with its reconstructed row houses, grew up along the Delaware River north and south of **Market Street,** extending west to 6th Street by 1776. The 19th century saw the development of the western quadrants of the city (including most museums and cultural centers) and the growth of the suburbs in every direction. The city blocks planned by Pennsylvania founder William Penn included five parks spaced between the two rivers. Four parks have been named for local notables (including George Washington, who headed the federal government here in the 1790s). The fifth supports City Hall. The broad northwest boulevard of Benjamin Franklin Parkway divides the grid, ending in the majestic neoclassical portico of the Philadelphia Museum of Art in the west. The area west of City Hall has been the site of intensive development and redevelopment of hotels, office buildings, and apartment houses.

To the west of this, the winding Schuylkill separates Philadelphia from West Philadelphia—if you're looking for an address between 24th Street and about 30th Street in this area, ask which side it's on. **Fairmount Park** lines both sides of the Schuylkill for miles north of the Philadelphia Museum of Art.

Helpful directional signs were posted at every Center City corner in 2000, displaying the name and a color-coded ID of the district you're in as well as listings of nearby destinations.

FINDING AN ADDRESS   Addresses on these streets add 100 for every block away from the axis of Market Street (north-south) or Front Street (east-west): 1534 Chestnut St. is between 15th and 16th streets, and 610 S. 5th St. is between 6 and 7 blocks south of Market.

STREET MAPS   The **Independence Visitor Center,** 6th and Market streets (© **800/537-7676** or 215/636-1666), has a very good street map in its "Official Visitors Guide." You can pick it up at the center and at all hotels.

THE NEIGHBORHOODS IN BRIEF

Philadelphia is more of a collection of neighborhoods than a unified metropolis. Here are short descriptions of those that you're likely to find yourself in.

CHESTNUT HILL This enclave of suburban gentility, with its "Main Street" flavor, is centered around upper Germantown Avenue, and is the highest point within city limits. It's filled with galleries and boutiques, tearooms, and comfortable restaurants.

CHINATOWN Nowadays it's largely commercial rather than residential, but there are lots of good restaurants, a growing number of hotels, and cheap parking only 5 minutes from the Convention Center. And it stays awake all night.

GERMANTOWN One of Philadelphia's most ancient settlements, this area was founded by German émigrés, attracted by Penn's religious tolerance. Outside of its wonderful historic mansions, however, it is not especially attractive now.

MANAYUNK This neighborhood, 4 miles up the Schuylkill River from Center City, has been gentrified over the last 15 years, and now boutiques, furniture and art galleries, and cafe/restaurants line Main Street, overlooking a 19th-century canal adjoining the river. It's a picturesque place for an afternoon stroll and an alfresco snack. Visit it virtually at www.manayunk.com.

OLD CITY Think New York's SoHo or Chelsea, in the shadow of the Benjamin Franklin Bridge just north of Independence National Historical Park, with an eclectic blend of 18th-century row houses, 19th-century warehouses, and 20th-century rehabs. This is now the city's hottest neighborhood for the 20- and 30-something set, with chic restaurants, bars, and boutiques set in historic buildings and storefronts. The first Friday of every month is a pleasant block party, with galleries and stores open until 9pm.

QUEEN VILLAGE This is a leafy neighborhood of old houses between Society Hill and South Philly, along the Delaware or 2nd Street (known as "Two Street" among old Philadelphians). There are lots of small, reasonably priced cafes and bistros here, and pedestrian bridges constructed over I-95 have recently reconnected the area to the waterfront.

RITTENHOUSE SQUARE This beautifully landscaped park ringed by elegant condominiums built during the 1930s and historic mansions illustrates the elegance, wealth, and culture of Philadelphia. Now, sleek outdoor cafes and luxury hotels line the park, also. From the Rittenhouse Hotel on a sunny day, walk through the square to Walnut Street, which rivals the shopping areas of Boston and San Francisco in charm and sophistication.

SOCIETY HILL This heart of reclaimed 18th-century Philadelphia is loosely defined by Walnut and Lombard streets and Front and 7th streets. Today, it's a fashionable section of the old city, just south of Independence National Historical Park, where you can stroll among restored Federal, Colonial, and Georgian homes—even the contemporary architecturally modern

Philadelphia Neighborhoods

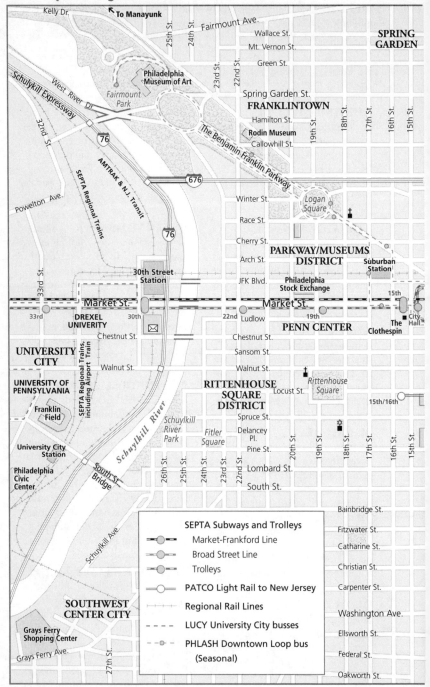

is interesting and immaculately maintained.

SOUTH PHILADELPHIA It's Rocky Balboa and more. Three hundred years of immigration have made South Philadelphia the city's most colorful and ethnically diverse neighborhood, although the overwhelming feel is distinctly Italian (think 1910s Calabria). Stroll the gritty, redolent Italian Market at 9th and Christian, heading south, snacking on cheeses, cured meats, and pastries.

SOUTH STREET Located below Society Hill and above Queen Village, South Street was the city limit in William Penn's day. The 1960s saw bohemian artists reclaiming this street in the name of peace and love; tattooed teenagers have replaced the previous hipsters. The place is undeniably loud and crowded day or night. If you have the patience, look for good restaurants and bars, bookstores, hoagie shops, contemporary handcrafted furniture stores, natural-food stores, European-style cafes, and art galleries. The neighborhood has a website at www.south-street.com.

UNIVERSITY CITY West Philadelphia was farmland until the University of Pennsylvania moved here from 9th and Chestnut streets in the 1870s. Wander through the main campus for the architecture and the cultural attractions. The original college quadrangle, built in 1895, was modeled on Oxford and Cambridge, with the added touch of Dutch gables. Penn has enticed a cool new cinema, retail, and bookstores to gentrify the area, following a long slump.

2 Getting Around

BY PUBLIC TRANSPORTATION

SEPTA (Southeastern Pennsylvania Transportation Authority) operates a complicated and extensive network of trolleys, buses, commuter trains, and subways. Ridership has increased since Center City has encouraged less auto traffic on historic streets, so it's crowded but safe. Busy Suburban Station is in the heart of Center City at 16th Street and JKF Boulevard.

Fares for any SEPTA route are $2 cash or $1.30 for tokens purchased before you ride (at stations, Rite Aid stores, and machines in various city concourses). Transfers are 60¢, and exact change is required. Seniors pay only during rush hours, and passengers with disabilities pay half-fare during off-peak hours. Certain buses and trolleys run 24 hours a day.

If you have questions about how to reach a specific destination, call SEPTA at ✆ **215/580-7800** between 6am and midnight—but expect to wait—or hit the website www.septa.org.

BY SUBWAY-SURFACE LINE This "local" connects City Hall and 30th Street Station, stopping at 19th and 22nd streets along the way. West of the Amtrak station it branches out, moving aboveground beyond U. Penn to the north and south.

BY RAPID TRANSIT In Center City, these fast cars speed under Broad Street and Market Street, intersecting under City Hall. The Broad Street line now connects directly to Pattison Avenue and Philadelphia sporting events to the south. The Market Street line stops at the 2nd, 5th, 8th, 11th, 13th (Convention Center), 15th, and 30th Street stations and stretches to the west and northeast. Both lines run all night, but exercise caution during late-hour use.

Tips **Ride Cheap**

A $5.50 DayPass is good for all buses, subways, and one ride on the Airport loop. A weekly TransPass, good from Monday to the next Sunday, is $19.

BY PATCO This commuter rail line (℗ 215/922-4600) begins at Walnut and Locust streets around Broad Street, connects with rapid transit at 8th and Market, and crosses the Ben Franklin Bridge to Camden. Visit www.drpa.org/patco for information. To get to the aquarium, transfer at Broadway in Camden to the New Jersey Transit's Aqualink Shuttle. Transfers connect to the Jersey shore from Lindenwold.

BY BUS Those purple trolley-style buses go pretty much everywhere tourists want to go. Every 12 minutes between 10am and 6pm in summer (May 1–Nov 30) the **PHLASH Bus** service (℗ 215/636-1666) links Independence Park sites, the Delaware waterfront, the Convention Center, Rittenhouse Square shopping, and the cultural institution at Logan Circle. The total loop takes 50 minutes and makes 30 stops. A one-time pass is $1, or get an all-day unlimited-ride pass for $4 per person or $10 per family. Passes are not transferable to SEPTA. Children under 5 ride free, as do seniors, outside of 4:30 to 5:30pm.

For a straight cross-town route, head to Chestnut Street and take bus no. 42, which swoops along Chestnut from West Philadelphia to 2nd at all hours. Several bus routes serve Market Street. Route 32 goes up Broad Street and the Parkway and through Fairmount Park to Andorra; the full trip is 15 miles.

BY TROLLEY There are no more actual city trolleys such as you would find in Boston or San Francisco, but **Philadelphia Trolley Works and 76 Carriage Company** operates buses that resemble 1930s open-air trolleys (℗ 215/925-8687). Guides point out all the highlights along the way. Tour prices range from $5 for children to $20 for adults, depending on family size. The tour originates at the Bourse Building at 5th Street between Market and Chestnut, or at your hotel, and the 90-minute ride includes 18 stops all the way to the Art Museum.

BY TRAIN The Philadelphia area is served by one of the best commuter-rail networks in America. Chestnut Hill, a wealthy enclave of fine shops and restaurants, can be reached from both Penn Center (Suburban) Station at 16th Street and John F. Kennedy Boulevard and Reading Terminal at 12th and Market streets; the two are now connected by the new rail link. In the beautiful suburbs west of the city, Merion is home to the great Barnes Foundation art collection. Bryn Mawr, Haverford, Swarthmore, and Villanova are sites of noted colleges. Devon hosts a great horse and country fair in late May and early June. One-way fares for all destinations are $5.50 or less, and you can buy tickets at station counters or vending machines.

BY CAR

Be forewarned that *all streets are one-way*—except for lower Market Street, the Parkway, Vine Street, and Broad Street. The Convention and Visitors Bureau at the foot of the Parkway offers a Center City traffic map. Traffic around City Hall runs counterclockwise, but traffic lights seem to follow a logic of their own.

Since Philadelphia is so walkable, it's easier to leave your car while you explore. Many hotels offer free or reduced-rate parking to registered guests.

If you need emergency car repair, try **Sargon Sunoco,** 1135 Vine St. (© 215/928-9574), or **Mina Motors,** Broad and Fitzwater streets (© 215/735-2749), for same-day service. **Keystone AAA** is at 2040 Market St. (© 215/864-5000).

RENTALS   Philadelphia has no shortage of rental cars and very good rates as a consequence. For example, you can pick up a weekend sedan from **Avis** (© 800/331-1212) from $50 per day, with unlimited mileage, at one of their lots: 2000 Arch St. (© 215/563-8976), from which site Avis will also deliver cars to 30th Street Station, and at the Hyatt at 201 S. Columbus Blvd. (© 215/629-1333). Avis and all other major renters maintain offices at the airport. These include **Alamo** (© 800/327-9633); **Budget** (© 800/527-0700, 215/492-9043 at the airport, or 215/564-3957 at 21st and Market); **Dollar** (© 800/800-4000); and **Hertz** (© 800/654-3131 for all locations). Also check smaller local companies and car dealers like **Chapman Ford** (© 215/698-7000).

On top of the standard rental prices, other optional charges apply to most car rentals, including liability insurance (if you harm others in an accident), personal accident insurance (if you harm yourself or your passengers), and personal effects insurance (if your luggage is stolen from your car). If your own insurance or credit card company doesn't cover you for rentals, you should consider the additional coverages. But weigh the likelihood of getting into an accident or losing your luggage against the cost of these coverages (as much as $20 per day combined), which can significantly add to the price of your rental.

PARKING   Call the **Philadelphia Parking Authority** (© 215/683-9600) for current information, or visit www.philapark.org. It's the expected mix of metered, free limited on-street, and garage parking. Parking tickets are $20 and up. Garage rates are fairly uniform: Outside of hotels, no place exceeds $25 per day, with typical charges of $5 per hour and $12 for an evening out.

Parking can be found for **Independence Mall and Park** underneath the new Visitor Center between 5th and 6th streets and Market and Arch streets; 125 S. 2nd St. (Sansom St. is the cross street); Spruce Street between 5th and 6th streets (private lot); and Head House Square, 2nd and Lombard streets (city meters). **Convention Center Area** parking includes Kinney Chinatown at 11th and Race streets (private garage); Kinney underneath the Gallery II mall at 11th and Arch streets; the Autopark beside the Gallery mall at 10th and Filbert streets; or the garage underneath the adjoining Marriott at Arch and 13th streets. **City Hall Area** parking is underneath Lord & Taylor (formerly Wanamaker's), between Market and Chestnut streets at 13th Street; a private garage adjoining the Doubletree Hotel at Broad and Spruce streets; and Kennedy Plaza, 15th Street and John F. Kennedy Boulevard (underground city garage; enter on Arch, 1 block north of the plaza).

BY TAXI

Fares are currently $1.80 for the first ¼ mile and 30¢ for each additional ¼ mile or minute of the motor running. Tips are expected, usually 15% of the fare.

If you need to call for a cab while in the city, two good operators are **Olde City Taxi** (© 215/338-0838) and **Quaker City** (© 215/728-8000).

FAST FACTS: Philadelphia

American Express There is an Amex office at 16th Street and John F. Kennedy Boulevard (☎ 215/587-2300).

Area Code Philadelphia's telephone area code is **215**. Bucks County and half of Montgomery County also use **215**, but the Brandywine Valley area of Delaware, Chester, and half of Montgomery have switched to **610**. Lancaster County and the Pennsylvania Dutch region use area code **717**.

Babysitters Check with your hotel.

Business Hours Banks are generally open Monday through Friday from 10am to 6pm, with some also open on Saturday from 9am to noon, or later. Most bars and restaurants serve food until 10 or 10:30pm (some Chinatown places stay open until 3am), and bars are open Friday and Saturday until 1 or 2am. Offices are open Monday through Friday from 9am to 5pm. Stores are open daily from 9am to 6pm, and most Center City locations keep the doors open later on Wednesday evening. Old City, South Street, and the Delaware waterfront are the most active late-night districts. Some SEPTA routes run all night, but the frequency of buses and trolleys drops dramatically after 6pm.

Business Services Most hotels have on-site business facilities, but for quick professional production of materials, try the various 24-hour FedEx/Kinko's, whose downtown locations include 1201 Market St. (☎ 215/923-2520) at the Marriott Convention Center, and 2001 Market St. (☎ 215/561-5170). For shipping, the local UPS is at ☎ 215/567-6006.

Car Rentals See "Getting Around," earlier in this chapter.

Dentist Call the **Philadelphia County Dental Society** ☎ 215/925-6050 in a dental emergency.

Doctor Call the Philadelphia County Medical Society (☎ 215/563-5343). You can always dial ☎ **911** in an emergency. Every hospital in town has an emergency room.

Embassies & Consulates See p. 55.

Emergencies In an extreme emergency, dial ☎ **911**. In case of accidental poisoning, call ☎ **215/386-2100**. For police, call ☎ **215/686-3010**; for fire and rescue, call ☎ **215/922-6000**. Ambulance and emergency transportation can be summoned through Network Ambulance Service (☎ **215/482-8560**), or SEPTA Paratransit (☎ **215/580-7700**). For 24-hour pet emergencies, call the referral office of the University of Pennsylvania Veterinary Hospital at ☎ **215/898-4685**.

Hospitals Medical care in Philadelphia is excellent. Major hospitals include Children's Hospital, 34th Street and Civic Center Boulevard (☎ **215/590-1000**); Graduate Hospital, 1800 Lombard St. (☎ **215/893-2000**); Hahnemann University Hospital, Broad and Vine streets (☎ **215/762-7000**); University of Pennsylvania Hospital, 3400 Spruce St. (☎ **215/662-4000**); Pennsylvania Hospital, 8th and Spruce streets (☎ **215/829-3000**); and Thomas Jefferson, 11th and Walnut streets (☎ **215/955-6000**).

Information See "Visitor Information," earlier in this chapter.

Liquor Laws The legal drinking age is 21, and closing time for bars (as opposed to private clubs) is 2am, 7 days a week. You can buy wine and spirits only in state stores, which are usually open Monday through Wednesday from 9am to 5pm and Thursday through Saturday from 9am to 9pm, and some on Sunday from noon to 5pm. Beer and wine coolers are available at most delis. See p. 191 for the best state store locations.

Lost Property If you lose something on a SEPTA train or subway, try the stationmaster's office in Suburban Station (© 215/580-7800).

Newspapers & Magazines Philadelphia has two main print journals, both now owned by the same firm. You'll want to check out the Friday "Weekend" supplement of the *Inquirer* for listings and prices of entertainment as well as special events and tours, and visit both papers online at www.philly.com. The *Daily News* has more local news. Free tabloid weeklies with helpful listings include *City Paper* and *Philadelphia Weekly;* you'll find them in street-corner boxes. *Philadelphia* magazine is the widely read, upscale city magazine, sold at bookstores and at newsstands, and available online at www.phillymag.com. For the most complete selection of journals and newspapers, try **Avril 50,** 3406 Sansom St. (© 215/222-6108), in University City. Center City has a **Barnes & Noble** at 1805 Walnut St. (© 215/665-0716), and a large new **Borders** bookstore at 1 S. Broad St. (© 215/568-7400), both near Rittenhouse Square.

Pharmacies There's a 24-hour **CVS** at 1826 Chestnut St., corner of 19th Street (© 215/972-0909), and at 10th and Reed streets (© 215/465-2130) in South Philadelphia. West of Center City, try the 24-hour **Pathmark** at City Line and Monument avenues (© 215/879-1322).

Police The emergency telephone number is © 911.

Post Office The main post office at 2970 Market St. (© 215/895-8000), just across the Schuylkill and next to 30th Street station, has a 24-hour window. The post office on the subway concourse at 2 Penn Center, 15th Street and John F. Kennedy Boulevard, is open Monday through Friday from 7am to 6pm, Saturday from 9am to noon. You can also go to the post office Ben Franklin used, at 316 Market St.

Radio All news, WKYW (1060 AM); album-oriented rock, WMMR (93.3 FM); classic rock, WYSP (94.1 FM) and WMGK (102.9 FM); oldies, WOGL (98.1 FM); soft rock, WIOQ (102.1 FM); country, WXTU (92.5 FM); ethnic urban orientation, WUSL (98.9 FM); R&B and classic soul, WDAS (1480 AM); jazz, WJJZ (106.1 FM); National Public Radio, WHYY (91.0 FM); and for independent rock and pop, WXPN (88.5 FM).

Restrooms Public restrooms can be found at 30th Street Station; the Independence National Historical Park Visitors Center; and at major shopping complexes such as Liberty Place, the Bourse, the Gallery, and Downstairs at the Bellevue. You can usually use hotel lobby and restaurant facilities.

Safety See "Staying Safe," on p. 21.

Taxes Lodging charges add 14% onto room rates, 6% for state tax and 8% city surcharge. There is a 7% tax on restaurant meals and general sales, and a 10% tax on liquor. Clothing is tax-free.

Taxis See "Getting Around," earlier in this chapter.

Time Zone Philadelphia is in the Eastern Time zone—Eastern Standard Time (EST) or eastern daylight saving time, depending on the time of year—making it the same as New York and 3 hours ahead of the West Coast.

Transit Information To find out how to reach a specific destination, call SEPTA headquarters at © **215/580-7800**—but expect to wait—or visit www.septa.org.

Weather Call © **215/936-1212** for weather information.

5

Where to Stay

Philadelphia has a tradition of inns, bed-and-breakfasts, and European-style hotels for all budgets and tastes; grand hotels such as the Bellevue-Stratford (now the Park Hyatt at the Bellevue) built in 1904, served as meeting places for the city's elite. During the 1970s, glitzy, modern towers became the fashion. Today, after decades of some disappointing choices, Philadelphia is again paying serious attention to the comfort of its guests, and this renewed interest shows.

Philadelphia geared up for the Republican National Convention in 2000, increasing Center City hotel rooms from 6,000 to 11,000 and airport rooms to 4,500 in order to accommodate the 55,000 delegates and press. The glut of rooms has resulted in wonderful deals, especially on weekends, when you can stay in a luxury hotel such as the Ritz-Carlton or Four Seasons for far less than you might expect.

Due to excellent tourism marketing efforts, there has been an upsurge in visitors over the past 2 years. Occupancy rates for the first 6 months of 2004 were almost 69%, a significant increase from 2002—but the average room rate in Philadelphia is still very low, at $120 per night (down from $142 in 2000). Discounts and promotions, especially at luxury hotels on weekends, abound.

So how to approach the choices? Concentrate on the great weekend packages around town. Find several hotels that look appealing, call their toll-free numbers, check out their websites, or use the websites of the many travel discounters to find out about package deals. Many hotels also advertise in the travel sections of major newspapers. Ask about senior discounts, or holiday, family, or all-inclusive packages with meals or sight-seeing tours. No matter where you decide to stay, *always ask for the lowest-priced package available.* Remember that reservation agents won't necessarily volunteer the cheapest rates—you might have to insist. And check out bed-and-breakfast and smaller inn listings for a cheaper, unique alternative. Ask about hotel and special admissions packages offered through coordinated city tourism (© **800/537-7676,** or visit www.gophila.com).

Geographically, look to hotels in the Rittenhouse Square area for larger, more individualized pre-World War II spaces. Other large hotels in town serve corporate headquarters in the northwest quadrant between City Hall and the Philadelphia Museum of Art. Business amenities such as Internet access ports, voice mail, and functional desks have become standard in all accommodations.

There are also 16,400 hotels in the four-county circumference outside of town (including Bucks, Chester, Delaware, and Montgomery counties). These offerings include a full complement of good airport hotels, only 20 minutes away. Outside the city, you can find plenty of lovely, historic inns, such as Evermay on the Delaware in Bucks County, and upscale hotels such as the Inns at Doneckers in Ephrata, Lancaster

County—see chapters 11 and 12 for listings of inns in the surrounding areas. The **Independence Visitor Center,** 6th and Market streets, Philadelphia, PA 19106 (© **800/537-7676;** www.independencevistorcenter.com), can help with accommodations questions.

RATES   Unless otherwise specified, all prices quoted are for double occupancy and all rooms have private bathrooms and phones. You can count on a state tax of 7%, plus a city surcharge of 6%, and a county tax of 1% (total hotel tax is 14%). Remember that the prices listed here are "rack rates"—the room rate charged without any discount—and you can usually do better. Be sure to ask about parking and/or arrangements for children.

B&B AGENCIES   The region has more than 250 bed-and-breakfasts, each as charming and/or eccentric as its owner. One good agency to contact is **A Bed & Breakfast Connection/ Bed & Breakfast of Philadelphia,** Box 21, Devon, PA 19333 (© **800/ 448-3619** or 610/687-3565; fax 610/ 995-9524; www.bnbphiladelphia. com). This reservation service represents more than 100 personally inspected accommodations in Philadelphia, Valley Forge, the Brandywine Valley, and in Lancaster, Montgomery, and Bucks counties. The agency has assembled a group of interesting, warm hosts, including linguists, gourmet cooks, and therapists. Philadelphia B&B accommodations include a contemporary loft with a spectacular view of the Delaware River, a mid-18th-century inn, a Victorian home with a magnificent three-story open staircase, and a town house tucked in an alley seconds from Rittenhouse Square. In greener pastures, you can pick from the second oldest house in Pennsylvania, a former stagecoach stop, or a converted carriage house complete with pool.

Prices range from $60 to $245 for a couple. Many accommodations at lower prices have shared bathrooms. Children are a point to discuss when booking since they are sometimes not welcome under a certain age and sometimes are especially welcome. The B&B agency listed above will select a compatible lodging for you or send you its free brochure. American Express, Visa, and MasterCard are accepted; phone reservations can be made Monday through Friday from 9am to 5pm.

Another website that lists 39 top bed-and-breakfasts and inns in Center City and in surrounding areas such as Chadds Ford and Bucks County, complete with photos, listings of amenities, and contact information, is **Bed and Breakfasts Online.** Rates start at about $60 and range up to about $250 for separate luxury cottages (www.bbonline.com/pa/philadelphia.html).

1 Historic Area

VERY EXPENSIVE

Hyatt Regency Philadelphia at Penn's Landing ⚐   The most recently constructed (Dec 2000) major hotel in town towers above the Delaware River waterfront, easily accessible from I-95. With its solid Deco-style angles and boxes, it's impossible to miss. Walkways over the highway at Walnut and Dock streets mean 5 easy Colonial blocks separate you from the historic sights. The well-lit, marble-floored lobby features a sofa encircling an enormous flower urn, flanked by warm cherry walls and swoops of fabrics; check-in is tucked near the elevator banks. The guest rooms continue the Art Deco theme, with patterns in browns and cherry furniture. Rooms have stupendous views of the riverfront or city. I-95 noise does percolate up, so choose a river-view room if quiet is

Philadelphia Accommodations

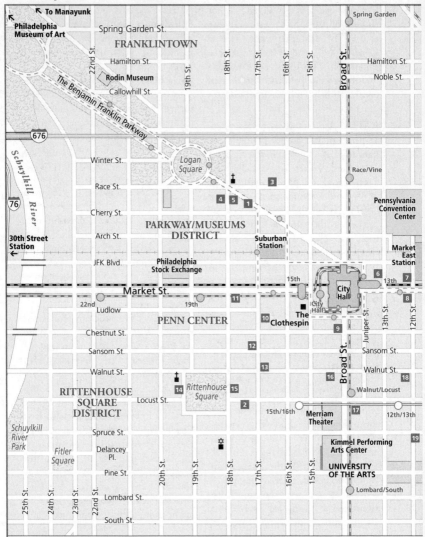

Alexander Inn **19**
Bank Street Hostel **24**
Best Western
  Independence Park Inn **23**
Comfort Inn
  Downtown/Historic Area **27**
Courtyard by Marriott **6**
Crowne Plaza Philadelphia
  Center City **11**

Doubletree Hotel Philadelphia **17**
Embassy Suites Center City **5**
Four Seasons Hotel **4**
Holiday Inn—Independence Mall **26**
Hotel Windsor **1**
Hyatt Regency Philadelphia
  at Penn's Landing **28**
The Latham **13**

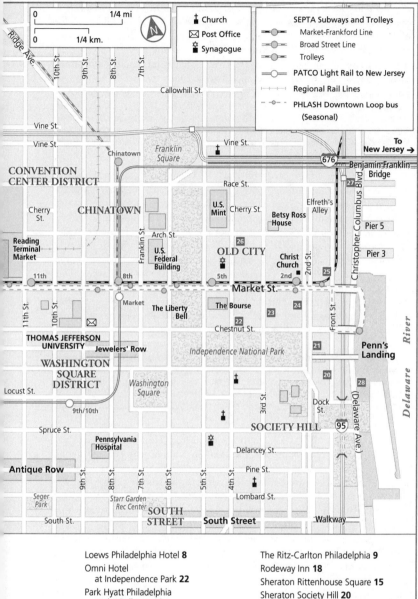

Map Legend

Scale: 0 — 1/4 mi, 0 — 1/4 km.

✝ Church
⊠ Post Office
☼ Synagogue

SEPTA Subways and Trolleys
- Market-Frankford Line
- Broad Street Line
- Trolleys
- PATCO Light Rail to New Jersey
- Regional Rail Lines
- PHLASH Downtown Loop bus (Seasonal)

Ridge Ave.
10th St.
9th St.
8th St.
7th St.
Callowhill St.
Vine St.
Vine St.
To New Jersey →
Chinatown
Franklin Square
Vine St.
676
Benjamin Franklin Bridge

CONVENTION CENTER DISTRICT

Cherry St.
CHINATOWN
Race St.
Cherry St.
Elfreth's Alley
27
Pier 5

U.S. Mint
Betsy Ross House
Pier 3

Reading Terminal Market
Franklin St.
Arch St.
U.S. Federal Building
OLD CITY 26
Christ Church
Christopher Columbus Blvd
2nd St.
25

11th
8th
5th
Market St.

11th St.
10th St.
Market
The Liberty Bell
The Bourse
22
23
24
Front St.
Penn's Landing
Delaware River

THOMAS JEFFERSON UNIVERSITY
Jewelers' Row
Chestnut St.
Independence National Park
21

WASHINGTON SQUARE DISTRICT
Washington Square
20
28
Locust St.
9th/10th
Dock St.

Spruce St.
Pennsylvania Hospital
3rd St.
SOCIETY HILL
95
(Delaware Ave.)

Antique Row
9th St.
8th St.
7th St.
6th St.
5th St.
4th St.
Delancey St.
Pine St.

Seger Park
Starr Garden Rec Center
SOUTH STREET
South Street
Lombard St.
Walkway
South St.

Loews Philadelphia Hotel **8**
Omni Hotel at Independence Park **22**
Park Hyatt Philadelphia at the Bellevue **16**
Penn's View Hotel **25**
Philadelphia Marriott **7**
Rittenhouse Hotel **14**
Rittenhouse Square Bed & Breakfast **2**

The Ritz-Carlton Philadelphia **9**
Rodeway Inn **18**
Sheraton Rittenhouse Square **15**
Sheraton Society Hill **20**
Hotel Sofitel **12**
Thomas Bond House **21**
Westin Philadelphia **10**
Wyndham Philadelphia at Franklin Plaza **3**

important to you. Bathrooms are marbled and swanky. Self-parking can be tedious here, with a small garage elevator and long waits for it, so go with the valets for only $5 more (you can drive in and out as many times as you like without extra fees). Keating's River Grill (Dan Keating owns the site, which Hyatt manages) can seat 200 guests indoors and 75 outdoors on an elegant plaza featuring artist-commissioned wrought iron rails and overlooking the Delaware River.

201 S. Columbus Blvd., Philadelphia, PA 19106. © 800/233-1234 or 215/928-1234. Fax 215/521-6543. www.hyatt.com. 350 units. $220 double. Weekend rates available from $150. Children 21 and under stay free in parent's room. AE, DC, MC, V. Valet parking $20 per day, self-parking $15 per day. Bus: 21. **Amenities:** Restaurant; lounge; glass-enclosed indoor lap pool (no lifeguard); large health club; sauna; concierge; great meeting facilities; 24-hr. room service; laundry service. *In room:* A/C, cable TV w/pay movies, dataport, minibar, coffeemaker, hair dryer, iron.

Omni Hotel at Independence Park ☆

This small, polished hotel, opened in 1990, has a terrific location fronting onto Independence National Historical Park, and is near many of the best Old City restaurants and galleries. All rooms have park views and were recently renovated, though there's a sense of history, too, as horse-drawn carriages clip-clop past the valet parking drop-off and elegant glass-and-steel canopy. The lobby is classic, with huge vases of flowers, and a clubby adjacent bar featuring a pianist. Every room is cheery, with plants and original pastels of city views. The staff here is noteworthy for its quality and its knowledge of the park. The hotel's Azalea serves New American fare. The restaurant is open for breakfast, lunch, brunch, and dinner, and the comfortable lounge serves excellent hamburgers and light pastas. The Ritz Five movie theater is next door in the Bourse complex.

4th and Chestnut sts., Philadelphia, PA 19106 (3 blocks south of Ben Franklin Bridge [Chestnut St. runs one way east, so approach from 6th St.]). © 800/843-6664 or 215/925-0000. Fax 215/931-1263. www.omni hotels.com. 150 units. $239 double; from $575 suite. Weekend rates available, from $169. Children stay free in parent's room, up to 4 people per room. AE, DC, DISC, MC, V. Self-parking $20 (no in and out), valet parking $28 (unlimited in and out). Bus: PHLASH, 21, or 42. **Amenities:** Restaurant; lounge; indoor lap pool; health club; Jacuzzi; sauna; concierge; 24-hr. room service. *In room:* A/C, TV/VCR, 2 dataports, minibar, hair dryer, iron, voice mail.

Sheraton Society Hill *(Kids)*

Located 3 blocks from Head House Square and 4 blocks from Independence Hall, the 1986 Sheraton Society Hill sits among the tree-lined cobblestone streets of this historic district. Set on a triangular 2½-acre site between Dock and South Front streets, the building is modern, but was designed in keeping with the area's Georgian architecture and Flemish Bond brickwork. Its skylit, four-story atrium is entered via a circular courtyard with a splashing fountain.

The guest rooms are on the long low second, third, and fourth floors (the only Delaware River views are from the fourth floor). Rooms are a bit smaller than you'd expect (as are the bathrooms); half have one king-size bed, and the others have two double beds. Rooms are furnished in Drexel Heritage mahogany, an upholstered love seat and chair, and glass-and-brass coffee tables. In each bathroom, dark marble tops the vanity, and Martex bathrobes are provided. The decor is rich and patterned, with American art prints on the walls.

On Dock St. at 2nd and Walnut sts., Philadelphia, PA 19106. © 800/325-3535 or 215/238-6000. Fax 215/ 238-6652. www.sheraton.com/societyhill. 365 units. From $199 double, depending on view; $350–$650 suite. Weekend rates available, from $169. Children 17 and under stay free in parent's room. AE, DC, MC, V. Valet parking $25 per day. Bus: PHLASH, 21, or 42. **Amenities:** 2 restaurants; lounge and courtyard bar; indoor pool (daily 6am–10pm); small health club with trainers; Jacuzzi; sauna; concierge; free weekday shuttle van to Center City; superior meeting facilities; 24-hr. room service; laundry service. *In room:* A/C, TV, dataport (high-speed in some rooms), minibar, coffeemaker, hair dryer, iron.

Tips **Smoke Gets in Your Eyes**

Accommodations reserved for nonsmokers—often in blocks as large as several floors—are so common that we no longer single out hotels that offer them. However, nonsmokers should not assume that they'll get a smoke-free room without specifically requesting one, except at the totally smoke-free Sheraton Rittenhouse Square. As smokers are squeezed into fewer and fewer rooms, the ones they are allowed to use become saturated with the smell of smoke, even in hotels that are otherwise antiseptic. Be sure to stress your need for a smoke-free room to avoid this disagreeable situation.

EXPENSIVE

Holiday Inn Independence Mall   This eight-floor Holiday Inn, set back from the street, is the closest you can sleep to the Liberty Bell—just turn the corner and you're at the pavilion that houses it. A renovation of the bedrooms and public spaces 5 years ago, and the addition of dataports, voice mail, and a concierge have given it a "commendable" rating within the Holiday Inn organization. Rooms are standard size and decor.

4th and Arch sts., Philadelphia, PA 19106. (℃) **800/843-2355** or 215/923-8660. Fax 215/829-1796. 364 units. $150 standard with double or king bed. Excellent weekend rates available. Extra person $10 (up to 5 in a room). Children under 12 stay and eat free; under 18 stay free in parent's room. AE, DISC, DC, MC, V. Parking $20 per day. Bus: PHLASH. **Amenities:** Restaurant and lounge; rooftop outdoor pool; children's programs in the summer; game room; concierge and room service 6am–midnight; laundry room. *In room:* A/C, TV, dataport, coffeemaker, voice mail.

Penn's View Hotel 𝒦 *Finds*   Tucked behind the Market Street ramp to I-95 in a renovated 1856 hardware store, this small, exquisite inn exudes European flair—when you enter you'll feel like you're in a private club. It was developed by the Sena family, which owns La Famiglia restaurant 450 feet south (p. 93). The decor is floral and rich. The main concern is traffic noise, but the rooms are well insulated and contain large framed mirrors, armoires, and efficient bathroom fixtures. The ceilings have been dropped for modern heat and air-conditioning, and you'll find Jacuzzis and fireplaces in 12 of the rooms. A third bed can be wheeled into your room for $15. Ristorante Panorama, adjacent to the lobby, offers excellent contemporary Italian cuisine at moderate prices. Also in the hotel is Il Bar, a world-class wine bar that offers 120 different wines by the glass.

Front and Market sts., Philadelphia, PA 19106. (℃) **800/331-7634** or 215/922-7600. Fax 215/922-7642. www. pennsviewhotel.com. 51 units. $120–$250 double. Weekend rates available; $316 package includes 2 nights, champagne upon arrival, and $70 Panorama restaurant voucher. Rates include European continental breakfast. Guarantee requested on reservation. AE, MC, V. Bus: PHLASH or 21. Parking $18 at adjacent lot. **Amenities:** Restaurant; wine bar. *In room:* A/C, TV, dataport, hair dryer, iron.

MODERATE

Best Western Independence Park Hotel 𝒦   This top choice for bed-and-breakfast-style lodging has a great location, 2 blocks from Independence Hall. Now a Best Western franchise, the inn is housed in a handsome 1856 former dry-goods store with renovated rooms and a renovated exterior.

The guest rooms, on eight floors, are normal size, but the ceilings are nice and high. The bathrooms have big beveled mirrors, dropped ceilings, and hair dryers. Although all the windows are triple casement and double-glazed, specify an interior room if you're sensitive to noise, since some rooms face the traffic on Chestnut Street. A third bed can be wheeled into your room for a child at no additional charge. The hotel serves a generous continental breakfast with a make-your-own Belgian waffle bar in a glass-enclosed garden courtyard, with a complimentary afternoon tea.

235 Chestnut St., Philadelphia, PA 19106. (C) **800/624-2988** or 215/922-4443. Fax 215/922-4487. www. independenceparkhotel.com. 36 units. $119–$199 double. Rates include breakfast and afternoon tea. Children 12 and under stay free in parent's room; 15% AAA discount. AE, DC, DISC, MC, V. Parking $13 at nearby enclosed garage. Bus: PHLASH, 21, or 42. Pets accepted. **Amenities:** Special discount coupons to nearby restaurants and a nearby health club ($10) are available. In room: A/C, TV, dataport (dial-up or wireless), hair dryer.

Comfort Inn Downtown/Historic Area   Comfort Inn at Penn's Landing is the area's only moderately priced waterfront hotel (sometimes offering specials from $69), in a corner of the Old City between I-95 and the Delaware River. It tends to attract a lot of student or senior groups. There is a courtesy shuttle van to Center City, and the cross-town subway line is 2 blocks away. Comfort Inn has been built to airport-area noise specifications, with insulated windows and other features to lessen the din of traffic. The eastern views of the river from the upper floors are stupendous. A complimentary continental breakfast is served in the cocktail lounge. There's a coin laundry on the second floor, and half the rooms are designated for nonsmokers. The fitness room stocks weights and has cardio-fitness machines.

100 N. Columbus Blvd., Philadelphia, PA 19106 (3 blocks from the northbound ramp off the expwy.). (C) **800/ 228-5150** or 215/627-7900. Fax 215/238-0809. www.comfortinnphila.com. 185 units. From $99 double. Rates include continental breakfast. Children 18 and under stay free in parent's room. Ask about discounts for AAA members. AE, DC, DISC, MC, V. Parking $15 (unlimited in-and-out) in adjacent lot. SEPTA: 2nd St. Bus: PHLASH or 42. In room: A/C, TV, dataport, coffeemaker, iron.

Thomas Bond House (Finds)   This 1769 Georgian row house sits almost directly across from the back of Independence Park in busy Old City, and is owned by the federal government, which kept the shell and gutted the interior. The guest rooms are cheerful, comfortable, Colonial-style accommodations, renovated completely in 2002. The entrance is decorated with map illustrations and secretary desks. The charming parlor has pink sofas and a replica Chippendale double chair, while the breakfast room has four tables for four. All rooms are individually decorated and feature private bathrooms and period furnishings. Fresh-baked cookies are put out each evening for bedtime snacking. The hotel is named for its first occupant, the doctor who co-founded Pennsylvania Hospital with Benjamin Franklin.

129 S. 2nd St., Philadelphia, PA 19106. (C) **800/845-2663** or 215/923-8523. Fax 215/923-8504. 12 units. $95–$175 double; $175 suite. Rates include breakfast and afternoon wine and cheese. AE, MC, V. Parking $13 at adjacent lot. Bus: PHLASH, 21, or 42. Children over 10 welcome. **Amenities:** Exercise room; limited business services and conference room. In room: A/C, TV, hair dryer.

2 Center City

VERY EXPENSIVE

Four Seasons Hotel (stars) (Kids)   It was rated the best hotel in Philly in the 2003 Zagat Guide, has earned five diamonds from AAA, and been named one of the top 20 U.S. hotels in *Condé Nast Traveler:* the Four Seasons' luxury is refined and understated. Built in 1983, the Four Seasons is an eight-story curlicue on Logan Square, with views of the exquisite Swann Fountain and a lush interior courtyard, and has just been completely renovated throughout with beautiful new fabrics and furnishings. The pale-toned lobby has enormous masses of flowers, intimate seating areas, and honey-colored woods. The peach-hued lounge and promenade serve as foyers to the dining and meeting facilities and are paneled in a rare white mahogany. Guest rooms have a rich American elegance: The overstuffed chairs and rich carpets are in tones of pale yellow and sage, and in-room business and tech capabilities are tops. The bathrooms have a wonderful marble dressing area, and excellent lighting. All the rooms have windows or private verandas boasting marvelous views of Logan Circle or the interior courtyard. If you can get a room with a view down the Parkway to the Art Museum and across to the Free Library, you will be dazzled both by day and at night.

The Four Seasons restaurants regularly collect raves from local reviewers. The Fountain Restaurant, under executive chef Martin Hamann, is a classic, a favorite among Philly residents for unstuffy service and a fabulous Sunday brunch. Natural light streams over 150 wide armchair seats and tapestries, fresh flowers, and walnut paneling. Another great option is dining in the hotel's cafe room, which offers slightly more casual fare from Hamann's kitchen at about half the price of a Fountain dinner. The Swann Lounge has marble-top tables and a colorful, civilized look like something out of a Maurice Prendergast sketch. It's open for an extensive lunch, afternoon tea, and cocktails.

1 Logan Sq., Philadelphia, PA 19103. ℂ **800/332-3442** or 215/963-1500. Fax 215/963-9506. www.four seasons.com. 365 units. Doubles from $320. Weekend rates available from $230. AE, DC, MC, V. Valet parking $32, self-parking $24. SEPTA: Suburban Station. Bus: PHLASH. Pets allowed. **Amenities:** 2 restaurants; cafe; indoor heated pool; health club with Universal machines, Exercycles, and exercise mats; spa; Jacuzzi; concierge; town-car service within Center City; salon; 24-hr. room service; babysitting; laundry service; dry cleaning. *In room:* A/C, TV w/pay movies, fax available, hi-speed dataport, minibar/fridge, iron, safe, in-room exercise equipment available.

Hotel Sofitel ★★
Sofitel is the premier French luxury chain, and this 5-year-old hotel set in a limestone-and-glass tower exudes hospitality and chic, with its modern-Deco vibe and popular bar off the marble lobby. The location, half a block from the Walnut Street shopping corridor, is wonderful for business or pleasure visitors, located between Rittenhouse Square and the Avenue of the Arts. Downstairs, the lobby is filled with inlaid marble, sleek wood, and flower arrangements; upstairs, guest rooms are very upscale and Deco-contemporary, with a glass coffee table, two armchairs, and an opulent bed with wall-mounted bedside lights on walls of handsome checkerboard cherrywood. The bathrooms are huge, with luxurious travertine marble throughout. Business travelers will find high-speed Internet jacks on the desk with easy table-top plug-ins.

Chez Colette is a traditional French brasserie that serves decadent breakfasts (and complimentary coffee to guests). The lobby bar is a popular gathering spot: a New York–style lounge, with tall windows overlooking Sansom Street, a long blue Brazilian granite bar, cozy seating areas, and varied wines by the glass.

17th and Sansom sts., Philadelphia, PA 19103. ℂ **800/SOFITEL** or 215/569-8300. Fax 215/569-1492. www. sofitel.com. 306 units. $269 double. Weekend packages available. AE, DC, DISC, MC, V. Valet parking $29 per day in underground garage. SEPTA: Suburban Station. Bus: PHLASH, 21, or 42. Pets allowed under 25 pounds; they incur a $50 surcharge. **Amenities:** Brasserie; lounge; fully equipped fitness center; 24-hr. room service. *In room:* A/C, TV w/pay movies, dataport, hair dryer, iron.

Park Hyatt Philadelphia at the Bellevue ★★
The "grande dame of Broad Street" was the most opulent hotel in the country when it first opened in 1904. It's still a grand experience in a great location: All guest rooms were renovated in 2002, and the Park Hyatt ranks just below the Four Seasons, the Rittenhouse,

---

Finds **Historic Bed & Breakfasts**

Many B&Bs are listed through A Bed & Breakfast Connection/Bed & Breakfast of Philadelphia (see p. 73 for contact information). However, some B&Bs list themselves independently. My favorite among the latter is **Shippen Way Inn** *⋆*, 418 Bainbridge St. (© **800/245-4873** or 215/627-7266), set in two pretty row houses in Queen Village built around 1750 and lovingly maintained. During the summer, you can wake up in a four-poster bed and have breakfast in the back herb garden for $85 to $120 per night. You might also try **Ten Eleven Clinton,** 1011 Clinton St. (© **215/923-8144**), an elegant 1836 Federal town house (that means high ceilings!) on a beautiful tree-lined residential street near Pine and 11th. Rates run $145 to $200.

---

and the Ritz-Carlton. The dazzling marble-mosaic ground floor houses high-end retailers like Tiffany & Co. and Polo/Ralph Lauren, and a lower level features Pierre & Carlo Spa Salon, Zanzibar Blue jazz bar and restaurant, and a gourmet food court. A separate elevator lifts you to the domed 19th-floor registration area and foyer for the hotel restaurants. The rooms, occupying floors 12 to 17, are large and all slightly different, with wall moldings reproduced from the 1904 designs. Each room boasts extra large goose-down pillows, three two-line phones with dataports, a VCR, a large bed, a writing desk, a round table, and four upholstered chairs. The bathrooms are marble, with amenities like hair dryers, TVs, and illuminated mirrors.

Founders (p. 98), voted one of the top 50 restaurants in the nation by *Condé Nast Traveler,* has two spectacular semicircular windows draped with dramatic swags of brown and cream, and offers dancing to a swing trio on weekends. The Library Lounge is quiet and comfortable, with a fireplace and a collection of books by and about Philadelphians. The Park Hyatt Bellevue is adjacent to the Sporting Club, one of Philadelphia's top health clubs, a Michael Graves–designed facility with 93,000 square feet of health club space, including a half-mile jogging track; a four-lane, 25m junior Olympic pool; and squash and racquetball courts.

Broad and Walnut sts., or 1415 Chancellor Court (between Walnut and Locust sts.), Philadelphia, PA 19102. © **800/223-1234** or 215/893-1234. Fax 215/732-8518. www.parkphiladelphia.hyatt.com. 172 units. $265 double; $340 suites. Weekend packages often available. AE, DC, DISC, MC, V. Self-parking $16 at connected garage, valet parking $25. SEPTA: Walnut-Locust. Bus: PHLASH, 21, or 42. **Amenities:** Restaurant; lounge; indoor pool at health club; use of the excellent health club facilities at the Sporting Club; full-day child-care facility at the Sporting Club; concierge; 24-hr. room service; laundry service; dry cleaning. *In room:* A/C, TV/VCR w/pay movies, dataport, minibar, hair dryer, iron.

Rittenhouse Hotel *⋆⋆⋆* *Kids*   Among Philadelphia's luxury hotels, the Rittenhouse has the fewest and largest rooms and the most satisfying views. Built in 1989, it's a jagged concrete-and-glass high-rise off the western edge of Philadelphia's most distinguished public square. The lobby is tranquil and lovely, with inlaid marble floors and a series of frosted-glass chandeliers and sconces. Along with the Four Seasons and the Ritz-Carlton, it's the only AAA Five-Diamond Award holder in the state—which may be why Bruce Willis, Mel Gibson, and Kevin Bacon have all made this their home for months at a time while filming movies in Philly.

Every room at the Rittenhouse is actually a suite with a full living room area, bay windows, reinforced walls between rooms, and solid-wood doors. All have great views: The park is leafy and beautiful most of the year, and the western view of the Schuylkill River and the Parkway is dramatic. City scenes by local artists decorate the walls.

Jean-Marie Lacroix, a superb chef formerly at the Four Seasons, helms Lacroix at the Rittenhouse, a chic restaurant overlooking the park, offering modern French cuisine. Smith & Wollensky, the New York steakhouse, has an outpost with a convivial bar off the main lobby, and the more casual Boathouse Row Bar & Grill has a late-night menu. The site was the original town house of painter Mary Cassatt's brother, and there is a charming trellised private garden adorned with three drypoints by Cassatt.

210 W. Rittenhouse Sq., Philadelphia, PA 19103. (C) **800/635-1042** or 215/546-9000. Fax 215/732-3364. www.rittenhousehotel.com. 98 units. Doubles from $310. Weekend rates and packages including health club, dinners, and other amenities available ($450 package includes parking, a three-course dinner for two at Lacroix, and the health club). AE, DC, MC, V. Valet parking $24. Bus: 21 or 42. **Amenities:** 3 restaurants; bar; lounge; 5-lane indoor pool; Adolf Biecker fitness club with sun deck, Cybex weight machines, and aerobic equipment; spa; sauna; steam room; concierge; executive business center; 24-hr. room service; massage; laundry service; dry cleaning. In room: A/C, TV/VCR w/pay movies, fax, dataport, minibar, hair dryer, iron.

The Ritz-Carlton Philadelphia ★★★

The Ritz-Carlton, which opened in 2000, is the jewel of the Avenue of the Arts, set in a 1908 domed bank designed by McKim, Mead, and White, and an adjacent 30-story marble-clad neighboring building. The tower has been converted into the hotel rooms, and the soaring 140-foot-high lobby is a domed rotunda with rococo Versace furnishings, two restaurants, a clubby bar called the Vault, and a downstairs ballroom. Many architectural details have been preserved, including marble flooring and a bank teller desk.

The hotel rooms occupy floors 4 to 29, with a spectacular concierge/club area in a paneled former boardroom on the 30th floor. (If you can upgrade to this level, you'll consider it money well spent—the room is gorgeous, and the hors d'oeuvres, champagne, and lavish breakfast are the best club-floor spread we've ever seen.) In guest rooms, you'll find more space than normal allotted to generous bathrooms with opulent marble tub/shower alcoves, and less to the snug bedrooms, decorated with stippled paper in peach and warm ochers. The furnishings and amenities are lovely, from the old Philadelphia prints and engravings to plush terry robes to the high-speed Internet access for laptops.

Pantheon, with its marble Ionic columns and 18-foot high windows, serves breakfast daily and weekend brunch. **The Grill** ★, a clubby space on the City Hall side, features an open kitchen, with former Striped Bass chef Terence Feury serving exceptional lunches and dinners. On weekends, a lavish 40-dessert buffet is served in the lobby.

10 Avenue of the Arts (corner of S. Broad and Chestnut sts.), Philadelphia, PA 19102. (C) **800/241-3333** or 215/523-8000. Fax 215/568-0942. www.ritzcarlton.com. 331 units. $279 double. Weekend rates available from $230. AE, DC, DISC, MC, V. Valet parking $32, no self-parking. SEPTA: 15th St./City Hall. Bus: PHLASH, 21, or 42. Dogs permitted under certain conditions, with a $25 surcharge. **Amenities:** 2 restaurants; lounge; fitness center; spa; sauna; steam room; concierge; 24-hr. room service; massage; laundry service; dry cleaning. In room: A/C, TV w/pay movies, 2 dataports, minibar, hair dryer, iron, safe.

Westin Philadelphia ★★ Value

The Westin opened with great fanfare as a gorgeous, paneled Ritz-Carlton in 1990. Although it's been fumbled with a bit by its owners, Starwood Hotels, this wonderful place seems to have emerged intact, with a blend of luxury amenities and service. And the location is convenient for business or leisure visits—it is part of the Liberty Place shopping complex and a block from Walnut Street. While it's a bit higher priced than other Westins, it's a value compared to its luxury peers.

A small porte-cochere and a ground-floor entrance on 17th Street lead to elevators that lift you up to the main lobby, which is a series of a living-room-like sitting rooms, plus a clubby bar and grill. The guest rooms feature bedside walnut tables, desks, firm beds with spindle-top headboards (and a luxurious four pillows), and Wedgwood or Sandwich glass lamps. Large walnut armoires house TVs, clothing drawers, and minibars. All rooms are provided with two phone lines and dataports. The modern bathrooms, improved by Westin, are outfitted with black-and-white marble, silver plate fixtures, magnifying mirrors, and lots of toiletries. The hotel runs frequent packages in tandem with museum exhibitions or other events.

17th and Chestnut sts. (at Liberty Place), Philadelphia, PA 19103. © **800/228-3000** or 215/563-1600. Fax 215/564-9559. www.westin.com. 290 units. $259 and up double. Weekend rates available from $99. AE, DISC, MC, V. Self-parking $22, valet parking $15-$31. SEPTA: Suburban Station. Bus: PHLASH, 21, or 42. **Amenities:** Restaurant; lounge; small exercise facility; sauna; 24-hr. concierge; $8 transport to and from airport; fully equipped business center and meeting rooms; internal connection to the 70 Shops at Liberty Place (p. 180); 24-hr. room service; laundry service; dry cleaning. *In room:* A/C, TV w/pay movies, fax, dataport, minibar, coffeemaker, hair dryer, iron, safe.

EXPENSIVE

Doubletree Hotel Philadelphia ⭐   The Avenue of the Arts location of this hotel is good for culture-seekers and families. The garage entrances ingeniously keep traffic flows separate for three floors of meeting facilities. The decor features rich paisleys and Degas-style murals alluding to the orchestral and ballet life at the Academy of Music across the street. Thanks to the saw-toothed design of the building, each of the guest rooms, which have been upgraded with new TVs and mattresses, has two views of town. Obviously, the higher floors afford the better views. The views of the Delaware River (eastern corner) or City Hall (northeastern corner) are the most popular. The bathrooms are clean and bland, and the Doubletree signature is a box of great chocolate chip cookies delivered to your room upon arrival.

Broad St. at Locust St., Philadelphia, PA 19107. © **800/222-8733** or 215/893-1600. Fax 215/893-1664. www.doubletreehotels.com. 427 units. $189 double. Weekend packages available. Children under 18 stay free in parent's room. AE, DC, DISC, MC, V. Self-parking $18 in adjoining garage, valet parking $22. SEPTA: Walnut-Locust. Bus: PHLASH, 21, or 42. **Amenities:** 2 restaurants; lounge; indoor lap pool; health club, and a small jogging track circling a huge rooftop deck; Jacuzzi; steam room; activities desk; laundry service; dry cleaning. *In room:* A/C, TV w/pay movies, 2 dataports, minibar, coffeemaker, hair dryer, iron.

Embassy Suites Center City ⭐ *Value*   The big 28-story cylinder of marble and glass on the Parkway at 18th Street, started out as a luxury apartment building in the 1960s. The all-suite structure coupled with the location and the price makes this a good choice for families, and all the guest rooms were renovated and improved in late 2004.

The kitchenette includes microwave, under-the-counter refrigerator, and coffeemaker (no oven or dishwasher); dishes and silverware are provided upon request. A table with four chairs overlooks the small balcony terrace, which is accessible through a sliding door. Bathrooms have large Italian marble tiles, plush white towels, and hair dryers. Bedrooms can offer one or two beds, and there is a pull-out couch in the living room.

TGI Friday's, connected on two levels, is open until 1am daily; full complimentary breakfast is served in the atrium. A manager's reception happy hour is included in your room rate.

1776 Benjamin Franklin Pkwy. (at Logan Sq.), Philadelphia, PA 19103. © 800/362-2779 or 215/561-1776. Fax 215/963-0122. www.embassysuites.com. 288 units. $149 suite. Excellent weekend packages available. Children under 18 stay free in parent's room. Rates include full breakfast. AE, DC, DISC, MC, V. Valet parking $24. SEPTA: Suburban Station. Bus: PHLASH, 21, 33, or 42. **Amenities:** Restaurant; fitness center with Nordic Track, Stairmasters, and rowing machines; sauna; laundry service; dry cleaning. *In room:* A/C, 2 TVs w/pay movies, dataport, minibar, coffeemaker, hair dryer, iron, microwave.

Hotel Windsor 🎀 *Value* This all-suite hotel located on the flag-flanked Parkway is convenient to shopping, the Convention Center, and the Art Museum, and has a pleasant lobby and balconies off most rooms. Living rooms and bedrooms are spacious and bland, with large, fully equipped kitchens, including pots, pans, dishware, and utensils, making it a good spot for families. All suites were renovated in 2003, and have marble bathrooms; the one-bedroom suites have a king-size bed, and there is a pull-out sofa in the living room.

There is a rooftop pool, and in the lobby, **Peacock on the Parkway** restaurant has a bar, and serves Italian fare for lunch and dinner; breakfast is available at nearby cafes and delis. Adjacent to the hotel, **Mace's Crossing** tavern is popular for alfresco martini-sipping in the summer months.

1700 Benjamin Franklin Pkwy., Philadelphia, PA 19103. © 215/981-8379. Fax 215/981-5608. www.windsorhotel.com. 350 units. $129–$179 suite. Children under 18 stay free in parent's room. AE, DC, DISC, MC, V. Valet parking $22. SEPTA: Suburban Station. Bus: PHLASH, 21, 33, or 42. **Amenities:** Restaurant; rooftop pool; 24-hr. fitness center; use of nearby Bally's Fitness Center included in room rate; laundry service. *In room:* Cable TV, dataport, kitchen, coffeemaker, hair dryer, iron.

The Latham 🎀 *Value* A landmark apartment house from 1915 to 1970, the Latham's charm, congeniality, and small attentions bring to mind a small, superbly run Swiss hostelry in a great setting off Walnut Street. On weekday mornings, the lobby—a high-ceilinged salon with terrazzo highlights—is filled with refreshed executives, though the hotel does no convention business. Weekend packages are great bargains. The reception staff is quick and professional. The guest rooms, redone in Victorian motif in 1998, are not huge or lavish but perfectly proportioned and decorated with cheerful striped silk. Full-wall and lighted facial mirrors, large marblelike basins, and over-size towels highlight the white-toned bathroom interiors.

135 S. 17th St. at Walnut St., Philadelphia, PA 19103. © 877/528-4261 or 215/563-7474. Fax 215/568-0110. www.lathamhotel.com. 139 units. $129 double. Weekend packages from $109. Up to 2 children stay free in parent's room. AE, DC, DISC, MC, V. Valet parking $20. SEPTA: Walnut-Locust. Bus: PHLASH, 21, 42. **Amenities:** Restaurant; lounge; small fitness center; concierge; laundry service; dry cleaning. *In room:* A/C, TV, dataport, minibar, coffeemaker, hair dryer, iron.

Loews Philadelphia Hotel 🎀 The Loews, opened in spring 2000 in the former PSFS Bank tower, is the fine product of the marriage of an Art Deco architectural landmark and a prestigious hotel chain. The tower, located across from the Reading Terminal and the Convention Center, was the nation's first skyscraper of modern design and construction, with gleaming polished stone and clocks by Cartier. Loews Hotels turned the 1932 granite and glass building into a first-class property. The three-story entrance hall has been preserved, and rooms feature 10-foot ceilings, modern-Deco interiors, and miles of spectacular views. Business aids are extensive, but watch out for the surcharges levied on phone use. For convention travelers, the location is ideal, though this stretch of Market Street is a bit grittier than it is near Society Hill or Rittenhouse Square

Solefood is the hotel's seafood restaurant, and there is a pleasant lobby lounge off the restaurant; Channel 10, the local NBC affiliate, often uses the lobby as a set for interviews.

1200 Market St., Philadelphia, PA 19107. © **800/235-6397** or 215/627-1200. www.loewshotels.com. 585 units. $199–$250 double. Weekend packages available from $169. AE, DC, DISC, MC, V. Parking $30. SEPTA: 11th St. Station. Bus: PHLASH, 21, or 42. **Amenities:** Restaurant; bar; library lounge; 15,000-sq.-ft. fitness facility with 2-lane lap pool available for $10/day; concierge service; laundry service; dry cleaning. *In room:* A/C, TV w/pay movies, fax, high-speed dataport, minibar, hair dryer, iron.

Philadelphia Marriott and **Courtyard by Marriott** 🐼🐼 (*Value*   The Marriott chain opened the biggest hotel in Pennsylvania in January 1995, linked by an elevated covered walkway to the Reading Terminal Shed of the Convention Center. And it's gotten bigger. In late 1999 Marriott converted the historic 1926 City Hall Annex across 13th Street at Filbert into a 500-room Courtyard by Marriott, the largest in the Courtyard division. So all together, you have your choice of 1,910 rooms, two fitness centers, and 10 restaurants and lounges—all linked with one another and with the Convention Center.

The hotel's major auto entrance is on Filbert Street (two-way between Market and Arch sts.), with an equally grand pedestrian entrance adjoining Champions Sports Bar and retail on Market Street. The lobby is sliced up into a five-story atrium, enlivened by a 10,000-square-foot water sculpture, a lobby bar, and a Starbucks. Setbacks and terraces provide plenty of natural light and views from the rooms on floors 6 to 23. Rooms are tastefully outfitted with dark woods, maroon and green drapes and bedspreads, a TV armoire, a desk, a club chair and ottoman, and a round table, but, overall, rooms are slightly less elegant than those of the top hotels. Comfortably sized bathrooms have heavy chrome fixtures and tuck sinks and counters in the corners for more dressing room space. Closets are spacious; there are large desks with dataports in the Courtyard's rooms. Service is impeccable, thanks to the well-trained, knowledgeable staff.

12th and Market sts., Philadelphia, PA 19107. © **800/228-9290** or 215/625-2900. Fax 215/625-6000. www.marriott.com. 1,410 units. $249 double; $259–$279 concierge-level rooms. Weekend rates available. *Courtyard by Marriott:* 13th and Filbert sts., Philadelphia, PA 19107. © **215/496-3200.** 498 units. $189 standard; $279 suite. AE, DC, DISC, MC, V. Valet parking $30. Bus: PHLASH, 21, or 42. SEPTA: Direct internal connection to Market East station and airport train. **Amenities:** *Philadelphia Marriott:* 2 restaurants; bar; 3 lounges; coffee bar; indoor lap pool; health club; Jacuzzi; saunas. Concierge-floor rooms have special amenities. *Courtyard by Marriott:* Restaurant; indoor pool; fitness center. *In room for both hotels:* AC, TV w/pay movies, dataport, minibar, coffeemaker, hair dryer, iron.

Rittenhouse Square Bed and Breakfast 🐼🐼🐼 (*Value*   Steps from chic Rittenhouse Square, the pristine park ringed by million-dollar apartments and historic mansions, Rittenhouse Square Bed and Breakfast is the city's best incarnation of a small, European-style luxury hotel. The inn is located at the heart of Center City, a 10-minute walk to the Convention Center, the Franklin Institute, and City Hall, but feels private on its tiny, leafy street a block from Walnut Street's shopping corridor. Set in a large mansion built around 1911, the lobby exudes haute-British style, and wine is served at 5pm. Upstairs, burrow under Frette linens and revel in cream-colored Berber carpets, antiques, and reproductions of Louis XIV and Chippendale furniture in one of 10 surprisingly large guest rooms and suites. Or check e-mail—the inn is equipped with DSL lines and workstations. All guest rooms have new marble bathrooms, and pastries and fruit are served in the morning from the city's best bakery, Metropolitan, to round out the sophisticated experience—so much so that children under 12 are not welcome.

1715 Rittenhouse Sq., Philadelphia, PA 19103. (C) **877/791-6500** or 215/546-6500. Fax 215/546-8787. www.rittenhousebb.com. 10 units. $209 double; $259 suite. AE, DC, MC, V. Parking from $20 at several nearby lots. SEPTA: Suburban Station. Bus: PHLASH, 21, or 42. **Amenities:** 24-hr. concierge; small meeting rooms; 2 dataports with DSL. *In room:* A/C, 100-channel cable TV, hair dryer, iron available, voice mail.

Sheraton Rittenhouse Square 🌟🌟   This attractive, renovated 1930s apartment building is spare and sleek, and one of the best values in its neighborhood, with its location right on urbane Rittenhouse Square. The hotel is marketed as the first "environmentally smart" hotel in the continental United States, with fresh filtered air, organic cotton bedding, bamboo plants and recycled granite in the lobby, energy efficient lighting, and no smoking anywhere. (You agree to pay $50 as a sanitizing fee if you smoke in the rooms.) Rooms are modern and very comfortable, with pretty striped wallpaper and deep chairs; a spacious 400 square feet on average, with 9½-foot ceilings and state-of-the-art technology. The same standards of care and cleanliness apply to the large, marbled bathrooms. Many have separate sitting areas and balconies, and kitchenettes are available. I'd avoid the interior rooms, facing all-night airshaft lighting instead of Rittenhouse Square.

    Bleu is the hotel's low-key bistro and cafe with outdoor seating, while **Potcheen Restaurant,** facing Locust Street, is very casual, with American fare.

227 S. 18th St. (at Rittenhouse Sq.), Philadelphia, PA 19103. (C) **800/325-3535** or 215/546-9400. Fax 215/875-9457. www.sheraton.com. 192 units. From $155 double. Excellent weekend packages and discounts available. Children under 18 stay free in parent's room. AE, DC, DISC, MC, V. Off-site valet parking $25. SEPTA: 15th–16th St. Station. Bus: PHLASH, 21, or 42. **Amenities:** 2 restaurants (1 with outdoor seating on Rittenhouse Sq.); fitness facility; room service 6am–midnight. *In room:* A/C, TV w/pay movies, dataport, coffeemaker, hair dryer, iron, voice mail.

Wyndham Philadelphia at Franklin Plaza *Value*   The Wyndham has been functioning as a convenient meeting center since 1980, and now the convention center, only 4 blocks away, fills this hotel sporadically. The complex dominates a full city block (unfortunately near the busy Vine St. Expwy.), and the lobby, lounge, and two restaurants are integrated under a 70-foot glass roof. The Wyndham lobby shows definite signs of fatigue, but is about to be renovated, and a 2004 update of the guest rooms has freshened their look. Request a west view above the 19th floor for an unobstructed peek at the Parkway, but be forewarned that the cathedral bells below ring at 7am, noon, and 6pm daily. Bathrooms are clean and bland.

17th and Race sts., Philadelphia, PA 19103. (C) **800/996-3426** or 215/448-2000. Fax 215/448-2864. www.wyndham.com. 758 units. From $119 double. Excellent weekend rates available. Children 18 and under stay free in parent's room. AE, DC, MC, V. Self-parking $20, valet parking $28. SEPTA: Race-Vine. Bus: PHLASH. **Amenities:** 2 restaurants; tennis courts; indoor pool; health club; Jacuzzi; sauna; limited room service; racquetball courts; squash courts; handball courts. *In room:* A/C, TV w/pay movies, dataport ($10/day fee), minibar, hair dryer, iron.

MODERATE

Alexander Inn 🌟 *Value*   The Alexander Inn bills itself as a four-star hotel at reasonable rates. It's got all the comfort and friendliness of a bed-and-breakfast, with a classy 1930s Art Deco/cruise boat feel to the furnishings. Rooms feature DirecTV with eight all-movie channels, direct dial phones with voice mail, and individual artwork, and bathrooms sparkle with cleanliness. Room rates include a breakfast buffet—until noon on weekends (though there's no restaurant)—and

Kids Family-Friendly Hotels

Family-Friendly Philadelphia (© 800/770-5889) offers special packages that include 2 nights at a number of hotels, free parking and breakfast, and free admission to attractions such as Sesame Place, the Franklin Institute, the Zoo, the Academy of Natural Sciences, the Please Touch Museum, and "The Liberty Tale Tour" run by the Historic Philadelphia guides near Independence Hall. Call for details and visit **www.gophila.com** for more ideas.

Four Seasons Hotel (p. 79) "Kids for All Seasons" amenities include child-size terry robes, toys, milk and cookies at bedtime, special menus at the Fountain restaurant, and playtime at the hotel's beautiful indoor pool. Should parents need any babysitting services—or car seats, strollers, night lights, or really anything imaginable—the staff will magically make it appear.

The Hilton Inn at Penn (p. 87) The comfortable and safe public areas, including the "Living Room" with its fireplace and thousands of books, give your kids a chance to let off steam indoors. Plus, it's across the street from the green lawns of the U. Penn campus. Frisbee, anyone?

Rittenhouse Hotel (p. 81) This hotel's large suites and living rooms in all guest suites make it ideal for families, and the pretty pool on the third floor has kid-size floats and games. You can even order lunch from the Boathouse Row restaurant and eat poolside with the kids .

Sheraton Society Hill (p. 76) There's a special children's check-in, free snacks, the use of the game room, and other kid-friendly features.

use of the fully equipped 24-hour fitness center and a business center. Note that the Alexander Inn is in the heart of the gay/lesbian district of Center City, and its clientele is both straight and gay.

12th and Spruce sts., Philadelphia, PA 19107. © **877/253-9466** or 215/923-3535. Fax 215/923-1004. www.alexanderinn.com. 48 units. $99–$149 double; $10 per additional person. Complimentary breakfast buffet. AE, DC, DISC, MC, V. Garage parking $10 nearby. SEPTA: Market East. **Amenities:** Fitness center; business center. *In room:* A/C, TV w/pay movies, dataport, hair dryer available, iron available.

Crowne Plaza Philadelphia Center City *(Value)* The Crowne Plaza offers solid, generic, primarily business-traveler-oriented accommodations. It's popular with conventioneers and relocating executives, and prices are competitive in an effort to maintain occupancy. The lobby, which dispenses coffee and apples all day, has entrances from both 18th Street and the garage. A parking garage and meeting halls occupy the next six floors, and rooms and several suites fill the next 17 floors. By Philadelphia standards, the rooms are large, and they were renovated in 2004. Furnishings include coffeemakers, telephones with dataports, and plush carpeting. Bathrooms are slightly shabby. Two floors are devoted to Executive Level suites, offering upgraded decor and complimentary breakfast. There is an espresso bar and a casual pub, the Elephant & Castle, on the lobby level.

18th and Market sts., Philadelphia, PA 19103. © 800/227-6963 or 215/561-7500. Fax 215/561-4484. www.crowneplaza.com/philadelphia. 515 units. $160 double. B&B and weekend packages available. Children 19 and under stay free in parent's room; children 12 and under eat free with parents. AE, DC, MC, V. Parking $24. SEPTA: 19th St. Bus: 21, 33, or 42. **Amenities:** Restaurant; outdoor pool; fitness room with rowing and Nautilus machines. *In room:* A/C, TV w/pay movies, dataport, hair dryer, iron.

Rodeway Inn This member of the Rodeway franchise chain is comprised of seven floors of comfortable, bigger-than-average rooms renovated 2 years ago, with solid-core doors, four-poster beds, and private bathrooms. Six rooms boast Jacuzzis, and all rooms have dial-up or wireless Internet access. The front desk is attended 24 hours a day. All suites have gas fireplaces. A state-of-the-art gym is available around the corner for $12.

1208 Walnut St., Philadelphia, PA 19107. © 800/887-1776 or 215/546-7000. Fax 215/546-7573. www. rodeway.com/hotel/pa271. 32 units. $100 double. Rates include continental breakfast and local calls. Garage parking nearby is $11. AE, DC, DISC, MC, V. Bus: 21 or 42. **Amenities:** Free local calls. *In room:* A/C, TV, dataport, hair dryer, iron.

3 University City (West Philadelphia)

EXPENSIVE

The Hilton Inn at Penn ★★ *Kids*   The handsome and elegantly appointed Inn at Penn is my favorite place to stay in the city limits when west of the Schuylkill River. The Inn, managed by Hilton Hotels, is the keystone of the block-long Sansom Commons, an attractive six-story brick area that includes the outstanding University Bookstore and collegiate trendy stores such as Urban Outfitters and a Cosi coffee and sandwich bar. While the front door faces the Penn campus across Walnut Street, you'll enter through a porte-cochere off the north side of Sansom Street. Expansive stairways and corridors connect entrances to registration and to the Living Room, a fully-stocked library where complimentary tea and coffee are dispensed until 4pm, and wine and spirits are sold thereafter. Artwork and bas-reliefs of U. Penn's athletic triumphs from decades past adorn the Mission-style walls. The rooms are done in warm olive and beige tones, with top-quality furnishings, firm beds, and individual temperature controls; some were recently renovated. The academic flavor translates into efficient lighting and amenities such as dual-line phones, voice mail, and coffeemakers.

Penne Restaurant and Wine Bar is a pleasant trattoria where chef Roberta Adamo hand-makes all the pasta. The **Faculty Club** restaurant serves breakfast and lunch. The futuristic Asian-themed **Pod,** with excellent pad Thai, sushi served from a conveyor belt, and sexy color-shifting decor, is within the Sansom Commons complex. University City is rich in ethnic restaurants, many within a block or two of the inn.

3600 Sansom St., Philadelphia, PA 19104. © 800/445-8667 or 215/222-0200. Fax 215/222-4600. www. innatpenn.com. 238 units. $219 double. Children 18 and under stay free in parent's room. Weekend packages available. AE, DC, DISC, MC, V. Valet parking $25. SEPTA: 34th St. Station. Bus: 21. **Amenities:** 2 restaurants; library lounge; 24-hr. exercise room; concierge. *In room:* A/C, WebTV w/pay movies, dataport, coffeemaker, hair dryer, iron, voice mail.

Penn Tower Hotel Penn Tower is a very convenient, if less than stellar, version of a former Hilton, built with a direct skywalk to University Hospital and within steps of the University of Pennsylvania, 30th Street Station, the Civic Center, and Drexel University. The hotel part of the tower comprises floors 17 and 18, and there is an enclosed garage. U. Penn takes over more floors every year for medical offices. You'll have to get used to spirited displays of red and blue, Penn's colors, and a long lobby corridor of rough-textured concrete that leads to the reception desk. A coffee cart serves pastries and sandwiches in the lobby starting at 6am. The rooms and bathrooms were renovated in 2004, and are efficient and clean.

Civic Center Blvd. at 34th St., Philadelphia, PA 19104. (©) 215/387-8333. Fax 215/386-8306. www.upenn. edu/penntower. 50 units. $165 double; $125 for relatives of patients in University of Pennsylvania and Children's Hospitals. Packages available. AE, DC, MC, V. Parking $9. Bus: 42. **Amenities:** Access for U. Penn indoor tennis court reservations; complimentary guest passes to Penn's nearby Hutchinson Health Complex for track and rowing machines; dry cleaning. *In room:* A/C, cable TV, dataport.

MODERATE

Sheraton University City   This concrete block of a Sheraton, midway between Drexel University and the University of Pennsylvania, has a new traditional theme throughout, thanks to a recent renovation, luxurious plush beds, over-size business desks with ergonomic chairs, and all new amenities as of June 2004. It still remains popular with visiting parents and conference attendees, and it's 1 block from the subway, and 4 from the Amtrak station and the three University City hospitals. The Sheraton offers a heated outdoor pool and sun deck on the Chestnut Street side of the building. The restaurant **Pallet** offers upscale dining, while **Java Concepts** serves coffee daily from 6:30am.

3549 Chestnut St., Philadelphia, PA 19104. (©) 800/325-3535 or 215/387-8000. Fax 215/387-7920. www. sheraton.com/universitycity. 374 units. $109–$299 double; all rates include continental breakfast. Children 18 years or under stay free in parent's room. Packages available. AE, DC, MC, V. Enclosed self-parking $15. SEPTA: 34th St. Station. Bus: 42. **Amenities:** Restaurant; lounge; heated outdoor pool; fitness center; Enterprise car rental adjacent to the hotel; dry cleaning. *In room:* A/C, TV w/pay movies, dataport, coffeemaker, hair dryer, iron, 2-line phones.

INEXPENSIVE

Gables *Value*   This lovely 1889 Victorian was one of West Philadelphia's first and finest mansions. The location is about 8 blocks west of the University of Pennsylvania's main campus. It's right at the SEPTA trolley line stop in Center City, 5 minutes from 30th Street Station, and 15 minutes from the airport. It's an excellent choice for visiting academics, parents of students, prospective applicants, and relaxed tourists.

Eight formal areas are filled with antiques. There are sitting rooms, a breakfast room, and a wraparound porch; five bedrooms with private bathrooms and four bedrooms with adjacent bathrooms are on the top two floors. All rooms have gorgeous inlaid wood floors, and three have charming corner turrets, and most rooms have private bathrooms. Closets, armoires, lamps, and desks fit in with the Victorian decor. There is a lovely yard and garden; home-baked muffins, breads, fresh fruit, and casseroles make up the breakfasts.

4520 Chester Ave. (at S. 46th St.), Philadelphia, PA 19143. (©) 215/662-1918. Fax 215/662-1918. www. gablesbb.com. 10 units, 8 with bathroom. $75–$125 double. Rates include full breakfast. AE, DISC, MC, V. Free off-street parking. SEPTA: #13 Green Line trolley stop. *In room:* A/C, TV, fax, dataport, fridge, hair dryer, iron available, private phone with answering machine, wireless DSL, microwave.

4 Near the Airport

Hotel chain options are very well represented at the moderate to inexpensive level in this area. Your choices include: **Holiday Inn Philadelphia Stadium,** 10th Street and Packer Avenue, Philadelphia, PA 19148 (© **800/424-0291** or 215/755-9500), which charges $159 for a double; **Airport Ramada Inn,** 76 Industrial Hwy., Essington, PA 19029 (© **800/277-3900** or 610/521-9600), with rates of $69 for a double; **Four Points by Sheraton Philadelphia Airport,** 4101a Island Ave. (between I-95 and Pa. 291), Philadelphia, PA 19153 (© **800/ 325-3535** or 215/492-0400), a slimmed-down version of the Sheraton suites across the way, charges $129; **Comfort Inn Airport,** 53 Industrial Hwy., Essington, PA 19029 (© **800/228-5150** or 610/521-9800), with rates of $98 for a double; and **Red Roof Inn,** 49 Industrial Hwy., Essington, PA 19029 (© **800/843-7663** or 610/521-5090), at $82 for a double.

EXPENSIVE

Philadelphia Airport Marriott Hotel ✦ *Value*   Opened in 1995 and renovated throughout in 2004, this is the only hotel linked by skywalk to Philadelphia International Airport, and the best of the airport options. The facility caters to business travelers with voice mail, speakerphone, free incoming faxes, and two dataport jacks. However, it's not a bad choice for families, since the soundproof rooms are mostly angled away from the runways, and it's very convenient to I-95. When you throw in the very complete fitness center and pool, the pleasant **Riverbend** restaurant, easy train or bus shuttle into Center City, and frequent weekend packages, it's well worth considering.

Arrivals Rd., Philadelphia, PA 19153. © **800/628-4087** or 215/492-9000. Fax 215/492-7464. www.marriott. com. 419 units. $209 double; $229 concierge-level room for up to 5 people. Excellent weekend rates. AE, DC, DISC, MC, V. Parking $10 in the airport garage at Terminal B. SEPTA: R1 Airport. **Amenities:** Restaurant; lounge; indoor pool; exercise room; Jacuzzi; laundry service; dry cleaning. *In room:* A/C, TV w/pay movies, dataport, voice mail, minibar, coffeemaker, hair dryer, iron.

Sheraton Suites Philadelphia Hotel *Value*   For just a bit more dough than the Four Points across the street requires, you get a suite with a beautifully furnished bedroom and living room that encircle a dramatic eight-story atrium. A 2001 rehab redecorated suites in white, brown, and maroon, with cherrywood furniture. The outer room contains a business desk and chair, convertible sofa bed, and armoire with TV. The bedroom, with the choice of a king or two twin beds, has another TV and phone, and bathrooms are similarly handsome. There is a wet bar with coffeemaker and small refrigerator in the kitchenette, and the bathroom has a marble-topped vanity. Airport noise is minimal.

4101b Island Ave., Philadelphia, PA 19153. © **800/325-3535** or 215/365-6600. Fax 215/492-9858. www. sheraton.com. 251 units. $159 double. Weekend and seasonal specials available. Children 18 and under stay free in parent's room. Some rates include full buffet breakfast. AE, DC, DISC, MC, V. Parking $5. SEPTA: Airport shuttle and courtesy bus. **Amenities:** Restaurant/lounge; indoor pool; exercise room; sauna; steam room; Jacuzzi; car-rental desk; complimentary shuttle to and from airport; same-day laundry service and dry cleaning. *In room:* A/C, 2 TVs w/pay movies, dataport, fridge, coffeemaker, hair dryer, iron, 2 dual-line phones, multi-port speakerphone.

MODERATE

Philadelphia Airport Hilton   The Philadelphia Airport Hilton is out of the way of flight patterns and features a just-renovated lobby and cocktail lounge built around a lushly planted indoor pool. Like all airport hotels, business travelers predominate during the week, and reservations are recommended. The guest rooms, with whirlpool-equipped bathrooms redone in 2000, are classically American—spacious and comfortable—and will all be renovated by 2005.

4509 Island Ave., Philadelphia, PA 19153. © **800/HILTONS** or 215/365-4150. Fax 215/937-6382. www. hilton.com. 331 units. $174 double. Children 18 and under stay free in parent's room. Weekend packages available. AE, DC, DISC, MC, V. Free parking, with courtesy transport to and from the airport. SEPTA: Airport shuttle and courtesy bus. **Amenities:** Restaurant; lounge; indoor pool; health club; Jacuzzi; sauna; 24-hr. room service; laundry service; dry cleaning. *In room:* A/C, TV w/pay movies, dataport, minibar, coffeemaker, hair dryer, iron.

5 City Line & Northeast

City Line Avenue (U.S. 1), just off the Schuylkill Expressway, is a good jumping-off point for the western suburbs or Lancaster County. Northeast Philly is close to Bucks County and the discount shopping at Franklin Mills Mall.

Thoroughly comfortable national chains dot this area, including **Holiday Inn City Line,** 4100 Presidential Blvd. (City Line Ave. at I-76), Philadelphia, PA 19131 (© **800/465-4329** or 215/477-0200) and the **Best Western Philadelphia Northeast,** 11580 Roosevelt Blvd., Philadelphia, PA 19116 (© **800/528-1234** or 215/464-9500).

MODERATE

Adam's Mark Philadelphia *Value*   The Adam's Mark looks like an airport control tower, but you'll find an extensive brick complex of connected restaurants and function rooms. Eighty percent of the hotel's business is conventioneers, and the lower levels contain 50,000 square feet of meeting space. Friendly service, good value, and individual touches such as customized safe keys make up for the hotel's somewhat ungainly size and its slow elevators. Rooms are on the large (and drab) side.

The Adam's Mark's food and beverage operation really shines. The gardenlike Appleby's is several notches above your average coffee shop, with all-you-can-eat meals, 30-foot ziggurat skylights, and local antiques. Lines start forming early at the Marker, an improbable re-creation (and improbable combination) of French château, paneled English library, and Western ranch that's relaxing, with well-done American cuisine. It seats 150 on three levels, and evenings bring American regional cuisine. Quincy's has hors d'oeuvres (complimentary until 7pm), nightly backgammon, big-band dancing, or jazz.

City Ave. and Monument Rd., Philadelphia, PA 19131. © **800/444-2326** or 215/581-5000. Fax 215/581-5069. www.adamsmark.com. 515 units. $119 double; $149 junior suite. Weekend packages and promotions available. AE, DC, DISC, MC, V. $5 parking in front lots or rear-connected garage, valet parking $15. SEPTA: R6 Bala Cynwyd stop ½ mile away. Bus: 1, 44, or 65. **Amenities:** 2 restaurants; lounge; bar; indoor pool and outdoor pool; 2 racquetball courts ($10/session); fitness facility with Stairmaster, Nautilus, and Lifecycle equipment; Jacuzzi; sauna; car-rental desk; salon; same-day laundry service and dry cleaning. *In room:* A/C, TV w/pay movies, dataport, voice mail.

6 Hostels

A $28 annual membership with **American Youth Hostels,** 733 15th St. NW, No. 840, Washington, DC 20005 (© **202/783-6161;** www.hiusa.org), will give you discounts on already-low hostel rates.

Bank Street Hostel   This 140-year-old former factory and its two neighbors, located in a very convenient part of town, offer spartan (although newly repainted) accommodations for travelers on a budget. The dormitory-style rooms are spread over four floors of the complex. Extras include free coffee and tea, a pool table, and a lounge with a large-screen TV. Kitchen facilities and washer/dryer are available for use. Clean, dorm-style bathrooms are shared. Discounts on food and other items at area merchants are available.

32 S. Bank St. (between 2nd and 3rd sts. and Market and Chestnut sts.), Philadelphia, PA 19106. © **800/392-4678** or 215/922-0222. www.hihostels.com. Fax 215/922-4082. 70 beds (shared bathroom). $18 for AYH members; $21 for nonmembers; $2 sheet charge. No credit cards. Check in from 8-11am or after 4:30pm. Parking $14 at nearby garages. SEPTA: 2nd St. Station. Bus: PHLASH, 21, or 42.

Chamounix Hostel Mansion The oldest building offering accommodations in town, this renovated 1802 Quaker farmhouse is also the cheapest. Chamounix Mansion is a Federal-style edifice constructed as a country retreat at what is now the upper end of Fairmount Park. It has six air-conditioned dormitory rooms for 44 people, with limited family arrangements, and another 37 spots in a fully renovated adjoining carriage house. Guests have use of the renovated self-serve kitchen, the TV/VCR lounge, free videos, and bicycles. Write or call ahead for reservations, since the hostel is often 90% booked in summer by groups of boat crews or foreign students. You can check in daily from between 4:30pm and midnight (which is the hostel's curfew) and show an American Youth Hostel card or IYHF card for member rates. Checkout is from 8 to 11am. Call **AYH** directly at ℂ **215/925-6004** for information on hostel trips in the area.

W. Fairmount Park, Philadelphia, PA 19131. ℂ **800/379-0017** or 215/878-3676. Fax 215/871-4313. www. philahostel.org. $15 Hostelling International members; $18 nonmembers; $2 sheet charge. MC, V. Closed Dec 15–Jan 15. By car: Take I-76 (Schuylkill Expwy.) to Exit 33, City Line Ave., turn right (south) on City Ave. to Belmont Ave., left on Belmont to first traffic light at Ford Rd., left on Ford, through stone tunnel to stop sign, then a left onto Chamounix Dr. and follow to the end. Bus: Take SEPTA route 38 from John F. Kennedy Blvd. near City Hall to Ford and Cranston sts. (a 30-min. ride), then walk under the overpass and left onto Chamounix Dr. to the end. **Amenities:** Free bike loan; game room with Ping-Pong and piano; coin-op washer and dryer; TV/VCR lounge; Internet kiosk; access to kitchen. *In room:* A/C.

6

Where to Dine

Philadelphia's restaurant scene has never been so sophisticated or exciting, and its reinvention over the past decade provides wonderful options at all price levels. There are stylish spots with star chefs such as Albert Portale for inventive cuisine, and charming neighborhood BYOBs around every corner. You can opt for serious dining at haute-French restaurants and exquisite spots in the city's top hotels, or pasta and gravy at South Philly Italian spots that haven't changed in decades. Philadelphia restaurants are consistently ranked among America's top 50 in *Condé Nast Traveler,* including Le Bec-Fin, and Fountain Restaurant at the Four Seasons Hotel, and six Philly spots were mentioned in *Gourmet's* "America's Top Restaurants" issue. Dozens of young culinary entrepreneurs have emerged in Philadelphia, reinventing the dining scene, especially in the Rittenhouse Square and Old City neighborhoods.

Don't neglect the rich "local favorites" culture in town: cheesesteaks, pizza, "hoagies" (large deli meat–based sandwiches on Italian rolls), and pretzels all claim fervent local connoisseurship.

This chapter unfortunately cannot include many renowned Main Line and other suburban restaurants. If you're heading out that way, your hotel concierge or volunteers who staff the desk at the **Independence Visitor Center,** 6th and Market streets, Philadelphia, PA 19107 (© **215/965-7676** or www.independencevisitor

center.com), can tell you more about the dining options there. For Web surfers, a good site I've seen for metro Philadelphia is **www.digitalcity.com/ philadelphia**, which combines its own breezy synopses about 1,500 restaurants with uncensored comments from the public. You can also visit **www.phillymag.com** for restaurant listings.

Lunch is a fantastic way to experience the city's high-end restaurants for a less daunting check: Lacroix, a fine French spot in the Rittenhouse Hotel, for instance, offers a $26 prix-fixe lunch that is an exceptional bargain.

This chapter will categorize **very expensive** restaurants as those charging $55 or more per person for dinner without wine; **expensive** as $40 to $55 per person; **moderate** as $20 to $40; and **inexpensive** as under $20. Meal tax is 7%, and standard tipping is 15% (the latter is occasionally included on the tab).

The service of wine and liquor is fraught with politics. Some restaurants are BYOB due to high fees to get a license, and restaurants with licenses may charge as much as 300% what they paid for a bottle of wine. The state Liquor Control Board does allow restaurants with licenses to permit customers to bring their own bottles, but don't look for quick acceptance of this policy.

Note: For most restaurants I have given only summer hours; you can expect 9pm (as opposed to 10pm) closings in other seasons.

1 Historic Area

VERY EXPENSIVE

Morimoto ★★★ FUSION/JAPANESE   The restaurant world buzzed when Masaharu Morimoto, the Japanese star of TV Food Network's *Iron Chef,* was lured by restaurant genius Stephen Starr to open his own place in Philadelphia. Starr hired designer Karim Rashid to build his chef a glowing, cool $1 million destination with a bamboo ceiling: The walls of the slim, narrow space are clad in undulating pale wood, illuminated by pastel lights that subtly change colors every few minutes. The menu is designed for a la carte ordering of appetizers (try the miso soup with tiny, delicate clams), sushi and entrees, or you can have the $80 to $120 *omakase* (chef's choice) multicourse menu—most dishes are spectacular. A warm whitefish carpaccio melts in the mouth, and chilled green tea noodles or buckwheat noodles are a revelation. Desserts range from citrus panna cotta to chocolate pot de creme. Starr and Morimoto are slated to open a second Morimoto in New York City after this book goes to print, in 2005.

723 Chestnut St. ② **215/413-9070.** www.morimotorestaurant.com. Reservations recommended. Sushi $4–$10 per piece; main courses $24–$36. AE, DC, MC, V. Mon–Fri 11:30am–2pm; Mon–Thurs 5–11pm; Fri–Sat 5pm–midnight; Sun 4–10pm.

EXPENSIVE

Buddakan ★★ *Moments* FUSION   There's one Philadelphian identified with the inventive theme restaurant: His name is Stephen Starr, and his Buddakan has been exceptionally popular since it opened 5 years ago, followed by Starr's Alma de Cuba, Jones, Washington Square, and other chic spots. The reason Buddakan continues to thrive: excellent food, served in a cool environment that's not just another pretty place. You'll find a shimmering water-wall, a double-height dining space, and a gold-coated, candle-bedecked, 10-foot Buddha who dominates the main room and the 22-seat onyx-topped community table under its belly. It's a noisy scene, but the fare is so fine and inventive that you won't care. Try the generous, made-for-sharing "angry lobster," wok-seared and served with lobster mashed potatoes, or the grilled lamb chops with Thai basil pesto. There's a young bar crowd, also.

325 Chestnut St. ② **215/574-9440.** www.buddakan.com. Reservations required. Main courses dinner $16–$28; lunch $12–$18. AE, DC, MC, V. Mon–Fri 11:30am–2pm and 5–11pm; Sat–Sun 5–11pm.

La Famiglia ★★ ITALIAN   The name La Famiglia refers to both the proprietors and the clientele of this refined Italian restaurant; the Neapolitan Sena family aims for elegant dining, service, and presentation. Several generations are involved in the business, and their success here has spawned Penn's View Inn and its Ristorante Panorama (see below). The Senas are particularly well-known for the excellent wine lists at La Famiglia and at Panorama.

The restaurant seats 60 in a warm, old-world setting of hand-hammered Venetian chandeliers, majolica tiles, and fresh flowers. The chefs at La Famiglia make most of their own pasta, and you might concentrate on such dishes as *pappardelle ai funghi,* served in appetizer or entree portions, or save room for an excellent veal chop with fresh garlic-basil sauce. The wine cellar is legendary. For dessert, try a *mille foglie,* the Italian version of the napoleon, or the profiteroles in chocolate sauce, accompanied by one of the grappas (kept over the fireplace). People often remain here well after the closing hour, lingering over sambuca while arias play in the background.

8 S. Front St. ② **215/922-2803.** www.la-famiglia.com. Reservations required. Main courses $28–$45; lunch $24 menu. AE, DISC, MC, V. Tues–Fri noon–2:30pm and 5:30–10pm; Sat 5:30–10pm; Sun 5–9pm.

Philadelphia Dining

To Manayunk

Philadelphia
Museum of Art

Spring Garden St.

Spring Garden

FRANKLINTOWN

Hamilton St.

Hamilton St.

Noble St.

Rodin Museum

Callowhill St.

The Benjamin Franklin Parkway

676

Winter St.

Logan
Square

Race/Vine

Race St.

**PARKWAY/MUSEUMS
DISTRICT**

Pennsylvania
Convention
Center

Cherry St.

76

Schuylkill River

Arch St.

Suburban
Station

**30th Street
Station**

JFK Blvd.

Philadelphia
Stock Exchange

Market
East
Station

15th

13th

Market St.

City
Hall

Juniper

Ludlow

City
Hall

PENN CENTER

Chestnut St.

Sansom St.

Sansom St.

Walnut St.

Walnut St.

Rittenhouse
Square

Walnut/Locust

Locust St.

15th/16th

Schuylkill
River
Park

Spruce St.

**RITTENHOUSE
SQUARE
DISTRICT**

Merriam
Theater

12th/13th

Fitler
Square

Delancey
Pl.

Kimmel Performing
Arts Center

Pine St.

**UNIVERSITY
OF THE ARTS**

Lombard St.

Lombard/South

South St.

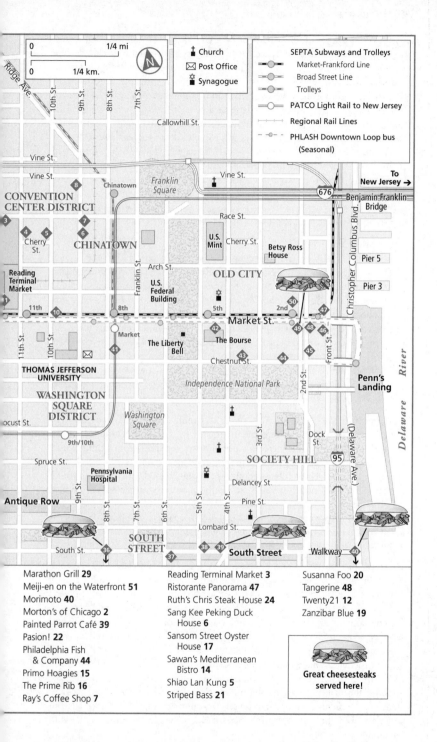

Map Legend

0 — 1/4 mi	
0 — 1/4 km.	

N

✝ Church
⊠ Post Office
🕎 Synagogue

SEPTA Subways and Trolleys
━●━ Market-Frankford Line
━●━ Broad Street Line
━●━ Trolleys
━○━ PATCO Light Rail to New Jersey
┼─┼─┼ Regional Rail Lines
─◇─ PHLASH Downtown Loop bus
(Seasonal)

Ridge Ave.

10th St.
9th St.
8th St.
7th St.

Callowhill St.

Vine St.
Vine St.

8

Chinatown

Franklin Square

Vine St.

To New Jersey →

676

Benjamin Franklin Bridge

CONVENTION CENTER DISTRICT

3

4 **5**
Cherry St.

7
6

CHINATOWN

Race St.

U.S. Mint

Cherry St.

Betsy Ross House

Pier 5

Christopher Columbus Blvd.

Franklin St.

Arch St.

U.S. Federal Building

OLD CITY

Pier 3

Reading Terminal Market

1

11th

10

8th

5th

2nd

50

47

Market St.

11th St.
10th St.

Market

41

The Liberty Bell

42 **The Bourse**

49 **48** **46**

45

Front St.

River

⊠

THOMAS JEFFERSON UNIVERSITY

Chestnut St.

43

44

2nd St.

Delaware

WASHINGTON SQUARE DISTRICT

Washington Square

Independence National Park

Penn's Landing

Locust St.

9th/10th

Spruce St.

3rd St.

Dock St.

95

SOCIETY HILL

(Delaware Ave.)

Pennsylvania Hospital

9th St.
8th St.
7th St.
6th St.
5th St.
4th St.

Delancey St.

Pine St.

Antique Row

Lombard St.

SOUTH STREET

South St.

36

38 **39**

South Street

Walkway **40**

37

Marathon Grill **29**
Meiji-en on the Waterfront **51**
Morimoto **40**
Morton's of Chicago **2**
Painted Parrot Café **39**
Pasion! **22**
Philadelphia Fish & Company **44**
Primo Hoagies **15**
The Prime Rib **16**
Ray's Coffee Shop **7**

Reading Terminal Market **3**
Ristorante Panorama **47**
Ruth's Chris Steak House **24**
Sang Kee Peking Duck House **6**
Sansom Street Oyster House **17**
Sawan's Mediterranean Bistro **14**
Shiao Lan Kung **5**
Striped Bass **21**

Susanna Foo **20**
Tangerine **48**
Twenty21 **12**
Zanzibar Blue **19**

Great cheesesteaks served here!

Tangerine ✿✿ MEDITERRANEAN   The theme of this Stephen Starr–designed extravaganza is Morocco, or Morocco as envisioned by a chic decorator. Open 5 years, with a recently renovated, modern lounge with low sofas and specialty cocktails, Tangerine has an inventive menu that riffs off Moroccan classics. In design terms, it's a brilliant division of a long, narrow space into chambers punctuated by curtains, extensive and eclectic lighting, and wild, exotic decor. A corridor festooned with hundreds of inset votive lights connects the various rooms. The restaurant is run by a cheerful, knowledgeable staff.

The menu offers couscous and wonderful tagine stews. A pan-seared red snapper comes with spinach ravioli and toasted pepper sauce. The sharing-size portions and big tables make this an ideal choice for large groups out to have some fun.

232 Market St. ✆ 215/627-5116. www.tangerinerestaurant.com. Reservations strongly recommended. Main courses $18–$28. AE, MC, V. Mon–Thurs 5–11pm; Fri–Sat 5pm–midnight; Sun 5–10pm.

MODERATE

Café Spice INDIAN   Café Spice, opened in 2000 by Sushil Malhotra (owner of Dawat in New York), is a contemporary Indian restaurant with a menu that tours the subcontinent. The interior features textured beige walls with recessed display boxes for spice jars, hanging lanterns, and cut-out windows—very dramatic and soothing all at once. All main courses include fragrant basmati rice, nan bread, and several vegetable dishes; I find the vegetarian entrees most satisfying for their size and complex textures. The restaurant looks more expensive than it is; most entrees are priced at $16 or less, and portions are large. And don't worry about the hours; the doors stay open until 2am on weekends.

35 S. 2nd St. ✆ 215/627-6273. www.cafespice.com. Main courses $14–$22. AE, DC, MC, V. Mon–Thurs 11:30am–3pm and 5–10:30pm; Fri 11:30am–3pm and 5–11:30pm; Sat 12:30–11:30pm; Sun 12:30–10:30pm.

Continental ✿✿ AMERICAN   With its comfy booths, olive-shaped light fixtures, and extensive cocktail menu, this 10-year-old vintage diner turned lounge/restaurant remains incredibly popular for everything from a casual lunch to a late-night snack. For such a busy spot, the food—from pad Thai to lobster spring rolls to burgers to filet mignon—is amazingly good. The crowd is young and loud on weekends, but you'll see plenty of families earlier on weeknights. The margaritas are particularly good.

138 Market St. ✆ 215/923-6069. www.continentalmartinibar.com. Main courses $12–$19. AE, DC, MC, V. Sun 10:30am–3pm and 5–11pm; Mon–Wed 11:30am–3:30pm and 5–11pm; Thurs–Fri 11:30am–3:30pm and 5pm–midnight; Sat 10:30am–3pm and 5pm–midnight.

DiNardo's Famous Crabs ✿✿ (Value) SEAFOOD   DiNardo's, now 27 years old, springs to mind as the best moderately priced spot in the area around the Betsy Ross House and Elfreth's Alley. The door nearest 3rd Street is the real entrance. DiNardo's is notable for three things: its site, its reasonable prices, and its staggering collection of fish lures. The building was an inn for Tory soldiers in 1776 and later served as an Underground Railroad stop and Prohibition-era brothel.

Prime catches from the Gulf of Mexico are flown up daily to the restaurant, where experienced hands season the crabs with the house blend of 24 spices and steam them to perfection. Only the DiNardo family mixes the secret crab seasonings. If you're not in a crabby mood, there are at least 30 other succulent items on the menu, from raw-bar oysters to seafood platters. Monday is all-you-can-eat crab night, now at $30. Service is especially patient with families with small kids.

312 Race St. ✆ **215/925-5115.** Reservations required for 5 or more. Crabs $3–$5 each; other main courses dinner $15–$30; lunch $7–$11; Wed 3-course prix-fixe dinner $34. AE, DC, MC, V. Mon–Thurs 11am–10pm; Fri–Sat 11am–11pm; Sun 3–9pm.

Fork ★★★ CONTINENTAL Fork, with its tall green banquettes, beautifully shaded light fixtures, oval-shaped bar, and open rear kitchen, is an affordable, stylish bistro and a local favorite. Set in a historic brick former warehouse, it is intimate and convivial, with 68 impeccable seats, and sought-after bar stools where regulars like to perch for a late-night pasta or cheese plate. Most of the ingredients come from organic farms and Amish purveyors; the menu is changed and reprinted daily. Signature dishes include pan-seared miso-ginger salmon with coconut sushi rice, and chimichurri-laced hanger steak with matchstick-thin yucca frites. Sunday brunch is an excellent break from big-hotel spreads.

306 Market St. ✆ **215/625-9425.** Reservations recommended. Main courses dinner $14–$26; lunch $7–$11. AE, DC, DISC, MC, V. Mon–Thurs 11:30am–10:30pm; Fri 11:30am–11:30pm; Sat 5–11:30pm; Sun 11am–4pm and 5–10:30pm. Late bar menu Thurs till midnight and Fri–Sat till 1am.

Philadelphia Fish & Company ★ *(Value* SEAFOOD/AMERICAN It's inevitable that you'll pass Philadelphia Fish & Company, given its location next to Independence National Historical Park. So it's great that owner Kevin Meeker and chef Kevin Cliggitt work so hard to deliver a reasonable, high-quality, exciting selection of fresh fish that's served with warmth and flair. The main courses run to innovative twists on classics such as towers of crab cakes on corn succotash. The $11 executive lunch is a great deal: a cup of soup, the fish special, vegetable, green salad, and beverage. And the $6 dinner special at the bar (often seared perch or a burger) has been rated the best tavern deal in the city by *Philadelphia* magazine. The wine list, skewed toward whites, is of a good quality and very reasonable for Philadelphia. There's outdoor dining in season.

207 Chestnut St. ✆ **215/625-8605.** Reservations recommended. Main courses dinner $17–$24; lunch $8–$13. AE, DC, MC, V. Mon–Thurs 11:30am–4pm and 4:30–10:30pm; Fri 11:30am–4pm and 5pm–midnight; Sat noon–3pm and 4:30pm–midnight; Sun 4–10:30pm.

Ristorante Panorama ★★ ITALIAN Although the Sena family's Ristorante Panorama is on the waterfront, its "view" is a colorful mural of the Italian countryside and of the charming Old City streets that surround it. Panorama, inside the Penn's View Inn, has a legendary wine bar, with 120 wines (not just Italian) served to a sophisticated, lively crowd. It's a lot of fun to order "flights," or a series of 3.5-ounce glasses of wines chosen to complement the food you order. The handmade pastas, especially the agnolotti with fresh spinach sauce and pappardelle with duck ragout, are memorable, and the grilled fish and veal chop are very good. The bread is served not with butter, but with a tiny bowl of pesto. Fish courses are usually grilled and lightly seasoned with garlic and tomatoes. The tiramisu, with its triple-cream mascarpone cheese drizzled with chocolate, is especially good with espresso or a dessert wine as an accompaniment.

Front and Market sts. ✆ **215/922-7800.** Reservations recommended. Main courses $18–$27. AE, DC, MC, V. Mon–Thurs noon–11pm; Sat 5–11pm; Sun 5–9pm.

INEXPENSIVE

Beau Monde ★ *(Value* FRENCH This pretty, Parisian-looking (but noisy) 65-seat restaurant specializes in crepes, and is usually filled with Gen-Xers or lively groups, thanks to the affordable dinner check. The restaurant prepares two types of crepes: savory, made with buckwheat flour and filled with anything from andouille sausage to mushrooms, goat cheese, and chicken; and a sweet wheat flour dessert crepe, filled with sliced fruits or berries. Appetizers and salads are also offered. There is a cozy bar and lounge upstairs, with occasional live music.

624 S. 6th St. (at the corner of Bainbridge, 1 block south of South St.). © 215/592-0656. Reservations accepted for 6 or more. Crepe main courses $6.50–$16 ($2 for each filling). AE, DC, DISC, MC, V. Tues–Fri noon–11pm; Sat 10am–11pm; Sun 10am–10pm.

Johnny Rockets *Kids* AMERICAN   Johnny Rockets, a national chain, is *Happy Days* retro for the kids and comforting for their parents. Clean red-and-white booths surround an open grill. Breakfast includes pancakes, eggs, and French toast. From midday on, burgers and sandwiches predominate, along with fries, onion rings, excellent malts and milkshakes, gooey desserts, and pies. The friendly staff does an energetic dance routine once an hour.

443 South St. © 215/829-9222. Sandwiches and burgers $4–$6. AE, DC, DISC, MC, V. Sun–Thurs 9am–11pm; Fri–Sat 9am–2am.

2 Center City

VERY EXPENSIVE

Founders *&* CONTINENTAL   Founders is on the top (19th) floor of the Park Hyatt at the Bellevue, and its location under the massive 45-foot dome of this French Renaissance landmark makes it attractive for fans of views at breakfast and lunch, as well as for anyone who is looking for romantic dinner and dancing on the weekends. The elegant dining room features arched windows, flourishes and swags of draperies, and plush armchairs. The "founders" are the statues of Philadelphia luminaries that surround you. At these prices, you will get fine American-European preparations from Charles Webber, the executive chef: Neiman ranch grilled pork chop with roasted potatoes and baby vegetables, or delicate Gulf Coast red snapper. The award-winning wine list includes over 400 selections, and there's dancing every Friday and Saturday from 8 to 11pm with the Eileen Duffy Trio. Jimmy Rudolph holds sway on piano most weeknights.

Broad and Walnut sts. © 215/790-2814. Reservations recommended. Main courses $22–$39. AE, DISC, MC, V. Mon–Sat 6:30–10:30am, 11am–2pm, and 5:30–10pm; Sun brunch 11am–2pm.

Fountain Restaurant *&&&* *Moments* INTERNATIONAL   Fountain Restaurant is Philadelphia's most nationally acclaimed restaurant, rated number one by the Zagat Survey and chosen as Philadelphia's Top Table by *Gourmet*. The views only add to the experience: plumes of water from Alexander Calder's Swann Fountain in Logan Circle are gorgeous. The decor was recently updated, and is rich and exquisite. The cuisine, under the brilliant chef Martin Hamann, is expertly prepared and quietly served in exquisitely comfortable surroundings, which turn romantic in the evening. The city's top lawyers, bankers, socialites, and artists gather here for breakfast and lunch, and marriage proposals are *de rigueur* at dinner.

The menu is understated but innovative, and many diners plunge into the $110 "spontaneous menu" of four savory and two sweet courses. A la carte choices include Maine lobster grilled with green-apple risotto and curried vegetables, and grilled Cervena venison chop with melted Swiss chard and prosciutto-wrapped Black Mission figs. The intimate Café room between the lounge and main dining room is a fantastic value, with Hamann's chefs turning out an intensely flavored Asian filet mignon for $30 and grilled chicken for $23. The Sunday brunch, which is $55 per person for a lavish buffet, is the setting for celebrations. A chocolate soufflé or selections from the cheese cart are

Stephen Starr: Restaurateur Extraordinaire

"The nightlife landscape in Philly has changed dramatically over the past 10 years," says restaurateur and lounge creator Stephen Starr, who should know—with the **Continental** (p. 96), he invented the cool martini bar in Philly in 1995 in Old City, and jump-started that neighborhood's bistro/bar boom.

Starr, a hometown boy who's a celebrity in Philly, has since gone on to create 13 hotspots, ranging from haute Japanese (the super-modern **Morimoto**, p. 93), to chic steakhouse (**Barclay Prime**, 237 S. 18th St.; ⓒ 215/732-7560), to groovy Middle-Eastern-mod (**Tangerine**, p. 96). Starr is so successful that he's been able to replicate the Continental in a second location near Rittenhouse Square, and bought and renovated the venerable, beautiful **Striped Bass** (p. 102) in 2004.

"Philadelphia went from rolling up the sidewalks at night to a 24/7 dining destination with areas of the city filled with new restaurants and bars," says Starr, who as a kid in the late 1970s ran a rock-'n'-roll club on South Street, but now dresses in Armani and saw many of his bars featured in the *Real World Philadelphia* show last season. "Now, we're always featured as one of the country's top 10 restaurant towns," he adds, noting that he's opening a spin-off of Morimoto in New York City this year, but remains loyal to his hometown. "Of course, I will always rank Philadelphia number one."

perfect ends to your meal. Service is the best in the city: formal, but totally unpretentious and still somehow friendly.

The Four Seasons Hotel, 1 Logan Sq. (between 18th St. and the Franklin Pkwy.). ⓒ **215/963-1500.** Reservations required. Main courses $44–$58; fixed-price "Spontaneous Taste" 6-course dinner menu $110; lunch $21–$29; set 3-course lunch menu $33; brunch $55 or a la carte, $46–$58, with an appetizer and dessert buffet included. AE, DC, MC, V. Mon–Fri 6:30am–11am and 11:30–2pm; Sat 7–11am and 11:30am–2pm; Sun 7am–2pm (brunch at 11); Mon–Sun 5:45–10pm.

Lacroix ⭐⭐⭐ *(Moments)* FRENCH   When French-born Jean Marie Lacroix left the Four Seasons Hotel and opened this eponymous haute restaurant in the Rittenhouse Hotel, the city buzzed: Would Lacroix be able to create the same magic in his new second-floor restaurant overlooking Rittenhouse Square? Absolutely: Lacroix's new setting is ethereal but unstuffy, with deep emerald-green armchairs and lovely limestone accents, as beautiful by day as it is at night. Service is impeccable and warm. The menu of interchangeable courses (choose from three to five dishes) might feature sautéed Virginia squab on pine leaves with bluefoot-mushroom torte, or lamb shank with parsley and lemon, with caramelized onion pudding. The $26 prix-fixe business lunch is an exceptional deal.

210 W. Rittenhouse Sq. ⓒ **215/790-2533.** Reservations recommended. Lunch a la carte from $13; prix-fixe lunch from $25; dinner $54–$75 prix fixe. AE, DC, DISC, MC, V. Mon–Fri 6:30–10am, 11:30am–2pm, and 5:30–10pm; Sat 7–10am and 5:30–10pm; Sun 7–10 am, 11am–2pm, and 5:30–10pm.

Le Bec-Fin ⭐⭐⭐ *(Moments)* FRENCH   For those who love jewel-box surroundings and multicourse, formal meals, Le Bec-Fin is the destination dining spot that has been ruled for almost 4 decades by owner/chef Georges Perrier. The chef, who is a celebrity in Philadelphia, hails from Lyon, France's gastronomic capital, and is a favorite of critics such as *Esquire*'s John Mariani. Perrier himself mans the stove and is frequently seen in the elegant dining room; young Gregory Castells is the sommelier. Perrier spent a fortune in the summer of 2002 transforming the interior from a Louis XVI homage to an elegant turn-of-the-20th-century Parisian salon setting, with a marble fireplace, 14 pilasters containing silk inlays, and sconces on floral fabric panels amid antiqued mirrors.

Perrier offers dinner at 6pm and 9pm on weekdays, with a 9:30pm seating on Friday and Saturday evenings; lunch is served at 11:30am or 1pm. You can choose from a six-course $135 prix fixe, or pull out the stops for a nine-course $155 menu, or a $235 menu with paired wines (yes, that's per person). All dishes are exquisite and change seasonally, with recent offerings including a first course of *cassolette d'escargots*, with champagne-hazelnut-garlic sauce; the signature *galette de crabe;* and duck magret with caramelized turnips, asparagus, red berries, and grain of paradise (spiced) sauce. The dessert cart is a grand vehicle for more than a dozen beautiful options, including opera cake topped with 24-karat gold leaf.

The set-course $45 lunch is a wonderful way to experience the restaurant (and dessert cart); or visit the tiny, lower-level **Le Bar Lyonnais,** with more affordable but very rich dishes from the same kitchen. Expect to spend about $18 a nibble and $11 for a glass of house wine. The later it gets, the more likely dishes from upstairs are to arrive—and M. Perrier himself, for that matter.

1523 Walnut St. ② 215/567-1000. Reservations required a week ahead for weeknights, months ahead for Fri–Sat. 3-course fixed-price lunch $45; fixed-price dinner $135; $155 for 9-course degustation. AE, DC, MC, V. Lunch seatings Mon–Fri at 11:30am or 1:30pm; dinner seatings Mon–Thurs at 6 and 9pm, Fri–Sat at 6 and 9:30pm. Bar Lyonnais downstairs serves food and drink Mon–Fri 11:30am–midnight; Sat 6pm–1am. Valet parking $16, available after 5:30pm.

Vetri ★★★ ITALIAN   Young Marc Vetri is a close friend of celebrity chef Mario Batali, and their road trips together through Italy have paid off. Vetri shares Batali's love of fresh ingredients, prepared with deceptive simplicity, so that they become something incredibly delicious, such as guinea hen breast stuffed with foie gras and prosciutto. Working in his tiny kitchen, hand-fashioning impossibly delicate pastas such as spinach gnocchi with shaved smoked ricotta cheese and brown butter, chef/owner Vetri is as quietly unassuming as his intimate 35-seat dining room in a historic town house. Meats are also a high point. It is very hard to get a reservation here, so call ahead. The sommelier is justly proud of the exceptional wine list.

1312 Spruce St. ② 215/732-3478. Main courses $30–$40; prix fixe $90 or $115 for 8 courses on Sat (Fri in summer). AE, MC, V. Mon–Fri 6–9pm; Sat 7–9pm. Closed Sat in summer.

EXPENSIVE

Alma de Cuba ★★★ LATIN AMERICAN   Douglas Rodriguez, who earned praise in New York at Pipa and Chicama, helms the kitchen in this Walnut Street town house with pre-Castro details located in the epicenter of fine dining. (Rodriguez also runs the kitchen at El Vez, a popular Mexican spot on 13th St.) Alma de Cuba, the "soul of Cuba," offers new interpretations of Cuban classics, from daiquiris to dishes like slow-roasted pork shank and crispy fried whole snapper. The atmosphere is evocative, with glass walls shimmering with tobacco leaf images, and there is an all-white lounge downstairs with mod seating, black-and-white photos projected onto the walls, and dim lighting. Alma de Cuba's dishes are rushes of strong flavors, ingredients, and heat. It's not perfect—quite loud, and service is rushed—but it is an original. And the mojitos will transport you to pre-Fidel Havana.

1623 Walnut St. © **215/988-1799**. Reservations recommended. Main courses $18–$31. AE, DC, DISC, MC, V. Mon–Thurs 5–11pm; Fri–Sat 5pm–midnight; Sun 5–10pm.

Brasserie Perrier ★★ FRENCH Proprietor Georges Perrier opened this brasserie in 1997. Now with chef Chris Scarduzio at the helm, it's more a French restaurant with international influence than a bistro, although there's a lounge menu throughout the day alongside the lunch and dinner menus. The Art Deco–style venue has colorful banquettes in the front bar area, silver leaf ceilings, and a more formal, stylish 88-seat dining area toward the back of the large space. It's built around a retro-cubist version of Marcel Duchamp's *Nude Descending a Staircase.* Don't expect anything too casual here, though there is a classic steak frites in the popular bar for $16; in the dining room, choose pan-roasted branzino with cockle clam risotto and lobster butter, or veal tenderloin with lobster dumplings in verjus-lobster sauce. The wine list features small, quality-oriented French, Italian, and U.S. varietals in the $35 to $75 range, with specially priced gems from southern France.

1619 Walnut St. © **215/568-3000**. www.brasserieperrier.com. Reservations usually required. Main courses $24–$37; lunch prix-fixe 3-course $28. AE, DC, MC, V. Mon–Sat 11:30am–4pm and 5–10:30pm; Sun 5–9pm.

Friday Saturday Sunday AMERICAN/CONTINENTAL A romantic survivor of Philadelphia's 1970s "restaurant renaissance," Friday Saturday Sunday has adapted to the times by offering informality, a renovated bar upstairs, and relaxed cuisine. It's charming and casual, dimly lit, with an adorable and romantic bar upstairs. Every bottle on the wine list is marked up $10, making it the best value in town.

Friday Saturday Sunday is pretty but not ostentatious: The cutlery and china don't match, flowers are rare, and the menu is a wall-mounted slate board. Pin lights frame a row of rectangular mirrors set in wood paneling. An aquarium bubbles behind the upstairs Tank Bar. Dress is everything from jeans to suits, and the service is vigilant but hands-off.

The cuisine is not complicated: The restaurant is famous for its rich mushroom soup, made from local Kennett Square mushrooms, chicken broth, cognac, and cream. Specials are written in colorful chalk on the board, and are very good; from the menu, try the pear and fennel salad, wild mushroom ravioli, and grilled filet mignon. The wine card lists about 30 vintages. The desserts change often.

261 S. 21st St. (between Locust and Spruce sts.). © **215/546-4232**. www.frisatsun.com. Reservations accepted. Main courses $16–$25. AE, DC, MC, V. Tues–Fri 11:30am–2:30pm; Mon–Sat 5:30–10:30pm; Sun 5–10pm.

Morton's of Chicago ★★ STEAK Oh, those rolling carts of aged, marbled double-cut filets, sirloins, and T-bones—choose your own, and prepare to indulge as it travels back to the kitchen. Morton's of Chicago, a clubby enclave, has become a staple for business dinners and celebratory evenings. The house porterhouse weighs in at 24 ounces. The cauliflower soup is highly touted, and the Sicilian veal chop with garlic bread crumbs is a "hometown" hit. For appetizers, sample the crab cocktail or the smoked salmon served on dark bread with horseradish cream, capers, and onions.

Morton's looks as welcoming and sedate as you'd expect, with glass panels between the tables and booths and dim lighting that makes the brass glow. There's a cigar lounge for postprandial puffing, and petite filet mignon sandwiches are served at the bar. The wine list, which features quality American reds like cabernets, is marked up at least 300%.

1411 Walnut St., 2nd floor. ℭ **215/557-0724.** Reservations recommended. Jacket and tie required for men. Main courses $25–$42. AE, DC, MC, V. Mon–Sat 5:30–11pm; Sun 5–10pm.

Pasion! ℛℛ LATIN AMERICAN/FUSION   Pasion!'s chef Guillermo Pernot, author of the cookbook *Ceviche,* is a young star, named as one of *Food & Wine*'s 10 best new American chefs. The stylish restaurant is Philadelphia's finest Nuevo Latino destination with authentic Latin ingredients, exotic presentation, and various preparation styles. The food is incredible, the atmosphere upscale but fun.

Pasion!'s dining rooms have warmth and mystery, with stone walls, louvered, draped windows, and candlelit sconces. Floral prints and stripes, sea grass cloth, and bamboo details evoke a tented tropical courtyard. The 12 stools at the granite and weathered wood bar in the rear—a great, relaxed dining spot—perch near the unhurried and spotless open kitchen. Cuisine itself is intense. Many people start and end with one of five ceviche courses (marinated fresh, raw fish) offered daily (three for $28), and move on to cumin-crusted roasted salmon, Argentinean sirloin, or unusual grilled or baked root vegetables. Desserts feature sweet pastries and custards, and wines are the expected California and South American vintages, with bottles averaging $45 and glasses at about $8.50.

211 S. 15th St. ℭ **215/875-9895.** Reservations recommended. Main courses $18–$32. AE, DC, MC, V. Mon–Thurs 5–10pm; Fri–Sat 5–11pm; Sun 5–9pm. Closed Sun in summer.

The Prime Rib ℛℛ STEAK   Step back into the 1940s (with modern steakhouse offerings and prices) at the Prime Rib, a small chain from Washington, D.C., which Zagat's has called the best steakhouse in town. Excellent meat and stellar side dishes (creamed spinach, of course, and very good potato skins) make this a regular spot for the city's power elite. The service and decor are classic, with sleek leopard-print carpeting, black leather furniture, and black walls trimmed in gold. Nightly jazz piano and bass duets play cocktail and dining background music.

1701 Locust St. ℭ **215/772-1701.** Reservations recommended. Jackets required for men. Main courses $22–$38. AE, DC, MC, V. Sun–Mon 4:30–9pm; Tues–Thurs 4:30–10pm; Fri–Sat 4:30–11pm.

Striped Bass ℛℛℛ SEAFOOD   The most glamorous setting in Philadelphia is this renowned, seafood-focused restaurant, set in a lofty, 100-year-old former brokerage house. Recently bought by prolific Stephen Starr, the room, with its sexy banquettes, columns, marquetry ceiling, and chic tented bathrooms, is even more beautiful with the recent addition of crystal modern light fixtures and dramatic triple-length gray velvet curtains on the tall antique windows. Still, the place is cool enough that you can wear either a Prada dress, or jeans and Manolo Blahniks, and feel equally comfortable at the intimate bar. Striped Bass is now under the direction of chef Alfred Portale and his young colleague Christopher Lee, and the menu still emphasizes exquisite seafood: choose wild striped bass ceviche, then roasted Canadian lobster with hon shimeji mushrooms and rhubarb-lemon butter. There is also a wonderful steak, and an interesting wine list.

1500 Walnut St. ℭ **215/732-4444.** Reservations recommended. Main courses $28–$42. AE, DC, MC, V. Sun–Thurs 5–10pm; Fri–Sat 5–11pm.

MODERATE

McCormick & Schmick's ℛ SEAFOOD   A lofty room with paneled walls, tall windows over Broad Street, and a happy vibe, plus a bar facing City Hall, McCormick & Schmick draws a business crowd at lunch for its affordable fresh fish, flown in from Maine, Hawaii, and points around the world, plus steaks.

(We do mean affordable—you can get fresh grilled salmon or more exotic Costa Rican mahimahi for about half what you would pay at neighboring stylish spots along the Avenue of the Arts.) At night, an early dinner with the kids in one of the "snuggeries," roomy booths that can be closed off with curtains, means they can dine on chicken fingers from a children's menu while you sip a nice sauvignon blanc and nibble oysters. There's also a bargain happy hour.

1 S. Broad St. ✆ **215/568-6888.** www.mccormickandschmick.com. Reservations recommended. Main courses $9.95–$37 (for a 2-lb. lobster). AE, DC, DISC, MC, V. Mon–Thurs 11:30am–11pm; Fri 11:30am–midnight; Sat–Sun 4pm–midnight.

Rouge ★★ AMERICAN-FRENCH   A stylish crowd gathers at the cafe tables right on Rittenhouse Square from April through October to sip and flirt, but the secret of Rouge, a tiny bistro with a circular white bar and velvet curtains, is its amazing food. Subtly spiced mussels, a peerless roasted chicken, chiffon-thin carpaccio of beef on pristine arugula—chef Michael Yeamans excels at French classics with a twist. He also does a lavish $15 hamburger with amazing frites—this two-hander with caramelized onions and bleu cheese is considered by burger-meisters to be the best in the city, and has won numerous awards.

205 S. 18th St. ✆ **215/732-6622.** Reservations taken depending on the season. Main courses $15–$33. AE, DISC, MC, V. Mon–Fri 11:30am–1am; Sat 10am–1am; Sun 10am–midnight.

Ruth's Chris Steak House ★ STEAK   Perfectly situated for the Kimmel Center or any performance on the Avenue of the Arts, Ruth's Chris has gotten rave reviews since 1989 for food, although the service-bashing is unfortunately justified. Ruth's Chris only serves U.S. prime beef that's custom aged, never frozen, and rushed to Philadelphia by the New Orleans distributor for the chain. Their steak is more charred on the outside than the steak at most other steakhouses, but the charring does lock in the flavors. The rib-eye steak in particular is presented lovingly, almost ritually, in a quiet and respectful setting, and with almost no garnishes. The portions are so large that you might want to skip the side dishes, although Ruth's Chris boasts nine ways of cooking potatoes. Several fish and chicken choices are also available. The desserts, mostly Southern recipes with lots of sugar and nuts, average $6. Several tables are partially in the hallway, so make sure you request to avoid these.

260 S. Broad St. ✆ **215/790-1515.** www.ruthschris.com. Reservations recommended. Main courses $18–$68. AE, DC, DISC, MC, V. Mon–Sat 5–11:30pm; Sun 4–10:30pm.

Sansom Street Oyster House ★ SEAFOOD   Sansom Street knows everything there is to know about oysters—where they come from, how their flavors differ, and how to prepare them. The space is colorful and you can watch the practiced shuckers at their craft, if you choose to sit at the bar at lunchtime. Blackboards listing the daily specials perch beside a large collection of antique oyster plates and nautical lithographs. Inventive chef-owner Cary Neff has added Asian and contemporary notes to the traditional fresh seafood menu.

The oysters are air-freighted several times a week here, and you'll probably want an appetizer of several types: metallic belons; cooler, meatier Long Island half-shells; the new, fruity hybrids like Trevenen and Westcott from the Northwest; and larger, fishier box oysters. All are opened right at the raw bar. For dinner, most people choose from the daily selections of 8 to 10 fresh fish, often including local shad or tilefish. The homemade bread pudding is the most reliable dessert. The liquor prices are moderate and draft beer starts at $3.75. There is discount parking after 5pm at 15th and Sansom with a $20 meal minimum.

1516 Sansom St. ✆ **215/567-7683.** Reservations accepted for 5 or more. Main courses dinner $17–$41; 4-course fixed-price dinner $21; lunch $8.50–$13. AE, DC, DISC, MC, V. Mon–Sat 11am–10pm; Sun 3–9pm.

Susanna Foo ⭐⭐⭐ *Finds* CHINESE   Susanna Foo has been touted in *Gourmet, Bon Appétit, Esquire* and just about everywhere else for serving one of

A Taste of Ethnic Philly: Reading Terminal Market

The **Reading Terminal Market,** at 12th and Arch streets (✆ **215/922-2317;** see map on p. 105, [not drawn to scale]), has been a greengrocer, snack shop, butcher, fish market, and sundries store for Philadelphians since the late 1800s. The idea was to use the space underneath the terminal's tracks for food vendors so that commuters and businesspeople could stock up easily and cheaply; now, it's lively, charming, redolent, and noisy, a great place to have lunch or breakfast, or pick up a picnic. Half of the stalls make up an English-style covered market with cool brick floors and the scent of fresh food and baked bread; the other vendors are gourmet grocers.

Scrapple, mangoes, clam chowder, pretzels—you name it, if it's fresh, you can find it here. You can still see the Amish in the city on their market days (Wed and Sat), and you can buy sticky buns at **Beiler's Bakery,** soft pretzels made before your eyes at **Fisher's,** and individual egg custards ($1) and chicken potpies ($6) at the **Dutch Eating Place.** If you're in the market for meat, **Harry Ochs** and **Halteman Family** have the most extensive selections, with great country hams and local honey as well. **Downtown Cheese Shop** offers gourmet cheeses; visit **Salumeria** for hoagies. The best coffee is sold at **Old City Coffee.**

If your stomach is rumbling uncontrollably by now, **Termini Brothers Bakery** will satisfy it with Italian cannoli pastries or **Braverman's** will fill it with an egg challah, Danish, or other pastry. For more protein, **Pearl's Oyster Bar** practically gives away six cherrystone clams for $4.25, and a shrimp platter with french fries, bread, and coleslaw goes for $8.50. Or try **Coastal Cave Trading Co.,** which has great clam chowder, oyster crackers, and smoked fish. Just inside 12th Street, **Bassett's** ⭐ (see "Best Restaurant Bets," p. 12) purveys Philadelphia's entry in the best American ice-cream contest at $1.75 a cone. The shakes ($3.75) are no less enticing.

The 1990s renovation of the market has left it with more seating. The **Down Home Diner** ⭐ (see "Best Restaurant Bets," p. 11) is an excellent choice for breakfast or lunch. The **12th Street Cantina** sells not only tasty enchiladas and burritos, but also authentic ingredients, like blue cornmeal. **Rick's Philly Steaks**—a third generation of Pat's down in South Philly—serves up one of the city's best cheesesteaks. The **Beer Garden** draws pints of Yuengling Porter and Dock Street Beer, among other more mass-market brews.

The market is open Monday through Saturday from 8am to 6pm, but many vendors close at 5pm. Prices vary by vendor, and about half accept cash only. Every second Friday, the Reading Terminals, a rock band, plays during lunchtime. There are public restrooms here.

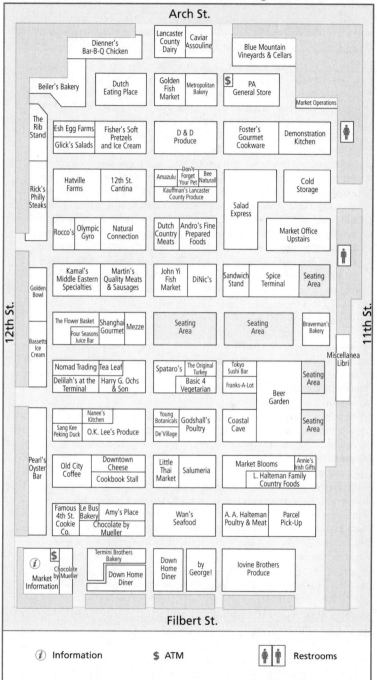

Arch St.

Dienner's Bar-B-Q Chicken

Lancaster County Dairy

Caviar Assouline

Blue Mountain Vineyards & Cellars

Beiler's Bakery

Dutch Eating Place

Golden Fish Market

Metropolitan Bakery

$ PA General Store

Market Operations

The Rib Stand

Esh Egg Farms

Glick's Salads

Fisher's Soft Pretzels and Ice Cream

D & D Produce

Foster's Gourmet Cookware

Demonstration Kitchen

Rick's Philly Steaks

Hatville Farms

12th St. Cantina

Amazulu

Don't Forget Your Pet

Bee Naturall

Kauffman's Lancaster County Produce

Salad Express

Cold Storage

Rocco's

Olympic Gyro

Natural Connection

Dutch Country Meats

Andro's Fine Prepared Foods

Market Office Upstairs

Golden Bowl

Kamal's Middle Eastern Specialties

Martin's Quality Meats & Sausages

John Yi Fish Market

DiNic's

Sandwich Stand

Spice Terminal

Seating Area

Bassetts Ice Cream

The Flower Basket

Four Seasons Juice Bar

Shanghai Gourmet

Mezze

Seating Area

Seating Area

Braverman's Bakery

Miscellanea Libri

Nomad Trading

Delilah's at the Terminal

Tea Leaf

Harry G. Ochs & Son

Spataro's

The Original Turkey

Basic 4 Vegetarian

Tokyo Sushi Bar

Franks-A-Lot

Beer Garden

Seating Area

Pearl's Oyster Bar

Sang Kee Peking Duck

Nanee's Kitchen

O.K. Lee's Produce

Young Botanicals

De'Village

Godshall's Poultry

Coastal Cave

Seating Area

Old City Coffee

Downtown Cheese

Cookbook Stall

Little Thai Market

Salumeria

Market Blooms

Annie's Irish Gifts

L. Halteman Family Country Foods

Famous 4th St. Cookie Co.

Le Bus Bakery

Amy's Place

Chocolate by Mueller

Wan's Seafood

A. A. Halteman Poultry & Meat

Parcel Pick-Up

$ Chocolate by Mueller

i Market Information

Termini Brothers Bakery

Down Home Diner

Down Home Diner

by George!

Iovine Brothers Produce

12th St.

11th St.

Filbert St.

i Information $ ATM   Restrooms

(*Tips* **Simple Pretheater Choices**

Not every performance on the Avenue of the Arts requires a pretheater extravaganza. Since the December 2001 opening of the Kimmel Center, simple restaurants serving mostly no-frills Italian pastas and quickly done main courses have sprung up in the neighborhood, to get you in and out before your show. **Bliss,** 220 S. Broad St. (© **215/731-1100**), next to the Kimmel Center, has a winning, eclectic menu with pasta, Asian, and grilled dishes. You could also dine superbly at the bar at **Pasion!** (p. 102) or **Striped Bass** (p. 102), or take your chances with the Kimmel Center's own preconcert fare, but if you want something less exalted, try the soups, salads, sandwiches, and simple platters at yuppie coffee shop **Cosi,** 235 S. 15th St. (© **215/893-9696**); the affordable wines and strip steak, squash-stuffed ravioli, and grilled salmon with basil at **Ernesto's 1521 Café,** 1521 Spruce St. (© **215/546-1521**); the homemade pasta and pizza (cooked in a wood-burning oven) at **Girasole Ristorante,** 1305 Locust St. (© **215/985-4659**); or the rustic antipasti and marinara at charming **Trattoria Primadonna,** 1506 Spruce St. (© **215/790-0171**), where the owner chooses a "prima donna" nightly to receive a free meal and sit in a throne seat.

---

the best blends of Asian and Western cuisines in the country. She is an elegant chef, and her decor reflects that aesthetic: The refined cuisine is enhanced by the space, which is comprised of stone, glass, and silks, and a collection of Chinese art and textiles. The second-floor dining room is more colorful, and also beautiful.

The cuisine is the main thing, but be forewarned: If you're the type that finds exquisite but small portions at high prices off-putting, you may find these dishes too delicate. Dim sum (entrees at lunch) features such delicacies as curried chicken ravioli with grilled eggplant, slightly crispy but not oily. Noodle dishes, salads, and main courses combine East and West: water chestnuts and radicchio, savory quail with fresh litchi nuts, smoked duck and endive, grilled chicken with Thai lemon grass sauce, and spicy shrimp and pear curry. Ms. Foo does caramelize some dishes in French style, but her menu contains no butter-based sauces or roux. The wine list, designed to complement these dishes, specializes in French and California white wines. Desserts such as ginger créme with strawberries and hazelnut meringue are light and delicate. The service is rather formal.

1512 Walnut St. © 215/545-2666. Reservations recommended for dinner. Main courses dinner $18–$35, with a $55–$75 prix-fixe option some evenings; lunch $14–$25, with 3-course prix fixe for $25. AE, MC, V. Mon–Fri 11:30am–2:30pm and 5–9pm (Fri until 10pm); Sat 5–10pm; Sun 5–9pm.

Zanzibar Blue ★★ CONTINENTAL   Philadelphia's premier venue for live jazz is also a great place to have dinner—witness the many happy pretheater and -symphony diners who take the Bellevue's escalator downstairs for Zanzibar Blue's glamorous surroundings and mixed, sophisticated group of patrons. The menu changes quarterly, but you can expect some Creole and Latin spices and seafood, along with basic steaks and fish. We love the jumbo lump crab cakes with two sauces: citrus beurre blanc and Creole sauce, with spinach and garlic mashed potatoes. Many people make a meal of appetizers while listening to a jazz set.

200 S. Broad St. ℂ **215/732-5200.** www.zanzibarblue.com. Reservations recommended; call or visit the website for listing of artists. Main courses $18–$29; Sun brunch $23; fixed-price 3-course pretheater dinner $27. AE, DC, DISC, MC, V. Daily 5:30pm–2am; Sun jazz brunch 11am–2pm.

INEXPENSIVE

Independence Brew Pub 🖈 AMERICAN   May 2000 brought this three-story brewpub and playground to Reading Terminal Headhouse inside the Convention Center complex. The main bar and dining room is on the first floor, with games and a second bar upstairs, all winding around enormous brewpub tanks. The all-day menu specializes in pizzas, grilled items in the $11 to $18 range, spectacular ice cream with fried bananas, and, of course, five or more fresh types of beer on tap, listed on a chalkboard. The atmosphere is woody and comfortable, with photos of the good old days of 1920s Center City and a very varied crowd of conventioneers and regulars. Happy hour is from 5 to 7pm, when draft beer is $3 a pint.

1150 Filbert St. (between Market and Arch sts. at 12th St.). ℂ **215/922-4292.** Main courses dinner $11–$18; lunch $9–$15, with $8.95 Express lunch menu; fresh-brewed tap beer $4 per 12-oz. glass; $3 beer of the day. AE, DC, DISC, MC, V. Mon–Fri 11:30am–2pm and 5–9pm; Sat–Sun 5–9pm. Bar menu until midnight.

⎛Kids Family-Friendly Restaurants

Ben's Garden Cafe   In the Franklin Institute at Logan Circle (p. 132), Ben's is well set up for kids, serving cafeteria food, hamburgers, and hot dogs. You can enter without museum admission.

Marathon Grill (p. 108)   You can dine on wonderful grilled salmon and have a nice glass of sauvignon blanc at this modern former diner just off Rittenhouse Square, while the kids choose from chicken fingers, pastas, and burgers. If they're noisy, no problem—the atmosphere is very casual. Weekend brunch is incredibly popular here, too.

Chinatown   You'll find loads of family-oriented places between 9th and 11th streets and Race and Vine streets.

Dave & Buster's (p. 211)   Children will love eating at this playground for all ages (carnival and arcade games are featured) on the Delaware Waterfront.

The Food Court at Liberty Place (p. 118)   Kids have their choice of cuisines from among 25 stalls.

Johnny Rockets (p. 98)   The location at 5th and South is convenient to South Street or the pedestrian walk from Penn's Landing, and the cheerful 1950s diner theme (red-and-white vinyl, indestructible booths) goes well with the very reasonable prices. The milkshakes are a favorite.

Capogiro   This Italian ice-cream spot at 13th and Sansom has all the classic flavors, plus more exotic gelato flavors such as Mexican-spiced chocolate.

Marathon Grill 🌟 *Kids* AMERICAN   Since 1984, the Borish family has run laps around the competition. They now have seven modern, comfortable Marathon Grills, each with gigantic menus boasting an enormous selection of comfort foods, from seven versions of grilled chicken breast sandwiches, to filet mignon under $10, to award-winning soups. Casual brunches are great here, too, on the weekends. The Commerce Square, West Philly, and Rittenhouse Square locations have liquor licenses: This last one, at 19th and Spruce, seats 60, and is perfect for a casual dinner with the kids, or for a post-theater meal on the way back to Rittenhouse Square. You can take out from any of these branches.

Locations: 121 S. 16th St. 🕐 **215/569-3278**; 1613 John F. Kennedy Blvd 🕐 215/564-4745; 1818 Market St. 🕐 215/561-1818; 1339 Chestnut St. 🕐 215/561-4460; 1839 Spruce St. 🕐 215/731-0800; 2 Commerce Sq., 2001 Market St. 🕐 215/568-7766; 40th and Walnut sts. 🕐 215/222-0100. Reservations not accepted. Main courses $6–$14. AE, DC, MC, V. Daily 8:30am–2am, depending on location.

Monk's Café 🌟 BELGIAN   It's the mussels—generous bowls of dark-shelled mollusks dressed in five sauces, from spicy Thai to classic white-wine-and-garlic—that Monk's legions of regulars return for every week. Or is it the 18 artisan beers on tap, and the dozens of interesting brews such as bottled Chimay made by Trappist monks? This is a no-nonsense tavern for satisfying burgers, fries with bourbon mayonnaise, or hearty salads, for when you crave comfort food. The kitchen is open till 1am.

264 S. 16th St. 🕐 **215/545-7005**. No reservations. Main courses $11–$24. AE, DC, DISC, MC, V. Mon–Sat 11:30am–2am; Sun 11am–2am.

3 South Philadelphia

South Philly is the colorful, down-to-earth neighborhood in which to find south and central Italian dishes adapted to American palates. You can always tell by the decor, menu, and music what decade a particular restaurant is frozen in. That said, these classic "red gravy" places are slowly depleting in numbers, as a younger generation of chefs shies away from the heavily sauced cuisine and moves to a more nuanced style of cooking.

EXPENSIVE

The Saloon 🌟🌟 ITALIAN/CONTINENTAL   The Santore family has been serving fresh, quality cuisine here since 1965. The restaurant is probably better known for its wonderful, huge herbed and marinated steaks than for its classic Italian dishes. The decor is solid wood paneling, sconces, antiques, and Tiffany lamps. The Saloon has a long menu and many daily specials to consider as you savor the pesto tapenade, Parmesan, and olive oil delivered automatically with your bread. The Santores favor standards such as clams casino and crabmeat salads but also serve sautéed radicchio with shiitake mushrooms and superb salads. Heavy artillery includes the 12-ounce prime sirloin, the Fiorentina (the seasoned 26-ounce porterhouse), or the lightly breaded veal slices with sweet and hot peppers. The wines are expensive. Desserts are exquisite.

750 S. 7th St. 🕐 **215/627-1811**. Reservations required. Main courses $16–$39. AE. Mon 5–10:30pm; Tues–Fri 11:30am–2pm and 5–10pm (Fri until 11pm); Sat 5–11pm.

MODERATE

Victor Cafe 🌟 *Finds* ITALIAN   Victor's is a South Philly shrine to opera, with servers who deliver arias along with hearty Italian classics. Opened in the 1930s by John Di Stefano, who covered the walls with photos of Toscanini, local Mario Lanza, and the like, the restaurant still has more than 45,000 classical recordings from which to choose and hires the best voices it can find. The menu changes frequently, with such classic Italian choices as meat lasagna, two fresh fish offered daily, three types of veal (including a hefty veal chop), and a filet. Pastas are homemade.

1303 Dickinson St. (C) **215/468-3040.** Reservations recommended. Main courses $17–$28. AE, MC, V. Mon–Thurs 5–10pm; Fri–Sat 4:30–11pm; Sun 4:30–9:30pm. SEPTA: Board & Tasker sts.; 1 block north of Tasker; make a right onto Dickinson. By car: Follow Broad Street 15 blocks south of City Hall, then 2 blocks east on Dickinson.

INEXPENSIVE

Marra's *Value* ITALIAN   Marra's, in the heart of South Philadelphia (supposedly the oldest surviving restaurant here, in fact), has brick ovens that give its thin-crust pizzas (and the walls, and the cozy booths) a real Italian smokiness. Marra's has a large, comprehensive Italian menu and is noted for its homemade lasagna, its tomato sauce, and its squid on Friday.

1734 E. Passyunk Ave. (between Morris and Moore sts.). (C) **215/463-9249.** Reservations not necessary. Main courses $6–$15; basic pizza $8 small, $9.50 large. DISC, MC, V. Tues–Thurs 11:30am–10pm; Fri 11:30am–midnight; Sat 11am–midnight; Sun 2–10pm.

Ralph's Italian Restaurant ITALIAN   Garlic-lovers alert: This two-story restaurant a few blocks north of the Italian Market is the epitome of the "red gravy" Italian style: unpretentious, comfortable, reasonable, and owned by the same family for decades. The baked lasagna, spaghetti with sausage, and chicken Sorrento have fans all over the city, and the extensive menu is long on veal and chicken dishes. The service, by tuxedoed pros, is friendly and attentive. To park, try the Rite Aid lot nearby, but don't get caught without buying something.

760 S. 9th St. (C) **215/627-6011.** Reservations recommended. Main courses $9–$16; steaks and chops to $27; pasta $10. No credit cards. Sun–Thurs noon–9:45pm; Fri–Sat noon–10:45pm.

4 University City (West Philadelphia)

MODERATE

Pod *Finds* JAPANESE   Pod has a fun, all-white, futuristic decor, generously sized Asian dishes, and a great selection of sushi. The young waitstaff is clad in what looks like Star Trek outfits, and the bathrooms resemble airplane loos, but the cuisine is not as kitschy. One gimmick is the three pods or curved semi-private seating areas, where you can self-select the color of your pod from nine possible pastels, depending on your mood. The other is the conveyor belt that carries sushi or small, delectable Japanese dishes like sesame-crusted scallops, miso-glazed sea bass, and crepes around an oval seating area with sit-down-light-up stools. (Dishes revolve unclaimed only 20 min. before they're disappeared.) The decor dazzles, with molded rubber, sculpted plastic, and video displays punctuated by a glass exterior curtain wall and bold lighting. Specialty drinks are $8.

3636 Sansom St. (C) **215/387-1803.** Reservations recommended. Main courses $16–$60 (for lobster; most others are in the $25 range); small plates $7–$14. AE, DC, MC, V. Mon–Thurs 11:30am–11pm; Fri 11:30am–midnight; Sat 4pm–midnight; Sun 4–10pm.

White Dog Café *Finds* AMERICAN   Judy Wicks is one of Philadelphia's great citizens: a fun-loving entrepreneur who gives generously to charities, holds thought-provoking dinners with authors and international academics, and always buys from and promotes small local farmers. She and her partner/chef Kevin von Klause have even written a cookbook. You'll enter two row houses with the dividing wall knocked out and an eclectic mix of checkered tablecloths,

---

Fun Fact **The Best Vegetables in Philly**

In restaurants such as the White Dog Café, Fork, and the Fountain, you'll see special mention on menus of the tiny heirloom tomatoes, baby herbs, and the smallest leaves of arugula you've ever seen from Branch Creek Farms in Bucks County. The 20-acre organic farm, owned by a former college professor and psychologist, produces vegetables so flavorful and beautiful they've inspired special dinners at Fork (p. 97), planned around the harvest of such items as zucchini blossoms and Silver Queen corn.

---

antique furniture, lights, and white dogs galore. The friendly pups are everywhere—on the menu, holding matchbooks, pouring milk, and in family photographs. The decor is charming, but a bit tired.

Off Sansom Street, the three-counter bar specializes in such all-American beers as McSorley's Ale, New Amsterdam, and Anchor Steam, as well as inexpensive American wines by the glass or bottle. Several dining areas lie to the rear and right, and there's a glassed-in porch across the rear.

The staff offers frequently changing menus as well as "theme" dinners based on the season or a particular American region. We prefer to come for a simple brunch at the bar rather than dine here in the evening. Next door at 3424 Sansom St., **The Black Cat** (© 215/386-6664) offers more of Judy's antiques and crafts.

3420 Sansom St. © 215/386-9224. Reservations recommended. Main courses dinner $15–$25; lunch $6–$18. AE, DC, DISC, MC, V. Mon–Fri 11:30am–2:30pm and 5:30–10pm (Fri until 11pm); Sat 11:30am–2:30pm and 5:30–11pm; Sun 10:30am–2:30pm and 5–10pm.

INEXPENSIVE

New Deck Tavern IRISH/AMERICAN   Virtually next door to the White Dog (see above), Mike Doyle's New Deck Tavern is less of a restaurant than a relaxed watering hole, with real Irish beers and bartenders and a 37-foot solid cherrywood bar. The Tavern specializes in crab cakes, homemade soups, and Irish fare such as shepherd's pie. Specials abound during the 5-to-7pm happy hour.

3408 Sansom St. © 215/386-4600. Main courses $7–$13. AE, DC, MC, V. Daily 11am–2am.

New Delhi INDIAN   New Delhi is a fairly good Indian restaurant near the U. Penn campus, with a 26-item all-you-can-eat buffet, including desserts like pistachio ice cream and sweet rice pudding. It boasts quality ingredients, a tandoor clay oven, and friendly service. Given these prices, it's often crowded with students and teachers from the university. Look for discount coupons in student newspapers.

4004 Chestnut St. © 215/386-1941. Reservations not required. Main courses $8.95–$11; all-you-can-eat lunch buffet $6.95; dinner buffet $9.95. AE, DISC, MC, V. Mon–Thurs noon–3pm and 4:30–10pm; Fri noon–3pm and 4:30–11pm; Sat noon–11pm; Sun noon–10pm.

The Restaurant School at Walnut Hill College ✸ *Value* ECLECTIC Housed in an elegant Victorian complex with a courtyard and several mansion-like wings, the Restaurant School is a respected and major institution among Philadelphia restaurateurs. After 8 months of instruction, teams of students plan a menu and kitchen protocol, then take over the ground floor for 8 weeks at a time; 96% of them find relevant jobs immediately upon graduation.

You have four dining choices, and since the students are paying for the right to cook your meal, the prices are extremely low. The formal restaurant, Great Chefs of Philadelphia, is housed in a totally renovated parlor dining room, and the city's premier chefs, who serve as mentors to student staffers, designed its $35 to $75 fixed-price menus. Three casual restaurants—one American, one an Italian trattoria, with three set courses for $13, one a brasserie in a pleasant courtyard environment—also have students in the kitchen, and you'd be hard-pressed to spend more than $25 for appetizer and entree without wine. The restaurant has acquired a liquor license and offers a fine selection of aperitifs, wines, and cocktails.

4207 Walnut St. ⓒ 215/222-4200. Reservations required on weekends, accepted after 3pm. $35–$75 fixed price for formal restaurant; $5–$25 at more casual student-run rooms. AE, DC, MC, V. Tues–Sat 5:30–9pm. Great Chefs opens at 6pm; brasserie closes at 10pm.

Zocalo ⓐ MEXICAN   This restaurant, 4 blocks from the U. Penn campus, offers contemporary Mexican cuisine from all the provinces. It's grown to sprawl through four or five separate dining areas, so it's quiet and civilized. You'll find everything from such traditional dishes as *carne asada* to such modern classics as fresh shrimp in chile sauce. They pat out the tortillas by hand before your eyes using fresh-flown or -grown ingredients. There's lively Latin music on most nights, with a pleasant deck in back for use in summer.

36th St. and Lancaster Ave. (1 long block north of Market St.). ⓒ 215/895-0139. Reservations recommended. Main courses $15–$21. AE, DC, MC, V. Mon–Fri noon–10pm (Fri until 11pm); Sat 5:30–11pm.

5 Chinatown

MODERATE

Rangoon Burmese Restaurant ⓐⓐ BURMESE   The most modern and sleek spot in busy Chinatown, Rangoon is more hip than its typically brightly lit, bare-bones neighbors. It even has a faux bamboo hut inside, plus hammered metal accents. There are no pretensions to perfect authenticity here, but the place is fun and lively, and we enjoy the basil- and curry-laced dishes: basil chicken, Kung Pao chicken, and calamari are all affordable and great to share with a group. The noodle soups are a lunchtime bargain.

112 N. 9th St. ⓒ 215/829-8939. Reservations for 5 and above. Main courses $8.50–$20. MC, V. Sun–Thurs 11:30am–9pm; Fri–Sat 11:30am–10pm.

Sang Kee Peking Duck House ⓐ CHINESE   A stalwart since 1980, Sang Kee still churns out Chinatown's best Peking duck (crispy on the outside, juicy inside, and delectable in a wrap with scallions and hoisin sauce), Szechuan duck, and barbecued pork. Its fans are many, fervent, and varied, and service is quick and bilingual. The dining rooms are basically devoid of atmosphere, but there are large, fun groups and multi-generational Asian families here. Other menu highlights are the spare ribs, fried dumplings, and the wonton noodle soup, and just about every fish dish.

238 N. 9th St. ℭ **215/925-7532.** Reservations recommended. Main courses $8.50–$25. No credit cards. Sun–Thurs 11am–10:45pm; Fri–Sat 11am–11:45pm.

INEXPENSIVE

Harmony Vegetarian Restaurant ★ VEGETARIAN/CHINESE Despite the menu listings for "meat" and "fish," absolutely everything here is made with vegetables (no eggs or dairy either). George Tang makes his own gluten by washing the starch out of flour. This miracle fiber is then deep-fried and marinated to simulate beef, chicken, even fish. The decor is intimate and candlelit, and there's no smoking. Raves go to the hot-and-sour soup and the various mushroom dishes. BYOB.

135 N. 9th St. ℭ **215/627-4520.** Reservations recommended. Main courses $6.50–$12. AE, MC, V. Sun–Thurs 11:30am–10:30pm; Fri–Sat 11:30am–11:30pm.

Imperial Inn CHINESE This longtime citizen of Chinatown (I find the decor outdated) serves an enormous variety of Szechuan, Mandarin, and Cantonese dishes. Lunch here features dim sum: appetizer-size dishes trundled around on carts that you can take or leave as you like; each dish is $2.50 or so. It's a great form of instant gratification. For dinner, the lemon chicken features a sautéed boneless breast in egg batter, laced with a mild lemon sauce. You can order a full-course dinner, which includes a choice of soup, rice, a main course, and a dessert for about $3 more than the main course alone. Service is efficient. If your party is eight or more, you can order a 10-course feast in advance for the bargain price of $19 per person.

142–6 N. 10th St. ℭ **215/627-5588.** Reservations recommended. Main courses $9–$17. AE, DC, MC, V. Mon–Thurs 11am–midnight; Fri–Sat 10:30am–1:30am; Sun 10am–11:30pm.

Ray's Coffee Shop ★ CHINESE/COFFEE BAR This unlikely precursor to the city's penchant for coffee bars, with 30 seats in a pleasant room located near the Convention Center, features an unusual combination of subtle Taiwanese cuisine (the dumplings are especially recommended) and dozens of exotic coffees, each smartly priced and brewed to order in lovely little glass siphons. The iced coffee and house special noodle soup here are great.

141 N. 9th St. ℭ **215/922-5122.** Main courses $9–$19; coffee $3.50–$8. AE, MC, V. Mon–Thurs noon–9pm; Fri–Sat 10am–10pm.

Vietnam ★ VIETNAMESE This attractive spot with recently upgraded, glossy wood tables and black-and-white photos serves sweet, oversize cocktails and wonderful, affordable dishes such as charbroiled pork, crispy spring rolls, lime-glazed chicken, and flavorful pho noodle soups. We love those cocktail names—especially the Virgin's Downfall.

221 N. 11th St. ℭ **215/592-1163.** Main courses $7–$14. AE, MC, V. Mon–Thurs 11am–9:30pm; Fri–Sat 11am–10:30pm; Sun 11am–9:30pm.

6 Manayunk

This neighborhood, 8 miles up the Schuylkill from the Art Museum and Center City, soared in popularity in the mid-1990s, with its shops and restaurant (see p. 185 for a shopping guide). It has cooled dramatically, but is still nice for a stroll and a casual dinner or brunch. Getting there is simple: From the I-76 Belmont Avenue exit, go north onto Green Lane, crossing the Schuylkill River and its adjoining canal; or 1 block south of the Green Lane SEPTA stop on the R6 line. Most restaurants are on Main Street from the 4400 to the 3900 addresses. A cohesive local development group runs a continuous series of weekend festivals and events to attract business. Parking is plentiful, and store hours tend to run late to match dinner reservations.

EXPENSIVE

Jake's 🏵🏵🏵 AMERICAN   Just redecorated in shades of amber, gold, and light brown leather, with richly textured fabrics on the cozy booths, this 16-year-old fine dining spot is Manayunk's upscale destination for dinner or brunch. Moneyed families gather here, as do romantic couples. Owner Bruce Cooper is famous for his crab cakes and wonderful spring roll and tuna tartare appetizers. Meats and dishes are inventive and perfectly prepared. At lunch, you can have a pristine but hearty salad, or a hefty and flavorful burger—the Sunday brunch omelet is a voluptuous beauty, with asparagus and cave-aged Gruyère. There is a cozy six-seat bar in front for people-watching.

4365 Main St. (𝄐 **215/483-0444.** www.jakesrestaurant.com. Main courses dinner $22–$32; lunch $11–$18. AE, DC, MC, V. Mon–Sat 11:30am–2:30pm and 5–9:30pm (till 10:30pm Fri–Sat); Sun 10:30am–2:30pm and 5–9:30pm.

MODERATE

Hikaru 🏵 JAPANESE   This restaurant has top-notch Japanese cuisine, with a high, elegant greenhouse and more traditional tatami room. With other branches in Queen Village and Rittenhouse Square, Hikaru is known for its sushi selection, but the teppan grill is great fun for tabletop drama, with a server searing meat, fish, or vegetables before your eyes.

4348 Main St. (𝄐 **215/487-3500.** Reservations recommended. Main courses $18–$26. AE, DC, DISC, MC, V. Mon–Thurs noon–2:15pm and 5–10pm; Fri–Sat noon–2:15pm and 5–11pm; Sun 5–9:30pm.

Le Bus Main Street AMERICAN/ECLECTIC   Bring the babies, the toddlers, and the grandparents: Le Bus got its name dishing out funky homespun food from a van on the University of Pennsylvania campus, and still dishes out fresh, affordable, home-style cuisine featuring American classics. Homemade breads and pastries are baked fresh daily, and the weekend brunch features omelets, frittatas, and pancakes. The menu, featuring everything from meatloaf to simple pastas, and the wholesomeness of the place make it especially attractive to families. There's outdoor seating, weather permitting. Watch out for lines at peak hours.

4266 Main St. (𝄐 **215/487-2663.** Reservations accepted. Main courses dinner $10–$18; lunch $5–$9. AE, MC, V. Mon–Thurs 11am–10pm; Fri 11am–12:30pm; Sat 9:30am–12:30pm; Sun 9:30am–10pm.

Sonoma 🏵 AMERICAN/ITALIAN   In 1992, Sonoma was the original hot Manayunk restaurant, and its Italian/California cuisine and service are still here. Set in a double storefront with 35-foot windows, three levels of seating, and a decor of black-and-brushed steel as a backdrop, there is a stainless-steel exposed kitchen and a thin waitstaff. The second-floor bar serves dozens of varieties of vodka. The menu includes Italian specialties like risotto and pizza and American standards such as roasted chicken. With this noise level, kids won't be noticed.

4411 Main St. (𝄐 **215/483-9400.** Reservations recommended. Main courses $11–$17. AE, DC, DISC, MC, V. Mon–Sat 11:30am–10:30pm (Fri–Sat till midnight); Sun 11am–10:30pm; late bar. Sun nights from 5–7pm, $10 entrees.

Zesty's GREEK/ITALIAN   Tom and Shelley Konidaris have transformed a small Roxborough diner to this agreeable, unpretentious cafe (one person called it the "anti-Sonoma"), featuring gourmet grilled fish (some flown in from

Greece) and meat along with Italian and Greek dishes such as pastas and moussaka. Don't rule out the meatier stuff like grilled lamb chops. The enormous espresso and cappuccino machine in the center of the room turns out coffee drinks that complement sweet desserts as well.

4382 Main St. Ⓒ 215/483-6226. Reservations not necessary. Main courses dinner $13–$30; lunch $8–$14. AE, DC, DISC, MC, V. Mon 5–10pm; Sun and Tues–Thurs 11am–10pm; Fri–Sat 11am–11pm.

7 Local Favorites: Cheesesteaks, Hoagies & More

CHEESESTEAKS & HOAGIES

Philadelphia cheesesteaks are nationally known. Preparing a cheesesteak is an art here—ribbons of thinly sliced steak are cooked quickly on a steel diner grill with onions (unless you order otherwise) and then slapped onto a roll on top of overlapping slices of provolone or a thick smear of Cheez Wiz. The perfect cheesesteak achieves a flavorful but not soggy balance between the cheese, onion, meat, and roll. Hoagies are the local name for the sandwiches known variously throughout the Northeast as submarines, grinders, or torpedoes. Remember, if you hate onions, you have to specify "Widout!" or they come chopped into the meat.

Jim's Steaks ⋩ *Value* AMERICAN   A fine practitioner of the fine art of "hoagistry" in this area is Jim's Steaks on South Street, which also offers the mightiest steak sandwiches in town. Jim's has a certain Art Deco charm, with a black-and-white enamel exterior, tile interior, and omnipresent chrome. Containers and ovens take up most of the ground floor, but there is a counter with bar stools along the opposite wall. Takeout is highly recommended in pleasant weather.

Proper hoagie construction can be debated endlessly, but Jim's treatment of the Italian hoagie with prosciutto is a benchmark. A fresh Italian roll is slit before your eyes and layers of sliced salami, provolone, and prosciutto are laid over the open faces. You choose your condiment: mayonnaise or oil and vinegar. Salad fixings—lettuce, tomatoes, and green peppers, with options of onion and hot peppers—come next, with more seasoning at the end. The result may not be subtle, but it's pungent, filling, and delicious. The steak sandwiches are really good here, at $6.15 (melted cheese or Cheez Wiz additional).

400 South St. Ⓒ 215/928-1911. Reservations not accepted. Lunch and main courses $6–$8. No credit cards. Mon–Thurs 10am–1am; Fri–Sat 10am–3am; Sun noon–10pm. SEPTA: 5th and Market sts.

Pat's King of the Steaks, and Geno's Steaks ⋩ AMERICAN   It's the quintessential American competition, the city's most famous two 24-hour-a-day South Philadelphia neighborhood joints on the same corner duking it out for the hearts of cheesesteak lovers. Pat's, so its adherents claim, invented the steak sandwich, without the cheese, in the 1930s, and still serves the best one this side of the equator. Geno's, to my palate, serves a more succulent and memorable version these days. The location and 24-hour competition make for an interesting mix at the takeout counters, especially at 3am.

Pat's: 1237 E. Passyunk Ave. (between 9th and Wharton sts.). Ⓒ 215/468-1546. $6.25–$10. Geno's: 1219 S. 9th St. Ⓒ 215/389-0659. $6.25 and up. Both: always open, no credit cards.

Primo Hoagies ⋩ AMERICAN   Primo has the right pedigree. It's from South Philadelphia and the Jersey shore, and bustles during the weekday with office orders. Size-wise they carry a small, medium, and giant; the regular is basically an elongated spicy cold-cuts sandwich measuring 7 inches long, the giant about twice as long. Various lauded combinations are the spicy tuna; a Sicilian made with capicola ham and sharp provolone; and an Abruzzi of roast pork, topped with provolone and broccoli rabe. The menu also includes plenty of low-fat, low-sodium healthy choices.

2043 Chestnut St. © 215/564-1264. Sandwiches $3.50–$14. Credit cards for orders over $25. Mon–Fri 9am–3pm.

PRETZELS

Soft, salted pretzels served warm with a dollop of mustard are an authentic local tradition, dating from the German settlers of the early 1700s. The best in town continue to be made by the Amish farmers who bring them to Reading Terminal Market. If you're outdoors, check out the vendor stand in front of the Franklin Institute.

PIZZA

I think **Marra's** (see "South Philadelphia," earlier in this chapter) is the best of Philadelphia's hundreds of pizza parlors and restaurants, and **Bertucci's,** 1515 Locust St. (© **215/731-1400**), is also a good bet for pizza and more. The following is a good bet as well.

Tacconelli's ★★ *Finds* ITALIAN   A real insider recommendation for pizza is Tacconelli's—not, as you'd think, in South Philly, but way up in Port Richmond, a long cab ride north of Old City. The greatly expanded Tacconelli's is open until whenever the crusts run out (about 9pm). It's imperative to call ahead to reserve the type of pizza you want, which is prepared in a brick oven. The white pizza with garlic oil, and the spinach and tomato pies are heavenly.

2604 E. Somerset St. at Aramingo Ave. © 215/425-4983. Reservations required; place pizza orders in advance. Pizzas $11–$18. No credit cards. BYO wine. Wed–Sat 4:30–9pm; Sun 4–8pm. SEPTA: Frankford subway line from Market St. to Somerset St., then walk 8 blocks east. Driving directions: from Society Hill, take Front St. north, make a right onto Kensington Ave., then another right onto Somerset.

COFFEE BARS

In the last few years, Center City has been transformed with the addition of dozens of coffee bars serving everything from inky espresso to frozen mochas. Depending on where you are, you can blow in for a 2-minute respite at a stand-up counter, or linger for an hour at a window seat.

The top restaurateurs, artists, hairstylists, and writers love **La Colombe,** both as a supplier of beans for New York's best, such as Daniel, and as its own very French-style shop at 130 S. 19th St. **Old City Coffee,** at 221 Church St., behind Christ Church (© **215/629-9292**), and at Reading Terminal Market (© **215/592-1897;** see the box "A Taste of Ethnic Philly: Reading Terminal Market," on p. 104), is relaxed to the point of somnolence and somewhat expensive, but the coffee selection is rich, varied, and strong. The Church Street location has eclectic acoustic acts during Old City's "First Friday" festivals. **Cosi** is a popular chain with a *Friends*-like ambience during the day at seven locations, including 235 S. 15th St. at Locust Street (© **215/893-9696**); 1720 Walnut St. near Rittenhouse Square; near Independence Hall at 4th and Chestnut streets (© **215/399-0214**); and by U. Penn at Sansom Commons. They add cocktails (p. 204) to the mix after 4:30pm.

In a more corporate vein, **ING Direct,** the Dutch financial giant, has a bright orange and glass cafe at the corner of Walnut and 17th streets; you can get a very decent cup of coffee, and then surf the Internet for free on one of eight flat-screen computers. **Starbucks** has set up outposts at 1528 Walnut St. (© **215/**

The Ultimate Cheesesteak Taste Test

Cheesesteak taste test? You think, *Aren't they all basically the same?* Don't say that out loud in this city. We Philadelphians take our cheesesteaks very seriously, though we know the quest to find the perfect cheesesteak requires patience and a hearty stomach. So hats off to Richard Rys at *Philadelphia* magazine, who wolfed down 50 cheesesteaks in 34 days in a quest to crown a Cheesesteak King. Richard ordered steaks with American cheese and no extras, also known as an "American, without": "This leaves only the three essential elements to any good steak—meat (judged on taste and quality), cheese (amount and thorough distribution throughout the sandwich), and roll (freshness, consistency, proper meat-to-bread ratio). A great steak shouldn't hide behind onions or condiments."

Here's a sample of his top picks closest to Center City, rated on a scale of 1 to 5 Clogged Arteries (clogged arteries are a good thing in the world of cheesesteaks). See map on p. 94 for locations:

Cosmi's Deli, 1501 S. 8th St. (© 215/468-6093), is just around the corner from famous rivals Pat's and Geno's, but Richard swear's Cosmi's is the real king of steaks. "Fresh roll, meat chopped with a samurai's precision, and melted cheese embracing each piece like Mama giving Raj a bear hug on *What's Happening*." Richard's rating: 5.

Swann Lounge at Four Seasons (p. 79) serves a $16 plate of four dainty cheesesteak spring rolls. "It's the culinary equivalent of flipping cheesesteak purists everywhere the bird. But you know, this is good. Meat, cheese distribution—perfect." Rating: 4.5.

Tony Luke's, 39 E. Oregon Ave. (© 215/551-5725), is in South Philly, near the Walt Whitman Bridge. "Strips of meat stuffed into a hearty, rugged roll that was built for handling a serious payload. My only complaint is that for all its mass, it's a little light on cheese." Rating: 4.5.

Chubby's, 5826 Henry Ave. (© 215/487-2575), is a favorite in Manayunk. "That wet-hot dairy goodness is mixed in well. Perfectly sized roll filled well with meat that's tasty and gristle-free." Rating: 4.

D'alessandro's, 600 Wendover Ave. (© 215/482-5407), also in Manayunk, has an ongoing rivalry with Chubby's. "They give up the crown this year. Not a bad sandwich, but it has its flaws. The roll is way overstuffed, leaving as much meat in my lap as in my mouth, and the meat is dry." Rating: 3.5.

Doce Carini, 1929 Chestnut St. (© 215/567-8892), is near Rittenhouse Square. "Healthy roll, stuffed well. Could use a wee bit more cheese, perhaps. Maybe a bit more density of bread would serve it well. But really, a fine sandwich." Rating: 3.5.

732-0708) and in the Convention Center Marriott at Market and 11th streets (© 215/569-4223). Don't forget about the cafes inside the bookstores of **Borders** at 1 S. Broad St. (© 215/568-7400) and **Barnes & Noble** at 1805 Walnut St. (© 215/665-0716); the former is lauded for its café au lait.

Jim's Steaks (p. 114) is just south of Society Hill. "The roll looks like it just wandered in off the set of a Sally Struther's infomercial, the meat is only moderately chopped, and the cheese is barely melted. Yet the damn thing is inexplicably good." Rating: 3.5.

John's Roast Pork, Weccacoe and Synder avenues (© **215/463-1951**), is close to Tony Luke's (above), near the Walt Whitman. "I was thrown off by the sesame seed–speckled roll, which wasn't nearly as crusty as it appeared—thin, but strong enough to handle the healthy portion of tasty meat stuffed inside it. Perfect amount of cheese." Rating: 3.5.

Lazaro's, 1743 South St. (© **215/545-2775**), claims to have the biggest steaks in town, at 18 inches. Richard ordered a half. "Soft roll, though maybe a bit too much so. Steak diced nicely, but I detected a subtle, unidentifiable spice that I didn't enjoy. There also could have been a little more meat on this puppy." Rating: 3.

Rick's Philly Steaks, Reading Terminal Market, 12th and Arch streets (© **215/925-4320**), is run by the Oliveri family who owns Pat's. "The meat is chopped, but not finely diced, and it's greasy, but perfectly so. Could load it up with extra meat, though—the last two bites were all roll and cheese." Rating: 3.

Sonny's, 228 Market St. (© **215/629-5760**), gets a lot of traffic in Old City. "Good cheese distribution and loads of meat, but although it's well diced, is a bit stringy at times. The roll is too thin for the load." Rating: 3.

Geno's Steaks (p. 114) is a Philly landmark, but Richard gives it modest praise. "Decent amount of cheese. Good roll. The meat is another story. It's riddled with pockets and veins of fat and contains a rainbow of colors from brown to gray. Oddly enough, the taste isn't bad." Rating: 2.5.

Pat's King of Steaks (p. 114), around the corner from Geno's, gets no special treatment, either. "The cheese distribution on my sandwich makes me think Stevie Wonder is working dairy duty on the grill line. It's spotty, leaving some regions bare. Like Geno's, a good roll, but a frightening amount of fat in the meat." Rating: 2.

So how much weight did Richard gain from his cheesesteak binge? He tells us that he was stunned to find that his cholesterol actually went down and his weight stayed the same, though he admits that he worked out four times a week during the taste-test period. "Either I have a superhuman metabolism, or I should get to work on a Cheesesteak Diet book. That South Beach thing was overrated, anyway."

—*courtesy of Richard Rys and* Philadelphia *magazine*
(*www.phillymag.com*)

FOOD COURTS & MARKETS

The **Reading Terminal Market,** 12th and Arch streets (© **215/922-2317**), in the space underneath the train terminal, has served Philadelphians since the turn of the 20th century. For a full description, see the box "A Taste of Ethnic Philly: Reading Terminal Market," on p. 104.

The Bourse Food Court This location has 11 snack/restaurant operations, all moderately priced and designed for takeout to be eaten at the tables that fill this cool and stunning restoration of the 1895 merchant exchange. The entire operation was recently upgraded, and representative stalls include **Sbarro's** for pizza and pasta, **Bain's Delicatessen** for turkey sandwiches, and **Flamers** for burgers.

111 S. Independence Mall E. (just east of the Liberty Bell). Mon–Sat 10am–6pm; Sun 11am–5pm summers only.

Downstairs at the Bellevue Upscale, and very quiet, with bright tiles, great lighting, and public restrooms, this is a great spot for a quick lunch when shopping on Walnut Street. Center tables surround food-court vendors such as **Montesini Pizza, Saladworks,** and **Rocco's Italian Hoagies** ($5 and up).

The Hyatt Regency at the Bellevue Hotel, S. Broad and Walnut sts. Mon–Fri 10am–6pm; Sat 10am–5pm.

The Food Court at Liberty Place 𝄞 *Kids* This court, in a gleaming urban mall in the heart of Center City, hosts branches of Reading Terminal favorites like Bain's Deli, Bassett's Original Turkey, and Original Philly Steaks, along with Teriyaki Boy for sushi and a Chick-Fil-A. It's spotless, large, and reasonably priced, with full lunches from $3.75. You'll find it easy to keep your eyes on the kids as they wander.

Second level (accessible by escalator or elevator) of Liberty Place between Chestnut and Market sts. and 16th and 17th sts. Mon–Sat 9:30am–7pm; Sun noon–6pm.

Italian Market 𝄞 *Value* While touring South Street or South Philadelphia, be sure to visit the Italian Market for fresh produce, pasta, seafood, and other culinary delights. It is very gritty and very fragrant (smelly?), but it's most interesting to see fast-talking vendors, opera-singing butchers, and try-it-before-you-buy-it cheese merchants hawk their wares here. The Market is also a great place to pick up ultracheap clothing, if you're willing to wade through racks of items. **Fante's Cookware** is famous nationally, and **DiBruno Bros. House of Cheese** combines a great selection with upscale savvy.

9th St. between Christian and Federal sts. Daily, dawn to dusk. Bus: 47 or 64.

Exploring Philadelphia

Consider Philadelphia's sightseeing possibilities—the most historic square mile in America; more than 90 museums; innumerable Colonial churches, row houses, and mansions; an Ivy League campus; more Impressionist art than you'll find in any place outside of Paris; and leafy, distinguished parks, including the largest one within city limits in the United States. Philadelphia has come a long way since 1876, when a guidebook recommended seeing the new Public Buildings at Broad and Market streets, the Naval Yards, the old YMCA, and the fortresslike prison (which is still a tourist site as the Eastern State Penitentiary!).

Most of what you'll want to see within the city falls inside a rectangle on a map between the Delaware and Schuylkill rivers in width, and between South and Vine streets in height. It's easy to organize your days into walking tours of various parts of the city—see chapter 8 for suggestions. Nothing is that far away. A stroll from City Hall to the Philadelphia Museum of Art takes about 25 minutes, although the flags and flowers along the Parkway will undoubtedly sidetrack you. A walk down Market or one of the parallel streets named for trees (Chestnut, Spruce, Pine, Locust) to Independence National Historical Park and Society Hill should take a little less time—but it probably won't, since there's so much to entice you on the way. If you'd rather ride, the spiffy

PHLASH buses loop past most major attractions every 13 minutes, and the all-day fare is $4, or pay $1 each time you ride (service runs May–Nov, and seniors ride for free except 4:30–5:30pm weekdays). SEPTA also has an all-day $5.50 fare for city buses, but the two systems do *not* accept each other's passes.

The city is trying to wrap some of its attractions together in various packages. The Independence Visitor Center and other locations have two "package priced" offers. The first is the **combined RiverPass ticket** for Independence Seaport Museum, the cruiser *Olympia,* and the submarine *Becuna,* plus Camden attractions such as the Aquarium (which is closed for renovations until May 2005), and the ferry between them; prices vary, but the deluxe version is $24 adults, $21 seniors, and $19 children 3 to 12. The second is **Philadelphia Citypass,** which offers admission to six major attractions, including the Philadelphia Museum of Art, the Franklin Institute, the National Constitution Center, and the Seaport Museum; prices are $36 for adults and $23 children 3 to 11, and they may be purchased in advance on http://citypass.net/cgi-bin/citypass (click on "Philadelphia") or at any one of the attractions. Tickets are good up to 9 days from first use, and they represent about a 50% discount from full admissions to all of the attractions.

SUGGESTED ITINERARIES

If You Have 1 Day

Start at the **Independence Visitor Center** and the adjacent **Liberty Bell Pavilion** in Independence National Historical Park, spend an hour or two at the **National Constitution Center,** then move south through **Independence Hall** and on to **residential Society Hill,** which is steeped in U.S. history. In the evening, if you've still got the history bug, stay for the multimedia **"Lights of Liberty"** show that uses the Park as backdrop. If not, see what's on at the **Academy of Music,** the **Kimmel Center for the Performing Arts,** the **Annenberg Center** at the University of Pennsylvania, or the **CoreStates Spectrum** for sports.

If You Have 2 Days

Follow the itinerary above for Day 1. On **Day 2,** starting at **City Hall,** walk up the Benjamin Franklin Parkway to **Logan Circle** and spend the afternoon at the **Franklin Institute Science Museum** or the **Philadelphia Museum of Art.** Try to circle back to Rittenhouse Square and the **Liberty Place** complex before it closes (7pm most nights, Wed to 8pm).

If You Have 3 Days

On Days 1 and 2, follow the itinerary given above. On **Day 3,** spend the morning in Old City viewing its **Christ Church** and **Elfreth's Alley,** then explore the expanding Delaware River waterfront attractions and the **Independence Seaport Museum** at **Penn's Landing.** Finally, either take the ferry to Camden for the **Adventure Aquarium** and the newly docked **Battleship** *New Jersey* or stay on land and stroll along the eclectic **South Street.**

If You Have 4 Days or More

Days 1 through 3, follow the itinerary given above. On **Day 4,** explore the Rittenhouse Square/South Broad Street area, with a visit to the **Pennsylvania Academy of Fine Arts,** winding up with a stroll through **Reading Terminal Market** and **Chinatown.** On **Day 5,** hit **Fairmount Park's Philadelphia Zoo** and the many restored Colonial mansions. Farther out, **Franklin Mills** and **King of Prussia Court and Plaza** have become magnets for millions of tourists who want to save on clothing from America's finest stores, retail and discounted, with no state sales tax.

1 Independence National Historical Park: America's Most Historic Square Mile ⋆⋆

Is there anyone who doesn't know about the Liberty Bell in Independence Hall? The bell is now housed across the street, but you get the point: The United States was conceived on this ground in 1776, and the future of the young nation was assured by the Constitutional Convention held here in 1787. The choice of Philadelphia as a site was natural because of its centrality, wealth, and gentility. The delegates argued at Independence Hall (then known as the State House) and boarded and dined at City Tavern. Philadelphia was the nation's capital during Washington's second term, so the U.S. Congress and Supreme Court met here for 10 years while awaiting the construction of the new capital in Washington, D.C. From the first penny to the First Amendment, Philadelphia led the nation.

The **Independence National Historical Park** ⋆ comprises 40 buildings on 45 acres of Center City real estate (see the "Walking Tour: Historic Highlights

Travel Tip: He who finds the best hotel deal has more to spend on facials involving knobbly vegetables.

Hello, the Roaming Gnome here. I've been nabbed from the garden and taken round the world. The people who took me are so terribly clever. They find the best offerings on Travelocity. For very little cha-ching. And that means I get to be pampered and exfoliated till I'm pink as a bunny's doodah.

travelocity®

1-888-TRAVELOCITY / travelocity.com / America Online Keyword: Travel

Plan your vacation

- flights, hotels, car rentals
- cruises & vacation packages
- destination guides
- fare alerts
- go to yahoo.com, click travel

DO YOU YAHOO!?

& Society Hill" map, p. 163). Independence Hall and the Liberty Bell, in its new pavilion, lie between 5th and 6th streets at Chestnut Street, and the Park has just been overhauled, with some $300 million poured into new attractions, renovations, and landscaping. The Independence Visitor Center 1 block north is well equipped to illustrate the early history of this country, and the new National Constitution Center explores the U.S.'s core document.

This neighborhood is a superb example of successful revitalization. Fifty years ago, this area had become glutted with warehouses, office buildings, and rooming houses. The National Park Service stepped in, soon followed by the Washington Square East urban renewal project now known as Society Hill, after the historic neighborhood it's in. To the east, gardens replaced buildings as far as the Dock Street food market, which was replaced by Society Hill Towers in 1959. Graff House, City Tavern, Pemberton House, and Library Hall were reconstructed on their original sites. Liberty Bell Pavilion and Franklin Court are contemporary structures erected for the Bicentennial of the Declaration of Independence celebrations. The most questionable project was the condemnation and destruction of 3 blocks' worth of commercial buildings to create Independence Mall, a wide swath of greenery opposite Independence Hall.

September 11, 2001, had an inevitable impact on the spontaneous excitement of stepping into the birthplace of American independence: You must pass through a security screening center on Market Street before visiting the Liberty Bell and Independence Hall, but most days the process moves fairly quickly.

Between March and October, and during Thanksgiving and end-of-year holidays, everyone in your group will need a ticket to visit Independence Hall. They're free, but it's preferable to pay the $1.50 handling charge by calling © **800/967-2283** or visiting http://reservations.nps.gov and reserving up to 12 months ahead, than to count on same-day walkup service. If you do take the latter course, go to the Visitor Center as early as possible (it opens at 8:30am), to claim up to 6 tickets for a time slot. The line for $2 tickets to take one of the frequent interior tours of the Second Bank of the United States, Bishop White House, and the Todd House is less intense.

The place to get tickets and most everything else is the **Independence Visitor Center,** 6th and Market streets (© **800/537-7676,** or 215/965-7676; www.independencevisitorcenter.com). The Visitor Center should be your first stop in the park, since it's the official visitors service for the Park, and also provides general tourism services and trip planning information. There's a cafe and a gift shop selling mementoes and park publications, and every 30 minutes the center shows a John Huston feature, *Independence,* free of charge.

To get here, you can take the SEPTA Market-Frankford Line to 5th and Market streets or 2nd and Market streets. By bus, take the PHLASH or any Chestnut Street bus from Center City.

If you're driving, from I-76, take I-676 east to 6th Street (last exit before the Ben Franklin Bridge), then turn south (right) along Independence Mall. From the Ben Franklin Bridge, make a left onto 6th Street and it's right there after the National Constitution Center. From I-95 southbound, take the Center City exit to 2nd Street. From I-95 northbound, use the exit marked "Historic Area." Turn left on Columbus Boulevard (formerly Delaware Ave.) and follow it to the exit for Market Street (on the right). There's metered parking along most streets, as well as parking facilities ($9.50–$15 per day) under the Visitor Center, at 2nd and Sansom streets, and at the corner of Dock and 2nd streets.

Philadelphia Attractions

Academy of Music **12**
Academy of Natural Sciences **5**
The African–American Museum
  in Philadelphia **15**
Arch Street Meeting House **22**
Athenaeum of Philadelphia **34**
Atwater Kent Museum **28**
Benjamin Franklin Bridge **14**
Betsy Ross House **19**
Carpenters' Hall **29**

Christ Church **21**
Christ Church
  Burial Ground **20**
City Hall **11**
Declaration House
  (Graff House) **23**
Edgar Allen Poe
  National Historic Site **41**
Elfreth's Alley **18**
Franklin Court **27**

Franklin Institute
  Science Museum **4**
Free Library of Philadelphia **3**
Independence Hall **31**
Independence Seaport
  Museum **28**
Independence Visitor Center **25**
Kimmel Performing Arts
  Center **13**
The Liberty Bell **24**

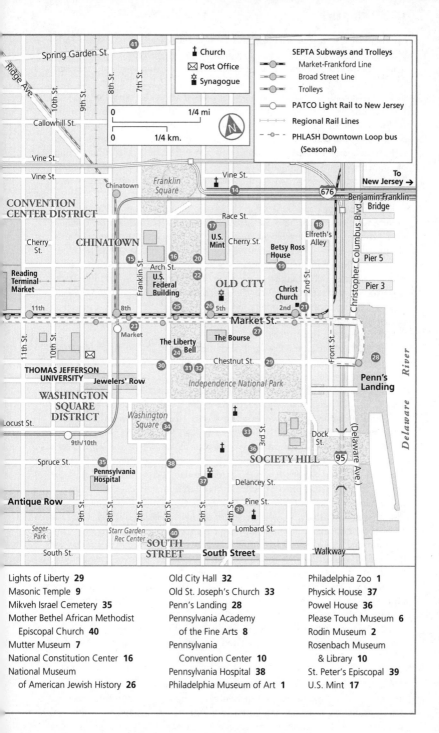

Lights of Liberty **29**

Masonic Temple **9**

Mikveh Israel Cemetery **35**

Mother Bethel African Methodist
Episcopal Church **40**

Mutter Museum **7**

National Constitution Center **16**

National Museum
of American Jewish History **26**

Old City Hall **32**

Old St. Joseph's Church **33**

Penn's Landing **28**

Pennsylvania Academy
of the Fine Arts **8**

Pennsylvania
Convention Center **10**

Pennsylvania Hospital **38**

Philadelphia Museum of Art **1**

Philadelphia Zoo **1**

Physick House **37**

Powel House **36**

Please Touch Museum **6**

Rodin Museum **2**

Rosenbach Museum
& Library **10**

St. Peter's Episcopal **39**

U.S. Mint **17**

Independence Hall ★★★ *(Moments)* Even if you knew nothing about Independence Hall, you could guess that noble and important events took place here. Although these buildings are best known for their national role, they also functioned as the seat of government for the city of Philadelphia and the state of Pennsylvania both before and after Philadelphia was the capital of the U.S. From an architectural standpoint, the edifice is graceful and functional; from the standpoint of history and American myth, it's unforgettable. Independence Square sets you thinking about the bold idea of forming an entirely sovereign state from a set of disparate colonies and about the strength and intelligence of the representatives who gathered here to do it. For some historical context, try the wonderful website of the **Independence Hall Association** at www.us history.org.

When the French and Indian War (1754–63) required troops, which required money, King George III believed the colonists should pay for their own defense through taxes. The colonists disagreed, and the idea that the king harbored tyrannical thoughts swept through the Colonies. Philadelphia, as the wealthiest and most cultured of the seacoast cities, was leery of radical proposals of independence. Even Ben Franklin himself, an American agent in London at the time, was wary of this scheme. But the news that British troops had fired on citizens defending their own property in Concord pushed even the most moderate citizens to reconsider what they owed to England and what they deserved as free people endowed with natural rights.

The Second Continental Congress convened in May 1775, in the Pennsylvania Assembly Room, to the left of the entrance to Independence Hall. Each colony had its own green baize-covered table, but not much of the original room's furnishings escaped use as firewood when British troops occupied the city in December 1777. The Congress acted quickly, appointing a tall Virginia delegate named George Washington as commander of the Continental Army. After the failure of a last "olive branch" petition, the Congress, through John Adams, instructed each colony's government to reorganize itself as a state. Thomas Jefferson worked on a summary of why the colonists felt that independence was necessary. The resulting Declaration of Independence, wrote noted historian Richard Morris, "lifted the struggle from self-interested arguments over taxation to the exalted plane of human rights." Most of the signatories of the Declaration of Independence used Philip Syng's silver inkstand, which is still in the room. The country first heard the news of the Declaration on July 8 in Independence Square.

Before and after the British occupied the city, Independence Hall was the seat of the U.S. national government. Here, the Congress approved ambassadors, pored over budgets, and adopted the Articles of Confederation, a loose and problematic structure for a country composed of states. Congress moved to New York after the war's end, and it grudgingly allowed delegates to recommend changes to the Articles.

The delegates who met in the Assembly Room in Philadelphia in 1787 created a new Constitution that has guided the country for more than 200 years. Jefferson's cane rests here, as does a book belonging to Franklin. Washington, as president of the convention, kept order from his famous "Rising Sun Chair." Delegates were mature, urbane (24 of the 42 had lived or worked abroad), and trained to reason, and many had experience drafting state constitutions and laws. They decided on approaches to governance that are familiar today: a bicameral Congress, a single executive, an independent judiciary, and a philosophical belief in government by the people and for the people. No wonder John Adams called

"Self-Evident" Not So Self-Evident

In the Declaration of Independence, Thomas Jefferson boldly declares, "We hold these truths to be self-evident"—but not in the rough draft. Jefferson originally found those truths to be "sacred and undeniable" before changing his mind. You can read his first handwritten copy along with documents like Ben Franklin's will and William Penn's 1701 Charter of Privileges, at **Library Hall,** 36 S. Pine St. at Spruce Street.

the convention "the greatest single effort of national deliberation that the world has ever seen."

Across the entrance hall from the Assembly Room, the courtroom served as Pennsylvania's Supreme Court chamber. Like the court at Williamsburg, Virginia, this room exemplifies pre–Bill of Rights justice. For example, your ranger guide will probably point out the tipstaff, a wooden pole with a brass tip that was used to keep onlookers subdued. Other period details include little coal-burning boxes to keep feet warm on chilly days. This was one of the first courtrooms in America to hear the argument that disagreement with a political leader isn't sedition, one of the great concepts in modern Anglo-American law.

The stairwell of Independence Hall held the Liberty Bell until 1976. The ranger will conduct you upstairs to the Long Gallery. Now it's set up as a banquet hall with a harpsichord (some of the guides even play) and a rare set of maps of the individual 13 colonies. Its view of Independence Mall is superb.

Two smaller rooms adjoin the Long Gallery. To the southwest, the royal governors of Pennsylvania met in council in a setting of opulent blue curtains, silver candlesticks, and a grandfather clock. Beneath a portrait of William Penn, governors met with foreign and Native American delegations, and conducted their everyday business. On the southeast side, the Committee Room fit the whole Pennsylvania Assembly while the Second Continental Congress was meeting downstairs. When it wasn't being used to house the Assembly, it stored the Assembly's reference library or arms for the city militia.

As you descend the stairs, look at leafy, calm **Independence Square,** with its statue of Commodore John Barry. The clerk of the Second Congress, John Nixon, first read the Declaration of Independence here, to a mostly radical and plebeian crowd. (Philadelphia merchants didn't much like the news at first, since it meant a disruption of trade, to say the least.)

Chestnut St. between 5th and 6th sts., flanked by Old City Hall to the left and Congress Hall to the right. ⓒ 215/965-2305. www.nps.gov/inde. Free admission. Daily 9am–5pm, later in summer. Free tours are led by park rangers every 15 min. 9am–4:45pm. You must take a tour in order to see the interior of the building. As noted above, if you haven't reserved a time slot in advance, go to the Visitor Center at 6th and Market sts., at or around 8:30am, to pick up time-reserved tickets so that you won't have to wait all day to get inside. Bus: PHLASH, 21, or 42.

The Liberty Bell ★★★   You can't leave Philadelphia without seeing the Liberty Bell. The Bell is housed in a new 13,000-square-foot, $12.4 million glass pavilion, 235 feet long and 50 feet wide, angled so you can see it against the backdrop of Independence Hall, but avoiding the brutal modern Penn Mutual skyscraper flanking the Hall.

The Liberty Bell, America's symbol of freedom and independence, was commissioned in 1751 for the Pennsylvania State House to mark the 50th anniversary of a notable event: William Penn, who governed Pennsylvania alone under

Crown charter terms, decided that free colonists had a right to govern them-selves, so he established the Philadelphia Assembly under a new Charter of Priv-ileges. The 2,000-pound bell, cast in England, cracked while it was being tested, and the Philadelphia firm of Pass and Stow recast it by 1753. It hung in Inde-pendence Hall to "proclaim liberty throughout the land" as the Declaration of Independence was read aloud to the citizens. In 1777, it survived a trip to an Allentown church so the British wouldn't melt it down for ammunition. The last time it tolled was to celebrate Washington's birthday in 1846. The term *Liberty Bell* was coined by the abolitionist movement, which recognized the relevance of its inscription, "Proclaim Liberty throughout all the land unto all the inhabi-tants thereof," in the fight against slavery.

The new building offers excellent information and interactive exhibits, including an X-ray of the bell's crack and a film produced by the History Chan-nel about how the bell became an international icon of freedom. Language options for the narrative videos range from Russian to Chinese to German.

Chestnut St. between 5th and 6th sts. ⓒ **215/965-2305.** Free with ticket from the Visitor Center (p. 121). The pavilion is open daily 9am–5pm, visitors must clear security by 4:45pm. You can see the bell at all times from 6th and Chestnut sts.

National Constitution Center 🌟🌟   Opening July 4, 2003, on Philadel-phia's redesigned Independence Mall, the stunning, modern National Constitu-tion Center is the first museum in the world devoted to the United States Constitution—its history and its relevance in the daily lives of Americans. The 160,000-square-foot, state-of-the-art facility, designed by Pei, Cobb Freed and Partners, in angular glass, steel, and limestone, has departments of history, edu-cation, and outreach, all using a blend of the most exciting and attention-grab-bing technological tools to offer something for everyone, from scholars to casual visitors. While same-day tickets are usually available, it's a good idea to buy tick-ets in advance, and arrive 20 minutes early for the timed theater shows that wel-come visitors twice each hour.

As you stroll north from Independence Visitor Center, you'll cross Arch Street and a broad walk to the gleaming white stone entrance to the Constitution Cen-ter, emblazoned with those three magic words, "We the People . . ." A 12-minute multimedia show with an inspiring live actor and 360-degree movie screen explain the Constitution's early history. From there, visitors learn how the Con-stitution affects the functioning of government—you can take your own Presi-dential Oath of Office, explore a national family tree, try on a Supreme Court robe, and check out the Bill of Rights. Signers Hall has bronze life-size figures of the 39 men who signed the Constitution, and the three who dissented. Espe-cially good are exhibits featuring a voting machine from Palm Beach, Florida, from the contested 2000 election, and one featuring tools used by G. Gordon Liddy at the Watergate burglary. There will be plenty of daily events, talks, and programs, as well as a 225-seat, glass-enclosed restaurant and store.

Note: Watch for special events at the National Constitution Center on and around Ben Franklin's 300th birthday, Jan 17, 2006, still in the works as we go to print. See **www.benfranklin300.org** for details.

525 Arch St. ⓒ **215/409-6600,** or 215/409-6700 for advance ticket sales. www.constitutioncenter.org. Admission $7 adults; $5 seniors, active military, and children 4–12. Sun–Fri 9:30am–5pm; Sat 9:30am–6pm. SEPTA: 5th St. Station. Bus: PHLASH.

Franklin Court 🌟🌟 *(Kids*   Franklin Court is an imaginative, informative, and downright fun (and free) museum run by the National Park Service. Designed by noted architect Robert Venturi, it was very much a sleeper when it opened in

April 1976, because Market and Chestnut streets' arched passages give little hint of the court and exhibit within.

Franklin Court was once the home of Benjamin Franklin, who had resided with his family in smaller row houses in the neighborhood prior to living here. Like Jefferson at Monticello, Franklin planned much of the interior design of the house, though he spent the actual building period first as Colonial emissary to England, and then to France. His wife, Deborah, oversaw the construction, as the flagstones engraved with some of her correspondence show, while Ben sent back continental goods and a constant stream of advice. Sadly, they were reunited in the family plot at Christ Church Burial Ground, since Deborah died weeks before the end of Ben's 10-year absence. Under the stewardship of his daughter Sarah and her husband, Richard Bache, Franklin Court provided a comfortable home for Ben until his death in 1790.

Since archaeologists have no exact plans of the original house, a simple frame in girders indicates its dimensions and those of the smaller print shop. Excavations have uncovered wall foundations, bits of walls, and outdoor privy wells, and these have been left as protected cutaway pits. It is all very interesting, but enter the exhibition for the really fun part. After a portrait and furniture gallery, a mirrored room reveals Franklin's far-ranging interests as a scientist, an inventor, a statesman, a printer, and so on. At the Franklin Exchange, dial various American and European luminaries to hear what they thought of Franklin.

The middle part of the same hall has a 15-minute series of three climactic scenes in Franklin's career as a diplomat. On a sunken stage, costumed doll figures brief you, and each other, on the English Parliament in 1765, the Stamp Act, the Court at Versailles (when its members were wondering whether to aid America in its bid for independence), and the debates of the Constitution's framers in 1787, which occurred right around the corner at Independence Hall. Needless to say, Ben's pithy sagacity wins every time.

On your way in or out on the Market Street side, stop in the 1786 houses that Ben rented out. One is the Printing Office and Bindery, where you can see Colonial methods of printing and bookmaking in action. The house at 322 Market St. is the restored office of *The Aurora and General Advertiser,* the newspaper published by Franklin's grandson. Next door, get a letter postmarked at the Benjamin Franklin Post Office (remember, Ben was Postmaster General, too!). Employees still stamp the marks by hand. Upstairs, a postal museum is open in summer.

Chestnut St. between 3rd and 4th sts., with another entrance at 316–322 Market St. ℭ 215/965-2305. Free admission. Daily 10am–5pm, including the post office and postal museum. SEPTA: Market East. Bus: PHLASH, 21, or 42.

Lights of Liberty ⭐ *Kids*   Since the summer of 1999, the most important park sights have been the backdrop for the world's first interactive sound-and-light walking tour, providing visitors with a lively, fun, high-tech immersion into the drama of the American Revolution as it happened and where it happened. You'll walk as night falls over Old City past trendy bars and restaurants, but be transported into Philadelphia 2 centuries ago: Five-story projections on historic buildings and wireless headsets equipped with movie-style "surround" sound make it the closest "virtual" Colonial experience money can buy.

The ground floor of the PECO Energy Center, next to Independence and Congress Halls on Chestnut Street, has been transformed into a group ticketing and holding area. Try to arrive at dusk, especially with kids, since there's a maximum of 50 per tour and it's first-come, first-served. You'll pick up headsets automatically tuned to a script read by such actors as Ossie Davis and Charlton

Heston, and which are triggered automatically as your group arrives at the planned Park destinations. Younger children might prefer the alternative kids' headsets.

Led by a guide, you'll walk across the moonlit cobblestone streets to Park sites, where the Revolutionary story is compressed into five acts. Rifles crackle, cannons boom, and the founders of America argue with actual quotes interwoven into the script. They're backed with choral music and a soundtrack performed by members of the Philadelphia Orchestra. The visuals are somewhere between shadow-box projections and animation, with superb color and resolution. The finale of 1776 takes place right in back of Independence Hall, and it's irresistibly thrilling.

1-hr. tour shows depart from PECO Energy Center, 6th and Chestnut sts. ⓒ 877/462-1776 or 215/LIBERTY. www.lightsofliberty.org. Admission $18 adults, $16 seniors, $12 children 6–12; family pack (2 adults, 2 children) $50. AAA discount of 10%. Up to 6 shows per hour. Tues–Sat dusk–11:15pm Apr–Oct. Shows available in Chinese, French, German, Italian, Japanese, and Spanish, as well as English; Hebrew, and Russian available in print versions. SEPTA: Market East. Bus: PHLASH, 21, or 42.

2 The Top Museums

Barnes Foundation ★★★ *(Finds* The magnificent Barnes Foundation, just outside the city limits in suburban Merion, will enchant you. Albert Barnes crammed his French provincial mansion, built around 1925, with more than 1,000 masterpieces—180 Renoirs, 69 Cézannes, innumerable Impressionists and post-Impressionists, and a generous sampling of European art from the Italian primitives onward. Each wall is filled with masterpieces, hung, literally, from floor to ceiling. The Barnes reopened in November 1995 after a world tour of more than 80 masterworks from the collection and a $12-million renovation of the galleries.

Barnes believed that art has a quality that can be explained objectively—for example, one curve will be beautiful and hence art, and another that's slightly different will not be art. That's why the galleries display antique door latches, keyholes, keys, and household tools with strong geometric lines right next to the paintings. Connections beg to be drawn between neighboring objects—an unusual van Gogh nude, an Amish chest, New Mexico rural icons. Virtually every first-rank European artist is included: Degas, Seurat, Bosch, Tintoretto, Lorrain, Chardin, Daumier, Delacroix, Corot, and more. Not a bad use of a fortune made from patent medicine!

The bad news is that the Barnes organization is rife with lawsuits, and due to complaints of "not in my backyard" neighbors who object to crowds, visiting hours are extremely limited and require reservations far in advance. Summer hours in July and August are Wednesday through Friday; in other months, the museum is open Friday through Sunday. In fall 2002, the Trustees filed court papers to move the museum to a new downtown home on Benjamin Franklin Parkway, against the wishes of Dr. Barnes; this has brought a raft of new controversy, though many Philadelphians would love to see the collection in a more accessible venue near other top museums. The historic building could then remain as an educational facility. Stay tuned, and call well ahead of your anticipated visit for reservations.

300 N. Latch's Lane, Merion Station. ⓒ 610/667-0290. Fax 610/667-8315 for reservations, or e-mail reserve@barnesfoundation.org. www.barnesfoundation.org. Admission $5 per person, but reservations at least a month in advance are essential. Sept–June Fri–Sun 9:30am–5pm; July–Aug Wed–Fri 9:30am–5pm. On-site parking $10. SEPTA: Take Paoli local train R5 to Merion Station; walk up Merion Rd. and turn left onto Latch's Lane. Bus: 44 to Old Lancaster Rd. and Latches Lane. Car: I-76 (Schuylkill Expwy.) west to City Line

Ave. (Rte. 1), then south on City Line 1½ miles to Old Lancaster Rd. Turn right onto Old Lancaster, continue 4 blocks, and turn left onto Latch's Lane.

Philadelphia Museum of Art ★★★   Even on a hazy day you can see America's third-largest art museum from City Hall—a resplendent, huge, beautifully proportioned Greco-Roman temple on a hill. Because the museum, established in the 1870s, has relied on donors of great wealth and idiosyncratic taste, the collection does not aim to present a comprehensive picture of Western or Eastern art. But its strengths are dazzling: It houses undoubtedly one of the finest groupings of art objects in America, and no visit to Philadelphia would be complete without at least a walk-through; allow 2 hours minimum. Late hours on Friday have become a city favorite, and there is a new bar open in summer in the elegant front courtyard overlooking the city skyline.

The museum is designed simply, with L-shaped wings off the central court on two stories. A major rearrangement of the collections was recently completed, and paintings, sculptures, and decorative arts are grouped within set periods. The front entrance (facing City Hall) admits you to the first floor. Special exhibition galleries and American art are to the left; the collection emphasizes that Americans came from diverse cultures, which combined to create a new, distinctly national aesthetic. French- and English-inspired domestic objects, such as silver, predominate in the Colonial and Federal galleries, but don't neglect the fine rooms of Amish and sturdy Shaker crafts. The 19th-century gallery has many works by Philadelphia's Thomas Eakins, which evoke the spirit of the city in watercolors and oils.

Originally controversial 19th- and 20th-century European and contemporary art galleries highlight Cézanne's monumental *Bathers* and Marcel Duchamp's *Nude Descending a Staircase,* which doesn't seem nearly as revolutionary as it did in 1913. The recent gift of the McIlhenny $300-million collection of paintings is one of the great donations of this type and adds strength in the French Impressionist area.

Upstairs, spread over 83 galleries, is a chronological sweep of European arts from medieval times through about 1850. The John G. Johnson Collection, a Renaissance treasure trove, has been added to the museum's holdings. Roger van der Weyden's diptych *Virgin and Saint John* and *Christ on the Cross,* one of the Johnson Collection, is renowned for its exquisite sorrow and beauty. Another, Van Eyck's *Saint Francis Receiving the Stigmata,* is unbelievably precise (borrow the guard's magnifying glass). Other masterpieces include Poussin's frothy *Birth of Venus* (the USSR sold this and numerous other canvases in the early 1930s, and many were snapped up by American collectors) and Rubens's sprawling *Prometheus Bound.* The remainder of the floor takes you far away—to medieval Europe, 17th-century battlefields, Enlightenment salons, and Eastern temples.

The museum has excellent dining facilities. A cafe, open Tuesday through Sunday from 10am to 4:30pm, dispenses simple and reasonable lunches and salads. The museum restaurant down the hall is open Tuesday through Saturday from 11:30am to 2:30pm, Sunday from 11am to 3:30pm. All main courses are under $20. There's also a lovely little Balcony Café just up the stairs as you enter the museum, for espresso, soups, sandwiches, and pastries.

The PMA has brought millions into the economy over the past decade with blockbuster exhibits of works by Picasso, Cézanne, van Gogh, and Degas, plus mounted wonderful fashion exhibits of Schiaparelli. The Museum recently acquired a massive Art Deco former insurance headquarters a block away, though they are not sure what they will feature here.

Ben Franklin Lives! An Interview With Ralph Archbold

You didn't just hallucinate Ben Franklin eating a cheesesteak in Independence Square Park. Philadelphia's official Ben Franklin, Ralph Archbold, performs frequently at museums and attractions throughout the city—and even Ben needs to eat between gigs. Archbold has been featured in various television specials, including a 2004 History Channel bio that touted Franklin as an "ambassador, scientist, and ladies man." He was also appointed by the president and Congress to a 15-member federal commission to oversee the celebration of Franklin's 300th birthday (Jan 17, 2006), still in the works as we go to print (see **www.benfranklin 300.org** for details). We caught up with Archbold to ask about his career and the man he portrays.

Frommer's: How did you start performing as Ben Franklin?

Ralph Archbold: I started performing at historic Greenfield Village in Dearborn Michigan in 1973. (That is the village that Henry Ford started.) I came to Philadelphia in 1981 and have been performing here ever since.

F: What's the best part of playing Franklin?

RA: I love the variety of audiences I perform for and the affection people seem to have for Mr. Franklin. The presentations I do are in storytelling form and I love telling stories.

F: What's the most challenging?

RA: Trying to fit in all the requests for my services as Ben is my biggest challenge. I love performing and the demand is great. I especially love interacting with the visitors in Independence National Historical Park during the summer.

F: What's your favorite of Franklin's proverbs?

RA: "A true friend is the best possession" is one of my favorites. I really love them all.

F: Why do you think Ben Franklin appeals to children so much?

RA: I think he appeals to the childlike enthusiasm and excitement in people of all ages and with his variety of inventions and adventures he is an inspiration to us all.

F: What's the most common misconception about Franklin?

RA: That he fathered a lot of children. He was the father of three: William, Sarah, and Francis.

F: Can you explain in your own words the "ladies man" connection? How much of a romancer was Franklin, and did his affairs end once he got married?

RA: Most of the ladies man reputation came when Ben was in France and his wife had died 2 years earlier. As far as we know there is no proof he cheated on his wife. His son William, born around the time he and Deborah Read became man and wife Sept. 1, 1730, was illegitimate.

F: What were some of Ben Franklin's flaws? Did he have any?

RA: He always said he was accused of lacking Humility but if he were able to conquer it he would be so proud.

F: Of all the museums and bridges and other Franklin tributes through-out the city, which one does the best job of conveying his character and spirit?

RA: It would be impossible to pick any one historic site in Philadelphia that does the "best" job of conveying the Franklin spirit and character. That is why if visitors want the complete picture they need to stay several days and visit the Independence Visitor Center (p. 121), Franklin Court (p. 126), the Franklin Institute (p. 132), the Lights of Liberty Show (p. 127), the National Constitution Center (p. 126), Independence Hall (p. 124), Fireman's Hall (p. 173), Pennsylvania Hospital (p. 140), and all the streets and buildings among the many places Franklin worked and walked.

F: What would Franklin think of these tributes?

RA: The variety and number of statues and locations talking about him would amaze him.

F: What would Franklin think of the current political landscape? Would he identify with any particular politicians today? Do you see any "heirs to Ben Franklin"?

RA: Ben would be fascinated how our nation and our government have grown. He would perhaps be pleased that we have lasted this long. Remember, as he remarked when asked what sort of government we had been given, he replied, "a republic, if you can keep it."

I don't think he would identify with any one particular politician but perhaps a composite of a number of those to whom we have entrusted our government.

As to "heirs," we all are heirs to the values, the courage, and the integrity our founders left to a nation with the hope that each of us would treasure freedom and work to maintain America as a symbol of freedom and a beacon of hope to the world.

F: Where's the single best spot to get a glimpse of "Old Philadelphia"?

RA: If you want the true flavor of a neighborhood, visit Elfreth's Alley (p. 140). If you want the feel of the beginning of our nation, walk the area around Independence Hall, Congress Hall, and Old City Hall.

F: What's your favorite bar or pub in the city?

RA: While I have many places I love I don't think anyone should miss the City Tavern (p. 171), at 2nd and Walnut, which no less a figure than John Adams proclaimed "the most genteel tavern in America."

F: Where can visitors expect to see you perform?

RA: I perform at the Franklin Institute (p. 132) for special occasions. You can find me more easily in the area of Franklin Court (p. 126) where his former home was located. There is a wonderful courtyard, print shop, and museum there, and no one should miss it.

26th St. and Ben Franklin Pkwy. ℂ **215/763-8100**, or 215/684-7500 for 24-hr. information. www.phila museum.org. Admission $10 adults; $7 students, seniors, and children 12–18; free for children under 12; pay-what-you-wish Sun. Tues–Sun 10am–5pm; Fri evening hours to 8:45pm with music, talks, movies, and social-izing. Bus: 7, 32, 38, 43, or 48. Car: From the parkway headed west (away from City Hall), follow signs to Kelly Dr. and turn left at the first light at 25th St. to the lots at the rear entrance. Plentiful parking, free Tues–Fri, $5 Sat–Sun.

Pennsylvania Academy of the Fine Arts ★★ Located 2 blocks north of City Hall is the Pennsylvania Academy of the Fine Arts (PAFA), a wonderful museum and teaching facility that was the first art school in the country (1805) and at one time the unquestioned leader of American Beaux Arts. After a major renovation in late 1994, the academy, housed in a stunning Frank Furness build-ing, unveiled a major reinstallation of 300 works from the past 200 years; another 2004–2005 restoration effort is brightening the jewel tones of the gor-geous, hand-painted decorative ceilings and the overall look of the landmark museum and school.

The ground floor houses an excellent bookstore, a cafe, and the academy's offices. A splendid staircase, designed by Furness, shines with red, gold, and blue. Each May the annual academy school exhibition takes over the museum. The school itself moved to 1301 Cherry St. years ago, but has acquired and is renovating the factory building to its north to recentralize operations.

As is evident from the PAFA galleries, such early American painters as Gilbert Stuart, the Peale family, and Washington Allston congregated in Philadelphia, America's capital and wealthiest city. The main galleries feature works from the museum's collection of more than 6,000 canvases. The rotunda has been the scene of cultural events ever since Walt Whitman listened to concerts here. The adjoining rooms display works from the illustrious mid-19th-century years, when PAFA enjoyed its most innovative period.

118 N. Broad St. at Cherry St. ℂ **215/972-7600**. www.pafa.org. Admission $7 adults, $6 seniors and stu-dents with ID, $5 children 5–18. Tues–Sat 10am–5pm; Sun 11am–5pm. Special exhibition rates may apply. Bus: 48.

Franklin Institute Science Museum ★★★ (*Kids*) The Franklin Institute Sci-ence Museum isn't just kid stuff. All ages love it because it's a thoroughly imag-inative trip through the worlds of science that demonstrates the influence of science in our lives. The complex has four parts. The first is the home of the Franklin National Memorial, with a 30-ton statue of its namesake and a collec-tion of authentic Franklin artifacts and possessions.

The second part is a collection of science- and technology-oriented exhibition areas, with innovative hands-on displays such as the recent "Titanic" show, from a gigantic walk-through heart (beloved by Philadelphians, and just restored after years of climbing and exploration by curious children) to the Train Factory, an interactive setting where you can play engineer for a 350-ton locomotive. For a hair-raising experience, plug into a Van de Graaff generator at the lightning gallery. On the third floor, an energy hall bursts with Rube Goldberg contrap-tions, noisemakers, and light shows. The nearby Discovery Theater gives after-noon shows featuring liquid air and other oddities. The fourth floor specializes in astronomy and mathematical puzzles. The basement **Fels Planetarium** (ℂ **215/563-1363**), just renovated and accompanied by the new "space station" on the first floor, rounds out the offering here.

The third part of the Franklin Institute is the result of an ambitious 1991 campaign, funded by $22 million from the city and state, and $36 million from private donors, to construct the **Mandell Futures Center** addition. Just past the

Franklin National Memorial on the second floor, you'll enter an atrium with cafes, ticket counters, and ramps and stairs leading to the new exhibits. Just beyond is a separate-admission IMAX arena, showing films ranging from undersea explorations to the Rolling Stones in spectacular 70mm format. Eight permanent interactive exhibits, including space, earth, computers, chemistry, and health, take you into the 21st century with Disney World–style pizazz. My personal favorites are "The Sports Challenge," an exploration of the science behind popular sports like surfing and rock climbing, a video driving exercise in "Future Vision," "The Jamming Room" of musical synthesizers, and the "See Yourself Age" computer program in "Future and You." The texts throughout are witty and disarming. Quite thrilling is the **Skybike,** which you can ride along a 1 inch cable three stories above the Bartol Atrium floor and its huge new sci-store.

The fourth section is the 1995 **CoreStates Science Park,** a collaboration with the Please Touch Museum. It uses the 38,000-square-foot lawn between the two museums—it's free with admission to the museum. The imaginative urban garden is filled with high-tech play structures, including a high-wire tandem bicycle, 12-foot tire, step-on organ, maze, and optical illusions.

Of course, you'll eventually get hungry—with a family, the institute is a full afternoon. Your choices are excellent: a vending-machine space in the **Wawa Lunchroom** on the first floor, open only to museum-goers; the all-American-with-a-nutritional-twist **Ben's Garden Cafe** on the second floor, accessible without museum admission, and open Monday through Friday from 8:30am to 2:30pm and Saturday and Sunday from 9am to 3:30pm; and the **Snack-A-Rama** in the Mandell Center lobby, open daily from 11am to shortly before museum closing, serving beer and wine. Vendors outside sell Philadelphia soft pretzels with plenty of mustard.

Note: Watch for special events at the Franklin Institute on and around Ben Franklin's 300th birthday, Jan 17, 2006. Citywide events are still in the works as we go to print. See **www.benfranklin300.org** for details.

Logan Circle, 20th St. and Benjamin Franklin Pkwy. ✆ **215/448-1200.** www.fi.edu. Basic admission to exhibitions, Fels Planetarium, and 3-D Theater $13 adults, $10 children; with IMAX Theater included, $17 adults, $14 children. Daily 9:30am–5pm, IMAX only open until 9pm Fri–Sat. CoreStates Science Park May–Oct daily 10am–4pm. Bus: 33 or PHLASH.

3 More Attractions

Reading Terminal Market (p. 104) is an attraction in itself, as is the **Italian Market** (p. 118) if you're exploring South Philadelphia.

ARCHITECTURAL HIGHLIGHTS

Benjamin Franklin Bridge 🎯 Great cities have signature bridges, and this is Philadelphia's. The Benjamin Franklin Bridge, designed by Paul Cret (one of the architects of the Parkway across town) was the largest single-span suspension bridge in the world (1¾ miles) when it was finished in 1926. The bridge carries cars and commuter trains and also has a foot/bicycle path along its south side, more reachable than ever since Independence Mall has been expanded to the edge of the bridge. For the bicentennial of the U.S. Constitution, a Philadelphia team including Steven Izenour, a leading American architect and planner, created a computer-driven system for illuminating each and every cable. At night, Philadelphians are treated to the largest lighting effects show since Ben Franklin's kite.

Entrance to free bicycle/pedestrian walkway at 5th and Vine sts. 6am–dusk. Bus: 50.

City Hall 🔎   When construction of City Hall began in 1871, it was planned to be the tallest structure in the world. But plans were scaled back, other buildings surpassed it, and the elaborate 1901 wedding cake by John McArthur, Jr., with an inner courtyard straight out of a French château, quickly became outdated. The charming building is still in use as the mayor's office and is home to offices from the Register of Wills to city courtrooms to City Council's quarters. Philadelphians love the crowning 37-foot statue of William Penn by A. M.

Mural, Mural, On the Wall

Philadelphia's Mural Arts Program (MAP) was established in 1984 and has since completed more than 2,400 murals throughout the city—indoors and outdoors, on buildings, schools, houses, and other structures. The MAP says it works "to help beautify the city; help create a sense of community; and turn graffiti-scarred walls into scenic views, portraits of community heroes, and abstract creations."

The murals can be quite striking, from the poignant (*Underground Railroad*, by Sam Donovan, at 908 Chestnut St.) to the psychedelic (*Larry Fine*, by David McShane, at 3rd St. and South) to the postmodern (*Symbolic Building of a City*, by Michael Webb, at 17th St. and Arch). They range in size from small one-story designs (*Fringe Festival*, by Tom Judd, at 35 N. 2nd St.) to eight-story projects (*Common Threads*, by Meg Fish Saligman, at Broad St. and Spring Garden), each take about 2 months to complete, and cost about $10-15,000 to commission and produce.

Here are a few more of our favorite murals in the city. You can find an online gallery, with walking tour suggestions, plus listings of the MAP's excellent children's outreach programs at their website, **www. muralarts.org**. You can find a comprehensive database with maps at **muralBase** (www.cml.upenn.edu/murals).

Children of Philadelphia, by Burt Dodge, at 16th Street and Fitzwater, depicts children with a preacher, with the city as a backdrop.

Goldfish, by David Sanner, in West Philly at 45th Street and Chestnut, looks like a koi pond that got way out of hand.

Frank Sinatra, by Diane Keller, at Broad Street and Wharton, is a woozy, blue-toned portrait of the Chairman of the Board.

Untitled, by Keith Haring, at 22nd Street and Ellsworth, features the artist's iconic colorful figures, which brighten the side of an aging building.

Peace Wall, by Jane Golden and Peter Pagast, at 29th Street and Wharton, is a famous mural of overlapping children's hands.

Pride and Progress, by Ann Northrup, in the Gayborhood at 13th Street and Spruce, is a large, elaborate tribute to the gay community.

Philadelphia on a Half Tank, by Paul Santoleri, near the airport at 26th Street and Passyunk Avenue, is a vivid pastel portrait of the city on the side of an oil tank.

Calder. For years the structure appeared rather rusty and grimy, but now, with repainting, new cast iron work, and cleaning, City Hall has reclaimed its pride.

You may wish to wander inside the vast floors, which range from the breath-taking to the bureaucratically forlorn. Both inside and out, City Hall boasts rich sculptural decoration. The Mayor's Reception Room (no. 202) and the City Council Chamber (no. 400) are especially ornate.

The highlight of City Hall is the **tower view.** The Juniper Street entrance is most convenient, but you can take any corner elevator to the seventh floor and follow the red tape (always indicative of city government). In this case, it leads to two escalators and a waiting area for the tower elevator. The elevator up to Penn statue's recently cleaned shoestrings, at 548 feet, can hold only eight peo-ple, and the outdoor cupola cannot hold many more. On the way, notice how thick the walls are—City Hall is the tallest building ever constructed without a skeleton of steel girders, so that its white stone is 6 feet thick at the top and 22 feet thick at ground level. The view from the top encompasses not only the city but also the upper and lower Delaware Valley and port, western New Jersey, and suburban Philadelphia. It's windy up there, though. If you look straight down, you can see more of the hundreds of sculptures designed by Calder, the works of whose descendants—Alexander Stirling Calder (1870–1945) and Alexander Calder (1898–1976)—beautify Logan Circle and the Philadelphia Museum of Art. You could spend hours, although 45 minutes should do it for the highlights.

Broad and Market sts. ℂ 215/686-2840. Free admission. Tower tours weekdays 9:30am–4:30pm. During school year, Mon–Fri 10am–noon reserved for school groups. Last tour at 2:45pm. Interior tours daily from the East Portal courtyard at 12:30pm. Bus/Subway: Most lines converge beside or underneath the building.

Fisher Fine Arts (Furness) Library   Like the Pennsylvania Academy of the Fine Arts building (see above), this citadel of learning has the characteristic chis-eled thistle of Frank Furness, although it was built a decade later from 1888 to 1890. The use of 1890s leaded glass here is even richer than on the Pennsylva-nia Academy of Fine Arts building. Originally the University's library, the build-ing now houses, appropriately, the fine arts library of the University of Pennsylvania. It's best viewed in a quick look while on the U. Penn quadrangle.

220 S. 34th St. (at Locust Walk on the U. Penn campus). ℂ 215/898-8325. Free admission. During academic year Mon–Fri 9am–10pm; summer hours Mon–Fri 9am–5pm. Bus: 44.

Pennsylvania Convention Center ℱ   With the July 1993 opening of the Pennsylvania Convention Center (PCC), Philadelphia made it clear that the future of the area depends on its ability to welcome tens of thousands of visitors weekly. The statistics are staggering: With 440,000 square feet of exhibit space, the center is larger than 30th Street Station. But what's really great about the $522-million Convention Center is how solid and elegant it is, and how nicely it fits in with its surroundings. Architects Thompson, Ventulett, Stainback & Associates shoehorned blocks of brick and limestone between I-76 in the back and Market Street in the front. Though the building is enormous, there is talk of expanding it so that it can host larger groups, and there have been problem-atic labor disputes with local unions who work the Center and set up for shows and meetings.

Unless you're one of the millions the PCC hopes to lure in for a meeting, you'll need to take the public tour for a peek inside, though a walkway between wings of the adjoining Marriott does overlook a section. The highlight is a stu-pendous Grand Hall on the second level, evoking the train shed and headhouse of the Reading Terminal, which was the first incarnation of this building. Gray and black Mexican marble alternates with waterfalls, steel, and terrazzo, plus huge granite pylons for heating and cooling the mammoth space. Judy Pfaff's vast, kaleidoscopic *Cirque* extends airy steel and aluminum tubes over 70,000 square feet of space. Esplanades and corridors contain a veritable museum of 52 living artists (35 from Philadelphia) in one of the most successful public art projects of our time. In 1995, the Market Street entrance, the original Reading Railroad facade, was restored, with an escalator up to the Train Shed. The Marriott next door has a skywalk into the Great Hall. The 37-foot rotating electric guitar, tucked into the southwest corner outside, signals the popular Hard Rock Cafe. If you don't want to dine at Hard Rock, head for the beers and burgers of the Independence Brew Pub. And don't forget that Reading Terminal Market is downstairs.

Between 11th and 13th sts. and Market and Race sts. ℂ 215/418-4700. www.paconvention.com. Public tours by arrangement with the sales office. Enter at the northwest corner of 12th and Arch sts. Subway: Rail lines (including Airport Express) stop at Market East Station; SEPTA at 11th and Market and 13th and Market. Bus: 12, 17, 33, 44, or PHLASH. Car: Separate exit from I-676, between I-95 and I-76.

CEMETERIES

Christ Church Burial Ground   This 1719 expansion of the original graveyard of Christ Church (see below) contains the graves of Benjamin Franklin and his wife, Deborah, along with those of four other signers of the Declaration of Independence and many Revolutionary War heroes. There are always pennies on Ben's grave; tossing them there is a local tradition that is supposed to bring good luck.

5th and Arch sts. ℂ 215/922-1695. Closed to the public. Bus: 48, 50, or PHLASH.

Laurel Hill Cemetery ⭐ (Finds   How come you find Benjamin Franklin buried in a small, flat plot next to a church (see above), while Civil War General George Meade is buried in a bucolic meadow? Basically, the view of death and contemplation of nature changed as the 19th-century Romantic movement grew, and Laurel Hill reflects that romanticism. Laurel Hill, designated a National Historic Landmark in 1998, was the second American cemetery (after Mount Auburn in Cambridge) to use funerary monuments—some are like small Victorian palaces. Set amid the rolling, landscaped hills overlooking the Schuylkill, its 100 acres also house plenty of tomb sculpture, pre-Raphaelite stained glass, and Art Nouveau sarcophagi. People picnicked here a century ago, but only walking is allowed now.

3822 Ridge Ave., East Fairmount Park. ℂ 215/228-8200. Entrance may be restricted, since it's still in use as a private institution. Grounds open Mon–Fri 8am–4pm; Sat 9:30am–1:30pm. The Friends of Laurel Hill arranges tours (ℂ 215/228-8817); $10 donation per person. Bus: 61. Car: Go north on East River Dr., make a right on Ferry Rd., go 1 block to Ridge Ave., and turn right. The entrance is a half-mile down on the right. Free parking.

Mikveh Israel Cemetery   Philadelphia was an early center of American Jewish life, with the second-oldest synagogue (1740) organized by English and Sephardic Jews. While this congregation shifted location and is now adjacent to the Liberty Bell, the original cemetery—well outside the city at the time—was bought from the Penn family by Nathan Levy and later filled with the likes of Haym Solomon, a Polish immigrant who helped finance the revolutionary government, and Rebecca Gratz, the daughter of a fine local family, who provided the model for Sir Walter Scott's Rebecca in *Ivanhoe*.

Spruce St. between 8th and 9th sts. ℂ 215/922-5446 (synagogue number). Summer Sun–Thurs 10am–3pm; off season, contact synagogue or park service. Bus: 47 or 9.

CHURCHES

Arch Street Meeting House   This plain brick building dates from 1804, but William Penn gave the land to his Religious Society of Friends in 1693. In this capital city of Quakers, the Meeting House opens its doors to 12,000 local Friends for worship during the last week in March each year. Quakers believe in direct, unmediated guidance by the Holy Spirit; individuals publicly search their souls during "threshing sessions" in a spartan chamber with no pulpit, only hand-hewn benches that face one another. Other areas of the Meeting House display Bibles, clothing, and implements of Quaker life past and present, along with a simple history of the growth of the religion and the life of William Penn.

4th and Arch sts. © 215/627-2667. Suggested donation $2. Guided tours year-round Mon–Sat 10am–4pm. Services Wed 7pm and Sun 10:30am. Bus: 17, 33, 48, 50, or PHLASH.

Christ Church ★★ *Moments*   The most beautiful Colonial building north of Market Street has to be Christ Church (1727–54). Its spire gleams white from anywhere in the neighborhood, now that a grassy park and a subway stop have replaced the buildings to the south. The churchyard has benches, tucked under trees or beside brick walls.

Christ Church, dating from the apex of English Palladianism, follows the proud and graceful tradition of Christopher Wren's churches in London. As in many of them, the interior spans one large arch, with galleries above the sides as demanded by the Anglican church. Behind the altar, the massive Palladian window—a central columned arch flanked by proportional rectangles of glass—was the wonder of worshipers and probably the model for the one in Independence Hall. The main chandelier was brought over from England in 1744. As in King's Chapel in Boston, seating is by pew instead of on open benches—Washington's seat is marked with a plaque.

With all the stones, memorials, and plaques, it's impossible to ignore history here. William Penn was baptized at the font, sent over from All Hallows' Church in London. Penn left the Anglican church at age 23 (he spent most of his 20s in English jails because of it), but his charter included a clause that an Anglican church could be founded if 20 residents requested it, which they did. Socially conscious Philadelphians of the next generations adopted Anglicanism, then switched to Episcopalianism after the Revolution.

2nd St. ½ block north of Market St. © 215/922-1695. Donations welcome. Mon–Sat 9am–5pm; Sun 1–5pm. Sun services at 9am and 11am, Mon–Fri 8am, Wed noon. Closed Mon–Tues in Jan–Feb. Bus: 5, 17, 33, 48, or PHLASH.

Gloria Dei (Old Swedes' Church) *Finds*   The National Park Service administers this church, the oldest in Pennsylvania (1700). Inside the enclosing walls, you'll think you're in the 18th century, with a miniature parish hall, a rectory, and a graveyard amid the greenery. The one-room museum directly across from the church has a map of the good old days. The simple church interior has plenty of wonderful details. Everybody loves the ship models suspended from the ceiling: The *Key of Kalmar* and *Flying Griffin* carried the first Swedish settlers to these shores in 1638. And note the silver crown in the vestry; any woman married here wears it during the ceremony.

916 Swanson St., near Christian and Delaware aves. © 215/389-1513. Apr–Oct daily 9am–5pm; by appointment in the off season. Bus: 5, 64, or 79. By foot or car: Take Swanson St. under I-95 at Christian St. in Queen Village, opposite Pier 34, then turn onto Water St.

Mother Bethel African Methodist Episcopal Church   This National Historic Landmark site is the oldest piece of land continuously owned by blacks in the United States. Richard Allen, born in 1760, was a slave in Germantown who bought his freedom in 1782, eventually walking out of St. George's down the street to found the African Methodist Episcopal order. The order today numbers some 2.5 million in 6,200 congregations, and this handsome, varnished-wood-and-stained-glass 1890 building is their mother church. Allen's tomb and a small museum, featuring his Bible and hand-hewn pulpit, are downstairs; open by appointment only.

419 S. 6th St. ✆ **215/925-0616.** Donations welcome. Tues–Sat 10am–3pm; Sun noon–1pm. Sun services 8am and 10:45am.

Old St. Joseph's Church *(Finds)*   When it was founded in 1733, St. Joseph's was the only place in the English-speaking world where Roman Catholics could celebrate Mass publicly. The story goes that Benjamin Franklin advised Father Greaton to protect the church, since religious bigotry wasn't unknown even in the Quaker city. That's why the building is so unassuming from the street, a fact that didn't save it from damage during the anti-Catholic riots of the 1830s. Such French allies as Lafayette worshiped here. The present interior (1838, and renovated in 1985 to its late-19th-century appearance) is Greek Revival merging into Victorian, with wooden pews and such unusual colors as mustard and pale yellow. The interior has also preserved a Colonial style unusual in a Catholic church.

321 Willings Alley, near 4th and Walnut sts. ✆ **215/923-1733.** Mon–Fri 11am–3pm; Sat 11am–6:30pm; Sun 8:30am–3pm. Masses are held weekdays at 11:30am, Sat 11:30am and 5:30pm, and Sun 7:30am, 9:30am, and 11:30am.

St. Peter's Episcopal   St. Peter's (1761) was originally established through the bishop of London, and has remained continuously open since. Like all pre-Revolutionary Episcopal churches, St. Peter's started out as an Anglican shrine. But what was wrong with Christ Church at 2nd and Market? In a word: mud. As a local historian put it, "the long tramp from Society Hill was more and more distasteful to fine gentlemen and beautiful belles."

Robert Smith, the builder of Carpenters' Hall, continued his penchant for red brick, pediments on ends of buildings, and keystoned arches for gallery windows. The white box pews are evidence that not much has changed. Unlike most churches, the wineglass pulpit in St. Peter's is set into the west end and the chancel is at the east, so the minister had to do some walking during the service. George Washington and Mayor Samuel Powel sat in pew 41. The 1764 organ case blocks the east Palladian window. The steeple outside, constructed in 1842, was designed by William Strickland to house bells, which are still played.

Seven Native American chiefs lie in the graveyard, victims of the 1793 smallpox epidemic. Painter C. W. Peale, Stephen Decatur of naval fame, Nicholas Biddle of the Second Bank of the United States, and other notables are also interred here.

3rd and Pine sts. ✆ **215/925-5968.** Mon–Fri 9am–4pm; Sat 11am–3pm; Sun 1–3pm. Services Sun 9am and 11am. Bus: 50, 90, or PHLASH.

HISTORIC BUILDINGS & MONUMENTS

Betsy Ross House *(Kids)*   One Colonial home everybody knows about is this one near Christ Church, restored in 1937, and distinguished by the Stars and Stripes outside. Elizabeth (Betsy) Ross was a Quaker needlewoman who, newly widowed in 1776, worked as a seamstress and upholsterer out of her home on Arch Street. Nobody is quite sure if no. 239 was hers, though. And nobody knows for sure if she did the original American flag of 13 stars set in a field of

13 red-and-white stripes, but she was commissioned to sew ships' flags for the American fleet to replace the earlier Continental banners.

The tiny house takes only a minute or two to walk through. The house is set back from the street, and the city maintains the Atwater Kent Park in front, where Ross and her last husband are buried. The upholstery shop (now a gift shop renovated in 1998) opens into the period parlor. Other rooms include the cellar kitchen (standard placement for this room), tiny bedrooms, and model working areas for upholstering, making musket balls, and the like. Note such little touches as reusable note tablets made of ivory; pine cones used to help start hearth fires; and the prominent kitchen hourglass. Flag Day celebrations are held here on June 14 (see "Philadelphia Calendar of Events," p. 15).

239 Arch St. ✆ 215/686-1252. www.betsyrosshouse.org. Suggested contribution $3 adults, $2 children. Apr–Oct daily 10am–5pm; Oct–Mar Tues–Sun 10am–5pm. Bus: 5, 17, 33, 48, or PHLASH.

Carpenters' Hall ★★ Carpenters' Hall (1773) was the guildhall for—guess who?—carpenters. At the time, the city could use plenty of carpenters, since 18th-century Philadelphia was the fastest-growing urban area in all the Colonies and perhaps in the British Empire outside of London. Robert Smith, a Scottish member of the Carpenters' Company, designed the building (like most carpenters, he did architecture and contracting as well). He also designed the steeple of Christ Church, with the same calm Georgian lines. The edifice is made of Flemish Bond brick in a checkerboard pattern, with stone windowsills, superb woodwork, and a cupola that resembles a saltshaker.

You'll be surprised at how small Carpenters' Hall is given the great events that transpired here. In 1774, the normal governmental channels to convey Colonial complaints to the Crown were felt inadequate, and a popular Committee of Correspondence debated in Carpenters' Hall. The more radical delegates, led by Patrick Henry, had already expressed treasonous wishes for independence, but most wanted to exhaust possibilities of bettering their relationship with the Crown first.

What's here now isn't much—an exhibit of Colonial building methods; some portraits; and Windsor chairs that seated the First Continental Congress. If some details seem to be from a later period, you're right: The fanlights above the north and south doors date from the 1790s, and the gilding dates from 1857. Hours are short because the Carpenters' Company still maintains the hall.

320 Chestnut St. ✆ 215/925-0167. www.carpentershall.org. Free admission. Mar–Dec Tues–Sun 10am–4pm; Jan–Feb Wed–Sun 10am–4pm. Bus: 9, 21, 42, or PHLASH.

Declaration House (Graff House) ★ Bricklayer Jacob Graff constructed a modest three-story home in the 1770s, intending to rent out the second floor for added income. The Second Continental Congress soon brought to the house a thin, red-haired tenant named Thomas Jefferson, in search of a quiet room away from city noise. He must have found it, because he drafted the Declaration of Independence here between June 10 and June 18, 1776.

The 1975 reconstruction used the same Flemish Bond brick checkerboard pattern (only on visible walls), windows with paneled shutters, and knickknacks that would have been around the house in 1775. Compared to Society Hill homes, it's tiny and asymmetrical, with an off-center front door. You'll enter through a small garden and see a short film about Jefferson and a copy of Jefferson's draft (which would have forbidden slavery in the United States had that clause survived debate). The upstairs rooms are furnished as they would have been in Jefferson's time.

7th and Market sts. 𝒞 **215/965-2305.** Free admission (part of Independence National Historical Park). Daily 9am–5pm in summer; daily 10am–1pm off season. Bus: 17, 33, 48, or PHLASH.

Elfreth's Alley 👁👁   The modern Benjamin Franklin Bridge shadows Elfreth's Alley, the oldest continuously inhabited street in America. Most of Colonial Philadelphia looked like this: cobblestone lanes between the major thorough-fares; small two-story homes; and pent eaves over doors and windows, a local trademark. Note the busybody mirrors that let residents see who was at their door (or someone else's) from the second-story bedroom. In 1700, most of the resident artisans and tradesmen worked in shipping, but 50 years later haber-dashers, bakers, printers, and house carpenters set up shop. Families moved in and out rapidly, for noisy, dusty 2nd Street was the major north-south route in Philadelphia. Jews, blacks, Welsh, and Germans made it a miniature melting pot in the 18th and 19th centuries. The destruction of the street was prevented in 1937, thanks to the vigilant Elfreth's Alley Association and a good deal of luck. The minuscule, sober facades hide some ultramodern interiors, and there are some restful shady benches under a Kentucky Coffee Bean tree on Bladen Court, off the north side of the street.

Number 126, the 1755 **Mantua Maker's House** (cape maker), built by black-smith Jeremiah Elfreth, now serves as a museum. An 18th-century garden in back has been restored, and the interior includes a dressmaker's shop and upstairs bedroom. You can also buy Colonial candy and gifts and peek into some of the open windows on the street. On the first weekend in June all the houses are open for touring—don't miss this.

2nd St. between Arch and Race sts. 𝒞 **215/574-0560.** www.elfrethsalley.org. Street is public; Visitor Center and gift shop at no. 124 free admission; Mantua Maker's House at no. 126 admission: $2 adults, $1 children. Mar–Oct Mon–Sat 10am–5pm, Sun noon–5pm; Nov–Feb Thurs–Sat 10am–5pm, Sun noon–5pm. Bus: 5, 48, or PHLASH.

Masonic Temple   Quite apart from its Masonic lore, the temple—among the world's largest—is one of America's best on-site illustrations of the use of post–Civil War architecture and design—no expense was spared in the con-struction, and the halls are more or less frozen in time. There are seven lodge halls, designed to capture the seven "ideal" architectures: Renaissance, Ionic, Oriental, Corinthian, Gothic, Egyptian, and Norman (notice that Renaissance was the newest style that architect James Windrim could come up with!). This is the preeminent Masonic Temple of American Freemasonry; many of the Founding Fathers, including Washington, were Masons, and the museum has preserved their letters and emblems.

1 N. Broad St. 𝒞 **215/988-1917.** Free admission. Tours Mon–Fri 10am, 11am, 1pm, 2pm, and 3pm; Sat 10am and 11am. Bus: 17, 33, 44, or 48.

Pennsylvania Hospital   The original Pennsylvania Hospital, like so much in civic Philadelphia, owes its presence to Benjamin Franklin. This was the first hospital in the Colonies, and it seemed like a strange venture into social welfare at the time. Samuel Rhoads, a fine architect in the Carpenters' Company, designed the Georgian headquarters; the east wing, nearest 8th Street, was com-pleted in 1755, and a west wing matched it in 1797. The grand Center Build-ing by David Evans completed the ensemble in 1804. Instead of a dome, the hospital decided on a surgical amphitheater skylight. In spring, the garden's azal-eas brighten the neighborhood. The beautifully designed herb garden (high-lighting plants used as medicines in the 18th c.) is very popular.

Aesthetics aside, the hospital still functions quite well, and in 2003 *U.S. News & World Report* ranked it as one of the top ten hospitals in America.

8th and Spruce sts. ℂ **215/829-3720.** www.pennhealth.com/pahosp. Free admission. Mon–Fri 8:30am–4:30pm. Guided tours are no longer obligatory; copies of a walking tour itinerary available from the Marketing Department on the 2nd floor of the Pine St. building. Bus: 47 or 90.

Powel House ★★   If Elfreth's Alley (see above) leaves you hungry for a taste of more well-to-do Colonial Philadelphia, head for the Powel House. Mayor Samuel Powel and his wife, Elizabeth, hosted every founding father and foreign dignitary around. (John Adams called these feasts "sinful dinners," which shows how far Powel had come from his Quaker background.) He spent most of his 20s gallivanting around Europe, collecting wares for this 1765 mansion.

It's hard to believe that this most Georgian of houses was slated for demolition in 1930, because it had become a decrepit slum dwelling. Period rooms were removed to the Philadelphia Museum of Art and the Metropolitan Museum of Art in New York. But the Philadelphia Society for the Preservation of Landmarks saved it, and has gradually refurnished the entire mansion as it was. The yellow satin Reception Room, off the entrance hall, has some gorgeous details, such as a wide-grain mahogany secretary. Upstairs, the magnificent ballroom features red damask drapes whose design is copied from a bolt of cloth found untouched in a Colonial attic. There is also a 1790 Irish crystal chandelier and a letter from Benjamin Franklin's daughter referring to the lively dances held here. An 18th-century garden lies below.

244 S. 3rd St. ℂ **215/627-0364.** www.philalandmarks.org/powel. Admission $5 adults, $12 for a family. Guided tours only. Thurs–Sat noon–5pm; Sun 1–5pm. Be sure to arrive at least 30 min. before closing. Bus: 50 or 90.

LIBRARIES & LITERARY SITES

Athenaeum of Philadelphia *Finds*   A 15-minute peek into the Athenaeum will show you one of America's finest collections of Victorian-period architectural design and also give you the flavor of private 19th-century life for the proper Philadelphian. The building, beautifully restored in 1975, houses almost one million library items for the serious researcher in American architecture. Visitors are welcome to the changing exhibitions of rare books, drawings, and photographs in the recently reconstructed first-floor gallery; tours of the entire building or collections require an appointment.

219 S. 6th St. (Washington Sq. E.). ℂ **215/925-2688.** www.philaAthenaeum.org. Free admission. Mon–Fri 9am–5pm. Permission to enter and guided tours given on request. Bus: 21, 42, or 90.

Edgar Allan Poe National Historical Site   The acclaimed American author, though more associated with Baltimore, Richmond, and New York City, lived here from 1843 to 1844. "The Black Cat," "The Gold Bug," and "The Tell-Tale Heart" were published while he was a resident. Just reopened following structural work, it's a simple place—after all, Poe was poor most of his life—and the National Park Service keeps it unfurnished. An adjoining building contains basic information on Poe's life and work, along with a reading room and slide presentation. The Park Service also runs intermittent discussions and candlelight tours on Saturday afternoon.

532 N. 7th St. (near Spring Garden St.). ℂ **215/597-8780.** www.nps.gov/edal. Free admission. Wed–Sun 9am–5pm. Bus: 47 or 63.

Free Library of Philadelphia   Splendidly situated on the north side of Logan Circle, the Free Library of Philadelphia rivals the public libraries of

Boston and New York for magnificence and diversity. The library and its twin, the Municipal Court, are copies of buildings in the Place de la Concorde in Paris (the library's on the left).

The main lobby and the gallery always have some of the institution's riches on display, from medieval manuscripts to exhibits of modern bookbinding. Greeting cards and stationery are sold for reasonable prices, too. The second floor houses the best local history, travel, and resource collection in the city. The local 130,000-item map collection is fascinating. The third-floor rare book room hosts visitors Monday through Friday from 9am to 5pm, with tours by appointment. If you're interested in manuscripts, children's literature, early printed books, and early American hornbooks, or you just want to see a stuffed raven, this is the place.

If you're hungry, the Skyline Cafe (Mon–Fri 9am–4pm) is a very nice location for a snack and one of the only dining options on the Parkway. There's also an active concert and film series.

Central Library, Logan Circle at 19th and Vine sts. ℂ 215/686-5322. www.library.phila.gov. Free admission. Mon–Thurs 9am–9pm; Fri 9am–6pm; Sat 9am–5pm; Sun 1–5pm. Bus: 2, 7, 27, 32, 33, or PHLASH.

Rosenbach Museum and Library *(Finds)*   The Rosenbach specializes in books: illuminated manuscripts, parchment, rough drafts, and first editions. If you love the variations and beauty of the printed word, they'll love your presence.

The opulent town-house galleries contain 30,000 rare books and 270,000 documents. Some rooms preserve the Rosenbachs' elegant living quarters, with antique furniture and Sully paintings. Others are devoted to authors and illustrators: Marianne Moore's Greenwich Village study is reproduced in its entirety, and the Maurice Sendak drawings represent only the tip of his iceberg (or forest). Holdings include the original manuscript of Joyce's *Ulysses* and first editions of Melville, in the author's own bookcase. Small special exhibitions are tucked in throughout the house, and don't miss the shop behind the entrance for bargains in greeting cards and a superb collection of Sendak.

You are welcome to wander around the rooms unaccompanied, but you are not allowed to sit down and leaf through the books. For access to the books, you need to call and arrange a special admission. For the most part, you will only be allowed to arrange to peruse the books if you are visiting with a specific scholarly purpose.

An expansion and renovations for access for those with disabilities were recently completed.

2010 Delancey Place (between Spruce and Pine sts). ℂ 215/732-1600. www.rosenbach.org. Admission $8 adults; $5 children under 18, students, and seniors. Tues and Thurs–Sun 10am–5pm; Wed 10am–8pm. Bus: 17 or 90.

MORE MUSEUMS & EXHIBITIONS

Academy of Natural Sciences *(Kids)*   If you're looking for dinosaurs, the Academy is the best place to find them. Kids love the big diorama halls, with cases of various species mounted and posed in authentic settings. A permanent display, "Dinosaurs Galore," features more than a dozen specimens, including a huge *Tyrannosaurus rex* with jaws agape. The Dig (weekends only) gives you an opportunity to dig for fossils in a re-created field station. The North American Hall, on the first floor, has enormous moose, buffalo, and bears. A small marine exhibit shows how some fish look different in ultraviolet light and how the bed of the Delaware River has changed since Penn landed in 1682.

Fun Fact   **Philadelphia's Oddball Museums**

Philadelphia has an amazing assortment of small single-interest museums, built out of the passions of, or inspired by, a single individual. Maybe you and your family are ready for these!

- The Mummer's Parade on New Year's Day is uniquely Philadelphian; dozens of crews spend months practicing their musical and strutting skills with spectacular costumes. Talk about multicultural—mumming comes out of both Anglo-Saxon pagan celebrations and African dancing. The **Mummers Museum,** 2nd Street and Washington Avenue (© **215/336-3050**), is devoted to the history and display of this phenomenon. It's open Tuesday through Saturday from 9:30am to 4:30pm and Sunday from noon to 4:30pm.
- In the northeast district of the city (we know, it's a schlep), Steve Kanya's **Insectarium,** 8046 Frankford Ave. (© **215/338-3000**), has taken off (mostly as a school-class destination) thanks to a write-up in the *Wall Street Journal.* Can you believe an admission of only $5 to watch more than 40,000 cockroaches, assorted bugs, and their predators (scorpions, tarantulas, and so on) scurry around? It's open Monday through Saturday from 10am to 4pm.
- Also not for the squeamish is the **Mutter Museum** 🐾, 19 S. 22nd St. (© **215/587-9919**), a collection of preserved human oddities assembled in the 1850s by a Philadelphia physician. Skeletons of giants and dwarves and row upon row of plaster casts of abnormalities inhabit this musty place. It's open daily from 10am to 5pm.

The second floor features groupings of Asian and African flora and fauna. Many of the cases have nearby headphones that tell you more about what you're seeing. Five or six live demonstrations are given here every day; the handlers are experts in conducting these sessions with rocks, birds, plants, and animals. The Egyptian mummy, a priest of a late dynasty, seems a bit out of place. Several daily demonstrations (called "Eco Shows") are given on the second floor and in the auditorium downstairs.

Upstairs, "Outside In" is a touchable museum designed for children under 12, with a model campsite, fossils, minerals, and shells. It stimulates almost every sense: Children can see, feel, hear, and smell live turtles, mice, bees in a beehive, and snakes (all caged), and wander around mock forests and deserts. An exhibit of live butterflies rounds out the picture, along with frequent films. There's a brown-bag lunchroom and vending area with drinks and snacks, or visit the Chocolate Café.

19th St. and Benjamin Franklin Pkwy. © **215/299-1000.** www.acnatsci.org. Admission $9 adults, $8.25 seniors, $8 children 3–12, free for children under 3. Mon–Fri 10am–4:30pm; Sat–Sun and holidays 10am–5pm. Bus: 32, 33, or PHLASH.

The African-American Museum in Philadelphia   This museum, 3 blocks northwest of the Liberty Bell, is built in five split levels of ridged concrete (meant to evoke African mud housing) off a central atrium and ramp. As you ascend, you follow a path leading from the African roots of black Americans to the role they have played in U.S. history. Specific exhibitions change.

The ground floor contains the admissions office, the gift shop, and the African Heritage Gallery. The second level, concentrating on slavery and captivity, is the most dramatic and informed part of the museum. It emphasizes that the slave trade was hardly exclusive to, or even predominant in, North America, and that it persisted in South America until 1870.

The upper three levels, dealing with black history and culture after emancipation, lose some focus. Black cowboys, inventors, athletes, spokespeople, and business-people are all presented, along with the history of such organizations as the NAACP and CORE and the civil rights movements of the 1960s.

7th and Arch sts. ✆ **215/574-0380.** www.aampmuseum.org. Admission $8 adults, $6 children and seniors. Tues–Sat 10am–5pm; Sun noon–5pm. Bus: 47, 48, or PHLASH.

American Swedish Historical Museum   Modeled after a 17th-century Swedish manor house, this small museum chronicles 350 years of the life and accomplishments of Swedish Americans. Traditional Swedish holidays are celebrated year-round, including *Valborgsmässoafton* (Spring Festival) in April, *Midsommarfest* in June, and the procession of St. Lucia and her attendants in December.

1900 Pattison Ave. ✆ **215/389-1776.** www.americanswedish.org. Admission $6 adults, $5 students and seniors, free for children under 12. Tues–Fri 10am–4pm; Sat–Sun noon–4pm. Bus: 17. Near the Naval Hospital and Veterans Stadium, at the southern edge of the city.

Atwater Kent Museum   The small and newly vitalized Atwater Kent Museum occupies an 1826 John Haviland building. The Atwater Kent shows you—with more artifacts than the Visitor Center—what Philadelphia was like from 1680 to today. Nothing, apparently, was too trivial to include in this collection, which jumps from dolls to dioramas, from cigar-store Indians to period toyshops. Sunbonnets, train tickets, rocking horses, ship models, and military uniforms all fill out the display. A hands-on history laboratory opened in 2001.

15 S. 7th St. ✆ **215/685-4830.** www.philadelphiahistory.org. Admission $5 adults, $3 seniors and children 13–17, free for children under 12. Wed–Mon 9am–5pm. Bus: 17, 33, 42, or PHLASH.

Independence Seaport Museum 🎯🎯 *Kids*   Opposite Walnut Street, between the two dock areas, is this great new facility in the contemporary poured-concrete structure north of the Olympia jetty. The match between the 1981 state-owned building and the 1961 museum took several years to achieve, but was consummated in July 1995. Now the user-friendly maritime museum is the premier attraction of the city's waterfront, and also boasts the docked cruiser *Olympia* and the submarine *Becuna.*

The museum is beautifully laid out, blending a first-class maritime collection with interactive exhibits for a trip through time that engages all ages. The 11,000-square-foot main gallery is the centerpiece for exhibits, educational outreach, and activities that are jazzy and eye-catching without being noisy or obtrusive. Twelve sections mix the personal with the professional—call up interviews with river pilots, navy personnel, and shipbuilders. There are stories of immigrants who flooded Philadelphia between 1920 and 1970, and the rich reminiscences and memorabilia that make the past come to life.

One of the museum's most attractive features is the **Workshop on the Water,** where you can watch classes in traditional wooden boat building and restoration throughout the year.

Penn's Landing at 211 S. Columbus Blvd. ✆ **215/925-5439.** www.phillyseaport.org. Combined admission to the museum and Historic Ship Zone (USS *Olympia* and USS *Becuna;* berthed at Penn's Landing) $9 adults, $8 seniors, $6 children, free Sun 10am–noon. Daily 10am–5pm except for major holidays. RiverPass tickets, including admission to the museum, the Riverbus Ferry, and the Adventure Aquarium at Camden $24 adults, $21 seniors, $19 children 3–11; this will take at least 5 hr. Ships Ticket including the museum, the Battleship *New Jersey* berthed in Camden, and round-trip ferry $22 adults, $17 seniors, $15 children 3–11. Bus: 5, 21, 33, or PHLASH.

Mutter Museum 🐸🐸 *Finds* Kids will be fascinated by this hugely entertaining collection of medical oddities in an appropriately dark, dank, horror-film setting in a grand 19th-century building in Center City. Three operative words apply: *goiters in jars*. You'll also see 20,000 other spooky objects at the Mutter Museum, including the "Secret Tumor of Grover Cleveland" and plaster casts of famously conjoined twins Chang and Eng, housed in a paneled, double-height gallery within the College of Physicians. This medical institution was founded by Dr. Benjamin Rush, a signer of the Declaration of Independence; it's not an active medical school, but is an educational society with an important historical library. Everything in the Mutter, which began as a private collection in the 1850s, is very Young Frankenstein: 10,000 horrifying antique surgical implements, shelves of swollen brains floating in fluid in vintage glass jars, and even the thorax of John Wilkes Booth.

19 S. 22nd St. ✆ **215/563-3737**, ext. 293. www.collphyphil.org. Admission $9 adults, $6 students and children under 18. Daily 10am-5pm. Closed Thanksgiving, Dec 25, and Jan 1. SEPTA: Suburban Station. Bus: PHLASH, 21, or 42.

National Museum of American Jewish History This is the only museum specifically dedicated to preserving and presenting Jewish participation in the development of the United States. The museum was established in 1976, although the congregation connected to it, Mikveh Israel, was established in Philadelphia in 1740. Enter close to 4th Street (passing Christ Church Cemetery, with Ben Franklin's grave) into a dark-brick lobby. The museum starts with a fascinating permanent exhibition, "Creating American Jews," combining reproductions of portraits and documents, actual diaries, letters, and oral histories from five diverse "snapshots" from today's six million American Jews and their predecessors. Smaller rotating exhibitions supplement this presentation, and there are moving and inspiring special events offered throughout the year. Attracting 40,000 visitors a year, the museum is usually cool and restful and makes a good break from a hot Independence Park tour. A small gift shop is attached.

55 N. 5th St. ✆ **215/923-8311**. www.nmajh.org. Admission $4 adults; $3 students, seniors, and children (some exhibits are free); free for children under 6. Mon–Thurs 10am–5pm; Fri 10am–3pm; Sun noon–5pm. Bus: 17, 33, 48, 50, or PHLASH.

Physick House 🐸 Like the Powel house (p. 141), the Physick (formerly Hill-Physick-Keith) House combines attractive design and historical interest. The house is the area's most impressive—freestanding but not boxy, gracious but solid. Built during the 1780s boom, with money from importing Madeira wine, it soon wound up housing the father of American surgery, Philip Syng Physick (a very propitious name for a physician). The usual pattern of neglect and renovation applies here, on an even grander scale.

All the fabric and wallpaper was fashioned expressly for use here, and the mansion as restored is an excellent illustration of the Federal style from about 1815. The drawing room opens onto a lovely 19th-century walled garden, and contains a Roman stool and 18th-century Italian art, collectibles that illustrate the excitement caused by the discovery of the buried city of Pompeii at that time. Look for an inkstand blessed by Ben Franklin's fingerprints. Dr. Physick treated Chief Justice Marshall, and Marshall's portrait and gift of a wine stand testify to the doctor's powers.

321 S. 4th St. ℭ **215/925-7866** or 215/925-2251. www.philalandmarks.org. Admission $5 adults, $4 students and seniors. Thurs–Sat noon–5pm; Sun 1–5pm. Guided tours only. Bus: 50, 90, or PHLASH.

Please Touch Museum ⭑ *Kids*   This is one of the best indoor activities in town for a family with young kids, and the location is great—just off the Parkway, 2 blocks south of the Franklin Institute (though the museum hopes to expand and move to Penn's Landing in the next decade). Dedicated to a unique fun-filled educational, cultural, hands-on experience, the converted factories help bring out the creative, exuberant, and receptive in us all.

Once you're in, you can park strollers, check coats, and buy tickets at counters that cater to kids. Exciting hands-on exhibits like "Growing Up" encourage parent/child participation and focus on specific social, cognitive, and emotional areas of child development. "Me on TV," installed in 1993, allows children to experience being behind the camera and on stage in a television studio, including sound effects and camera angles. An exhibit of oversize settings and creatures comes from celebrated author/illustrator Maurice Sendak. The museum collaborates with the Franklin Institute to operate the 38,000-square-foot CoreStates Science Park between May and September, on the lawn between the two institutions. It's a great playground for the mind and body. Small children particularly love the cloud that they can make "rain," and the miniature grocery store.

The Please Touch Museum is not a day-care center; you cannot simply drop the kids off, and you won't want to. Educational activities like storytelling and crafts are available daily from 11am to 3:30pm. It's also a great place to celebrate a child's birthday if you plan ahead.

210 N. 21st St. ℭ **215/963-0667**. www.pleasetouchmuseum.org. Admission $9.95 adults and children (free for infants); voluntary donation Sun 9–11am. No strollers inside, but Snuglis available. After Labor Day to June 30 daily 9am–4:30pm; July 1 to Labor Day daily 9am–5pm. Bus: 7 or 48.

Rodin Museum *Moments*   The beautiful, intimate Rodin Museum, in a 1929 Paul Cret building, exhibits the largest collection of the master's work (129 sculptures) outside the Musée Rodin in Paris. It has inherited its sibling museum's romantic mystery, making a very French use of space inside and boasting much greenery outside. Entering from the Parkway, virtually across the street from the Franklin Institute (see earlier in this chapter), you'll contemplate *The Thinker,* then pass through an imposing arch to a front garden of hardy shrubs and trees surrounding a fish pond. Before going into the museum, study the *Gates of Hell.* These gigantic doors reveal the artist's power to mold metal with his tremendous imagination.

The galleries had a top-to-bottom renovation 5 years ago. The main hall holds authorized casts of *John the Baptist, The Cathedral,* and *The Burghers of Calais.* Several of the side chambers and the library hold powerful erotic plaster models. Drawings, sketchbooks, and Steichen photographic portraits of Rodin are exhibited from time to time.

Benjamin Franklin Pkwy. between 21st and 22nd sts. ℭ **215/763-8100**. $3 donation requested. Free with same-day admission ticket from the Philadelphia Museum of Art (p. 129). Tues–Sun 10am–5pm. Bus: 7, 32, 38, 43, 48, or PHLASH.

U.S. Mint   The U.S. Mint was the first building authorized by the government, during Washington's first term. The present edifice, diagonally across from Liberty Bell Pavilion, turns out about 1.5 million coins every hour. As of September 2002, tours must be arranged through your representative in Congress in advance, and serious security measures are in place; see the mint website for details, or call ℭ 202/354-6700.

5th and Arch sts. © **215/408-0114.** www.usmint.gov. Free admission, but limited to Congressionally-sponsored groups of 6 or fewer, and school and veteran groups. Call in advance to arrange a tour. Bus: 5 or 48.

University of Pennsylvania Museum of Archaeology and Anthropology ⋒

The 115-year-old Museum got started early and well, and is endowed with Benin bronzes, ancient cuneiform texts, Mesopotamian masterpieces, pre-Columbian gold, and artifacts of every continent, mostly brought back from the more than 350 expeditions it has sponsored over the years. The taller structures that surround this museum give its Romanesque brickwork and gardens a secluded feel. The museum has had spectacular special exhibitions recently, with forays into ancient Iran, Roman glass, and works from ancient Canaan and Israel.

Exhibits are intelligently explained. The basement Egyptian galleries, including colossal architectural remains from Memphis and "The Egyptian Mummy: Secrets and Science," are family favorites. Probably the most famous excavation display, located on the third floor, is a spectacular Sumerian trove of jewelry and household objects from the royal tombs of the ancient city of Ur. Adjoining this, huge cloisonné lions from Peking's (now Beijing's) Imperial Palace guard Chinese court treasures and tomb figures. The Ancient Greek Gallery in the classical world collection, renovated in 1994, has 400 superb objects such as red-figure pottery—a flower of Greek art—and an unusual lead sarcophagus from Tyre that looks like a miniature house. Other galleries display Native American and Polynesian art and a small but excellent African collection of bronze plaques and statues.

The glass-enclosed Museum Cafe, overlooking the museum's inner gardens, serves cafeteria-style snacks and light meals from 8am to 3:30pm on weekdays, from 10am to 3:30pm on Saturday, and from 1 to 5pm on Sunday. The Museum Shop has cards and jewelry and crafts from around the world, and the Pyramid Shop has children's items. There's a very active schedule of events throughout the year.

33rd and Spruce sts. © **215/898-4000.** www.upenn.edu/museum. Admission $8 adults, $5 students and seniors, free for children under 6. Tues–Sun 10am–4:30pm. Closed holidays and Sun from Memorial Day to Labor Day. Bus: 21, 30 (from 30th St. Station), 40, or 42.

UNIVERSITY OF PENNSYLVANIA ⋒

You could call Philadelphia one big campus, with 27 degree-granting institutions within city limits and 50,000 annual college graduates. The oldest and most prestigious university is U. Penn. This private, coeducational Ivy League institution was founded by Benjamin Franklin and others in 1740. It boasts America's first medical (1765), law (1790), and business (1881) schools. Penn's liberal arts curriculum, dating from 1756, was the first to combine classical and practical subjects. The university has been revitalized in the last 30 years, thanks to extremely successful leadership, alumni, and fund-raising drives. Under President Judith Rodin, it's starting to reshape its neighborhood positively, with the successful Sansom Commons project across the street, including the wonderful Inn at Penn, retail stores, the stylish Bridge de Lux cinema at 40th and Walnut streets, and the massive Barnes & Noble–run university bookstore.

The core campus, based in West Philadelphia since the 1870s, features serene Gothic-style buildings and specimen trees in a spacious quadrangle. Visitors can hang out comfortably on the lawns and benches. More modern buildings are results of the 20th-century expansion of the university to accommodate 22,000 students enrolled in four undergraduate and 12 graduate schools, in 100 academic departments. Sights of most interest to visitors include the University

Museum of Archaeology and Anthropology, the Annenberg Center for the Performing Arts, and the always intriguing Institute of Contemporary Art, with its changing exhibits.

34th and Walnut sts. and surrounding neighborhood. Ⓒ 215/898-5000. www.upenn.edu. Bus: 21, 30, 40, 42, or 90. Car: 30th St. exit from I-76 (Schuylkill Expwy.), 6 blocks west toward West Philadelphia.

A ZOO & AN AQUARIUM

Philadelphia Zoo 🐾🐾 *(Kids)*   The Philadelphia Zoo, opened in 1874, was the nation's first. By the late 1970s, the 42 acres tucked into West Fairmount Park had become run-down, with few financial resources. The zoo has since become a national leader, with nearly 1,800 animals. The Zoo celebrated its 125th anniversary with the opening of the **PECO Primate Center,** a breathtaking pavilion that blurs the line between visitors and its 11 resident species. Note that the basic admission ($16 per adult, $13 for children) will not cover a lot of special attractions like the new Channel 6 **Zooballoon,** a 15-minute ascent on a helium balloon that goes 400 feet high.

The 1½-acre **Carnivore Kingdom** houses snow leopards and jaguars, but the biggest attraction is the rare white lions. Feeding time is around 11am for smaller carnivores, 3pm for tigers and lions. The monkeys have a new home on four naturally planted islands, where a variety of primate species live together naturally.

In the magical **Jungle Bird Walk,** you can walk among free-flying birds. Glass enclosures have been replaced with wire mesh so that the birds' songs can now be heard from both sides. The **Treehouse** ($1), opened in 1985, contains six larger-than-life habitats for kids of all ages to explore—oversize eggs to hatch from, an oversize honeycomb to crawl through, and a four-story ficus tree to climb and see life from a bird's-eye view. The very popular Camel Rides start next to the Treehouse. A **Children's Zoo** portion of the gardens lets your kids pet and feed some baby zoo and farm animals; this closes 30 minutes before the rest of the zoo.

Other exhibits include polar bears; the renovated Reptile House, which bathes its snakes and tortoises with simulated tropical thunderstorms; and cavorting antelopes, zebras, and giraffes that coexist in the "African Plains" exhibit. The zoo has a McDonald's across from the lion house. There is a Fidelity Bank MAC ATM machine at the North Gate. Try to arrive early in the day; it's a long hike from the more distant lots if you don't.

34th St. and Girard Ave. Ⓒ 215/243-1100. www.philadelphiazoo.org. Admission adults $11 Nov–Mar, $16 Apr–Oct; children 2–11, $11 Nov–Mar, $13 Apr–Oct; free for children under 2. For the Zoo and Zooballoon adults $26, children $23. Parking spaces for 1,800 cars, $8 per vehicle. Feb–Nov daily 9:30am–5pm; Dec–Jan daily 9:30am–4pm. Closed Thanksgiving, Christmas, and New Year's Day. Bus: 15, 32, or 38. Car: Separate exit off I-76 north of Center City.

Adventure Aquarium 🐾 *(Kids)*   Formerly the New Jersey State Aquarium, this venue, opened in 1992 as a first step in reclaiming the once-vital (and now denuded) Camden waterfront, is being totally renovated and revitalized in 2005.

Up to 4,000 aquatic animals live here, and more exotic species are coming. The main attraction is a 760,000-gallon tank, the second largest (next to Epcot Center's) in the country, with stepped seat/benches arranged in a Greek amphitheater on the first floor. Also on the first floor is a Caribbean outpost with 1,000 tropical fish and beach birds. The second floor features interactive exhibits and strange ocean dwellers. New exhibits will include crocodiles in a West African river setting, sharks swimming alongside a 40-foot glass tunnel, and even the opportunity to swim alongside sharks.

1 Riverside Dr., Camden, NJ. © **856/365-3300**. www.njaquarium.org. Admission $14 adults, $12 students and seniors, $11 children 3–11, free for children under 3. Apr 15–Sept 15 daily 9:30am–5:30pm; Sept 16–Apr 14 Mon–Fri 9:30am–4:30pm, Sat–Sun 10am–5pm. Closed Thanksgiving, Christmas, and New Year's Day. Ferry: The RiverLink Ferry from Independence Seaport Museum at Penn's Landing is $6 adults, $4 children over age 2, round-trip (see Independence Seaport Museum listing above for ferry/package admissions); hourly arrivals/departures. Car: From I-676 eastbound (Vine St. Expwy./Ben Franklin Bridge) or westbound from I-295/New Jersey Turnpike, take Mickle Blvd. exit and follow signs.

4 Parks, the Parkway & Penn's Landing ⌖

BENJAMIN FRANKLIN PARKWAY ⌖

The Parkway, a broad diagonal swath linking City Hall to Fairmount Park, wasn't included in Penn's original plan. In the 1920s, however, Philadelphians wanted a grand boulevard in the style of the Champs Elysées. In summer, a walk from the Visitor Center to the "Museum on the Hill" is a flower-bedecked and leafy stroll. And year-round, various institutions, public art, and museums enrich the avenue with their handsome facades. Most of the city's parades and festivals pass this way.

Logan Circle, outside the Academy of Natural Sciences, Free Library of Philadelphia, and Franklin Institute, used to be Logan Square before the Parkway was built, and it was a burying ground before becoming a park. The designers of the avenue cleverly made it into a low-landscaped fountain, with graceful figures cast by Alexander Stirling Calder. In June, look for students from neighboring private schools, getting a traditional graduation dunking in their uniforms! From this point, you can see how the rows of trees follow the diagonal thoroughfare, although all the buildings along the Parkway are aligned with the grid plan. Under the terms of the city permit, the Four Seasons Hotel now landscapes and tends Logan Circle, to magnificent effect.

The PHLASH bus goes up as far as Logan Circle every 12 minutes.

FAIRMOUNT PARK ⌖⌖

The northern end of the Benjamin Franklin Parkway leads into Fairmount Park, the world's largest landscaped city park, with 8,700 acres of winding creeks, rustic trails, and green meadows, plus 100 miles of jogging, bike, and bridle paths. In addition, this park (© **215/683-0200;** www.phila.gov/fairpark) features more than a dozen historical and cultural attractions, including 29 of America's finest Colonial mansions (most are open year-round with some wonderful Christmas tours, and are run by the Art Museum; standard admission is $3), as well as gardens, boathouses, America's first zoo, a youth hostel, and a Japanese teahouse. Visitors can rent sailboats and canoes, play tennis and golf, swim, or hear free symphony concerts in the summer. See the Fairmount Park map on p. 151 to find your way around the park. See below for information on renting bikes and inline skates at Drive Sports (next to Lloyd Hall at the start of Boat House Row) for a couple of hours; they're cheap, and can get you in and out of the heart of the park quickly.

If you're driving, there are several entrances and exits off I-76, such as Montgomery Drive; the Kelly Drive and the West River Drive are local roads flanking the Schuylkill River.

The park is generally divided by the Schuylkill River into East and West Fairmount Park. Before beginning a tour of the mansions, stop by the **Waterworks** (© **215/236-5465**). Philadelphia set the waterworks up here in 1812 to provide water for the city. They set aside a 5-acre space around the waterworks, which became a park in 1822.

The Greek Revival mill houses in back of the Art Museum and an ornamental post–Civil War pavilion connecting them are undergoing the end of a $23-million restoration. An upscale, year-round restaurant, open-air market, summer stage, and new bike path joined the renovated houses in summer 2003. Also on the east bank, don't miss **Boat House Row,** home of the "Schuylkill Navy" and its member rowing clubs. Now you know where Thomas Eakins got the models for all those sculling scenes in the Art Museum. These gingerbread Tudors along the riverbank appear magical at night, with hundreds of tiny lights along their eaves.

The four most spectacular Colonial houses are all in the lower east quadrant of the park. **Lemon Hill** (✆ 215/232-4337), just up the hill from Boat House Row, shows the influence of Robert Adam's architectural style, with its generous windows, curved archways and doors, and beautiful oval parlors. John Adams described **Mount Pleasant** (✆ 215/763-8100), built for a privateer in 1763 and once owned by Benedict Arnold, as "the most elegant seat in Pennsylvania" for its carved designs and inlays. **Woodford** (✆ 215/229-6115), the center of Tory occupation of the city in 1779, is not to be missed, both for its architecture and for the Naomi Wood Collection of Colonial housewares. Along with Winterthur (p. 225), this is the best place to step into 18th-century home life, with all its ingenious gadgets and elegant objects. The next lawn over from Woodford is the park's largest mansion, **Strawberry Mansion** (✆ 215/228-8364), with a Federal-style center section and Greek Revival wings.

Just north of this mansion is bucolic **Laurel Hill Cemetery** (p. 136), but if you cross Strawberry Mansion Bridge, West Fairmount Park also has many charms. Located in West Fairmount Park, **Belmont Mansion** (✆ 215/878-8844) hosted all the leaders of the Revolutionary cause. South of this area, you'll enter the site occupied by the stupendous 1876 Centennial Exposition. Approximately 100 buildings were designed and constructed in under 2 years. Only two remain today: **Ohio House,** built out of stone from that state, and the rambling Beaux Arts **Memorial Hall** (✆ 215/683-0200), now the park's headquarters and a recreation site. The **Japanese House and Gardens** (✆ 215/878-5097), on the grounds of the nearby Horticultural Center, is a typical 17th-century Japanese scholar's house, with sliding screens and paper doors in place of walls and glass. It was originally presented to the Museum of Modern Art in New York. Since the Centennial Exposition had featured a similar house, it wound up here. The waterfall, grounds, and house are serene and simple and were extensively refurbished in 1976 by a Japanese team as a bicentennial gift to the city. It's open during the summer only, Tuesday through Sunday from 11am to 4pm.

Two more major homes lie south of the Exposition's original concourses: **Cedar Grove** (✆ 215/763-8100), a Quaker farmhouse built as a country retreat in 1748 and moved here in 1928, and **Sweetbriar** (✆ 215/222-1333), a mixture of French Empire and English neoclassicism with wonderful river views. Continuing south past the Girard Avenue Bridge will bring you to the **Philadelphia Zoo** (see above), and then to Center City.

If you have some time and really want to get away from it all, Wissahickon and Pennsylvania creeks lie north of the park and don't allow access by automobile—only pedestrians, bicycles, and horses can tread here. The primeval trees and slopes of these valleys completely block out buildings and noise—right within the limits of the fifth largest city in the United States! Search out attractions like the 340-year-old Valley Green Inn and the only covered bridge left in an American city.

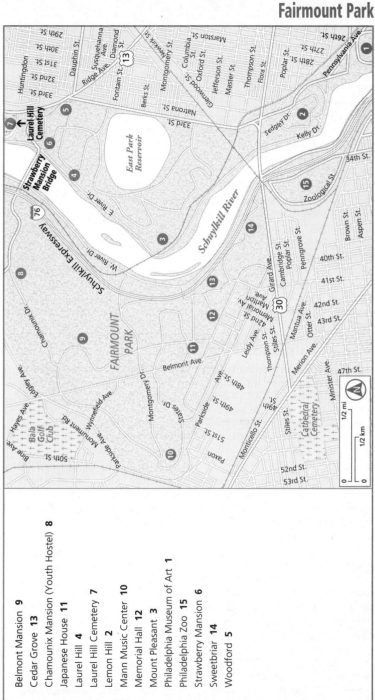

Belmont Mansion **9**

Cedar Grove **13**

Chamounix Mansion (Youth Hostel) **8**

Japanese House **11**

Laurel Hill **4**

Laurel Hill Cemetery **7**

Lemon Hill **2**

Mann Music Center **10**

Memorial Hall **12**

Mount Pleasant **3**

Philadelphia Museum of Art **1**

Philadelphia Zoo **15**

Strawberry Mansion **6**

Sweetbriar **14**

Woodford **5**

PENN'S LANDING ⊛

Philadelphia started out as a major freshwater port, and its tourism and services are increasingly nudging it back to the water after 50 years of neglect (typified by the placement of the I-95 superhighway between the city and its port). Two recent proposals for a full revitalization with shops and restaurants were not approved by the city, so for now, the options are rather limited at Penn's Landing, but it's still a pleasant place for a walk on a sunny day.

In 1945, 155 "finger" piers jutted out into the river; today, only 14 remain. The Delaware waterfront is quite wide, and the esplanade along it has always had a pleasant spaciousness. The challenge has been to give it a unified, coherent sense of destination. Since 1976, the city has added on parts of a complete waterfront park at Penn's Landing (© 215/629-3200; www.pennslandingcorp. com), on Columbus Boulevard (formerly Delaware Ave.) between Market and Lombard streets, with a seaport museum and an assembly of historic ships, performance and park areas, cruise facilities, and a marina. Further additions include more pedestrian bridges over I-95; a 1996 project to install wider sidewalks, lighting, and kiosks along Columbus Boulevard; and the new riverside Hyatt Penn's Landing hotel.

You can access the Penn's Landing waterfront by parking along the piers or by walking across several bridges spanning I-95 between Market Street, at the northern edge, and South Street to the south. There are pedestrian walkways across Front Street on Market, Chestnut, Walnut, Spruce, or South streets; Front Street connects directly at Spruce Street. Bus nos. 17, 21, 33, and the purple PHLASH go directly to Penn's Landing; the stop for bus no. 42 is an easy walk from 2nd Street. If you're driving from I-95, use the Columbus Boulevard/Washington Street exit and turn left on to Columbus Boulevard. From I-76, take I-676 across Center City to I-95 south. There's ample parking available on-site.

Walking south from Market Street, you'll see an esplanade with pretty new blue guardrails and charts to help you identify the Camden shoreline opposite. The hill that connects the shoreline with the current Front Street level has been enhanced with the addition of the festive **Great Plaza,** a multitiered, tree-lined space. In the other direction is a jetty/marina complex, perfect for strolling and snacking, anchored by the **Independence Seaport Museum,** the Hyatt hotel, and the Chart House restaurant. The lovely, sober 1987 **Philadelphia Vietnam Veteran Memorial** lists 641 local casualties. Nearby, you'll find the **International Sculpture Garden** with its obelisk monument to Christopher Columbus.

There's also plenty to do in and near the water. Just north of the Great Plaza at Columbus Boulevard and Spring Garden Street is Festival Pier. The Penn's Landing Corporation coordinates more than 100 events here annually, all designed to attract crowds with high-quality entertainment. Even on a spontaneous visit you're likely to be greeted with sounds and performances. Festival Pier is also the location of the Blue Cross RiverRink, Philadelphia's only outdoor skating rink, open daily from late November to early March.

Several ships and museums are berthed around a long jetty at Spruce Street, and the Independence Seaport Museum is slowly consolidating management of these attractions as the **Historic Ship Zone.** Starting at the north end, these attractions are the brig *Niagara,* built for the War of 1812 and rededicated as the official flagship of Pennsylvania in 1990; the **USS** *Becuna,* a guppy-class submarine, commissioned in 1944 to serve in Admiral Halsey's South

Pacific fleet; and the USS *Olympia,* Admiral Dewey's own flagship in the Spanish-American War, with a self-guided three-deck tour. (Separate admission to both the *Olympia* and the *Becuna* is $3.50 for adults, $1.75 for children under 12; both are open daily 10am–5pm.) The harbor cruise boats **Liberty Belle II** (© 215/629-1131) and *Spirit of Philadelphia* (© 215/923-1419), and the paddle-wheeler *Riverboat Queen* (© 215/923-BOAT), are joined by private yachts. In fact, Queen Elizabeth docked her yacht *Britannia* here in 1976. Anchoring the southern end is the **Chart House** restaurant, 555 S. Columbus Blvd. (© 215/625-8383), open for lunch and dinner, and the restored **Moshulu** four-masted floating restaurant, 401 S. Columbus Blvd (© 215/923-2500) in Penn's Landing marina.

Another group of boats occupies the landfill directly on the Delaware between Market and Walnut streets. The *Gazela Primiero,* a working three-masted, square-rigged wooden ship launched from Portugal in 1883, has visiting hours on Saturday and Sunday from 12:30 to 5:30pm when it's in port, as does the tugboat *Jupiter.* All boats mentioned in the paragraph are operated by the Philadelphia Ship Preservation Guild (© 215/238-0280); admission $3 adults, $2 students.

If you want to get out onto the water, the *RiverLink* (© 215/925-LINK), at the river's edge in front of the Independence Seaport Museum at Walnut Street, plies a round-trip route to the Camden attractions including the Adventure Aquarium, the Camden Children's Garden, and the Battleship *New Jersey,* next to the Tweeter concert arena. The ferry crosses every hour on the hour between 9am and 5pm during the summer months. The trip takes 10 minutes, and the round-trip fare without museum admission on either end is $6 adults, $4 children each way.

5 Especially for Kids

Philadelphia is one of the country's great family destinations. It has a variety of attractions for different ages, and because it's so walkable and neighborhood-based, a snack, a rest, or a new distraction is never far away. Since so many of the family attractions are explained in more detail elsewhere in this or other chapters, I'll restrict myself to a list of the basics.

The Independence Visitor Center, at 6th and Market streets, coordinates and sells several packages that combine free admission to many kid-friendly attractions with accommodations at hotels such as the Penn Tower, Sheraton Society Hill, and Embassy Suites Center City (© 215/965-7676). Visit www.gophila. org, the website of the Greater Philadelphia Tourism and Marketing Corporation, or call them at © 215/599-0776, for more great family-oriented hotel packages.

MUSEUMS & SIGHTS

In Center City, you'll find the **Please Touch Museum,** 210 N. 21st St. (until it moves to Penn's Landing); **Franklin Institute,** Benjamin Franklin Parkway and 20th Street; **CoreStates Science Park** between these two on 21st Street; and the **Academy of Natural Sciences,** the Parkway and 19th Street. The **Free Library of Philadelphia Children's Department,** across Logan Circle at Vine and 19th streets, is a joy, with a separate entrance, 100,000 books and computers in a playgroundlike space, with weekend hours. Around Independence Hall are the **Liberty Bell Center; Franklin Court,** between Market and Chestnut streets at

(Kids Connect the Docs

Here's a game to test your knowledge of Philadelphia's historical documents. Match each document—written and ratified or published in Philly—with its first full sentence:

1. The Declaration of Independence (1776)
2. The Articles of Confederation (1778)
3. The Constitution of the United States (1787)
4. The Bill of Rights (1791)
5. George Washington's Farewell Address (1796)

A. "We the People of the United States, in Order to form a more perfect Union, establish Justice, insure domestic Tranquility, provide for the common defence, promote the general Welfare, and secure the Blessings of Liberty to ourselves and our Posterity, do ordain and establish this [document name]."

B. "To all to whom these Presents shall come, we the undersigned Delegates of the States affixed to our Names, send greeting."

C. "When in the Course of human events, it becomes necessary for one people to dissolve the political bands which have connected them with another, and to assume among the powers of the earth, the separate and equal station to which the Laws of Nature and of Nature's God entitle them, a decent respect to the opinions of mankind requires that they should declare the causes which impel them to the separation."

D. "Friends and fellow citizens: The period for a new election of a citizen to administer the Executive Government of the United States being not far distant, and the time actually arrived when your thoughts must be employed in designating the person who is to be clothed with that important trust, it appears to me proper, especially as it may conduce to a more distinct expression of the public voice, that I should now apprise you of the resolution I have formed to decline being considered among the number of those out of whom a choice is to be made."

E. "The Conventions of a number of the States having, at the time of adopting the Constitution, expressed a desire, in order to prevent misconstruction or abuse of its powers, that further declaratory and restrictive clauses should be added."

Answers: 1) C, 2) B, 3) A, 4) E, 5) D. For the full text of the "Declaration of Independence," see p. 256.

4th Street; the waterfront at **Penn's Landing,** off Front Street; the new **National Constitution Center** at Arch and 5th streets; and, of course, the guided tour of **Independence Hall.** You can also take the ferry from Penn's Landing and the great new **Independence Seaport Museum** to the **aquarium, children's garden,** and **battleship** in Camden, New Jersey. In West Fairmount Park you'll find the **zoo.**

PLAYGROUNDS

Rittenhouse Square at 18th and Walnut streets has a small playground and space in which to eat and relax. Other imaginative urban playgrounds on this side of Center City are **Schuylkill River Park** at Pine and 26th streets, and at 26th Street and the Benjamin Franklin Parkway, opposite the art museum. Nearest Independence Hall, try **Delancey Park** at Delancey between 3rd and 4th streets (with lots of fountains and animal sculptures to climb on) or **Starr Garden** at 6th and Lombard streets. The best park in Fairmount Park is the **Smith Memorial** (head north on 33rd St., then take a left into the park at Oxford Ave., near Woodford).

ENTERTAINMENT

There is lots of children's theater in Philadelphia. **The Arden Theatre** at 40 N. 2nd St. (© 215/922-1122) is one of a dozen companies that produces children's theater year-round. **Mum Puppettheatre** at 115 Arch St. presents a season of thought-provoking and enjoyable plays for all ages; call © **215/925-8686** for schedule and details.

The **Philadelphia Museum of Art** at Suburban Station (bus: PHLASH, 21, or 42) has dedicated itself to producing Sunday-morning and early afternoon programs for children, at minimal or no charge. Your kids could wind up drawing pictures of armor or watching a puppet play about dragons, visiting a Chinese court, or exploring Cubism. Call © **215/763-8100,** or 215/684-7500 for 24-hour information.

OUTSIDE PHILADELPHIA

In Bucks County, there is **Sesame Place,** based on public TV's *Sesame Street,* in Langhorne, and the restored antique carousel at **Peddler's Village** in Lahaska. To the northwest, try the 20th-century entertainment areas connected with **Franklin Mills,** and **Ridley Creek State Park** and its 17th-century working farm in Montgomery County. For Revolutionary War history in action, try Valley Forge or Washington Crossing National Historical Parks. And for a fascinating experience, spend a couple of days in Lancaster County—you can even stay on a working Amish farm. See chapters 11 and 12 for directions and information.

6 Organized Tours

BOATING TOURS

Two choices are available at Penn's Landing. The *Spirit of Philadelphia* (© 866/211-3808) at the Great Plaza combines lunch, brunch, or dinner with a cruise on a 600-person passenger ship, fully climate-controlled, with two enclosed decks and two open-air decks. Trips, which require reservations, are $30 and up for 2 or 3 hours.

The *Riverboat Queen* (© 215/629-1131) also offers cruises and dining options.

The *RiverLink* (© 215/925-LINK) provides a 10-minute interstate crossing from landings just outside the Independence Seaport Museum and the Adventure Aquarium. The ferry is large inside, and the views of the Philadelphia skyline are great. Departures from Penn's Landing are on the hour, from Camden on the half-hour, from 9am to 5pm daily. Round-trip fares are $6 for adults, $4 for children. The packages including admission to various Camden attractions are a good deal. You can purchase the packages at the Independence Visitor

Center, the Seaport Museum, or at any attraction along the Philadelphia or Camden waterfront.

BUS TOURS

Big Bus is a new venture of double-decker, British-style tour vehicles (© **866/ 324-4287** or 215/923-5008; www.bigbustours.com). Tours of historic areas, conducted by guides in the climate-controlled vehicles, leave from the Visitor Center at 5th and Market. The tours cost $25 for adults, $22 for seniors, and $10 for children.

   Philadelphia Trolley Works and 76 Carriage Company (© **215/925- TOUR;** www.phillytour.com) offers 90-minute tours of the historic area in trolley-style buses, as well as special Fairmount Park tours, for $20 for adults and $4 for children; the trolleys pick up at 6th and Market streets. Short horse-drawn carriage tours start at $25.

HORSE & CARRIAGE TOURS

To get the feel of Philadelphia as it was (well, almost—asphalt is a lot smoother than cobblestones), try a narrated horse-drawn carriage ride. Operated daily by the **76 Carriage Co.** (© **215/923-8516**), tours begin at 5th and Chestnut streets in front of Independence Hall, from 10am to 5pm in fall, winter, and spring, and from 10am to 8 pm in summer. Fares range from $25 for 15 minutes to $70 for an hour-plus, with a maximum of four per carriage, additional people $5 each. Reservations are not necessary.

WALKING TOURS

The next chapter will give you some guided walking tours to follow. The most spectacular, the "Lights of Liberty" show using Independence National Historical Park as a backdrop, is described on p. 120. There are also many specific-interest tours, focusing on topics such as African-American Philadelphia, architecture, Jewish sights in Society Hill, and the Italian Market. Check with the Independence Visitor Center (© **215/965-7676;** www.independencevisitor center.com) for information.

---

7 Outdoor Activities

I can't begin to make a complete list of all that you can do outdoors while in Philadelphia, so the following is merely a sample.

BIKING/BLADING

Drive Sports in **Fairmount Park,** the most southerly Boathouse Row building along the Schuylkill (© **215/235-7368;** www.drivesports.com), is the jumping-off spot for these activities, full of bikes and skates for rental. It's an ideal spot, almost in the Art Museum's backyard, and at the tip of Fairmount Park. You can rent all kinds of bikes, blades, and baby joggers at $8 per hour or $20 for 4 hours, helmets and gear included. Once you're on wheels, the paths along the Schuylkill on Kelly (East River) Drive, West River Drive, and off West River Drive to Belmont Avenue are pure pleasure. The lower half of West River Drive along the Schuylkill is closed to vehicular traffic most weekend hours in summer. Rent bicycles from $25 a day at the **Bike Lines** at 226 S. 40th in University City (© **215/243-2453**), or 1028 Arch near the Convention Center (© **215/923-1310**). The ground is flat near the Schuylkill on either side but loops up sharply near Laurel Hill Cemetery or Manayunk. Anyone who enjoys cycling will love the outlying countryside, and you can rent bicycles in

Lumberville, 8 miles north of New Hope on the Delaware, at the **Lumberville Store,** 3741 River Rd. (© **215/297-5388**). Bicycles may be taken free on all SEPTA and PATCO trains, so you're within easy range of some nice country rides.

Visit the **Bicycle Club of Philadelphia** at www.phillybikeclub.org for specific neighborhood recommendations.

BOATING

Outside of the city, try **Northbrook Canoe Co.,** north of Route 842 at 1810 Beagle Rd. W., in West Chester on Brandywine Creek (© **610/793-2279**), or **Point Pleasant,** on Route 32, 7 miles north of the New Hope exit on I-95, with canoeing, inner tubing, and rafting on the Delaware River with **Bucks County River Country,** 2 Walter Lane (© **215/297-8823**).

FISHING

Pennypack Creek and **Wissahickon Creek** are stocked from mid-April to December with trout and muskie and provide good, even rustic, conditions. A required license of $17 for Pennsylvania residents, or $15 for 3 days, $30 for 7 days, and $35 for a season for out-of-staters, is available at the **Municipal Services Building,** located at 1401 John F. Kennedy Blvd., near the Visitor Center. Licenses are also available at the **Wal-Mart** at 1601 S. Columbus Blvd. (© **215/468-4220**). Outside the city, **Ridley Creek** and its **state park** (© **610/ 566-4800**) and **Brandywine Creek** at Hibernia Park of Chester County (© **610/383-3812**) are stocked with several kinds of trout.

GOLF

The quality and variety of public access golf is wonderful. The city of Philadelphia operates five municipal courses in the region. All have 18 holes, and current fees range from $15 to $25 Monday through Friday and $20 to $30 on Saturday and Sunday. Not everyone can get onto the legendary Pine Valley or Merion, but Hugh Wilson of Merion also designed the pretty and challenging **Cobbs Creek,** 7800 Lansdowne Ave. at 72nd Street (© **215/877-8707**). Since Meadowbrook Golf Group took over in April 1999, course conditions have improved dramatically. **Karakung** is the shorter 18-hole course, and preferred for seniors and juniors. **John F. Byrne,** Frankford Avenue and Eden Street in North Philadelphia (© **215/632-8666**), has an Alex Findlay design with Torresdale Creek meandering through or beside 10 holes, and plenty of rolling fairways and elevations. **Walnut Lane,** Walnut Lane and Henry Avenue in Roxborough (© **215/482-3370**), places a premium on short game skills, with 10 par-3 holes and deep bunkers set into hills and valleys. There's also a driving range in East Fairmount Park.

Among the better township courses outside the city are **Montgomeryville Golf Club,** Route 202 (© **215/855-6112**); **Paxon Hollow Golf Club,** Paxon Hollow Road in Marple Township (© **610/353-0220**), under 6,000 yards and demanding accuracy; and **Valley Forge Golf Club,** 401 N. Gulph Rd., King of Prussia (© **610/337-1776**). Expect fees of $65 and up.

HEALTH CLUBS

The Philadelphia Marriott, Four Seasons, Rittenhouse, and Sheraton Society Hill have in-house facilities that are free for guests but open to nonguests at an additional charge. The spectacular **Sporting Club** (© **215/985-9876**) offers $15 day-passes to guests of other hotels in Center City. Most other moderately priced hotels have at least a few Exercycles and an aerobics space; the

Buttonwood Square Hotel, 4 blocks from Logan Circle, has a full gym room, pool, and tennis court. Alas, you'll only have access to the facilities if you stay at the hotel. The **12th Street Gym,** 204 S. 12th St. (✆ **215/985-4092**), is a restored 1930s men's club (it's gay-friendly, and women are welcome these days), with a pool, full basketball court, courts for squash and racquetball, and weights and aerobics rooms. It's open Monday through Friday from 5:30am to 11pm, Saturday from 8am to 8pm, and Sunday from 8am to 7pm. The basic rate is $10 to $20 per guest, depending on whether your hotel has an arrangement with the gym.

HIKING

Fairmount Park (✆ **215/686-1776**) has dozens of miles of paths, and the extensions of the park into the Wissahickon Creek area are quite unspoiled, with dirt roads and no auto traffic. Farther afield, **Horseshoe Trail** (✆ **215/664-0719**) starts at Routes 23 and 252 in Valley Forge State Park and winds 120 miles west marked by yellow horseshoes until it meets the Appalachian Trail.

ICE SKATING

The **Blue Cross RiverRink at Festival Pier** is open for public skating near the intersection of Columbus Boulevard and Spring Garden Street daily, from late November to early March. Admission for one 2-hour session is $6, with skate rental only $3. Call ✆ **215/925-RINK** or visit www.riverrink.com for details; there's a nice food court, too.

RUNNING & JOGGING

Again, **Fairmount Park** has more trails than you could cover in a week. An 8.25-mile loop starts in front of the Museum of Art, goes up the east bank of the Schuylkill, across the river at Falls Bridge, and back down to the museum. At the north end, Forbidden Drive along the Wissahickon has loops of dirt/gravel of 5 miles and more, with no traffic. The Benjamin Franklin Bridge path from 5th and Vine streets is 1.75 miles each way.

SWIMMING

Philadelphia has 86 municipal swimming pools, and many hotels have small lap pools. Municipal pools are open daily from 11am to 7pm and are free. Two of the best are **Cobbs Creek,** 63rd and Spruce streets, and **FDR Pool,** Broad and Pattison in South Philadelphia. Call ✆ **215/686-1776** for details. Of the best indoor pools, try the Sporting Club at the Philadelphia Park Hyatt (p. 79).

TENNIS

Some 115 courts are scattered throughout **Fairmount Park,** and you can get a tourist permit to use them by calling ✆ **215/686-0152.** You might also try the University of Pennsylvania's indoor courts at the **Robert P. Levy Tennis Pavilion,** 3130 Walnut St. (✆ **215/898-4741**). Hours are limited, but guest fee and rates total $38 for two visitors until 4pm, $42 for two after 4pm.

8 Spectator Sports

Even in these days of nomadic professional teams, Philadelphia fields teams in every major sport, and boasts two new outdoor stadiums and two indoor venues at the end of South Broad Street to house them all. The brand-new, 43,000-seat **Citizens Bank Park** is a beautiful baseball stadium opened by the Phillies in 2004; the state-of-the-art **Lincoln Financial Field** seats 66,000 for Eagles games, and opened in fall 2003. The 21,000-seat **Wachovia Center** houses the

Philadelphia Flyers pro hockey team and the Philadelphia 76ers basketball team. It couples with the 17,000-seat **Spectrum,** which functions as a rock-concert forum and hosts the U.S. Pro Indoor Tennis Championships and other one-of-a-kind events.

All these facilities are next to each other and can be reached via a 10-minute subway ride straight down South Broad Street to Pattison Avenue ($1.60). The same fare will put you on the SEPTA bus C, which goes down Broad Street more slowly but is the safer choice late at night.

Professional sports aren't the only game in town, though. Philadelphia has a lot of colleges, and **Franklin Field** and the **Palestra** dominate West Philadelphia on 33rd below Walnut Street. The Penn Relays, the first intercollegiate and amateur track event in the nation, books Franklin Field on the last weekend in April. Regattas pull along the Schuylkill all spring, summer, and fall, within sight of Fairmount Park's mansions.

A call to Ticketmaster (📞 215/336-2000 in Philadelphia) can often get you a ticket to a game before you hit town.

BASEBALL

The **Philadelphia Phillies,** Box 7575, Philadelphia, PA 19101 (📞 **215/463-1000** or www.phillies.com for ticket information, or 215/463-5300 for daily game information), won the National League pennant in 1993 and made playoffs in 1995. They play at the gorgeous, intimate new **Citizens Bank Park,** where great local food options include Tony Luke's steaks, Bull's BBQ (owned by former Phillie Greg Luzinski, who signs autographs at all games), and Peace-a-Pizza. A giant lighted Liberty Bell rings after every Phillies home run. Don't miss a cocktail at lively McFadden's Pub behind the 3rd Base Gate. Day games usually begin at 1:05pm, regular night games at 8:05pm on Friday, 7:05pm on other days. When there's a twilight doubleheader, it begins at 5:35pm.

Box seats overlooking the field at Veterans Stadium are $20, and the cheapest bleacher seats are $6 to $12 if you're over 14.

BASKETBALL

Energized by superstar Allen Iverson, the **Philadelphia 76ers,** Box 25050, Philadelphia, PA 19147, play about 40 games at the Wachovia Center between early November and late April. Call 📞 **215/339-7676** for ticket information, or charge at 📞 **215/336-2000;** single tickets range $15 to $65. There's always a good halftime show, and the promotion department works overtime for the special event nights.

There are five major college basketball teams in the Philadelphia area, and the newspapers print schedules of their games. Most games are at the Palestra, with tickets going for $5 to $8. Call 📞 **215/898-4747** to find out about ticket availability.

BIKING

The **CoreStates Pro Cycling Championship,** held each June, is a top event in the cycling world. The 156-mile race starts and finishes along the Benjamin Franklin Parkway. Watching the cyclists climb "The Wall" in Manayunk is terrifying.

BOATING

From April to September, you can watch regattas on the Schuylkill River, which have been held since the earliest days of the "Schuylkill Navy" a century ago. The **National Association of Amateur Oarsmen** (📞 **215/769-2068**) and the

Boathouse Association (© **215/686-0052**) have a complete schedule of races, one of the best known being the Dad Vail Regatta.

FOOTBALL

Football is, without a doubt, Philadelphia's favorite sport, and current Eagles quarterback Donovan McNabb is especially popular. It will take all your ingenuity (and cash) to get tickets, since virtually 100% are sold to season-ticket holders. Call © **215/463-5500** for ticket advice; you may be able to score pricey club seats. The games start at 1 or 4pm, and tickets can cost more than $100.

HORSE RACING

Philadelphia Park (the old Keystone Track) is the only track left in the area, with races from June 15 to February 13, Saturday through Tuesday. (Post time is 12:35pm.) Admission, general parking, and a program are free. The park is at 3001 Street Rd. in Bensalem, half a mile from Exit 28 on the Pennsylvania Turnpike. Call © **215/639-9000** for information.

Philadelphia Park Turf Club, 7 Penn Center, 1635 Market St., on the concourse and lower mezzanine levels (© **215/245-1556**), features 270 color video monitors and an ersatz Art Deco design; it brings the wagering to you in the comfort of Center City.

ICE HOCKEY

The Wachovia Center rocks to the **Philadelphia Flyers** from fall to spring (when the NHL is not on strike). As with the Eagles, Flyers tickets aren't easy to find—80% of tickets are sold by the season's start in October. Call © **215/465-5500** for ticket information; if you can get them, they'll cost between $23 and $85.

TRACK & FIELD

The city hosts the **Penn Relays,** the oldest and still the largest amateur track meet in the country, in late April at Franklin Field. There's an annual **Marathon** in November and a September **Philadelphia Distance Run,** a half-marathon; the latter is becoming a world-class event. Call © **215/686-0053** for more details on any of these runs.

8

City Strolls

Philadelphia is probably the most compact, walkable major city in the United States, just as it was in 1776. Even on a random walk, you'll be fascinated by the physical illustration of the progress of the centuries, and the many unexpected juxtapositions between past and present. Many of the city's neighborhoods are still made up of tree-lined, intimate streets flanked by lovely Federal town houses, especially in Society Hill, along Pine Street's "Antique Row," and the residential streets west of Rittenhouse Square, such as Spruce, Locust, and Delancey. Keep in mind that the nearer you are to the Delaware, the older (and smaller) the buildings are likely to be. The walking tours mapped out below are specifically

designed to cover the most worthwhile attractions. *Note:* It is important that you purchase individual tickets for Independence Hall, Bishop White House, and Todd House (all on Tour 1) at the Independence Visitor Center (some are available in advance at www.independencevisitorcenter.org), as you will not be able to purchase tickets at the attractions themselves. Before you enter the Liberty Bell Center, Independence Hall, Congress Hall, and Old City Hall, you must pass through a security screening facility across from Independence Visitor Center; be sure to allow time to get through security when you are choosing timed tickets to Independence Hall during busy afternoon hours.

WALKING TOUR 1	HISTORIC HIGHLIGHTS & SOCIETY HILL

Start:	Independence Visitor Center, 6th and Market streets.
Finish:	City Tavern, 2nd and Walnut streets; optional extension to Penn's Landing.
Time:	From 6 to 7 hours.
Best Time:	Start between 9 and 11am to avoid hour-long waits for Independence Hall tours.
Worst Time:	Mid-afternoon.

Start your tour at the:
1 Visitor Center
The Independence Visitor Center (open 8:30am–5pm, till 7pm July–Sept) is located in Independence National Historical Park, on 6th and Market streets. This handsome brick building was built for the 21st-century renovation of Independence Mall. It maintains spotless rest rooms, a cafe

for that jump-start-your-day coffee, and a plethora of information about the Park, the city, and the region. This is where you pick up tickets to get inside Independence Hall (whether you've reserved in advance or are counting on walk-up access). Tickets to the Bishop White and Todd houses (see below), and information about special tours and special daily events are also available here. The John Huston–directed film *Independence* is shown free of charge every half-hour. There is a handsome exhibition area and a substantial quality gift shop and bookstore.

Just north of the Visitor Center is the:

2 National Constitution Center

This is a generous half-block-long space that is dramatically modern, made of limestone, steel, and glass. The center, which opened in July 2003, explores the history of the framing of the Constitution in 1787, and also challenges the visitor to think about the effect that this document has had on the lives of all Americans, from 1787 to the present day. Its designers, Pei, Cobb, Freed & Partners, have a great track record with the Holocaust Museum in Washington, the Rose Planetarium in New York, and Cleveland's Rock & Roll Hall of Fame. Walk under a doorway inscribed "We the People," receive a "delegate's card," a la the Constitution's authors in 1787, and you'll find architecture and creative multimedia exhibits that are informative and entertaining, if a bit mind-numbing. Families can split up during their visit to experience different parts of the center. The Epcot-esque multi-media introductory theater presentation isn't essential but will appeal to kids.

Backtrack across the Visitor Center block with its new landscaping to:

3 The Liberty Bell

Decades ago, the famously cracked giant bell was located in Independence Hall, but now it's in year-old Liberty Bell Center on Market between 5th and 6th streets, just behind the Visitor Center. There is a video presentation about the bell's history, and audio is offered in a dozen languages. You will need to go through a security screening before entering this glass-walled center. See p. 125 for a full description.

Just to the east of the Liberty Bell is:

4 The Bourse

This building is a superb example of late Victorian architecture. It has been renovated as a mall and offices, in the form of two arcades surrounding an expansive atrium with a skylight. Built from 1893 to 1895 as a merchants exchange, the Bourse handsomely combines a brick-and-sandstone exterior with a cool and colorful interior. You will probably not be allowed to explore upstairs (security concerns) but you can see a lot from the ground floor.

TAKE A BREAK

The Bourse's spacious, cool ground-floor **Food Court** is open Monday, Tuesday, and Thursday from 10am to 6pm; Wednesday, Friday, and Saturday from 10am to 8pm; and Sunday from 11am to 6pm.

Right ahead of you between 5th and 6th streets (the crowds and carriages will tip you off) is:

5 Independence Hall

Independence Hall is grand, graceful, and one of democracy's true shrines (see p. 124 for a full description). Ranger-led 35-minute tours depart every 15 minutes or so, starting at 9am. (Remember, you must stay inside the secure area of the park, or you will need to go through the screening process again to enter Independence Hall.)

The two flanking buildings, **Old City Hall** (built to house the Supreme Court) and **Congress Hall,** were intended to balance each other, and their fanlight-adorned doors, keystone-decorated windows, and simple lines are appealing from any angle. They were used by a combination of federal, state, county, and city governments during a relatively short period.

Walking Tour: Historic Highlights & Society Hill

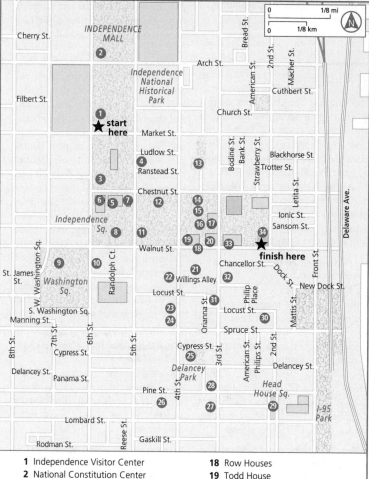

1 Independence Visitor Center
2 National Constitution Center
3 The Liberty Bell
4 The Bourse
5 Independence Hall
6 Congress Hall
7 Old City Hall
8 Independence Square
9 Washington Square
10 Athanaeum
11 Library Hall and Philosophical Hall
12 Second Bank of the United States
13 Franklin Court
14 Pemberton House
15 New Hall
16 Carpenters' Hall
17 First Bank of the United States
18 Row Houses
19 Todd House
20 Bishop White House
21 St. Joseph's Church
22 Philadelphia Contributionship
23 Episcopal Diocese of Philadelphia
24 Old St. Mary's Church
25 Hill-Physick-Keith House
26 Old Pine Presbyterian
27 St. Peter's Episcopal Church
28 Kosciusko National Memorial
29 Head House Square
30 Man Full of Troubles Tavern
31 Powel House
32 St. Paul's Episcopal Church
33 Philadelphia Exchange
34 City Tavern

Turn left as you exit Independence Hall and walk next door to:

⑥ Congress Hall

Built in 1787, this building housed the U.S. Congress for 10 years and witnessed the inaugurations of Washington and Adams. The wall-to-wall carpeting and Venetian blinds are disappointingly modern, but it's hard to get mahogany desks and leather armchairs of such workmanship nowadays. Look for the little corners where representatives could smoke, take snuff, and drink sherry during recess. Watching the House and Senate from the balconies was a popular social activity. If debate was boring, one could always admire the ceiling moldings.

Exit Congress Hall and turn right, passing Independence Hall, to reach:

⑦ Old City Hall

Built in 1790, and located at the corner of 5th and Chestnut streets, Old City Hall was home to the third branch of the federal government, the U.S. Supreme Court, under Chief Justice John Jay, from 1790 to 1800. From 1800 to 1870 the building was used as the city hall. An exhibit here describes the first years of the judiciary branch of the U.S. government.

In back of this central trio of buildings is the shady and hallowed:

⑧ Independence Square

On July 8, 1776, John Nixon read the Declaration of Independence to the assembled city on this spot. At night, from April to October, the "Lights of Liberty" sound-and-light tour/show ends with projections on the back wall of Independence Hall.

Cut through Independence Square to the greenery at the southwest corner. This is:

⑨ Washington Square

This square is just as expansive and even leafier than when it was the town's pasture. In the 1840s, this was the center of fashionable Philadelphia. Some modern apartment houses have risen here, but vintage buildings that ring the square include the magnificent Victorian Athenaeum literary society, and the grand Beaux Arts–style Locks art gallery. On the southwest corner, the **Meredith-Penrose House** and its neighbors, are lovely. On the west side, Deco buildings have been turned into condos, and there's a sleek restaurant and outdoor lounge called, simply, Washington Square. The square now houses the Tomb of the Unknown Soldier from the Revolutionary War, with its eternal flame. The square has also been the center of Philadelphia publishing for 150 years, with **Lea and Febiger** and **J. B. Lippincott** at no. 227. The massive white building on the north side of the square has been redeveloped, but the Curtis Publishing Co. (now the **Curtis Center**) once sent out the *Saturday Evening Post* and other magazines from here.

Turn to look east. The solid, Italianate Revival brownstone (1845–47) on Washington Square East is the:

⑩ Athenaeum

The Athenaeum is a virtually unchanged pocket of 19th-century society life (see p. 141 for a fuller description).

Returning to Independence Square, walk behind Old City Hall. Along 5th Street and opposite, you'll find the:

⑪ Library Hall and Philosophical Hall

Library Hall is the 1954 reconstruction of Benjamin Franklin's old Library Company, which was the first lending library in the Colonies. The Library Company is now at 1314 Locust St., and this graceful Federal building now houses the library of the American Philosophical Society, across the street. The collection is fascinating, including Franklin's will, a copy of William Penn's 1701 Charter of Privileges, and Jefferson's own handwritten copy of the Declaration of Independence. The exhibits focus on

Architectural ABCs

You'll enjoy your stroll around Society Hill and Queen Village even more if you know something about Colonial and Federal architecture, especially since many homes aren't open for individual tours. Brick is the constant, clay being abundant by the Delaware's banks—but construction methods have varied over the past 150 years.

Generally, houses built before the 1750s, such as the **Trump House** at 214 Delancey St., are two and one-half stories, with two rooms per floor and a dormer window jutting out of a steep gambrel roof (a gambrel roof consists of a roof with two slopes on each of the two sides, with the lower slope steeper than the upper). An eave usually separates the simple door and its transom windows from the second level. Careful bricklayers liked to alternate the long and short sides of bricks (called "stretchers" and "headers," respectively), a style known as Flemish Bond. The headers were often glazed to create a checkerboard pattern. Wrought-iron boot scrapers flank the doorsteps.

Houses built in Philadelphia's Colonial heyday soared to three or four stories—taller after the Revolution—and adopted heavy Georgian cornices (the underside of a roof overhang) and elaborate doorways. The homes of the truly wealthy, such as the **Powel House** at 244 S. 3rd St. and the **Morris House** at 235 S. 8th St., have fanlights above their arched brick doorways; the **Davis-Lenox House** at 217 Spruce St. has a simple raised pediment. Since the Georgian style demanded symmetry, the parlors were often given imaginary doors and windows to even things out. The less wealthy lived in "trinity" houses—one room on each of three floors, named for faith, hope, and charity. Few town houses were free-standing (most were row houses)—the **Hill-Physick-Keith House** at 321 S. 4th St. is an exception.

Federal architecture, which blew in from England and New England in the 1790s, is less heavy (no more Flemish Bond for bricks) and generally more graceful (more glass, with delicate molding instead of wainscoting). Any house like the **Meredith House** at 700 S. Washington Sq., with a half story of marble stairs leading to a raised mahogany door, was surely constructed after 1800. Greek Revival elements such as rounded dormer windows and oval staircases became the fashion from the 1810s on. Three Victorian brownstones at 260 S. 3rd St. once belonged to Michel Bouvier, Jacqueline Kennedy Onassis's great-great-grandfather.

If you're here in April through June, don't pass up the **Philadelphia Open House** to view the interiors of dozens of homes (volunteered by proud owners). Call © **215/928-1188** or visit www.friendsof independence.org for information.

the history of science in America. The library's hours follow the park schedule (daily 9am–5pm). **Philosophical Hall,** across the way, is the home of the American Philosophical Society. The society, founded by Ben Franklin, is made up of a prestigious honor roll of America's outstanding intellects and achievers. In Franklin's day, philosophers were more often than not industrious young men with scientific and learned interests. Current members of the society include former senator Bill Bradley, violinist Itzhak Perlman, poet Rita Dove, and commentator Bill Moyers. The building's interior is not open to the public, but look for traces of old Georgian springing into new Federal architecture, such as fan-shaped and larger windows and more elaborate doorsteps.

Next to Philosophical Hall is the:

⑫ Second Bank of the United States

Its strong Greek columns have worn away somewhat, but the beautiful bank still holds interest. The Second Bank was chartered by Congress in 1816 for a term of 20 years, again at a time when the country felt that it needed reliable circulating money. The building (1818–24), designed like the Philadelphia Exchange by William Strickland, is adapted from the Parthenon, and the Greeks would have been proud of its capable director, Nicholas Biddle. An elitist to the core, he was the man Andrew Jackson and his supporters had in mind when they complained about private individuals controlling public government. "Old Hickory" vetoed renewal of the bank's charter, increasing the money supply but ruining Biddle and the bank.

The building was used as a Customs House until 1934. Now the National Park Service uses it as a portrait gallery of early Americans. The collection contains many of the oldest gallery portraits in the country, painted by Peale, Sully, Neagle, Stuart, and Allston. Admission is $2 for persons 16 or over. The building is open daily from 9am to 5pm.

Walk east on Chestnut Street 1 block. The southern side of the block is 18th century all the way, passing New Hall Museum (we'll get back to that). Crossing the street brings you to a handsome collection of 19th-century banks and commercial facades, including the 1867 First National Bank at no. 315 and the Philadelphia National Bank at no. 323. Go into the marked alleyway to enter:

⑬ Franklin Court

See p. 126 for a full description of this wonderful tribute to Benjamin Franklin in his final home.

You can cross through to Market Street to the north to buy some stamps from Ben's own re-created post office, or return to Chestnut Street for more history at:

⑭ Pemberton House

Joseph Pemberton, a Quaker sugar and Madeira wine merchant, had just built this fine Georgian home when the Second Continental Congress, in the aftermath of the gunfire at Concord and Lexington, cut back on British imports. Pemberton went bankrupt, and the house was razed in 1862, only to be reconstructed a century later. It now houses a bookstore.

⑮ New Hall

This is a modern copy of a hall built in 1791 by the Carpenters' Company, who rented it out to various people. When the federal government was provisionally based in Philadelphia, this space was used as the headquarters for the first War (now Defense) Department. The building now houses the Military Museum, including some very early American flags. (The Marine Corps was founded at nearby Tun Tavern.) You'll see lots of uniforms, swords, and medals.

Walk south upon exiting New Hall. In mid-block sits the delicate:

⑯ Carpenters' Hall

This was a newly built guildhall when the First Continental Congress met here in 1774. See p. 139 for a more detailed description.

Walk to the east across the manicured walkways to find the:

⑰ First Bank of the United States (built in 1795)

This building is not open to the public but is a superb example of Federal architecture. This graceful edifice is the oldest surviving bank building in America. Initially, each of the new states issued its own currency. Dealing with 13 different currencies hampered commerce and travel among the states, so Alexander Hamilton proposed a single bank (originally in Carpenters' Hall) for loans and deposits. The classical facade, Hamilton's idea, is meant to recall the democracy and splendor of ancient Greece. The mahogany American eagle on the pediment over the Corinthian columns at the entrance is a famous and rare example of 18th-century sculpture.

The Park Service cleared many of the non-historic structures on the block behind the First Bank (and throughout the Historic Park area), creating 18th-century gardens and lawns.

You may be surprised to learn that Society Hill wasn't named after the upper crust who lived here in Colonial times. Rather, the name refers to the Free Society of Traders, a group of businessmen and investors persuaded by William Penn to settle here with their families in 1683. The name applies to the area east of Washington Square between Walnut and Lombard streets. Many of Philadelphia's white-collar workers, clerics, teachers, importers, and politicos have lived and worked here over the years.

Despite the Colonial facades, nobody would have considered walking through this decrepit and undesirable neighborhood a few decades ago. That's all changed now thanks to a massive urban-renewal project, which did a superb job of blending new housing developments in with their Georgian neighbors.

Of course, Society Hill isn't just residential. Georgian and Federal public buildings and churches, from **Head House Square** and **Pennsylvania Hospital** to **St. Peter's** and **St. Paul's,** may make you feel as if you've stumbled onto a movie set. But all of the buildings are used—and the area works as a living community today. A bit south of your present location fine restaurants and charming stores cluster south of Lombard, especially around Head House Square (1803) at 2nd and Lombard streets.

Continuing on your tour from the greenery in back of the First Bank, you'll see very typically restored row houses along the southern side of Walnut Street between 3rd and 4th streets. Take some time to explore these:

⑱ Row Houses

These restored row houses will catch your eye with their paneled doors and shutters, bands of brick or stone between floors, and small diamonds of painted metal. These last are fire-insurance markers—all early American cities were terrible fire hazards, and Philadelphia, led by Benjamin Franklin, was the first to do anything about it. The plaques functioned as advertisements for the various companies and also helped firemen identify which houses they were responsible for saving. Now the houses belong to park offices and the Pennsylvania Horticultural Association, which maintains an 18th-century formal garden open to the public.

At the corner of 4th and Walnut streets is the:

⑲ Todd House

Tours of the house (for 10 persons at a time) are required (you can't explore on your own), and tickets by advance reservation are required. They cost $2 at the Independence Visitor Center (you can't buy directly from Todd House, but the ticket price covers admission to both this and the Bishop White House). John Todd, Jr., was a young Quaker lawyer of moderate means. His house, built in 1775, cannot compare to that of Bishop White (see below), but it is far grander than Betsy Ross's. Todd used the ground-floor parlor as his law office and the family lived and entertained on the second floor. When Todd died in the 1793 epidemic of yellow fever, his vivacious widow Dolley married a Virginia lawyer named James Madison, the future president.

Double back down Walnut toward 3rd Street; at no. 309, is the other park-run dwelling, the:

20 Bishop White House

Tours (for 10 persons at a time) are the only way to see the house; $2 tickets can *only* be obtained at the Independence Visitor Center. This house is on one of the loveliest row-house blocks in the city, and it's a splendid example of how a pillar of the community lived in Federal America. Bishop White (1748–1836) was the founder of Episcopalianism, breaking with the Anglican church. He was a good friend of Franklin, as you'll see from the upstairs library. Notice how well the painted cloth floor in the entrance hall survived muddy boots and 20 varnishings. In case you take indoor plumbing for granted, remember that outhouses provided the only relief on most Colonial property. The library reveals the bishop's tastes, featuring Sir Walter Scott's *Waverley* novels, the *Encyclopaedia Britannica,* and the Koran alongside traditional religious texts.

Across the street, the park has purchased property and created a garden that exposes the side of:

21 Old St. Joseph's Church

This is the first Roman Catholic church in Philadelphia (see p. 138 for a description). It's much more intriguing if you enter through the iron gate and archway on Willing's Alley, off 4th Street between Walnut and Spruce.

Turn down 4th Street, and walk to 212 S. 4th St. to find the:

22 Philadelphia Contributionship (1836)

This building has sported the "Hand-in-Hand" fire-insurance mark since it was built in 1836 as the headquarters of the Hand-in-Hand fire-insurance company (which was founded in 1752). The facade of the building is Greek Revival, with a gorgeous limestone entrance, columns, and balustrades leading to the front door. The architect, Thomas U. Walter, also designed the dome and the House and Senate wings of the U.S. Capitol. Entrance to the building is free, and it's open Monday through Friday from 10am to 3pm. The normal exhibition displays old leather fire-fighting equipment and the original policy statement and list of members. If you call © 215/627-1752 ahead of time, you'll get to view two meeting rooms and a dining room, with their veined marble fireplaces and rare bird's-eye maple dining-room chairs.

Walk down 4th Street until you reach no. 240, which is the:

23 Episcopal Diocese of Philadelphia

This building combines two splendid row houses built in 1750 and 1826 for the Cadwallader family. Both houses are closed to the public. Look opposite the Diocese to see **Bingham Court,** a 1967 adaptation of the Society Hill style of brick row houses.

Continue down 4th Street to 248 4th St.:

24 Old St. Mary's Church

The most important Roman Catholic church during the Revolution, this was the "Sunday" church, as opposed to St. Joseph's which functioned as a weekday chapel. The interior is fairly prosaic, but the paved graveyard is a picturesque spot for a breather, with some interesting headstones and memorials.

Impressions

It is a handsome city, but distractingly regular. After walking about it for an hour or two, I felt that I would have given the world for a crooked street. The collar of my coat appeared to stiffen, and the brim of my hat to expand, beneath its Quakery influence. My hair shrunk into a sleek short crop, my hands folded themselves upon my breast of their own calm accord, and thoughts of taking lodgings in Mark Lane over against the Market Place, and of making a large fortune by speculations in corn, came over me involuntarily.

—Charles Dickens, *American Notes* (1842)

Walk a quarter of a block south of the church. The corner of Spruce and 4th streets is a good place to take a breath, with the town houses of **Girard Row** in front of you. Half a block to the west at 426 Spruce St., Thomas U. Walter, the architect of the Contributionship (see above), designed a Baptist church in 1830 that has been modified as the **Society Hill Synagogue,** run by Romanian immigrants at the turn of the 20th century and by Conservative Jews more recently.

Continue down 4th Street to no. 321, the:

㉕ Physick House

This is possibly the finest residential structure in Society Hill (see p. 145 for a fuller description). Take a few steps east on adjoining Cypress Street to reach **Delancey Park,** more popularly known as "Three Bears Park," a delightful playground with places to play and a group of stone bears that are perfect photo props.

Continue south along 4th Street. More Georgian and Federal church facades appear at the corners of 4th and Pine streets. Take a right down Pine Street. At 412 Pine St. you'll find:

㉖ Old Pine Presbyterian

With its enormous raised facade and forbidding iron fence, this building didn't always look like a Greek temple. The Penns granted the Presbyterians this land in perpetuity, and the first sanctuary took shape in 1768. The double Corinthian columns, inside

and out, were added in 1830, after the occupying British soldiers burned most of the interior. Everything is linear at Old Pine: The portico leads into a rectangle of pews, and slim pillars support a gallery with an elaborately carved rail of flowers and dentils. The altar will surprise you—it's just a dais backed by elaborate columns and entablature. You'll find it hard to believe that this filigree is of wood and not clay or plaster. Exploration of the lovely building is free. It's open daily from 9am to 5pm, and there are sometimes Sunday "Jazz Vespers" concerts held here.

If you like, take a detour and keep going south on 4th Street to Lombard and South streets, until South Street's funky shopping and nightlife district. If you've taken this detour, double back up to Pine Street. Walk east on Pine Street to:

㉗ St. Peter's Episcopal Church (1761)

This church is an example of classic Georgian simplicity (see p. 138 for a full description).

Farther north, at 301 Pine St., is the:

㉘ Kosciuszko National Memorial

This is the double 1775 Georgian building that housed Kosciuszko, the Polish engineer and soldier who turned the tide for American forces at Saratoga and West Point. It's part of the Park system and open daily from 10am to 5pm.

Now follow Pine Street to 2nd Street, the major north-south route through Philadelphia in Colonial days. Open markets were a big part of urban life. In fact, no Colonial native would recognize Market Street today without the wooden sheds that covered stalls from Front to 6th streets and its narrow cart paths on both sides. One place that would be recognizable, though, is:

㉙ Head House Square

This square was built in 1803 in the middle of 2nd Street as a place where shoppers could congregate. Head House itself, a brick shed with a cupola that once held a fire bell, trails a simple brick arcade between Pine and South streets. The building used to house fire companies and stables. In those days, market took place at dawn on Tuesday and Friday. Butter and eggs were sold on the west side, meat under the eaves, and herbs and vegetables on the river side. Fish sellers were relegated to the far sidewalks (it isn't hard to imagine why). Now craftspeople spread out their goods here in summer, especially on weekends.

TAKE A BREAK
Dark Horse Pub, 421 S. 2nd St., and several other Head House Square restaurants make excellent lunch or snack stopovers; the Dark Horse (open from 11:30am daily) offers classic British fare such as shepherd's pie, and more modern dishes such as chipotle flank steak quesadillas and Vietnamese mussels. **Chef's Market,** just around the corner at 231 South St., offers upscale baked goods, cheeses, sandwiches, and prepared foods.

Now head up 2nd Street to Spruce Street. Across the street from the 1765 Abercrombie House (one of the tallest Colonial dwellings in America), at 127 Spruce St., are the:

㉚ Society Hill Towers

Look just up the hill to see the **Society Hill Towers** (1964), three condominium buildings built around a plaza, designed by I. M. Pei. They are sleek, simple, and modern, with excellent landscaping.

It's best to walk west back to 3rd Street, then north to a stunning block of row-house mansions including Bishop Stevens at no. 232, with its cast-iron balcony; Atkinson House at no. 236, which today conceals an indoor pool; and Penn-Chew House at no. 242, owned by the grandson of William Penn and the last Colonial governor of Pennsylvania. The mansion that you can actually visit, at 244 S. 3rd St., is:

㉛ Powel House

This is the impressive home of Philadelphia's last Colonial and first U.S. mayor. (See p. 141 for more details.)

Across the street, at 225 S. 3rd St., is:

㉜ St. Paul's Episcopal Church (1761)

This is another church founded thanks to Philadelphia's religious tolerance. When the High Anglican Church refused to license the speech of William McClenachan, a young clergyman who preached such radical notions as the separation of church and state, St. Paul's was set up as his "bully pulpit." The money for the Georgian hall was raised through donations and lotteries. Now the building houses the headquarters of the denomination's community inside beautiful pre-Revolutionary wrought-iron gates and marble-topped enclosing walls. If you go up to the second floor (open Mon–Fri 9am–5pm), you can still see most of the original chancel.

Standing at the corner of 3rd and Walnut streets, you can't miss the:

㉝ Philadelphia Exchange (1832)

This building is a masterwork by William Strickland. It's not open to the public.

Head toward 2nd Street and the river, crossing one of my favorite spaces, a broad area of cobblestones covering Dock Street (Dock Creek in Penn's day) and the Delaware River beyond. The Ritz 5 movie house on your left shows fine independent movies. Soon you'll make a rear approach to the reconstructed restaurant and gardens of:

❸❹ City Tavern

Built in 1773, this was the most opulent and genteel tavern and social hall in the Colonies and the scene of many discussions among the founding fathers. Unlike most of the city's pubs, it was built with businessmen's subscriptions, to assure its quality. George Washington met with most delegates to the Constitutional Convention for a farewell dinner here in 1787. The park now operates the City Tavern as a concession, which serves continuously from 11am. The back garden seating is shady and cool—perfect for a mid-afternoon break in warm weather.

If you choose to continue toward the Delaware via the pleasant pedestrian extension of Walnut Street and the staircase at its end, you'll pass between the new **Sheraton Society Hill** hotel and the new incarnation of famous **Bookbinder's** restaurant, winding up more or less in front of the wonderful **Independence Seaport Museum** and the new Hyatt Regency on the waterfront. Consult the "Parks, the Parkway & Penn's Landing" section on p. 149 for more details on this area.

WALKING TOUR 2   OLD CITY

Start:	Welcome Park, 2nd and Walnut streets.
Finish:	Market Place East, 7th and Market streets.
Time:	From 3 to 5 hours.
Best Time:	Start no later than 3pm to avoid museum closings. If contemporary art and socializing is your interest, the first Friday of every month brings special late hours for all galleries, cafes, and many historic attractions.
Worst Time:	Afternoons.

Old City is an intriguing blend of 17th- and 18th-century artisan row houses, robust 19th-century warehouses and commercial structures, and 20th-century rehabs of all of the above featuring artist lofts and galleries. Many of the cast-iron and brick buildings are being carefully restored and preserved; even if they are modern condos outside, their facades retain a sense of history.

Across from the narrow lane adjoining City Tavern, on 2nd Street, near Walnut Street, is:

❶ Welcome Park

This is the site of the Slate Roof House, where William Penn granted the "Charter of Privileges" (now at the Library Hall off Independence Square) in 1701. The pavement bears a massive and whimsical map of Penn's City, with a timeline of his life on the walls.

Next door is the **Thomas Bond House,** a restored 1769 Georgian row house that's now a bed-and-breakfast (see p. 78 for more information).

Walk along the block-long Ritz East cinema to:

❷ Front Street

Front Street actually butted up to the river's edge in Colonial times. A walk north brings you past Warmdaddy's and La Famiglia restaurants, and the possibility of exploring Penn's Landing (p. 152) via a beautifully terraced park.

TAKE A BREAK
The block of "Two Street" between Chestnut and Market contains lots of good, casual restaurants such as **Cuba Libre, Serrano, Sassafras,** and **Café Spice.**

Impressions

[With its] streets of small, low, yet snug-looking houses . . . Philadelphia must contain in comfort the largest number of small householders of any city in the world.
    —*London Times* reporter William Bussell, *My Diary North and South*
                                                                    (1850)

Perhaps deterred by the large, blocky Hyatt Regency between you and the water, head back to the florid Corn Exchange Bank at 2nd and Chestnut streets, then turn right onto one of the liveliest blocks in the historic area. Once you hit the newly widened sidewalks of Market Street (High St. in Colonial times), you'll find a different world, where a burst of boutiques, bars, and upgraded bistros like Fork, Farmicia, and Continental have replaced discount clothing stores. The many alleyways between Front and 5th streets, with names like Trotter Street, Bank Street, and Strawberry Street, testify to the activities and preoccupations of Colonial residents. A particular favorite facade of mine is at 22 S. 3rd St. This is the:

③ Norwegian Seaman's Church

This William Strickland gem from 1837, with Corinthian columns and granite steps, is now a restaurant and club.

If you took the first walking tour, continue right through the Franklin Court stop (stop number 4) to Market Street and Christ Church. Otherwise continue on Market Street until you are between 3rd and 4th streets, where you will find:

④ Franklin Court

This was Ben Franklin's final home, and is now a post office (see p. 126 for a full description).

Standing on Market Street, you can't miss the graceful spire of:

⑤ Christ Church

Urban renewal removed the unsightly buildings that hid the church walls from Market Street. Christ Church, with its restful benches and adjoining cemetery, is Philadelphia's leading place of worship. See p. 137 for a full description.

> **TAKE A BREAK**
> It may be a bit early for another refueling stop, but the block of Church Street directly to the west of the church contains **Old City Coffee** at no. 221, a favorite place for marvelous coffee and light lunches. **Petit 4 Pastry Studio** at 160 N. 3rd St has handmade truffles, tarts, and pastries, plus coffee drinks in a charmingly funky setting. If the end of the day is approaching by the time you get here, duck underneath the Market Street ramp to I-95 at Front Street to reach **Panorama's** wine bar and bistro.

Walk east down Church Street and take a left at Front Street. Walk north along Front Street for 4 short blocks to get the flavor of the 1830s warehouses, such as Girard at 18–30 N. Front St. and Smythe Stores at 101 Arch St. If you continued north and east, you would come to the clubs and restaurants on the water, such as Hibachi and Rock Lobster. Instead, take a left onto:

⑥ Elfreth's Alley

Since 1702, this has been the oldest continuously occupied group of homes in America. See p. 140 for a full description of these tiny houses. Several courts are perfect for wandering into, and you can enter the house at no. 126 and shop at the gift boutique at no. 124.

Walk to the end of Elfreth's Alley and make a right back onto 2nd Street, with its china and restaurant-supply stores. Detour north for a minute to look at 2nd Street Art Building, which houses the Clay Studio and NEXUS galleries, and stop when you reach Quarry Street to visit the:

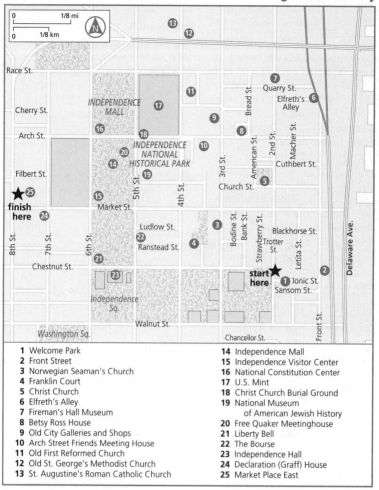

1 Welcome Park
2 Front Street
3 Norwegian Seaman's Church
4 Franklin Court
5 Christ Church
6 Elfreth's Alley
7 Fireman's Hall Museum
8 Betsy Ross House
9 Old City Galleries and Shops
10 Arch Street Friends Meeting House
11 Old First Reformed Church
12 Old St. George's Methodist Church
13 St. Augustine's Roman Catholic Church
14 Independence Mall
15 Independence Visitor Center
16 National Constitution Center
17 U.S. Mint
18 Christ Church Burial Ground
19 National Museum of American Jewish History
20 Free Quaker Meetinghouse
21 Liberty Bell
22 The Bourse
23 Independence Hall
24 Declaration (Graff) House
25 Market Place East

⑦ Fireman's Hall Museum

This restored century-old firehouse contains a hand pump used by Ben Franklin, who helped advance firefighting beyond tossing water from rudimentary wooden buckets. On display are 19th- and 20th-century fire wagons, along with assorted firefighting tools and memorabilia.

Head south now and turn right on Arch Street, where you'll come to no. 239, the:

⑧ Betsy Ross House

See p. 138 for full details on the house. The tour of the house is short, but there's a large garden to explore. Directly opposite the house, you'll find the **Mulberry Market,** an upscale deli with seating in the rear.

Continue west on Arch Street until you find 3rd Street. At the corner of 3rd Street, turn north (toward the Ben Franklin Bridge) to reach the:

⑨ Old City galleries and shops

This block of N. 3rd Street has some of the coolest Old City furniture, crafts, and art you can find. I love **Foster's Urban Homeware** at no. 124, and the **OLC** lighting store at no. 152.

Cross 3rd Street to the Hoop Skirt Factory at 309–313 Arch St., dating from 1875, and the charming Loxley Court just beyond, designed by carpenter Benjamin Loxley in 1741. (It stayed within the family until 1901.) On the south side of Arch Street is the:

⑩ Arch Street Meeting House

This is the largest Quaker meeting-house in America, a simple 1805 structure with a substantial history (see p. 137 for details).

Walk west on Arch Street and make a right when you reach 4th Street. Walk north on 4th Street to no. 151, the:

⑪ Old First Reformed Church

Built in 1837 for a sect of German Protestants, the building survived a stint as a paint warehouse in the late 19th century. The church functions as a small and always full youth hostel during July and August.

Continuing on 4th Street and crossing under the gloomy piers of the Benjamin Franklin Bridge, you'll see 235 N. 4th St., the:

⑫ Old St. George's Methodist Church

This was the cradle of American Methodism and the scene of fanatic religious revival meetings in the early 1770s.

Cross to the other side of 4th Street, below Vine, to find:

⑬ St. Augustine's Roman Catholic Church

This is another 18th-century building. This one was built for German and Irish Catholics who couldn't get to St. Joseph's, south of Market Street, because of muddy streets. Villanova University, and the Augustinian presence in the United States, started here. The building actually only dates from 1844; the original burned down during anti-Catholic riots.

Now, keep walking west along the bridge to 5th Street, then head south along:

⑭ Independence Mall

Independence Mall is a swath of urban renewal that has recently been graced with the new Independence Visitor Center, beautiful landscaping, and a new home for the Liberty Bell.

Walk over to the area between Market Street and Arch Street to visit the:

⑮ Independence Visitor Center

For a general rest stop, tickets to chief Independence National Historical Park sights, and information about the city and region, this facility is superb. See p. 121 for a fuller description.

Walk 1 block north to:

⑯ National Constitution Center

This attraction is described in Walking Tour 1 on p. 162, and in Chapter 7 on p. 126.

At the upper end of the Mall (Florist St.) is the bicycle and pedestrian entrance to the Benjamin Franklin Bridge; cycling or walking across the bridge makes for a thrilling but time-consuming expedition.

Continuing on, head down 5th Street, stopping at the:

⑰ U.S. Mint

Of the three mints in the country (the others are in Denver and San Francisco), Philadelphia's is the oldest and the largest. (See p. 146 for hours and description, but note that with security concerns the Mint is generally closed to walk-up traffic.)

Just south of the Mint, on Arch Street, is:

⑱ Christ Church Burial Ground

This is the resting place of Benjamin and Deborah Franklin and other notables (toss a coin through the opening in the brick wall for luck).

Walk south down 5th Street to 55 N. 5th St. to find the:

⑲ National Museum of American Jewish History

The city of Philadelphia has a history of distinguished Jewish involvement in town affairs that's almost as long as the life of the city itself. This museum, connected to the city's oldest congregation, commemorates the history of Jews in America (see p. 145 for a fuller description). You'll notice how much lower the street level used to be by looking at the statuary outside.

Turn up 5th Street, and look for a small building across from the Franklin graves, in Independence Mall. This is the:

20 Free Quaker Meetinghouse

"Fighting Quakers," such as Betsy Ross, were willing to support the Revolutionary War. But since this violated the tenets of pure Quakerism, they were forced to leave Arch Street Friends and establish their own meetinghouse, which they did—right here. The building is now run by the Park Service.

Cross Market Street on Independence Mall to see the:

21 Liberty Bell

See p. 125 for a description and history of the bell.

Walk east from the Liberty Bell Center on 5th Street where you'll find:

22 The Bourse

This was a 19th-century exchange that now contains a food court and pleasant urban mall (a "Take a Break" stop discussed in the Historic Highlights tour above).

Walk south on 5th Street and reenter Independence Mall via Chestnut Street, and you'll be in front of:

23 Independence Hall

Independence Hall is described, as are the two flanking buildings, **Congress Hall** and **Old City Hall,** on p. 124. Tour hours and security-screening information are also given on this page.

Continue west along Chestnut Street to 7th Street, and turn right onto a historic block containing the Atwater Kent Museum of city memorabilia and the:

24 Declaration (Graff) House

This is a reconstruction of the lodgings where Thomas Jefferson drafted the Declaration of Independence. It is run by the National Park Service, with free daily admission. You'll find a full description of the Declaration House on p. 139.

Directly opposite Graff House on Market Street is:

25 Market Place East

This is the converted and rehabilitated former home of Lit Brothers Department Store, a wrought-iron palace that's a block long (see the full description on p. 180).

9

Shopping

Philadelphia has a beguiling mix of small, homegrown boutiques and antiques stores, plus glossy designer shops along Rittenhouse Row, as Walnut Street's shopping corridor is called. You'll find unique gifts for the kids in a triple-story all-children's department store, and modern home accessories in an Old City neighborhood warehouse-turned-boutique. Especially in the past decade, Philadelphia has become a sophisticated and diverse place to shop (sleek Lagos Jewelers, upscale national chain Anthropologie, and teenagers' favorite Urban Outfitters were all born here, and have flagship stores in Center City).

Though downtown has few major department stores (look for Neiman Marcus and Nordstrom at the wonderful, huge King of Prussia Mall about 20 minutes west of the city), you can still find anything from Jimmy Choo sandals to Tiffany & Co. diamonds to the softest teddy bears imaginable in Center City Philly. As Ben Franklin's *Autobiography* put it, telling of his surprise upon coming to breakfast one morning to find a china bowl and silver spoon in his very own Colonial kitchen: "Luxury will enter families and make a progress in spite of principle."

1 The Shopping Scene

This chapter concentrates on Center City stores that carry unique, special, or unusual items. The best places to look for chic fashion, cosmetics, and international wares are the specialty shops around **Liberty Place** and **Rittenhouse Square.** You'll find some SoHo–style art, antiques, and crafts in the **Old City** area, north and east of the historic landmarks, and unique home and antiques stores along **Pine Street. Manayunk,** several miles up the Schuylkill River to the northwest of town, has some home stores and boutiques, plus chains such as Pottery Barn. The once-funky area on **South Street,** just south of Society Hill, is best suited for teenagers or fans of Gothic, multizippered clothing.

It's useful to note that the outskirts of Philadelphia contain prime examples of the enormous malls now ubiquitous at the interchanges of American superhighways—the 21st-century version of Colonial village squares. You'll find luxury chains and department stores at **King of Prussia Mall**—a 450-store behemoth, with Neiman Marcus, Nordstrom, J. Crew, Cartier, and Louis Vuitton, it's second only to Minnesota's Mall of America. **Franklin Mills,** a hugely popular and sprawling outlet mall that includes Off Fifth, a low-priced outlet of Saks Fifth Avenue, draws four times the traffic of the Liberty Bell.

There is no sales tax on clothing; other items are taxed at 7%. Most stores stay open during regular business hours, from 10am to 6 or 7pm Monday through Saturday, and later on Wednesday evening. Some are also open on Sunday.

MALLS & SHOPPING CENTERS

The Bellevue   The lower floors of the Park Hyatt/Bellevue Hotel have been turned into an upscale collection of the top names in retailing. Browsing here is a low-key affair—the space feels a little like a private club. The **Polo Ralph Lauren** store here is the third largest in the world, boasting three floors of mahogany-and-brass splendor. Other tenants include **Tiffany & Co.,** with its extraordinary jewelry, silver, and accessories; **Williams Sonoma** for gourmet snacks and high end kitchen supplies; a just-right fashionable **Nicole Miller; Hope Chest** for intimates and lingerie; **Suky Rosan** for women's fashion; **Vigant** luggage; and **Origins** cosmetics. Dine at the **Palm Restaurant,** grab a soy latte at **Starbucks,** or pick up spring rolls or pizza at the lower-level food court. Broad and Walnut sts. (© 215/875-8350. www.bellevuephiladelphia.com.

Franklin Mills *Value*   Fifteen miles northeast of Center City, on the edge of Bucks County, the former Liberty Bell is now Franklin Mills, the city's largest single-story mall, with 1.8 million square feet devoted to 220 discount and outlet stores. It generates 15 million shoppers annually, and there's parking for more than 9,000 cars in four color-coded zones. Franklin Mills is a discount shoppers' landmark, with designer clothing at outlets from Saks Fifth Avenue, Neiman Marcus, Nordstrom, Burlington Coat Factory, and Kaspar. If you are patient, you can find such brands as Chanel, Manolo Blahnik, and Gucci here. General Cinema has a 14-screen multiplex with stadium seating. For other amusement, **Jillian's** is a modern take on an old-fashioned bowling alley, with billiard table, games, casual American dining (and a hibachi grill), dancing on weekends, and bars—plus 18 softly lit, groovy lanes (Mon–Wed 11am–1am; Thurs–Sat 11am–2am; Sun 11am–midnight; must be 21 after 9:30pm; © **215/632-0333**). There's also a 30-store **Home and Design Centre.** Open Monday through Saturday from 10am to 9:30pm and Sunday from 11am to 7pm. 1455 Franklin Mills Circle. (© **800/336-6255** or 215/632-1500. Follow the signs from I-95 (take Exit 35 Woodhaven Rd.) or from the Pa. Turnpike (take Exit 351 south). SEPTA buses go right to the complex.

The Gallery at Market East   The Gallery at Market East, next to the Pennsylvania Convention Center, features four levels accommodating more than 170 lower-priced stores and restaurants around sunken arcades and a glass atrium, and includes a JCPenney department store, and a two-story Kmart. The **food court** has more than 25 snack bars and takeout spots, and top stores include **Gap** and the **Children's Place.** The **Hardshell Café,** at the street corner of 9th and Market, offers all-you-can-eat specials. Stores offer running shoes, books, pets, cameras, jewelry, fresh produce, toys, and clothing. **Strawbridge's** connects over 9th Street with merchandise of slightly higher quality and prices. You can pick up a substantial coupon discount book at the Gallery's Information Center

---

Finds Food & Shops at the Airport

Philadelphia International Airport (© **215/937-1200**) has more than 30 shops and eateries in the "Philadelphia Marketplace" between Terminals B and C, including a lively and spacious food court with seating for 400. Retail includes **Airport Wireless** for gadgets and PDA accessories, **GAP/GAP Kids, Discovery Channel Store, Brookstone,** and **Wilson's Leather,** while the **Dock Street Airport Brew Pub** headlines the food court operation. There are 70 other shopping and dining venues along the concourses near airline gates.

Philadelphia Clothing Shops, Malls & Shopping Centers

Adresse **8**

Anthropologie **6**

Banana Republic **17**

The Bellevue **18**

Born Yesterday **3**

Boyd's **5**

Brooks Brothers **16**

Burberrys Limited **10**

Children's Boutique **10**

Daffy's **12**

Franklin Mills **22**

The Gallery at Market East **20**

Gap **15**

H&M **14**

J. Crew **13**

Jaques Ferber **10**

Joan Shepp Boutique **9**

Kamikaze Kids **23**

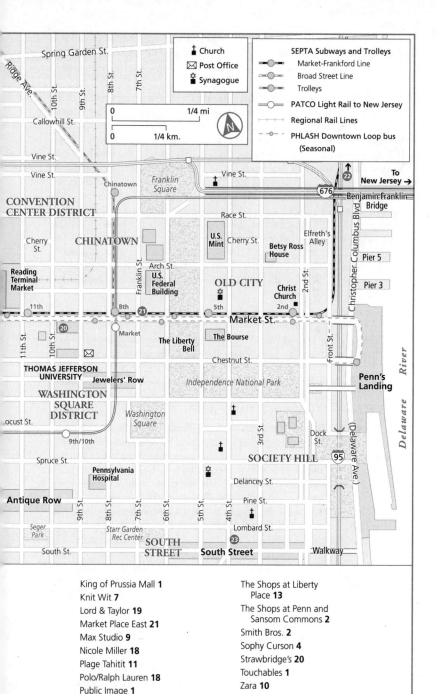

King of Prussia Mall **1**
Knit Wit **7**
Lord & Taylor **19**
Market Place East **21**
Max Studio **9**
Nicole Miller **18**
Plage Tahitit **11**
Polo/Ralph Lauren **18**
Public Image **1**

The Shops at Liberty Place **13**
The Shops at Penn and Sansom Commons **2**
Smith Bros. **2**
Sophy Curson **4**
Strawbridge's **20**
Touchables **1**
Zara **10**

(located just within the main entrance), which also provides city maps and sells SEPTA day passes. Open Monday, Tuesday, Thursday, and Saturday from 10am to 7pm, Wednesday and Friday from 10am to 8pm, and Sunday from noon to 5pm. 8th to 11th and Market sts. ✆ 215/925-7162.

King of Prussia Court and Plaza Aptly named, this is retail royalty: King of Prussia is the gleaming second-largest mall in the country, impeccably designed and marketed, with 450 establishments in three connected tiers, grouped roughly by price range. The major stores include Bloomingdale's, JCPenney, Lord & Taylor, Neiman Marcus, Nordstrom, Strawbridge's, and Sears. Other top-quality boutiques include Hugo Boss, Versace, Williams-Sonoma, Hermès, and Tiffany & Co. There's the expected food court in the Plaza, but the restaurant scene is also very popular, with lines at the Cheesecake Factory, Maggiano's Little Italy, Rock Bottom Brewpub, and Morton's of Chicago Steakhouse open beyond mall hours. And with 126 acres of parking, don't forget where you left your car. Open Monday through Saturday from 10am to 9:30pm, Sunday from 11am to 7pm. Near junction of U.S. 202 and Pa. 422. ✆ 610/265-5727. www.kingofprussiamall.com. ½ mile south of the Pennsylvania Tpk. Valley Forge Exit 326, take Route 202 north; 3 miles south of Valley Forge National Historical Park via Rte. 422.

Market Place East The century-old Lit Brothers Department Store was a beautiful, sprawling assembly of wrought-iron facades that has been recently resuscitated as the Market Place East. The ground floor has attracted tenants including **Ross Dress for Less, Dress Barn,** and **Expressions** for gifts and cards. The lower level has a food court with atrium seating. There is garage space nearby. Open Monday through Friday and Saturday from 10am to 6pm, until 8pm on Wednesday. Some stores are open from noon to 5pm on Sunday. 701 Market St., between 7th and 8th sts. ✆ 215/592-8905.

The Shops at Liberty Place *(Kids)* Liberty Place, the steely 60-story tower that supplanted City Hall as the city's tallest spire, has a bi-level shopping area that contains 70 stores and stalls that together achieve an ambience and a comfort level that are the finest in the city. It's not overwhelming, but there's still a great selection, and the space is beautifully designed, with a soaring, glass-domed rotunda. Retailers include **J. Crew, Benetton,** and **Express** for clothing, **Nine West** and **Aldo** shoes, **Brentano's** books, **Coach** for leather goods, **Ann Taylor Loft,** and **Victoria's Secret. Linde Meyer** is a small, high-end jeweler with both sleek new platinum, gold, and diamond jewelry and estate pieces. The second floor houses a convenient, reasonably priced food court where you can eat on the run, with hundreds of well-kept tables and chairs around quality food stalls. There are two ATMs inside, near the 16th and 17th Street entrances, and the garage directly underneath holds 750 cars. Open Monday through Saturday from 9:30am to 7pm, Wednesday to 8pm, and Sunday from noon to 6pm. 1625 Chestnut St. between 16th and 17th sts. ✆ 215/851-9055. www.shopsatliberty.com.

The Shops at Penn and Sansom Commons You'll find dozens of specialty, fashion, music, book, and gift shops, and a nine-store food court, as part of U. Penn's urban redevelopment around the campus. Naturally, stores are geared to fun, collegiate tastes and budgets, with offerings such as the **Gap, Urban Outfitters, Starbucks,** and **Eyeglass Encounters.** Close by, the Bridge Cinema de Lux movie theater has great films and a cafe and lounge. The Shops at Penn, 34th and Walnut sts; Sansom Commons, 36th and Sansom sts. ✆ 215/573-5290.

2 Shopping A to Z

ANTIQUES

With its tradition of fine furniture-making since the 1700s, Philadelphia is a trove of antiques, which range from fine locally made chairs and desks to beautiful French, English, and Swedish pieces sold in intimate shops. Pine Street from 9th to 12th streets boasts some 25 antiques stores, some of which do their own refinishing and silver restoration. Old City stores mostly specialize in Deco and mid-20th-century modern pieces, and Germantown Avenue in Chestnut Hill also has several fine antiques shops. As in any antiques market, you'll have to bring your own expertise to the store, and you'll have to trust your dealer. April brings several high-end antiques shows, including the prestigious Philadelphia Antiques Show, held at the 33rd Street Armory. There are usually dozens of antiques markets every week in the Delaware Valley. Consult the "Weekend" section of the *Philadelphia Inquirer* for details.

Calderwood Gallery   This is an international resource for very high-end French Art Nouveau and Art Deco furnishings, which are beautifully displayed in a recently renovated Rittenhouse Square town house. Though pieces run mostly $5,000 and up, the prices are reasonable compared to those in New York City. 1622 Spruce St. ✆ **215/546-5357.**

Freeman/Fine Arts of Philadelphia   The dean of Philly's auction scene since 1805, Freeman specializes in Americana, and eBay has started streaming their sales in real time for online antiques lovers. Fully cataloged auctions for jewelry and fine furniture are held about once a month, often on Saturdays. Regular auctions include antique and 20th-century modern home furnishings and some fine silver, rugs, jewelry, and decorative arts. 1808 Chestnut St. ✆ **215/563-9275.** www.freemansauction.com.

Gargoyles *(Value*   Among Society Hill antiques shops, Gargoyles stocks everything from toothpick holders to mantels and bars. Although much of the stock is American, there's also a delightful selection of English pub signs, dart boards, top hats, polo mallets, and the like. Several large items have been salvaged from 19th-century buildings and businesses. 512 S. 3rd St. ✆ **215/629-1700.**

Jansen Antiques   This corner store has a dazzling (if slightly overwhelming) mix of affordable, eclectic antique Italian chandeliers, mirrors, and English and American furnishings—and things you can easily pack to take home, such as silver objets and antique jewelry. We recently coveted a wide antique rhinestone necklace from the 1920s, for $75. 1042 Pine St. ✆ **215/922-5594.**

M. Finkel and Daughters   Finkel is one of the true anchors of Pine Street. Look here for fine folk art, furniture, and painting. And if you're looking for antique needlework samplers, this is the place—they publish the scholarly journal *Samplings* twice a year. Appointments are advised. 936 Pine St. ✆ **215/627-7797.**

W. Graham Arader III Gallery *(Finds*   Arader has become one of the country's leading rare book, map, and print dealers in the past 20 years thanks to its aggressive purchasing techniques (which translates into high prices). You'll find a variety of interesting items here. 1308 Walnut St. ✆ **215/735-8811.** www.arader galleries.com.

ART GALLERIES

The line between art "galleries" and art "shops" is more blurred here than in many cities, and the Old City scene is similar to New York's SoHo *after* the

Pottery Barn invasion. But a few galleries stand out for quality, and it's fun to stroll along Second and Third streets on the "First Friday" night of every month, when galleries stay open after hours and draw crowds with free wine and snacks.

The Eyes Gallery Isaiah and Julia Zagar have presented a cheerful assortment of Latin American folk art, including *santos* and *retablos* (portable religious shrine panels and sculptures), for 30 years now, in the same location. One-of-a-kind articles of clothing and sterling silver jewelry are also spread over three floors. Open every day of the week. 402 South St. *C* 215/925-0193. www.eyes gallery.com.

Fleisher/Ollman Gallery This gallery is known for carrying fine works by emerging contemporary and self-taught American artists such as Martin Ramirez. Style is variable. 211 S. 17th St. *C* 215/545-7562. www.fleisher-ollman gallery.com.

Larry Becker An intimate space for contemporary paintings and sculpture, Becker shows artists such as Jon Poblador. Becker has excellent taste. 43 N. 2nd St. *C* 215/925-5389.

Locks This is a powerhouse gallery for paintings, sculptures, and mixed-media works, set in a beautiful Beaux Arts building, known for its serenity and elegance. Works by artists such as Frank Stella, David Hockney, and Francesco Clemente are sold here. Stylish owner Sueyun Locks aims "to help collectors get savvy," and there's more for the beginner than you might think. 600 Washington Sq. S. *C* 215/629-1000. www.locksgallery.com.

Moderne Gallery Moderne is unique, specializing in vintage craft furniture. Owner Robert Aibel offers a very good selection of American and French iron-works—both furniture and decorative items. He's added inventory from the 1940s and 1950s, and features the world's largest selection of vintage pieces by renowned woodworkers such as George Nakashima. You'll also find books and fabrics with 20th-century designs. Ask about his other gallery, Mode Moderne, down the street, for affordable mid-20th-century finds. 111 N. 3rd St. *C* 215/923-8536.

Newman Galleries *(Finds)* The oldest gallery in Philadelphia (founded in 1865), Newman Galleries has a strong representation of Bucks County artists, American sculptors, and traditional painters in general. Custom framing and art conservation work is also available. Signed, limited edition prints start at $200. 1625 Walnut St. *C* 215/563-1779.

Philadelphia Art Alliance *(Finds)* Founded in 1915 in a striking mansion on Rittenhouse Square, the Alliance now boasts exhibition space and performing/literary programs. The alliance's committee of laypersons and artists chooses the three floors of local talent displayed here. Open Tuesday through Sunday from 9am to 5pm. Rittenhouse Square, 251 S. 18th St. *C* 215/545-4302. www. philartalliance.org.

University of the Arts Rosenwald-Wolf Gallery This gallery in the heart of the Avenue of the Arts presents works by the University of the Arts faculty and students. 333 S. Broad St. (Ave. of the Arts). *C* 215/717-6480.

BOOKSTORES

AIA Bookstore and Design Center This book and design store sells Aalto vases, lamps, tabletop items, and toys, along with architecture and design liter-ature. Visit here at Christmas for the best selection of cards; it also offers an excellent downstairs gallery of architectural renderings, watercolors, and drawings (see below, under "Crafts"). The AIA store is a triple "Best of Philly" award winner for its unique and delightful objects. 117 S. 17th St. at Sansom St. ⓒ 215/ 569-3188. www.aiaphila.org.

Barnes & Noble   B&N's rambling store with an upstairs cafe is right on Rittenhouse Square, in a lovely 19th-century building with tall windows overlooking the park; there are three floors stocked with every imaginable tome and magazine (but not music). Visiting authors and guest speakers abound, and top sellers are discounted to 40%. 1805 Walnut St. ⓒ 215/656-0716.

Big Jar Books *(Finds)*   In Old City, you'd expect a used bookstore to have a sizable collection of trendy and substantive fiction and nonfiction, supplemented by mouth-watering cookies, pastries, and espresso at the counter. It's all here. 55 N. 2nd St. ⓒ 215/574-1650.

Book Trader   If you're on South Street and feel like browsing or just resting, Book Trader has a fine paperback and fiction collection, along with benches and a resident cat. It's open until midnight every night. You can also find a good selection of out-of-print books and used LPs, tapes, and CDs. 501 South St. ⓒ 215/925-0219.

Borders   Started by the Borders brothers in Minneapolis, this was the first superstore of its kind in town, and it remains a cultural center. This 2-year-old location is a massive three-story space at the top of the Avenue of the Arts, 1 block south of City Hall and across from the Ritz-Carlton. Borders features a great staff, and a wider selection than B&N (see above). It has an active reading series in the evening that pays attention to local writers. Listening stations with headsets allow you to preview every CD in stock. There's a fine children's book section with toys and there are storytelling hours some Saturdays (call in advance). There is also a second-floor espresso bar with newspapers. 1 S. Broad St. (corner of S. Broad and Chestnut) ⓒ 215/568-7400.

Cookbook Stall   The space is tight at this cookbook shop in Reading Terminal Market, but the outstanding selection and helpful service draw many of Philly's top chefs. Open Monday through Saturday from 9am to 6pm. 12th St. at Filbert St. ⓒ 215/923-3170.

Joseph Fox Bookshop   This tiny shop is cozy, well-organized, and always has what we want to read, whether it's George Eliot's *Middlemarch,* or the new mystery by Janet Evanovich. Excellent for fiction and nonfiction. 1724 Sansom St. ⓒ 215/563-4184.

The University of Pennsylvania Bookstore   A 50,000-square-foot collaboration between U. Penn and Barnes & Noble, this store opened in 2000. It's a great academic bookstore, but you'll also find excellent selections of quality fiction and nonfiction and children's books; a 100-seat Starbucks cafe; a comprehensive music department with listening stations; and even clothes and accessories suitable for that hastily scheduled job interview. Open Monday through Saturday from 8:30am to 10:30pm, Sunday from 10am to 8pm. Sansom Commons, 3601 Walnut St. ⓒ 215/898-7595.

CRAFTS

Philadelphia artisanship has always commanded respect. The tradition lingers on, both in small individual workshops and in cooperative stores. The Craft Show held every November at the Convention Center is one of the best in the country.

For outdoor crafts vendors, **Head House Square** becomes a bustling bunch of booths from April to September, all day Saturday and Sunday afternoon. **Reading Terminal Market** has several booths devoted to tableware, wearable art, and South American and African crafts.

AIA Bookstore and Design Center This gallery specializes in small home furnishings, lighting, and drawings. They've also added custom framing to their list of services. In the fall, it becomes a gorgeous holiday shop and each spring, the center features Inuit sculpture and textiles. Connected to it is an excellent bookstore (see above, under "Bookstores"). 117 S. 17th St. ℂ **215/569-3188.**

The Black Cat *Finds* Next door to the White Dog Café, Judy Wicks has a charming arts-and-crafts store that's open Sunday and Monday till 9pm, Tuesday through Thursday till 11pm, and Friday and Saturday till midnight. Offerings include weaving, frames, clocks, and silverware among other crafts. There's a small collection of antiques and items that are contemporary but look antique. 3424 Sansom St. ℂ **215/386-6664.**

The Fabric Workshop and Museum This is the only nonprofit arts organization in the United States devoted to creating, displaying, and selling new work in fabric and other materials. You'll find an abundance of finished fabric crafts on sale. The store also operates as a workshop center and collaborates with both emerging and recognized artists. Don't miss the Venturi and Red Grooms–designed bags, scarves, ties, and umbrellas. The store is close to the Convention Center. 1315 Cherry St., 5th floor. ℂ **215/568-1111.**

Linu For gossamer, handmade linens—many from Latvia, where the store's owner was born—visit this modern Pine Street shop. The stylish spot also stocks towels, tabletop items, candles, and frames, and you can order custom bed linens and window treatments. 1036 Pine St. ℂ **215/206-8547.**

OLC *Finds* OLC, in the Old City, has 6,000 feet of sophisticated lighting and modern furnishings displayed in a museum-quality setting that's been lauded by the American Institute of Architects. It represents 30 European lighting lines and classic furniture by LeCorbusier, Bertoia, Breuer, and hard-to-get contemporaries like B&B Italia. 152–154 N. 3rd St. ℂ **215/923-6085.**

DEPARTMENT STORES

Lord & Taylor This landmark store was once Wanamaker's, a Philadelphia classic that was one of the first of the great department stores in the country. Now, Lord & Taylor is running the store (the setting for the 1980s movie "Mannequin"). The style of much of the apparel is "updated American classic." The present building (1902–10), which fills a city block, is ingeniously modeled on Renaissance motifs, giving its 12 stories proportion and grace.

On the first floor, there's the shoe salon, and fine and fashion jewelry. The retail area comprises three floors, with commercial offices on top. You'll see Polo Ralph Lauren, DKNY, Kate Spade, Ben Sherman for men, and other designers' clothing and accessories at a deep discount near the end of a season—watch the *Inquirer* for ads with coupons that can shave a further 20% to 30% off the price. A center courtyard presents wonderful Christmas shows with a massive 30,000-pipe organ; this court also hosts daily organ concerts at noon and 5pm (7pm on Wed). Café Americanstyle overlooks the scene from a third floor terrace. Between Market and Chestnut and 13th and Juniper sts. ℂ **215/241-9000.**

Strawbridge's Formerly Strawbridge & Clothier, this store, which was formerly family-run, quietly anchors the Market East neighborhood. Now

Manayunk Shopping

This neighborhood, 8 miles up the Schuylkill from the Art Museum and Center City, soared in popularity in the 1990s. It houses casual restaurants and shops (see chapter 6 for the former), and though it's no longer a hot spot, it's still a pleasant place to stroll and browse Main Street for contemporary crafts, clothing, antiques, and galleries. Getting there is easy: From the Belmont Avenue exit (north, crossing the Schuylkill River) off I-76, turn onto Green Lane, then right onto Main Street. Or from 1 block south of the Green Lane SEPTA stop, just follow Main Street east alongside the river from the 4400 to the 3900 addresses. A cohesive local development group runs a continuous series of weekend festivals and events to attract business. Parking can be difficult, but inexpensive lots are available and store hours tend to run late to match dinner reservations.

ARTS, CRAFTS & GIFTS   In recent years, quality branches of national brands like **Restoration Hardware,** 4130 Main St. (© 215/930-0300), selling everything from tea strainers to leather couches, have moved in. Among specialty stores, I like **Xcessories Inc. by Design,** 4321 Main St. (© 215/483-9665), for its elegant candlesticks, updated Tiffany-style lamps, and contemporary frames. **Owen Patrick Gallery,** 4345 Main St. (© 215/482-9395), has interesting glass and ceramics, as well as bigger furniture and sculptural art, and carries American West/Urbana upholstered pieces from California. **Belle Maison,** 4340 Main St. (© 215/482-6222), offers pretty French provincial home accessories in a roomy setting.

FASHION   In 6 years, **Nicole Miller,** 4249 Main St. (© 215/930-0307), has become the high priestess of high fashion, with little black dresses, cool sportswear, and whimsical men's neckties, formal wear, and boxers. **Public Image,** 4390 Main St. (© 215/482-4008), has two stories of hip designer labels such as Product, Vivienne Tam, Diesel, and Freelance; **Smith Bros.,** 4430 Main St. (© 215/508-2450), has the coolest jeans, including Seven for All Mankind; and **Touchables,** 4309 Main St. (© 215/487-7988), has a very extensive selection of lingerie and night wear, including Swiss cotton and silk loungewear and peignoirs. **Banana Republic Women,** 4313 Main St. (© 215/508-0772), offers the best of every season's collection (for the girls only), and has great sales.

FOOD   We like to linger over crab cakes at sophisticated **Jake's,** 4365 Main St. (© 215/483-0444); visit **Bucks County Coffee,** 4311 Main St. (© 215/487-3927), for a mocha and a scone; or have a fantastic margarita and a spicy sandwich at **Bourbon Blue,** 2 Rector St. (© 215/508-3360), in a lovely old canal house with terra-cotta walls set just above the river.

connected to the Gallery Mall, it covers three stories. Prices and boutiques are moderately scaled, with frequent sales. It contains an underrated but excellent food hall with cookies, ice cream, and a deli. 8th and Market sts. © 215/629-6000.

DISCOUNT SHOPPING

Daffy's   For the patient shopper, Daffy's offers value on name and house brands for men, women, and children in a beautiful 1920s Art Deco building (now a bit downscale) that once housed the luxurious Bonwit Teller store. Prices are 40% to 75% off regular retail, and men's and women's Italian suits, fine leather items (on the third floor), and lingerie are particular bargains. Sometimes the selection is very picked-over, occasionally it can be fun. 17th and Chestnut sts. © 215/963-9996.

H&M   A roomy one-floor selection of colorful trendy clothes by the European manufacturer—knockoffs of chic designs include sexy little blouses, trench coats, lingerie, and cargo pants. 1530 Chestnut St. © 215/561-6178.

FASHION

Rittenhouse Square and its surrounding blocks, known as Rittenhouse Row, is the fashion destination in Center City. Your fellow shoppers will be a stylish bunch, and sales staff are refreshingly friendly and sweet. Charge on! Remember, there is no state sales tax on clothing.

Anthropologie   A 1992 offshoot of Urban Outfitters, this exclusive chain was founded to bring the best of other cultures into our own, with party-style funky flair. The store's buyers and in-house designers troll bazaars and artisan shops in Europe, India, and the Far East for inspiration, and they adapt or reproduce apparel, accessories, home decor (think platters and comforters, for example), and gifts exclusively in their 20 U.S. stores. This one's a gorgeous turn-of-the-20th-century mansion on the corner of Rittenhouse Square, and shoppers' consorts will welcome the overstuffed sofas. 18th and Walnut sts. © 215/568-2114.

Banana Republic   This is a particularly nice, two-level setting for a Banana Republic, in a marble-clad former bank with high ceilings and two levels (men's clothing is downstairs). The well-made, stylish pieces for men and women range from slim coats, suits, and dresses to khaki miniskirts and silk tops and T-shirts. 1401 Walnut St. 215/751-0292.

Burburrys Limited   The rejuvenated Burberrys has the beautifully cut suits, raincoats, and accessories you'd expect for both men and women, but it also offers renaissance additions, from bikinis to headbands. 1705 Walnut St. © 215/557-7400.

J. Crew   This store offers a nice mix of casual and formal clothes, all brightly colored and softly styled. A highlight is the beautiful cable-knit sweaters. It's a popular rendezvous spot for high-school and college-age students. Liberty Place, 1625 Chestnut St. © 215/977-7335.

Max Studio   Flirty dresses in silk, cotton, and chiffon are a Max Studio staple, as are well-cut trousers, wrap sweaters, and chic blouses. These clothes can go to work, or to a cocktail party. 1616 Walnut St. © 215/545-6003.

Polo Ralph Lauren   Polo and RL typify American luxury style. The local outpost is in the Bellevue. The Bellevue, Broad and Walnut sts. © 215/985-2800.

CHILDREN'S FASHION

Born Yesterday   Right on Rittenhouse Square and recently doubled in size, this store outfits babies, boys to size 8, and girls to size 10 in current, stylish fashions. Trendy items such as adorable black velvet dresses with matching leggings are sold alongside traditional hand-knit baby sweaters and old-fashioned quilts.

This is a "Best of Philly" store for unique baby gifts and tapes of classical music for kids. Attentive staff. 1901 Walnut St. ℰ 215/568-6556.

Children's Boutique All the high-end labels are here, plus luxurious party clothes by local designers such as Joan Calabrese, and an excellent selection of adorable shoes, from classic to trendy. The store has a large infant's department and stocks some toys; sizes range up to 14-16. 1702 Walnut St. ℰ 215/732-2661.

Gap The ubiquitous children's clothing store is set within a mammoth Gap superstore, in the heart of shopping central. 1510 Walnut St. ℰ 215/546-7010.

Kamikaze Kids You'll find stylish, up-to-the-minute kid's fashion here. The stock ranges from tights to hair ornaments—everything the urban chic child needs. The store also stocks incredible Halloween costumes. Nothing is cheap, except for the 25¢ carnival rides. 527 S. 4th St. ℰ 215/574-9800.

MEN'S FASHION

Boyd's *(Finds* This gorgeous white-wedding-cake of a store has a grand entrance under a maroon canopy, a large parking lot across the street, and every major men's designer on hand, from Armani to Zegna. Family-owned, the place is pure luxury, from the gorgeous marble and columns to the "can we get you anything?" service. The store sells everything from shoes to formal coats to ties, with suits being the focus, and caters to top lawyers, bankers, and Philly's star athletes. Boyd's has 65 tailors on-site, and boasts European and American lines of all types, as well as alterations for a variety of fine designers; the store will be expanding its women's lines, and its mezzanine cafe will be overseen by *über-*French chef Georges Perrier. Sale periods are January and July. 1818 Chestnut St. ℰ 215/564-9000.

Brooks Brothers Even in conservative Philadelphia, this is not your father's Brooks. They won't steer you wrong on perfectly acceptable items for business and casual wear, but the handsome, paneled store is infused with pizazz and a playful conservative-but-fashionable style. Women can also find classic dresses, trousers, and knits here. 1513 Walnut St. ℰ 215/564-4100.

WOMEN'S FASHION

Adresse Fashionistas love this spare, unusual boutique, where you can find a gorgeous silk halter dress, a Paul Smith cashmere sweater, Lambertson Truex handbags, and handmade jewelry. It's been praised by *Vogue,* and has won awards from *Philadelphia* magazine. 1706 Locust St. ℰ 215/985-3161.

Boyd's *(Finds* Boyd's, a superb men's fashion mansion (see above), is adding even more designers to its first-floor women's boutique. Look for Armani, featuring classic suits, dresses, and casual wear, as well as hip names such as Philosophy, Genny, Sonia Rykiel, Isaac Mizrahi, and Krizia. The store provides free custom alterations and incorporates a cafe. 1818 Chestnut St. ℰ 215/564-9000.

Jacques Ferber In the market for a $60,000 sable coat, or a sheared-mink scarf for a few hundred dollars? This classic furrier, owned by Ken and Andre Ferber, is family-run, with exclusive designs by Pam Ferber. The atmosphere, with elegant Deco brass windows, is regal, but you can also find fun items such as a white-mink ski parka alongside full-length classics. Also look here for fabulous Longchamps handbags. 1708 Walnut St. ℰ 215/735-4173.

Joan Shepp Boutique The presentation is elegant, with an eclectic mix of accessories, antique jewelry, cosmetics, and home furnishings. Among the Yohji Yamamotos, Rifat Ozbeks, Prada, and Robert Clergeries, you'll occasionally find spectacular bargains on these two floors. Joan has moved back with the times, with some impeccable vintage by the likes of Trigere and Givenchy. 1616 Walnut St. ℂ 215/735-2666.

Knit Wit *Value* In a sleek spot with windows on Walnut Street, Ann Gitter's Knit Wit specializes in the latest in contemporary fashions and accessories for women, from designers such as Miu Miu, Paul Smith, and Blumarine. Sales come in March and September. Shoe maven Danielle Scott has an adorable boutique inside the stores, with Prada and Jimmy Choo among the labels. 1721 Walnut St. ℂ 215/564-4760.

Plage Tahiti A tiny, selective store and a frequent "Best of Philly" winner, Plage Tahiti has original separates with an artistic slant from Theory, Ghost, and Garfield + Marks. The second floor sale racks have some real steals in Betsey Johnson dresses and the like. As the name suggests, French bathing suits are a constant. 128 S. 17th St. ℂ 215/569-9139.

Sophy Curson An old-fashioned exterior and very clever window displays house a boutique with couture items inside, including exquisite designer dresses and gowns by Lacroix, Lanvin, and Blumarine. The store, open since 1929, does not display items in the modern vernacular; rather, the staff, led by owners Susan Schwartz and her son David, chat you up, gauge your style, then disappear into the back and return with several perfect options for you. It's like being back in the 1940s, but with very sophisticated, of-the-moment clothes. 19th and Sansom Sts. ℂ 215/567-6442.

FOOD

Also see the review of the **Reading Terminal Market** at 12th and Market streets, with its dozens of individual booths and cafes, on p. 104. In addition, see the "Local Favorites: Cheesesteaks, Hoagies & More" section on p. 114.

Caviar Assouline An astonishing selection of oils, chocolates, caviar, and other delicacies greets you at this superb gourmet market. There's an excellent selection of gift baskets. Open daily. 505 Vine St. ℂ 215/627-3511 and at Liberty Place, 1625 Chestnut St. ℂ 215/972-1616. Also at Marketplace at the Airport.

Chef's Market *Finds* The premier gourmet store in Society Hill is Chef's Market, offering a staggering array of charcuterie, cookbooks, and condiments. Would you believe this place stocks breads and cakes supplied by 20 bakeries? 231 South St. ℂ 215/925-8360.

Italian Market *Finds* The Italian Market feels like it's straight out of another era, with pushcarts and open stalls selling fresh goods, produce, and cheese Tuesday through Saturday (the end of the week is better). Many shops are open until noon on Sunday. Particular favorites are **DiBruno's** at 930 S. 9th St. (ℂ **888/ 322-4337** or 215/922-2876) for cheese, **Sarcone and Sons** at 758 S. 9th St. (ℂ **215/922-0445**) for bread, **Pasticceria** at 9th and Federal streets (no phone) for pound cake, and **Fante's** at 1006 S. 9th St. (ℂ **215/922-5557**) for kitchenware. To reach the market, head 5 blocks south of South Street; SEPTA bus no. 47 goes south on 8th Street from Market. 9th St. between Christian and Wharton sts.

Whole Foods Market A supermarket? Whole Foods, however, has a wonderful selection of the finest natural and organic foods, including a great assortment of prepared dishes and oven-baked goods. Generous samples in every aisle, too. 2001 Pennsylvania Ave. ℂ 215/557-0015 and 929 South St. ℂ 215/733-9788.

GIFTS & SOUVENIRS

You will run into your basic historic Philadelphia memorabilia all over Society Hill and Independence National Historical Park, beginning with the gift shop at Independence Visitor Center at 6th and Market streets. We like to recommend spots for more unique gifts.

Bluemercury   We love to walk into this sunny store a few steps up from street level and inhale the scents of Tocca and Diptyque candles, Occitane soaps and lotions, and the chic Fresh line of fragrances in scents such as fig and pomegranate. Nars and Laura Mercier cosmetics are sold here, and there is a small spa in the back. The gift wrapping, in crisp blue boxes filled with potpourri, is beautiful. 1707 Walnut St. ℂ **215/569-3100.**

Country Elegance   Unique gifts and home accessories, along with a great selection of fine and antique linens, are sold here. 269 S. 20th St. ℂ **215/545-2992.**

Details   Sumptuous gifts, such as invitation cards, Juliska glassware, high-end desktop accessories, picture frames, and the largest selection of fine stationery in town, are sold in this turn-of-the-20th-century town house. 131 S. 18th St. ℂ **215/977-9559.**

Foster's Urban Homeware   If you love modern home decor, you must visit Old City's Foster's for its cool, whimsical wares ranging from Karim Rashid's colorful acrylic chess set to Umbra bottle openers and trash cans. Great vases, plates, frames, and clocks as well as lamps and some toys fill out the space. 124 N. 3rd St. ℂ **267/671-0588.**

Scarlett Alley   Close by the Betsy Ross house is a cottage-y home boutique set in a vintage building that's the best place for engagement and birthday gifts in Old City. Italian cordial glasses, hand-painted bowls, clocks, candlesticks, table linens, and more. Sniff the fresh flowers as you walk in and slowly take in all the colors and textures; you'll no doubt meet the owners, adorable mother and daughter Liz and MK Scarlett, too. 241 Race St. ℂ **215/592-2898.**

Xenos Candy and Gifts   Miniature Liberty Bells? Snow globes featuring Independence Hall? Tea towels illustrated with the Betsy Ross story? All this and much more is available just around the corner from the sights themselves. 231 Chestnut St. ℂ **215/922-1445.**

JEWELRY & SILVER

Philadelphia is known for all types of jewelry—traditional, one of a kind, heirloom, and contemporary. Many of the city's jewelers can be found within a couple of city blocks at **Jeweler's Row,** centering on Sansom and Walnut streets and 7th and 8th streets, which touts itself as offering 30% to 50% off the retail price. This area contains more than 350 retailers, wholesalers, and craftspeople. Particularly notable is **Sydney Rosen** at 714 Sansom St. (ℂ **215/922-3500**). **Robinson Jewelers,** 730 Chestnut St. (ℂ **215/627-3066**), specializes in Masonic jewelry and watch repair.

Jack Kellmer   Kellmer imports diamonds by the dozen and sells unusual gold and diamond jewelry out of a magnificent marble showroom. This is an official Rolex jeweler, and carries almost all top watch brands. 717 Chestnut St., moving by 2005 to 1521 Walnut St. ℂ **215/627-8350.**

Lagos   Lagos is known for its striking fashion-forward settings and unusual colored gems, like evergreen topaz. Oprah is a fan, and you may have spotted the store's wares on TV's *Will & Grace.* 1735 Walnut St. ℂ **215/864-7800.**

Linde Meyer Gold & Silver *(Value)*   This nook on the ground floor passage to the central atrium of Liberty Place presents contemporary designer jewelry from Niessing, Georg Jensen, and Henrich+Denzel in precious metals, along with an adjoining collection of estate jewelry and giftware. Meyer's taste in jewelry is impeccable. Liberty Place, 1625 Chestnut St. ✆ **215/851-8555.**

Niederkorn Silver   Antique baby items, dressing-table adornments, napkin rings, picture frames, and Judaica are featured here. Also on display is Philadelphia's largest selection of period silver, including works of such fine crafters as Jensen, Tiffany, and Spratling. 2005 Locust St. ✆ **215/567-2606.**

Tiffany & Co. *(Finds)*   Tiffany & Co. is an American institution with an international reputation for quality, craftsmanship, and design. Today, the store has an extensive collection of sterling silver jewelry, but also offers china, crystal, timepieces, writing instruments, and fragrance. Though many items (diamonds!) are very expensive, there are many items under $100. The sales staff in this location are wonderful and helpful. The Bellevue, 1414 Walnut St. ✆ **215/735-1919.**

LUGGAGE

Bon Voyage   From airplane roll-ons to backpacks, adventure wear, and accessories, this Rittenhouse Square store offers a combination of outdoor necessities and the luggage you need to get where you're going. Liberty Place, 1625 Chestnut St. ✆ **215/567-1677.**

Robinson Luggage Company   At this flagship of six regional locations, you'll find a great selection of leather gear, along with discounted travel accessories and briefcases. Broad and Walnut sts. ✆ **215/735-9859.**

MUSIC

Borders   A vast selection is sold at this friendly 2-year-old superstore, from classical to jazz, pop, and rock, with all CDs available for previews at listening stations. 1 S. Broad St. ✆ **215/568-7400.**

Theodore Presser Music Store   Known primarily as a piano store (since 1900), this store (formerly known as Jacobs Music Co.) is Center City's best source of sheet music for classical and pop musicians alike. 1718 Chestnut St. ✆ **215/568-0964.**

Tower Records *(Value)*   The Los Angeles–based Tower Records stocks virtually all current recordings at low prices. For a last-minute gift, the Broad Street location is open every night till midnight—even Christmas Eve and Christmas Day. 100 S. Broad St. ✆ **215/568-8001** and 610 South St. ✆ **215/574-9888.**

SHOES

Aldo   Aldo has zoomed into prominence as a hip urban chain, with the latest styles for both sexes (though most of the inventory is geared to women). Most shoes are priced under $100. You'll also find handbags and jewelry here. This new shoe store in Liberty Place has high-energy service. Liberty Place, 1625 Chestnut St. ✆ **215/564-5736**; also Gallery at Market East, 901 Market St., ✆ **215/625-9854,** and at Franklin Mills Outlet Center.

Bottino Shoes   Look here for avant-garde European (particularly Italian) men's and women's shoes. 121 S. 18th St. ✆ **215/854-0907.**

Sherman Brothers   At this location for more than 35 years, and recently expanded into the suburbs, Sherman Brothers has the city's best collection of fine men's shoes like Cole Haan, Allen Edmonds, Clarks, and Rockport, as well as difficult sizes. Everything is discounted 10% to 25% all the time. 1520 Sansom St. ℭ **215/561-4550.**

Stiletto   Sexy is the operative word at this corner shoe boutique, where Carrie Bradshaw would have loved the high-heeled sandals, sleek boots, and European designer offerings. 124 S. 18th St. ℭ **215/972-0920.**

SPORTING GOODS

City Sports   This roomy, well-designed, full-service store for those who "do it" rather than dress the part (the urban runner, in-line skater, baseball or hockey player, swimmer, or racquet player) has captured the Center City market. 1608 Walnut St. ℭ **215/985-5860.**

Eastern Mountain Sports   This superstore adjoining U. Penn has a complete line for hiking, trekking, and camping. Brands include Timberland, Patagonia, Woolrich, and the excellent house EMS brand. Clothing and equipment are only the start; EMS has an extensive book and magazine selection. 130 S. 36th St. ℭ **215/386-1020.**

TOBACCO/CIGARS

Harry's Smoke Shop   Harry's has been puffing along since 1938 and retro-cool has caught up with its historic location. Premium cigars like Arturo Fuente, Macanudo, and Partegas are the specialty. You'll find shaving accessories here also. 15 N. 3rd St. ℭ **215/925-4770.**

Holt's   Holt's is renowned throughout the country for its selection of pipes and tobaccos. There are enough fresh cigars here to fill every humidor on Wall Street, plus an excellent pen selection. The opulent relocation and late hours fit perfectly with the neighborhood, and there is an upstairs cafe and bar. 1522 Walnut St. ℭ **215/732-8500.**

WINE & LIQUOR

After the repeal of Prohibition, Pennsylvania decided not to license private liquor retailing but to establish a government monopoly on alcohol sales. You can only buy wine and spirits in state stores (or at a vineyard), which are usually open Monday and Tuesday from 11am to 9pm, Wednesday through Saturday from 9am to 9:30pm. Thanks to new Liquor Control Board chairman Jonathan Newman, selections have improved greatly in recent years, but the system is widely regarded as an anti-consumer nuisance. Beer, wine coolers, and hard cider are exempt from the system; pick them up at some delis such as the Foodery at 10th and Pine streets, Kitchen USA at 19th and Spruce streets, or distributors.

In the Independence Hall area, try the Wine and Spirits state store at **Society Hill Shopping Center** at 5th and Delancey streets (ℭ **215/560-7064**). In the City Hall/Convention Center area, there is a Center City "super store," one of a few extra-large stores featuring up to 5,000 varieties of liquor, open from 9am to 9pm Monday through Saturday at 1218 Chestnut St. (ℭ **215/560-4381**).

Around Rittenhouse Square, there is a Wine and Spirits shop at 1913 Chestnut St. (ℭ **215/560-4215**). In University City, there's a state store at 4049 Walnut St. (ℭ **215/823-4709**).

10

Philadelphia After Dark

Most cultural attractions keep their box offices open until curtain time. Also check out **UPSTAGES** (☎ 215/569-9700), the city's premier nonprofit box-office service, representing smaller dance companies and theaters such as the Adrienne. They take phone orders Monday through Friday from 10am to 6pm, and the principal walk-up location is at the Prince Theater, at 1412 Chestnut St.; hours are from noon to 3pm Monday through Friday. There's a small service charge. The venues themselves generally sell tickets at their own box offices starting an hour before curtain.

For commercial attractions such as large concerts, Ticketmaster (☎ 215/336-2000; www.ticketmaster.com) is your best bet. Local ticket brokers such as the **Philadelphia Ticket Office,** 1500 Locust St. (☎ 215/735-1903), or **Ticket Warehouse** (☎ 800/252-8499) are also reliable. Out-of-state brokers may have better selections, though their prices could be exorbitant. Many of the fine performing arts such as the Philadelphia Orchestra have assigned their telephone box office to **Ticket Philadelphia,** at ☎ 215/893-1999 and www.ticketphiladelphia.org.

Seniors can receive discounts of about 10% or $5 per ticket or more at many theaters, including the Annenberg Center and Wilma Theater. Concert halls generally make rush or last-minute seats available to students at prices under $10; these programs sometimes extend to adults as well. Groups can generally get discounts of 20% to 50% by calling well in advance.

1 The Performing Arts

Music, theater, and dance are presented regularly all over the city. I have restricted the venues below to those located in Center City and West Philadelphia, where you'll be most of the time, and where the quality of entertainment tends to be highest. There's really no off season for the performing arts in Philadelphia; when the regular seasons of the Philadelphia Orchestra or Pennsylvania Ballet finish at the end of May, they move to the outdoor venues such as the Mann Music Center that make Philadelphia so pleasant.

PERFORMING ARTS COMPANIES & GROUPS
CLASSICAL MUSIC GROUPS

The Chamber Orchestra of Philadelphia This excellent orchestra, made up mostly of home-grown Curtis graduates such as music director Ignat Solzhenitsyn, and talent from New York, performs chamber music at the **Perelman Theater,** the smaller hall within the **Kimmel Center.** 338 S. 15th St. ☎ 215/545-5451 office, or 215/893-1999 box office. www.chamberorchestra.org. Tickets $33–$78.

Philadelphia Chamber Music Society (*Value*) This is a wonderful home-grown series: director Tony Cecchia knows all of the classical music greats from his time at the Marlboro Music Festival, and brings renowned international soloists, chamber musicians, and jazz and popular artists to the city. Most concerts take place at the Pennsylvania Convention Center's 600-seat hall, or the Perelman Theater of the Kimmel Center. Ticket prices are exceptionally low for the quality of the performances. 135 S. 18th St. ☎ **215/569-8080**. www.philadelphiachambermusic.org. Tickets $18–$20.

The Philadelphia Orchestra ★★   For many people, a visit to Philadelphia isn't complete without hearing a concert given by the smooth, powerful Philadelphia Orchestra, under the direction of the dynamic Christoph Eschenbach. Eschenbach followed an incredible string of 20th-century leaders: Leopold Stokowski, Eugene Ormandy (for 44 legendary years), Riccardo Muti, and Wolfgang Sawallisch. The ensemble has built a reputation for virtuosity and balance that only a handful of the world's orchestras can match. Verizon Hall, their modern home designed by Rafael Vinoly, has a soaring glass-roofed lobby, and the concert hall is built of warm, dark woods, with curved spaces, and plush seats ringing the stage.

Concerts are most Tuesday, Thursday, Friday, and Saturday evenings and Friday and Sunday afternoons. More tickets to individual performances are available than in the past, with certain dress rehearsals open and fewer subscriptions sold. Try to buy tickets well in advance for the best seats.

In the summer the orchestra moves to Mann Music Center for 4 weeks of concerts (see "Mann Music Center" review below). Regular season Sept–May at Verizon Hall in the Kimmel Center, Broad and Spruce sts. ☎ **215/893-1999**. www.ticketphiladelphia. org. Tickets $28–$130 for subscription concerts, $10–$45 family concerts. Student rush seats are $8 ½ hr. before concert time for subscription concerts. Community Rush tickets at $10 available from about 5:30pm on for same day 8pm concerts, 11:30am on for same day 2pm concerts.

Relâche Ensemble   This contemporary music group, with a particular affinity for young composers, strikes a refreshing balance between the interesting and the intellectual. Made up of a dozen or so instrumentalists, the group performs at the Arts Bank on South Broad Street (p. 196), the Painted Bride Art Center (p. 197), and Villanova University (located on the Main Line). If you're driving, it's at the intersection of Route 30 and Route 476. On public transportation, it's a 25-minute ride to Villanova's station on the R5 commuter line from Suburban Station. Office only at 715 S. 3rd St. ☎ **215/574-8246**. www.relache.org. Tickets $10–$20.

DANCE COMPANIES

Local troupes perform successfully alongside such distinguished visitors as White Oak Dance Project, Pilobolus, and the Dance Theater of Harlem.

Pennsylvania Ballet   Founded in 1963, this nationally renowned company has been a great success in the past decade under the leadership of Roy Kaiser, a former principal dancer. The company is known for diverse classical dance (with Jerome Robbins and Twyla Tharp choreography occasionally in the mix) with a Balanchine backbone. They perform at the Academy of Music during the annual season. The Christmas-season performances of Tchaikovsky's *Nutcracker,* with the complete Balanchine choreography, are a beloved city tradition. Each of the company's dozens of performances, held from September to June, offers something old, something new, and always something interesting. 1101 S. Broad St. at Washington Ave. ☎ **215/551-7000**; box office at Academy of Music 215/893-1999. www.paballet.org. Tickets $20–$99; Nutcracker holiday tickets $20–$99.

Philadanco   This 35-year-old company is now the Kimmel Center's dance world resident. The company has grown from a community arts group to 17 dancers blending African-American styles with ballet, jazz, and cutting edge styles. They tour frequently, but show off at home in November and May. Kimmel Center,

S. Broad and Spruce sts. © 215/387-8200, or for tickets call 215/893-1999. www.philadanco.org. Tickets $27–$35; limited $10 rush seats.

OPERA COMPANIES

Academy of Vocal Arts This exclusive opera school housed in a beautiful town house presents small but expertly produced full operas starring the AVA's students, many of whom head off to the Met and other renowned companies after graduation. Performances held in the town house's theater are especially intimate and charming, and are held October through May. 1920 Spruce St. © 215/735-1387. www.avaopera.org. Tickets $45–$75.

The Curtis Opera Theater This company presents full-scale productions, either in the beautiful Rittenhouse Square school's theater, at the Prince Music Theater, or at the Kimmel Center. 1726 Locust St. © 215/893-5252. www.curtis.edu. Tickets $20–$63.

Opera Company of Philadelphia The opera company, which is the star tenant of the Academy of Music, presents five fully staged operas per year. Performances take place Monday, Tuesday, Thursday, or Friday evenings, with Sunday matinees; seating preference is given to season subscribers. Advance tickets are sold at the Kimmel Center. Such international opera stars as Mary Mills, Kevin Glavin, and William Burden appear here. © 215/732-8400, or for tickets call 215/893-1999. www.operaphilly.com. Tickets $5–$155; half-price amphitheater tickets available on day of performance.

THEATER COMPANIES

At any given time there will be at least one Broadway show in Philadelphia, on its way into or out of New York. There are also student repertory productions, professional performances by casts connected with the University of Pennsylvania, small-theater offerings in the various neighborhoods of Center City, and cabaret or dinner theater in the suburbs.

Arden Theatre Company One of the city's most popular professional theaters, the Arden is set in a beautifully renovated brick building near the trendy galleries and restaurants of Old City. The Arden performs in an intimate 360-seat space and mounts five main stage shows (2004–2005 will include Steve Martin's *The Underpants* and August Wilson's *Fences*), and a children's show each season. 40 N. 2nd St. © 215/922-8900. www.ardentheatre.org. Tickets $24–$40.

InterAct Theatre Company InterAct was founded in 1988 as a theater with a social conscience, mirroring today's world. All plays are new to Philadelphia audiences, with four contemporary productions mounted annually between September and June. Performances are at the Adrienne Theater. 2030 Sansom St. © 215/568-8077. www.interacttheatre.org. Tickets $14–$25.

Philadelphia Theatre Company This company combines fine regional talent with Tony Award–winning actors and directors. They've world-premiered Broadway-bound productions like *Master Class* and *Side Man,* and done excellent versions of shows such as *Fully Committed.* Their "Plays and Players Theater" is a slightly antiquated but charming hall just off Rittenhouse Square. 1714 Delancey Place. Tickets available from UPSTAGES © 215/569-9700 or 215/985-1400. www.phillytheatreco.com. Tickets $30–$45.

Walnut Street Theatre This theater has been in business, incredibly, since 1809. The regional Walnut Street Company plays in this 1,052-seat theater. The resident company presents five plays from September to June; both subscriptions and single tickets are available. Wednesday is singles night, with half-price tickets and a mixer. The company's Studio Theater Season presents new and more experimental works in the 75- and 90-seat studio spaces at 825 Walnut St., adjoining the theater; independent producers also rent those spaces. Barrymore's Café is a welcome downstairs addition. 9th and Walnut sts. ℂ 215/574-3550. www.wst online.org. Tickets $50–$65, with $10 student rush. Same-day tickets (if available) are sold for half price between 6 and 6:30pm every day.

Wilma Theater   Philly's premier modern theater company, the Wilma has been led by its directors Blanka and Jiri Zizka to national acclaim. The 2004–2005 season features Tom Stoppard's *Night and Day,* and a new play by Sarah Ruhl. Their beautiful state-of-the-art 300-seat theater, designed by Hugh Hardy, has a distinctive jagged neon logo in the heart of the "Avenue of the Arts" district. Broad and Spruce sts. ℂ 215/546-7824. www.wilmatheater.org. Tickets $30–$48.

PERFORMING ARTS VENUES

In addition to musical performances held at the following major institutions, look for the many concerts presented in churches, especially around Rittenhouse Square.

Academy of Music   In the early 19th century, building an opera house/symphony hall was a proposal much discussed by the cultural movers and shakers in Philadelphia. At the time, opera was the hallmark of culture, and in 1852, Philadelphia followed New York and Boston in constructing a hall specifically equipped to handle opera. Modeled on La Scala in Milan, the Academy of Music is grand, ornate, and acoustically problematic. The academy underwent a major multimillion-dollar overhaul from 1997 to 2001, with construction of a level extended stage, replacement of an old bowl-shaped floor with a raked one, and better seating and lighting. It remains a symphony of Victorian crimson and gold, with original gaslights still flaming at the Broad Street entrance. The marble planned for the facade has never been added, but the brick and glass seem to suit Philadelphia far better.

The Philadelphia Orchestra, the owner of the building and chief resident since 1900, moved to the Kimmel Center (see below), 1 block south, in 2001. So the calendar's now a patchwork of touring orchestras and local groups such as the Pennsylvania Ballet and the Opera Company of Philadelphia. Tours of the academy (reservations required) are $5 (reserve at ℂ **215/893-1935**). Broad and Locust sts. ℂ **215/893-1935** for general information, or Ticket Philadelphia 215/893-1999 for ticket availability and purchase. www.academyofmusic.org. Advance sales are through the Kimmel Center Box Office, S. Broad and Spruce sts. 10am–6pm daily. Academy of Music Box Office open only 1 hr. before performances to ½ hr. after performance begins. Discounted $10 student tickets available. Prices vary.

Annenberg Center at the University of Pennsylvania   Located on the beautiful University of Pennsylvania campus and easily reached by bus or subway, the roomy, modern Annenberg Center presents a wide variety of performances by American and international companies from September to June. Of the two stages, the Harold Prince Theater generally has more intimate, and usually more avant-garde, productions. The Zellerbach Theater can handle the most demanding lighting and staging needs. There is also a small studio theater.

Since U. Penn established its own Penn Presents in 1999 as the professional performing arm of the campus, they've expanded the programming mix to include classical, world, and jazz music; Philadelphia's leading contemporary dance series, Dance Celebration; and each April, the International Children's Festival, with dance, theater, and music. 3680 Walnut St. ℂ 215/898-6791 (also the number for Penn Presents), or TDD 215/898-4939. Tickets through Penn Presents, www.pennpresents. org. Box office open 10am–6pm weekdays. Tickets $25–$50 depending upon event. Discounted tickets available for students and seniors.

Arts Bank   One of the cornerstones of the Avenue of the Arts, the Arts Bank is a gift of the William Penn Foundation, which realized that there wasn't enough quality, affordable performance space in Center City. The 230-seat theater (a former bank, of course) is owned and operated by the nearby University of the Arts and serves a large, diverse constituency. The stage has a sprung (bouncy) wood floor and state-of-the-art computerized lighting and sound. This is the place for excellent, cheap student and professional theater. Relâche and University of the Arts students are just a few of the performing artists. 601 S. Broad St. at South St. ⓒ **215/545-0590** or 215/717-6000. Tickets $10–$25.

Curtis Institute of Music   The most famous touring concert pianist in the world, 22-year-old Lang Lang, was trained at the Curtis, one of the country's finest music schools, housed in a rambling historic limestone mansion with its own theater. The world-famous Curtis Institute is headed by Gary Graffman. Curtis itself has a small hall just off Rittenhouse Square that's good for chamber works; call ⓒ **215/893-5261** for a schedule of the mostly free concerts, operas, and recitals. Student recitals are Monday, Wednesday, and Friday evenings at 8pm from October through May. As mentioned above, The Curtis Opera Theater presents full-scale productions at the school, at the Prince Music Theater, and one at the Kimmel Center. 1726 Locust St. ⓒ **215/893-5252**. www.curtis.edu. Most in-house concerts free; faculty and guest artist recitals $15–$25. Curtis Orchestra and Opera tickets $20–$66.

The Forrest   Of the commercial Philadelphia theaters, The Forrest—owned by the Shubert Organization—is the best equipped to handle big musicals like *Mamma Mia!*, and it hosts several of these during the year, along with other short-running plays and concerts. Performances are usually Tuesday through Saturday at 8pm (occasionally Sun night as well) and Wednesday, Saturday, and Sunday at 2pm. 11th and Walnut sts. ⓒ **215/923-1515**, or for group sales 866/886-7049. Tickets $25–$80.

Kimmel Center for the Performing Arts   Opened with tremendous fanfare in December 2001, Vinoly's dramatic glass and steel vault along the Avenue of the Arts encompasses **Verizon Hall,** a 2,500-seat cello-shaped concert hall built specifically to house the Philadelphia Orchestra; and **Perelman Theater,** a 650-seat hall for chamber music, dance, and drama with a turntable stage. Other features at Kimmel include an interactive education center; "black box" theater space; a daytime cafe and gift shop in the plaza along Spruce St.; and parking and restaurant facilities. Above all, there is space, acres and acres of it—space designed to sparkle and amaze, unlike anything else in the area.

Verizon Hall is a pleasure, with its comfortable mahogany interior and four levels of seating, and excellent acoustics. Perelman's design is also nice, with a metal-clad exterior and light woods and warm fabrics within.

Most of the jewels in Philadelphia's cultural crown—the city opera, orchestra, and ballet companies—perform either at Kimmel or at the historic Academy of Music (which is affiliated with Kimmel and located 1 block north). Prestigious visiting talent in music and dance (either renting the spaces themselves, or an incredible jazz series presented by the Kimmel Center) also use the venue frequently. Tickets for *both* locations are sold during the day only at the Kimmel

---

Tips **Blow Your Cover**

Borders, 1 S. Broad St. at Chestnut St. (© **215/568-7400**); and **Tower Records,** 610 South St. (© **215/574-9888**), have stacks of coupons for reduced admission to clubs and music venues.

Center box office. Broad and Spruce sts. © 215/790-5800 for general information, or ticket purchase from Ticket Philadelphia 215/893-1999 8am–8pm daily. Fax 215/790-5801. www.kimmel center.org. Advance sales at the box office, open 10am–6pm daily, and 2 hr. past performance times. Ticket prices depend upon performance event.

Prince Music Theater   Founded in 1984 by visionary Marjorie Samoff as the American Music Theater Festival, the Prince is a renovated 450-seat picture palace that hosts all original productions. Musical theater is presented in all major forms—opera, musical comedy, cabaret, and experimental theater, along with film. *Time* magazine has called the Prince Music Theater the foremost presenter of new and adventurous music theater in the country. 1412 Chestnut St. © 215/972-1000, or for tickets call Upstages 215/569-9700. www.princemusictheater.org. Tickets $25–$45.

Mann Music Center   The Mann Music Center, traditionally specializing in summer presentations of the Philadelphia Orchestra in the 4-week PNC Bank Summer Concert Series, also showcases artists such as Tony Bennett, Garrison Keillor, and Linda Ronstadt, and series such as Symphonic Pops, Jazz at the Mann, a Family Series, and rock-'n'-roll concerts.

A Mann concert is one of the delights of summer. Special SEPTA buses travel from Center City and there's plenty of paid parking available in lots around the Mann. Concerts are usually Monday, Wednesday, and Thursday at 8pm. Tickets for the covered amphitheater seats may be purchased at the box office there, if available, or by calling ahead.

If you prefer, you can enjoy music under the stars, on the grassy slopes above the orchestra, where picnicking is encouraged, and there is a great view of the city skyline. Seating is unassigned, but tickets are required. The food stall choices range from fine and ethnic to fast, and wine and beer are available. Don't forget the blankets and insect repellent. George's Hill near 52nd St. and Parkside Ave. © 215/893-1999. Tickets from Ticket Philadelphia at © 215/893-1999 or 215/546-7900. www. manncenter.org. Amphitheater (covered) seats $25–$49; lawn seating $20.

Merriam Theater   The Merriam, belonging to the newly rejuvenated University of the Arts, hosts many of Broadway's top touring shows such as *Chicago* and *Thoroughly Modern Millie,* in addition to popular artists like Patti LaBelle and Barbara Cook. The Merriam is an ornate turn-of-the-20th-century hall with 1,668 seats. The theater is renovated to some degree for uses never foreseen during the vaudeville era. 250 S. Broad St. at Locust St. © 215/732-5446, or call Ticketmaster 215/336-1234. www.broadwayacrossamerica.com. Tickets $30–$90.

Painted Bride Art Center   It's hard to know what to call the wonderful Painted Bride Art Center, located near the entrance to the Benjamin Franklin Bridge. This spot set the trend of cultural activity in Old City starting 35 years ago. It's an art gallery catering to contemporary tastes, but it also hosts folk, electronic, and new music, plus jazz, dance, and theater events. 230 Vine St. © 215/925-9914. www.paintedbride.org. Tickets $10–$20.

2 The Club & Music Scene

Club kids of all ages (and interested onlookers) will be happy to learn that Philadelphia has plenty of home-grown DJ talent and enjoys frequent visits from New York artists and DJs. Most of the clubs mentioned below are within blocks of the Delaware waterfront. The minimum legal drinking age in Pennsylvania is 21. Bars may stay open until 2am; establishments that operate as private clubs can serve until 3am.

NIGHTLIFE CENTERS
OLD CITY, RITTENHOUSE SQUARE, NORTHERN LIBERTIES & THE DELAWARE WATERFRONT

If you ask most Philadelphians in their 20s through mid-30s where the epicenter of Philly nightlife is, they'd answer that it has moved to young, stylish **Old City,** the restaurant- and lounge-heavy district that's close to both art galleries and the historic district. North of Old City, and even younger and more trend-obsessed, is **Northern Liberties,** a neighborhood of old warehouses and historic homes that is quickly being gentrified and boasts cool spots with excellent food, such as the popular and casual Standard Tap.

Beautiful people in their 30s and older gather at the sleek lounges and restaurants around **Rittenhouse Square:** Singles flirt at outside cafe tables at Rouge, sip pomegranate margaritas at Twenty Manning, or try to elbow their way into the VIP bar at Denim Lounge. With its huge, open spaces and lights shimmering off the water, the **Delaware Waterfront**—nightclubs built onto piers along Delaware Avenue (aka Columbus Blvd.), both north and south of the Ben Franklin Bridge—was popular in the mid-1990s, and is a little more seedy and rough 10 years later. One place that is pleasant is the summer-only Rock Lobster, where you should take a taxi or valet-park to avoid the dangerous drivers and traffic patterns along Delaware Avenue.

DANCE CLUBS

Brasil's Before its Old City neighborhood was hopping 10 years ago, Brasil's was sizzling, and it still is. Check out the amazing, authentic salsa moves on the small, mirrored second-floor dance floor on weekends. The music is irresistible, and the crowd of South Americans in Lycra is awesome. Open Wednesday, Friday, and Saturday. Salsa instruction given on Wednesday and Saturday is devoted to torrid Brazilian music and dance. 112 Chestnut St. ✆ **215/413-1700.** Cover $5 weekdays, $10 weekends.

Egypt Located on the west side of Delaware Avenue, this is one of the city's longest-running clubs. A bi-level dance floor features concert light and sound systems in a campy "oasis" setting in the main room, with different DJs (Q102 broadcasts on Sat) and atmospheres in two different areas. Some nights allow children as young as 14 to come and dance, though not to drink, of course. 520 N. Delaware Ave. at Spring Garden St. ✆ **215/922-6500.** Cover around $10.

Five Spot Just south of Market Street in Old City, the Five Spot is very popular with singles. They do a combination of lessons and dance sessions most nights. Themed nights range from swing dancing to electronica, with DJs, open-mic nights, reggae bands, and more. There is plenty of room on two floors to move or talk. Open Tuesday through Sunday 8pm to 2am. 5 S. Bank St. ✆ **215/574-0070.** Cover $5.

Fluid This is a great dance club in a cool space with blue wood floors. Depending on the night, you'll encounter hip-hop, swing, drum and bass, or

> ### *Tips* Sleepless in Philadelphia: Where the Nightlife Is
>
> The best places to start looking for entertainment after the sun goes down include:
>
> - Old City, where the sidewalks are filled with young hotties from sundown till sun-up, and the Continental, 32 Degrees, Cuba Libre, and other nightspots draw a cool crowd.
> - Northern Liberties, where you can sip and snack late with local artists and musicians at lounges and bistros such as the 700 Club, N. 3rd, Pigalle, and Standard Tap.
> - For sophisticated lounging, the most stylish eateries and bars near Rittenhouse Square are Striped Bass, the Continental Midtown, Twenty Manning, Rouge, Alma de Cuba, and Tria wine bar.
> - The fringes of the University of Pennsylvania, west of the Schuylkill, especially on Walnut and Sansom streets.
> - South Philly, for those craving cheesesteak or pasta.

house. The scene is always high energy. The entrance is an unmarked door in the alley just off 4th Street, above the Latest Dish. Open Thursday through Saturday 8pm to 2am. 613 S. 4th St. © **215/629-0565.** Cover $3–$10.

Polly Esther's Culture Club   A blast from the past, Polly Esther's has two dance floors, one for '70s disco, one for '80s retro. Lots of singles of both genders feel comfortable here, and bartenders get good marks. Open Thursday through Saturday 8pm to 2am. 1201 Race St. © **215/851-0776.**

Rock Lobster   At the corner of Race Street, just north of the Ben Franklin Bridge and on the Marina, this is a good approximation of a beach club overlooking the Delaware River. It's a fun spot to sip a margarita and feel relaxed and tropical. From May to mid-September, it serves hundreds of moderately priced lunches and dinners daily in a 4,000-square-foot tent or an alfresco area designed to look like a Maine yacht club. The restaurant opens for lunch at 11:30am and stays open until 2am for dancing. The crowd is in its 30s, 40s, and 50s. 221 N. Delaware Ave. © **215/627-7625.** There's no cover until 8:30pm, then it's usually $5–Thurs, $10 Fri–Sat, and $7 Sun. The cover is higher when national acts appear. Valet parking $10.

Shampoo   This spot spreads progressive music and trendy retro chic decor over two floors with eight bars and three dance floors. It's popular with a mixed gay and straight crowd, and summer brings a tent-covered Groove Garden with patio furniture, Jacuzzi, and an extra DJ. Open Wednesday, Friday, and Saturday from 9pm to 2am. 417 N. 8th St. © **215/922-7500.** www.shampooonline.com. Cover charges vary; usually $10 on a non-event night.

FOLK & COUNTRY VENUES

Grape Street Pub   Manayunk's best live music spot has moved to the former Chemistry nightclub digs. There's rock, indie music, and more here, with live bands most nights, and a friendly bar scene. 105 Grape St., Manayunk. © **215/483-7084.**

The Khyber   This is where bands like Garbage played their first Philly gigs, a rough-around-the-edges spot for cutting-edge music. See p. 203 for more details. 56 S. 2nd St. © **215/238-5888.** Cover $5–12.

Philadelphia Bars, Clubs & Lounges

12th Air Command **17**
The 2–4 Club **16**
32 Degrees **25**
Abilene **33**
Alma de Cuba **5**
The Angel Acoustic Café **25**
Bleu **3**
Brasil's **27**
Bridget Foy's South Street
   Grill **37**

Bump **15**
Chris' Jazz Club **11**
Continental **25**
Cosi **30**
Denim Lounge **4**
Devon Seafood Grill **3**
Drinker's Tavern **39**
Electric Factory **21**
Egypt **38**
Fado **8**

Five Spot **28**
Fluid **34**
Glam **26**
Il Bar **24**
Independence Brewpub
   at the Terminal **18**
Irish Pub **1**
Judy's Café **36**
The Khyber **26**
Le Bar Lyonnais **9**

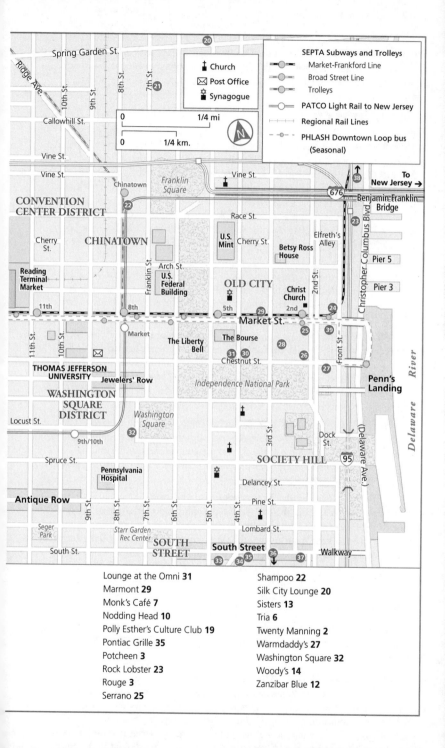

SEPTA Subways and Trolleys
- Market-Frankford Line
- Broad Street Line
- Trolleys

PATCO Light Rail to New Jersey

Regional Rail Lines

PHLASH Downtown Loop bus (Seasonal)

Church
Post Office
Synagogue

Spring Garden St.
Ridge Ave.
Callowhill St.
Vine St.
Vine St.
CONVENTION CENTER DISTRICT
Chinatown
CHINATOWN
Cherry St.
Reading Terminal Market
THOMAS JEFFERSON UNIVERSITY
WASHINGTON SQUARE DISTRICT
Jewelers' Row
Locust St.
Spruce St.
Pennsylvania Hospital
Antique Row
Seger Park
SOUTH STREET
South St.

Franklin Square
Vine St.
Race St.
U.S. Mint
Cherry St.
Betsy Ross House
Elfreth's Alley
Arch St.
U.S. Federal Building
OLD CITY
Christ Church
Market St.
The Liberty Bell
The Bourse
Chestnut St.
Independence National Park
Washington Square
SOCIETY HILL
Delancey St.
Pine St.
Starr Garden Rec Center
Lombard St.
South Street
Walkway

Benjamin Franklin Bridge
To New Jersey →
Christopher Columbus Blvd
Pier 5
Pier 3
Penn's Landing
Delaware River
Dock St.
(Delaware Ave.)

Tin Angel Acoustic Café   This conveniently located 105-seat club above Serrano restaurant/bar (p. 205) is riding the unplugged wave with artists like Lauren Hart, Livingston Taylor, and Maria Muldaur. Open Wednesday through Saturday. 20 S. 2nd St. ✆ 215/928-0770. No cover for Wed open-mic evenings; other nights run $10–$20.

JAZZ & BLUES CLUBS

Philadelphia is one of the great American hot spots for jazz, boasting performances from everyone from John Coltrane to current sax phenomenon Grover Washington, Jr., who still lives in the city, to bassist Christian McBride. The Kimmel Center now presents a popular jazz series, and the Mellon Jazz Festival is held in May (see "Philadelphia Calendar of Events," p. 15). The Philadelphia Clef Club on the Avenue of the Arts has given jazz an intimate performance home. Even the Philadelphia Museum of Art offers live jazz on most Wednesday and Friday evenings. For specific information, write or call **Mill Creek Jazz and Cultural Society,** 4624 Lancaster Ave., Philadelphia, PA 19131 (✆ 215/473-2880).

Chris' Jazz Club   This casual three-room bar in the shadow of the venerable Union League puts the stage in the corner of the front section of the bar, and the front and middle rooms get a fine show nightly. There are four beers on tap. 1421 Sansom St. ✆ 215/568-3131. Cover $5.

Ortlieb's Jazzhaus   This smoky, longtime jazz hangout in a former Northern Liberties brewery is the real, dark, bare-bones deal. Quartets headed by Shirley Scott and Mickey Roker are regulars here. There's a terrific seven-piece house band that performs nightly at 9:30pm, and there's no cover charge to enjoy the down-home ambience Sunday through Thursday. You can park in the small strip mall across the street for free. 847 N. 3rd St. at Poplar St. ✆ 215/922-1035. Cover $8–10.

Philadelphia Clef Club of Jazz & Performing Arts   The nonprofit Clef Club is dedicated solely to the preservation and promotion of jazz. In its handsome building on the Avenue of the Arts, it presents jazz workshops and instrumental training as well as concerts in a 250-seat performance hall. 736–738 S. Broad St. ✆ 215/893-9912. Ticket prices vary.

Warmdaddy's   Run by the Bynum brothers, who made jazz club Zanzibar Blue (see below) a success, this wine-colored, sophisticated addition to the historic district features authentic live blues from Koko Taylor, Murali Coryell, and the like, and excellent traditional Southern cuisine, with entrees ranging from $11 to $17. The stage and sound system are first rate, and the ambience is simultaneously sexy and familial. Monday night "gumbo" is a mix of comedy, music, and spoken-word performances. Front and Market sts. ✆ 215/627-2500. Cover $8 after 8pm waived with dinner. Cover $10–$12.

Zanzibar Blue   This place, down the escalator at the Bellevue, features the best of the city's and touring jazz bands. The ambience is elegant, so you may want to dress up for a visit. Open until 2am nightly. 200 S. Broad St. ✆ 215/732-5200. Sun jazz brunch $23. Cover $10–$12.

ROCK CLUBS & ROCK CONCERT VENUES

Two firms control the presentation of large rock concerts in town, and advance tickets are almost obligatory. **Clear Channel** (✆ 215/569-9416; www.electricfactory.com) usually books major talent into the **Wachovia Center** (box office ✆ 215/336-3600), the city's major indoor arena, in South Philly, as well as at the 25,000-seat **Tweeter Center on the Waterfront** in Camden (✆ 856/365-1300). Other venues include the **Electric Factory,** 421 N. 7th St., a plain industrial rehab with questionable acoustics; the **Tower Theatre,** at 69th and Market streets in Upper Darby (scene of recent Sting and Todd Rundgren concerts); and, in the summer, the **Mann Music Center** in Fairmount Park. The **Theater of Living Arts** at 334 South St. (© **215/922-1011**), now bereft of all seating, is used for smaller shows like Mary Chapin Carpenter.

Tickets are available in advance through **Ticketmaster** for most venues (© **215/336-2000**).

Abilene   Abilene opened way back in 1997 with a Southwestern menu and blues to match; more recently it's gone into straight-ahead American R&B and rock, live nightly. There are three dining rooms to choose from, including one nonsmoking. Call to see what band is playing when you're in town. 429 South St. © 215/922-2583. Cover $4–$10.

The Khyber   This is one of the most popular spots to hear rock nightly. There's live entertainment from 9:30pm until 1 or 2am, depending on the crowd and the day. Khyber Pass is named after the route the British took to get through Pakistan; it has a certain atticlike charm. English ales and Irish stout are served. 56 S. 2nd St. © 215/238-5888. Cover is usually $5.

North Star Bar   North Star, located north of the Philadelphia Museum of Art, hosts photo exhibits and poetry readings in addition to the rock groups that perform 5 nights a week. This old bar is a comfortable place to drink, and the spicy chicken wings are very tasty. 27th and Poplar sts. © 215/684-0808. www. northstarbar.com. Cover $7–$10.

Pontiac Grille   The Pontiac features live music Wednesday through Saturday, and DJs on Tuesday nights. It's a hard-drinking, hard-smoking place, with lots of energy when the band is good. Both floors are now hooked into a closed-cir-cuit live feed of the main stage. 304 South St. © 215/925-4053. Cover $6–$7.

3 The Bar Scene

Great drinking spots are everywhere in Philadelphia: They range from neighbor-hood bars to elegant hotel lounges to dimly lit hipster hangouts, where you need to buy an entire $200 bottle of champagne just to hold a table. The hottest bars in town now are in **Old City** and **Rittenhouse Square.** Ironically, Rittenhouse Square has always been a place where residents walk dogs, artists set up easels, and children play in fountains. Now, however, thanks to some smart entrepreneurs, the stretch along the entire east side (18th St.) glows with heat lamps and candles, and

---

Ben Franklin: "Bottom's Up!"

Believe it or not, Ben Franklin approves of your Philly bar crawl. Franklin was a wine and beer enthusiast and occasional winemaker, who coined the drinking proverbs still quoted in Philadelphia taverns:

"There cannot be good living where there is not good drinking."

"Beer is proof that God loves us and wants us to be happy."

"Wine makes daily living easier, less hurried, with fewer tensions and more tolerance."

Just remember that Franklin also valued moderation:

"Take counsel in wine, but resolve afterwards in water."

"Eat not to dullness; drink not to elevation."

Tips   Drink Like a Founding Father

If you want a taste of what our first representatives drank at the end (and sometimes in the middle) of their work day, try a glass of **Madeira,** a mixture of wine and brandy originally from an island off of Portugal. Madeira was considered a tasty, healthy drink that didn't spoil easily.

---

resounds with murmurs of conversation and the clink of glasses. Neil Stein initiated the alfresco movement in 1998 with his 1920s-style bistro **Rouge,** at 205 S. 18th St. It's a Mobil Travel four-star awardee, and it serves a great $15 burger. In 2000, he followed Rouge with **Bleu** at 227 S. 18th St., where whimsical murals enliven a great $29 three-course prix-fixe dinner. Also present are **Devon Seafood Grill,** and **Potcheen** around the corner on Locust Street. All are active until 11pm Sunday through Thursday, and until 1am Friday and Saturday. Just off the Square is **Twenty Manning,** on 20th Street between Locust and Spruce, where stylish, vibrant owner Audrey Claire Taichman draws a crowd of young professionals to her mod indoor-outdoor lounge, with excellent cocktails and appetizers.

BREWERIES & PUBS

Bridgid's   This tiny, very friendly horseshoe-shaped bar near the Philadelphia Museum of Art stocks a superb collection of Belgian beers, including an array of fruit-to-hops-originated brews. A varied menu is also available at the bar. Smoking is not allowed, except for the smoke that billows out of the warm fireplace. 726 N. 24th St. ℂ 215/232-3232.

Cosi   These bustling cafes serve coffee throughout the day and drinks starting at 4:30pm. In the evenings, the signature sliding bar front lifts to reveal a full liquor bar, table service begins, and lighting and music levels gradually shift for a hopping nightlife scene. Service is variable. Historic area: 325 Chestnut St. ℂ 215/399-0214; 215 Lombard St. ℂ 215/925-4910. Center City: 1128 Walnut St. ℂ 215/413-1608; 15th and Locust sts. ℂ 215/893-9696; 1700 Market St. ℂ 215/569-2833; 201 S. 18th St. ℂ 215/735-2004. University City: Sansom Commons, 3601 Walnut St. ℂ 215/222-4545.

Fado   Fado, an Atlanta-based chain that sells more Guinness than anyone else in the United States, is Kieran McGill's personal vision of Victorian-era Dublin, with carved mahogany, cast iron, cozy fireplaces, displays of antique china, and the finest Irish and European draft beers. Intimate nooks seat up to a dozen. Stop by for the Irish music on Tuesdays and Thursdays. 1500 Locust St. ℂ 215/893-9700.

Independence Brewpub at the Terminal   If you don't want to venture far from the Convention Center, you can't do better than this huge, attractive space with a great selection of freshly brewed beers and late-night munchies. Open to 2am daily. 1150 Filbert St. ℂ 215/922-4292.

Irish Pub   This Rittenhouse Square stalwart for serious drinkers packs in hundreds of college kids and young professionals. There is Irish and American folk music in the front, and a quieter area in the back. Open until 2am nightly. 2007 Walnut St. ℂ 215/568-5603.

Monk's Café   This small brewpub wins "Best of Philly" awards as the first and premier local importer of kegs of flavorful Belgian ales like Chimay. The back bar is more "authentically drafty," while the front bar is more decorous. Both serve from an extensive wine list and furnish a simple menu, with great mussels. 264 S. 16th St. ℂ 215/545-7005.

Nodding Head Brewery and Restaurant   This cozy brew house was opened in the late 1980s as an offshoot of the Sansom Street Oyster House downstairs, but now has its own identity. Three beers are regularly brewed right here: a light ale, an amber ale, and a dark porter. Try to secure one of the spacious booths in a semicircle opposite the bar. 1516 Sansom St. ✆ **215/569-9525.**

Serrano   Serrano, along with the Tin Angel Acoustic Café (p. 202), offers a wonderful collection of brews, along with eclectic world cuisine, in an intimate setting. It's located on one of the Historic District's nicest blocks. The old wooden bar has antique stained glass behind it, and a spiced wood fire burns in the fireplace. If you can't get out to Stoudt's own brewpub in Adamstown (p. 249), try their unpasteurized beer here ($5.95 per bottle). 20 S. 2nd St. ✆ **215/928-0770.**

LOUNGES & PIANO BARS

Alma de Cuba   The wonderful fusion–South American creation of Stephen Starr and Douglas Rodriguez has a swanky, evocative lounge on its first floor. Mambo classes once a week. 1623 Walnut St. ✆ **215/988-1799.**

South Street: The Hippest Street in Town (Sort Of)

The old Orlons' tune declared that South Street was "where all the hippest meet" and sang of "stomping down the street" and digging those "crazy sounds." That was in the '60s. South Street today isn't quite as hip, and mostly appeals to teens and 20-somethings looking for some trashy bars and goofy boutiques. But you'll find an interesting place to stroll around for an hour or so and browse the fabric shops and maybe grab a loud and lively cocktail.

Start at 4th and South and walk down to **Kinkus Fabrics,** 754 S. 4th St. (✆ 215/923-8836), on "Fabric Row."

Peek into **Django,** 526 S. 4th just off South (✆ 215/922-7151), the area's best BYOB restaurant, and a near-impossible dinner reservation (put your name on the waiting list). Get more immediate satisfaction at the old-fashioned diner that is now **Jim's Steaks,** 400 South St. (✆ 215/928-1911), an incredibly popular cheesesteak spot.

Check out the goods at **Elite Snowboard and Skateboard,** 611 South St. (✆ 215/238-1991).

The venerable **Book Trader,** 510–503 South St. (✆ 215/925-0219), has every new title, plus hard to find art, music, and fashion tomes, and a cool '60s-ish vibe.

Teens and crafty types love the **Eyes Gallery,** 402 South St. (✆ 215/925-0193), with its eclectic decorative arts, and **Mineralistic,** 319 South St. (✆ 215/922-7199), a groovy spot for affordable jewelry.

The most famous clothing shop is **Zipperhead,** 407 South St. (✆ 215/928-1123), for leather, pleather, and other naughty good stuff.

Snack at the excellent **Chef's Market,** 227 South St. (✆ 215/925-8360), which is great for cooks, but also has wonderful takeout.

Cocktails? We like the **Latest Dish,** 613 S. 4th St., and **North Bar and Lounge,** 222 South St. (✆ 215/238-0299).

South Street

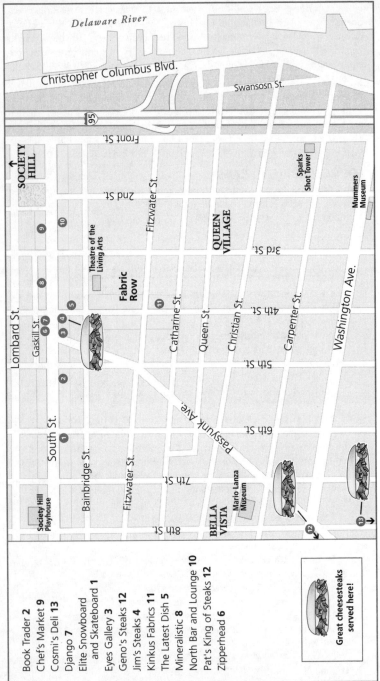

Delaware River

Christopher Columbus Blvd.

Swansosn St.

95

SOCIETY HILL ←

Front St.

2nd St.

Fitzwater St.

Theatre of the Living Arts

Fabric Row

QUEEN VILLAGE

3rd St.

Sparks Shot Tower

Mummers Museum

Lombard St.

Gaskill St.

Catharine St.

Queen St.

Christian St.

4th St.

Carpenter St.

Washington Ave.

5th St.

South St.

Passyunk Ave.

6th St.

Bainbridge St.

Fitzwater St.

7th St.

Mario Lanza Museum

BELLA VISTA

8th St.

Society Hill Playhouse

Great cheesesteaks served here!

Book Trader **2**
Chef's Market **9**
Cosmi's Deli **13**
Django **7**
Elite Snowboard and Skateboard **1**
Eyes Gallery **3**
Geno's Steaks **12**
Jim's Steaks **4**
Kinkus Fabrics **11**
The Latest Dish **5**
Mineralistic **8**
North Bar and Lounge **10**
Pat's King of Steaks **12**
Zipperhead **6**

Bridget Foy's South Street Grill   Newly renovated and featuring a fine open-style grill at reasonable prices, Bridget Foy's offers a nice, mellow atmosphere. There's no pressure to socialize if you don't feel like it, but plenty of company to keep you entertained if you do. Situated at the lower corner of Head House Square, the establishment features a lively sidewalk cafe in summer. It's open every evening until 1am. 200 South St. ℂ **215/922-1813.**

Continental Restaurant and Martini Bar   This Old City vintage diner, with its olive-shaped lamps and inventive cocktails, is one of the coolest spots in the city for dining and drinking. Owner Stephen Starr has also just replicated the concept with a second location at 18th and Chestnut, this one with an amazing three levels of funky modern decor, including a beautiful rooftop bar. The martinis deserve the *Food & Wine* magazine's "Best Chef Hangout" award that they won. Tapas from all over the world include pad Thai and miniature spring rolls. 138 Market St. ℂ **215/923-6069** and 1801 Chestnut St. ℂ **215/567-1800.**

Denim Lounge   A Philippe Starck–style series of rooms, each with a different decor, this restaurant and bar is a popular date spot (or place at which to find a date). You can nibble tuna tartare on sleek white banquettes lit by votive candles, or hang out in a funky back bar with red quilted walls punctuated by antlers. Lighting is low and flattering. There is a bottle service policy after 10pm for occupying a table. 1712 Walnut St. ℂ **215/735-6700.**

Le Bar Lyonnais   Downstairs from the famed Le Bec-Fin Restaurant (p. 99), you'll find this crowded, intimate, smoky bar, a favorite hangout of those with high bank balances, hormones, or hopes. 1523 Walnut St. ℂ **215/567-1000.**

Lounge at the Omni   This lounge is a pleasant, quiet spot, with dark woods and Oriental carpets, a crackling fireplace, a piano, and large picture windows surveying Independence National Historical Park across the street. Good if you're looking for a sophisticated backdrop to conversation. It stays open past midnight on weekends. 4th and Chestnut sts. ℂ **215/925-0000.**

Marmont   Marmont is a swanky narrow bar and restaurant, serving excellent tapas and more for dinner, followed by live music on Mondays and great DJs every other night. It's almost all candle-lit; summer brings a few street-side cafe tables. A great date location. 222 Market St. ℂ **215/923-1100.**

Silk City Lounge   With lava lamps and a young, ultrahip crowd, this is what would have been called a dive before the postmodern era. Occasional nights are devoted to music of the Sinatra era, although the owner likes to change themes every 6 months or so. Live bands play about once a week. The attached American Diner is open all night Friday through Sunday. 5th and Spring Garden sts. ℂ **215/592-8838.**

32 Degrees   When celebrities and athletes wander into Philly, they often end up lounging at 32 Degrees, with its sofas, chic bar, and pricey "bottle service" for champagne and vodka. Think J. Lo comes to Philly. 16 S. 2nd St. ℂ **215/627-3132.**

Impressions

I have never observed such a wealth of taverns and drinking establishments as are in Philadelphia. . . . There is hardly a street without several and hardly a man here who does not fancy one his second home.
—Thomas Jefferson, letter to a Virginia friend (1790)

Twenty Manning With its windows opening out onto a leafy corner, and a long, modern bar, this is a living-room-style bar and restaurant for professionals from their 20s into their 40s. In the back are black leather sofas for canoodling, and the outdoor tables are a favorite dinner-date destination. The Asian-influenced cuisine and wine list chosen by beautiful owner Audrey Taichman are as delightful as the people-watching—come at 5:30pm, or after 9pm on weekends. 261 S. 20th St. ℂ 215/731-0900.

Washington Square The city's most sophisticated outdoor lounging space is in this restaurant set in an Art Deco insurance building, where designer David Rockwell took an outdoor space, tented it, and installed sofas and banquettes. The tree-lined spot on Washington Square Park feels like Los Angeles in summer months, and the cocktails and menu by chef Marcus Samuelsson are enticing. In the winter, there are dark, cozy rooms and a sleek bar indoors. 210 W. Washington Sq. ℂ 215/592-7787.

WINE BARS

Il Bar ⭐⭐ Wine bar enthusiasts, this is your mecca. The Penn's View Hotel's first class wine bar features the world's largest *cruvinet* system for preserving up to 120 different bottles after they've been opened. Every selection is available by the glass, most for around $8, or by the "taste" (3 oz.). You can also order "flights" of five 1.5-ounce glasses, which makes for a convivial learning experience. There's piano entertainment to accompany your sipping and swirling, and you can order from the stellar menu of the adjoined Ristorante Panorama (p. 97). Sunday through Thursday until midnight, Friday through Saturday to 1am. 14 N. Front St. at Market St. ℂ 215/922-7800.

Tria This small, narrow bar looks more New York than Philly, with its neutral colors and mod light fixtures. Wines by the glass are categorized as Bold, Bubbly, and Zippy; come here also for boutique beers, cheeses, and tapas, served to a sophisticated crowd. 123 S. 18th St. ℂ 215/972-TRIA.

4 The Gay & Lesbian Scene

The area between Walnut and Locust streets south of the Convention Center—roughly from 9th Street to 13th Street—is the "Gayborhood," the heart of gay and lesbian Philadelphia, and it's filled with social services, bookstores, clubs, bars, and restaurants. Pick up a copy of *Philadelphia Gay News* at **Giovanni's Room** bookstore (345 S. 12th St.; ℂ 215/923-2960) for suggestions of places that cater to a variety of niches and sub-niches.

Bump This slick modern gay bar has warm orange lighting, titillating artwork, cute guys, and trendy cocktails including $2 happy-hour martinis. Sunday's popular prix-fixe brunch menu is $9.95. Open Tuesday through Sunday, 5pm to 2am. 1234 Locust St. ℂ 215/732-1800.

Judy's Café If you're looking for a friendly place just to hang out, Judy's front bar area is a hot spot for gay and lesbian singles and couples. 627 S. 3rd St. at Bainbridge. ℂ 215/928-1968.

Pure The Weiss family, who transformed the Eighth Street Lounge in Old City and Grape Street Pub in Manayunk, cleaned up this cavernous after-hours gay bar and dance club in 1999. Fabrics abound, from neon zebra fake fur to baroque red velvet and chandeliers. It's got three floors, and the top floor is filled with couches

---

Tips **Alexander Inn Knows the "Gayborhood"**

The **Alexander Inn** (p. 85) is Philadelphia's only gay-owned, gay-managed, and gay-staffed hotel, located in the heart of the "gayborhood" at 12th and Spruce Streets. Owner John Cochie gave us his nightlife tips for gay travelers:

1. "The *Philadelphia Gay News* is the city's leading gay periodical, but our other two weekly papers *Citypaper* and *Philadelphia Weekly* both cover local gay issues and events."
2. "Don't overlook **Westbury** (261 S. 13th St. at Spruce St; ✆ **215/546-5170**). This is a great neighborhood gay bar that's the most overlooked by tourists."
3. "After hours, you will find many of our local community taking breakfast at the 24-hour **Midtown Restaurant** (122 S. 11th St. at Sansom St.; ✆ **215/627-6452**)."
4. "Watch for **'Pride and Progress'** (1315 Spruce St. at 13th St.), a 7500-square-foot, four-story outdoor mural paying tribute to GLBT persons."
5. And a general note about Philly pride: "Remember that 'freedom started here' in Philadelphia and that gay civil rights demonstrations took place here well before the Stonewall Riots in New York."

---

and multimedia screens. Altogether the space holds nearly 1,000 people and hosts top-name DJs and drag hostesses. 1221 St. James St. ✆ **215/735-5772**.

Sisters   Unfortunately, this is the only game in town for single lesbians, but Sisters delivers big: three bars over three floors, covering over 5,000 square feet, with a diverse female crowd. It features Saturday "Liquid Sex" events (where the drink creations are supposed to be as good as sex, hence the name), Sunday vinyl dance parties, and Thursday karaoke. 1320 Chancellor St. ✆ **215/735-0735**.

12th Air Command   Gay men mingle on three floors and an open deck on 12th Street, open nightly until 2am. Crowds tend to spill outside on nice nights. Downstairs there's a lounge bar and game room. Burgers and hot dogs are served outdoors on the deck, and there's another bar and a crowded disco upstairs. No credit cards. 254 S. 12th St. ✆ **215/545-8088**. Cover $5 for dancing only Fri–Sat.

Uncles   The bartenders and their mature male patrons are on a first-name basis at this small, smoky neighborhood bar, complete with pale pink walls and slightly tacky tinsel decor. Younger crowds gather on weekends, but weekdays locals come to listen to the jukebox and watch the street scene pass by the bar's large folding windows. 1220 Locust St. ✆ **215/546-6660**.

Woody's   The party atmosphere and rugged Midwestern decor of Woody's attracts both a gay and straight clientele. The original bar is downstairs, and a sandwich counter and the **CyberBar** (with free Internet access) has been added alongside. The disco adjoining the upstairs lounge features *trompe l'oeil* Atlases holding up a roof of stars. Friday and Sunday nights are Country Western. 202 S. 13th St. ✆ **215/545-1893**. Cover Fri–Sat $5–$10.

5 Other Nighttime Entertainment

BOWLING

Philadelphia is not much of a bowling town; no lanes are found in Center City, but there are lanes out along the northern routes leading out of the city, or across the Delaware in New Jersey. Many lanes have adapted to a younger social crowd by offering special "cosmic" or "extreme" bowling nights on the weekends—same lanes but spiced up with loud music and black lights.

Boulevard Lanes   These lanes hold "Cosmic" evenings on Fridays and Saturdays. 8011 Roosevelt Ave. © 215/332-9200.

Jillian's   This groovy spot at the Franklin Mills Mall has 20 lanes, three bars, billiards tables, an arcade, and fun food, as well as music and dim, colorful lighting. 1995 Franklin Mills Circle. © 215/632-0333.

Thunderbird Lanes   Thunderbird gets high marks from devotees and daters alike. Rock 300, a bowling-alley-focused satellite radio station, plays over the whole scene; Saturday evenings are "cosmic bowling," and the wait for a lane can be up to an hour unless you're there early. Monday nights draw college and high school kids. There is no bar, but there are video games to entertain while you wait for a lane. You can bring canned beer, though. 3081 Holme Ave. © 215/464-7171.

CINEMA

Center City's movie-going options are clustered mainly in Old City and along the river. **United Artist Riverview,** 1400 S. Columbus Blvd. along the Delaware River waterfront (© 215/755-2219), features stadium seating and 17 screens, but it's a considerable taxi ride from Center City (though less than $10 from Society Hill and Old City).

In the historic district, **Ritz 5 Movies,** 214 Walnut St. (© 215/925-7900 or 215/440-1184), is the best choice for independent releases. It has five comfortable screening rooms and shows sophisticated, often foreign, fare. The first daily matinee performance is $4.

Its sister theater, the five-screen **Ritz at the Bourse,** 4th and Ranstead streets (© 215/925-7900), behind the Bourse and the new Omni Hotel, has the advantage of an espresso/cappuccino bar replete with long leather sofas. The minichain also owns the **Ritz East,** on 2nd Street between Chestnut and Walnut streets, with two screens (© 215/925-7900).

The **Tuttleman IMAX Theater** at the Franklin Institute, 222 N. 20th St. (© 215/448-1111), shows exciting adventure and nature movies *(Titanica, Whales)* on its four-story, domed screen.

In University City, there's the well-designed, upscale **Bridge Cinema de Lux,** 230 S. 40th St. at Walnut (© 215/386-3300). **International House,** 3701 Chestnut St. (© 215/387-5125), presents a fine series of foreign films, political documentaries, and work from independent filmmakers. **Cinemagic 3 at Penn,** 3925 Walnut St. (© 215/222-5555), screens intelligent releases from the U.S. and abroad.

READINGS

Borders, 1 S. Broad St. at Chestnut Street (© 215/568-7400), runs one of the country's top series of author readings in an elegant setting across the Avenue of the Arts from the Ritz-Carlton. Readings are usually at 7:30pm weekdays and 2pm weekends.

Barnes & Noble in Rittenhouse Square, 1805 Walnut St. (© **215/665-0716**), offers semi-regular 7pm readings. The main branch of the **Free Library of Philadelphia,** a beautiful limestone temple at 1901 Vine St. (© **215/686-5415;** www.library.phila.gov) offers regular author readings with names such as Carl Hiassen and Walter Mosley in residence.

SALONS
Several spots around town have started catering to the large pool of intellectu-ally curious singles in Philadelphia. Judy Wicks at the **White Dog Café,** 3420 Sansom St. (© **215/386-9224**), has instituted "salon meals," calling on local academics, artists, and her own contacts to address issues such as domestic and foreign policy, the arts, and social movements. The salon talks include a three-course dinner for $30 per person, and reservations are recommended.

SPECTACLES
The **Benjamin Franklin Bridge** has been outfitted with special lighting effects by the noted architectural firm Venturi, Rauch, and Scott Brown. The lights are triggered into mesmerizing patterns by the auto and train traffic along the span. Lighting plays on most of the major monuments and bridges leading in and out of Center City and on City Hall as well.

May through October, from dusk until 11:15pm, Independence National Historical Park becomes the backdrop for the mesmerizing **"Lights of Liberty"** show. Wearing special headsets you hear stereophonic sound and see 50-foot projections and surprising special effects that illustrate the struggle toward America's independence. See p. 127 for details.

A VIDEO ARCADE
Traffic is huge for **Dave & Busters,** Pier 19, 325 N. Delaware Ave. (© **215/ 413-1951**), an urban country club with video arcades, virtual-reality headsets, electronic golf, billiards, and blackjack. Downsides: Service to redeem coupons from prizes can be slow, and the burgers from the Bridgeside Grill get a mixed reaction. The cover is $5 Friday and Saturday after 10pm.

6 Late-Night Bites
Twenty years ago, this section wouldn't have existed; the fact is, Philadelphia does stay up late, but until recently the city was private about it. As the city becomes more oriented to tourism and service professions, hours are adapting to fit the clientele.

Fork   The cool bar here serves its full menu till 11:30pm weekends, then intro-duces a great late-night bar menu (truffled duck pâté, anyone?) until 1am. 306 Market St. © 215/625-9425. forkrestaurant.com.

Melrose Diner   The Melrose's logo of a coffee cup with a clock face and knife-and-fork hands, like the place in general, is somewhere between kitsch and post-modern. The Melrose dishes out scrapple (a local fried combination of pork, herbs, and cornmeal) and eggs, creamed chipped beef, and the like 10 blocks north of the sporting stadiums in South Philly. If you hanker for the type of place where you'll be called "Hon," this is for you. They bake pies three times a day to ensure fresh-ness and turn out wonderful butter cookies and a great butter-cream layer cake. Reservations not accepted. No credit cards. Open 24 hours. 1501 Snyder St. (intersec-tion of 15th St., Passyunk Ave., and Snyder St., 1 block west of S. Broad St.). © 215/467-6644.

Midtown Restaurant   This inexpensive, no-frills diner serves up a large menu of greasy food to hungry bar-hoppers, in the Gayborhood and Rittenhouse Square areas. Open 24 hours. 122 S. 11th St. at Sansom St. ℰ **215/627-6452.** Rittenhouse Square: 2013 Chestnut St. at 20th St., ℰ **215/567-3142;** and 28 S. 18th St. at Ludlow St., ℰ **215/567-5144.**

Silk City American Diner   This is what happens when a 1950s diner is given a real postmodern twist; in particular, the pastel pinks and grays in the decor combine with an eclectic song selection and the hip couture that patrons sport. Though Silk City serves breakfast all day, the menu aspires to be gourmet, with dishes such as spicy jerk chicken with grilled plantains, chocolate bread pudding, and huevos rancheros. Adjoins Shampoo nightclub. Open Sunday through Thursday until midnight, 24 hours on Friday and Saturday. No credit cards. 435 Spring Garden St. ℰ **215/592-8838.**

Tangerine   This is the closest you'll come to playing out a sophisticated fantasy of entering the Casbah for swank, exotic Moroccan fusion cuisine. The over-the-top, low-wattage decor varies from room to room. This place is somewhat pricey but service is excellent. Open Sunday through Thursday 5 to 10pm and Friday and Saturday 5pm to midnight. 232 Market St. ℰ **215/627-5116.**

The Real World Takes On Philly Nightlife

MTV's *The Real World* created a media storm when they filmed here in 2004, but the initial union protests and petitions didn't faze the cast or slow down their nightlife. We asked them about their favorite hangouts.

Karamo: "Five Spot (p. 198). On Tuesday nights, they have a neo soul night, 'Black Lily,' where young artists can get up and speak, and Sunday night is a hip-hop gay night. It's great and really cheap, only $5 both nights."

Landon: "Glam (52 S. 2nd St. at Chestnut St.; ℰ **267/671-0840)** because it's tight and hot, with dancing and drinking close to one another. It's in close proximity to many other bars and food joints."

Melanie: "Drinker's Tavern (124 Market St. at 2nd St.; ℰ **215/351-0142)** is the only bar in my heart. The bar staff is awesome. The atmosphere is great, just a small hole in the wall where you can hide out when being chased by a camera crew! It's dark and cozy and has a great jukebox."

Sarah: "I loved **Jones** restaurant (700 Chestnut St. at 7th St.; ℰ **215/238-9600).** You could get a burger or a nicer dish or a salad, and the atmosphere was really laid back and cozy."

Shavonda: "Soho Pizza (218 Market St. at N. 2nd St.; ℰ **215/625-3955)** had a cool staff, and you can order a whole pizza or just a slice. My favorite was the barbecue chicken pizza."

Willie: "Bump (p. 208) had a comfortable atmosphere, with great cocktails and decent food. And **Continental** (p. 207) was always packed and lively."

— *Thanks to Eileen Quast and MTV*

11

Side Trips from Philadelphia

Less than an hour from Philadelphia, you can drive north to tranquil Bucks County or southwest to the green and beautiful Brandywine River Valley, and find enchanting farms, classic stone farmhouses, antiques galleries, and art museums. The same boats that brought Penn's Quakers to Pennsylvania also brought the pioneers that fanned out into the Delaware Valley to the south, Bucks County to the north, and what is now Pennsylvania Dutch Country to the west. This chapter covers Bucks County and the Brandywine area; the next chapter guides you through the Amish heartland of Lancaster County.

Much of these areas remain lush and unspoiled, although, of course, development has encroached where land preservationists have not been able to save open space. The major attractions of the Bucks and Brandywine countryside are historical: Colonial mansions and inns, early American factories and businesses, and Revolutionary War battlegrounds. Both areas are known for inspiring renowned painters, also: Along with the New Hope School of Impressionist art, the Brandywine is and was home to three generations of Wyeths, the late N. C., as well as Andrew and Jamie Wyeth.

1 Bucks County & Nearby New Jersey

Bucks County, at most an hour by car from Philadelphia, is bordered by the Delaware River to the east and Montgomery County to the west. Historic estates and sights, antiques stores, and country inns abound. The natural beauty here, which has survived major development so far, has inspired many artists and authors, including Oscar Hammerstein II, Pearl Buck, and James Michener, and draws as many New Yorkers on weekends as it does Philadelphians. A new interest in this area is ecotourism—the landscape is great for gentle outdoor activities. Nearby New Jersey offers scenic routes for bicycling and walking, plus enjoyable restaurants. The rural-but-sophisticated area, especially the bustling village of New Hope, is also very gay-friendly and has a large population of gay and lesbian residents.

ESSENTIALS

GETTING THERE   The best automobile route into Bucks County from Center City is I-95 (north). Pa. 32 (which intersects I-95 in Yardley) runs along the Delaware past Washington Crossing State Park to New Hope, which connects to Doylestown by U.S. 202. By train, the R5 SEPTA commuter rail ends at Doylestown, with connections to New Hope and Lahaska.

From New York, take the New Jersey Turnpike to I-78 west; follow to Exit 29 and pick up Route 287 south to Route 202, which crosses the Delaware River at Lambertville, straight into New Hope. To stay a bit more north and rural, depart I-78 at Exit 15 in Clinton, and take Route 513 south 12 tranquil miles, crossing the Delaware at Frenchtown, New Jersey.

⌒ Fun Fact Where Washington Crossed the Delaware

A trip along the Delaware via Route 32 through Morrisville and Yardley will bring you to **Washington Crossing State Park** in New Jersey,
500 acres that are open year-round (there are another 400 acres of
parkland west of the Delaware in Pennsylvania). Most people know
that Washington crossed a big river in a small boat on Christmas Eve
of 1776, and many people are familiar with the heroic painting depict-
ing this event, with Washington standing in the boat, his eyes on the
farther shore (the painting is by Emanuel Leutze, a German, who
trained as an artist in Philadelphia). This was the spot, and an annual
reenactment of the historic crossing takes place here at Christmas. The
Durham boats that Washington and his troops used, which are on display in the boat barn, were hardly tiny—they held 30 soldiers each.

The Pennsylvania side of the park is divided into upper and lower
sections separated by 3 miles; Washington left from the site that is now
the lower park. You can tour the low-ceilinged **Old (McKonkey's) Ferry
Inn** (1752), where Washington ate before he crossed the river, and tour
the bird sanctuary and the Memorial Building at the point of embarka-
tion. The 30-minute film in the Visitors Center (closed Mon) is dated and
not worth sitting through—just start exploring on your own.

The **Wild Flower Preserve** in the upper park is really a 100-acre
arboretum, flower garden, and botanical preserve rolled into one; it
contains 15 different paths, each emphasizing different botanical won-
ders. The **Thompson-Neely House** was intact when General Washington,
Brigadier General Stirling, and Lt. James Monroe decided on the year-
end push into New Jersey. Next to the Wild Flower Preserve is the stone
Bowman's Hill Tower; it will reward you with a stunning view of this part
of the Delaware Valley, which would probably still belong to the British
Commonwealth if Washington's troops hadn't conquered the Hessians
(German soldiers who fought with the British) in 1776. Washington
Crossing State Park is located at Route 32, P.O. Box 103, Washington
Crossing, PA 18977 (© **215/493-4076;** www.fieldtrip.com/pa). A combination ticket, including a walking tour, Thompson-Neely House, Bowman's Hill and Tower, costs $5 for adults, $3 for seniors, and $2 for
children ages 4 to 12. Buildings are open Monday through Saturday
from 9am to 5pm, Sunday from noon to 5pm. Grounds open daily from
8:30am to 8pm or sunset. Parking is free. Located at the intersection of
Pa. 532 and Pa. 32 (River Rd.), 3 miles north of I-95 from Exit 31.

VISITOR INFORMATION   To find out more about the hundreds of historic
sites, camping facilities, and accommodations here, contact the **Bucks County
Convention and Visitors Bureau,** 3207 Street Rd., Bensalem, PA 19020
(© **800/836-2825** or 215/634-0300; www.experiencebuckscounty.com). You
can also write to or stop by the **New Hope Visitors Center,** South Main and
Mechanic streets, Box 141, New Hope, PA 18938 (© **215/862-5880** or 215/
862-5030; www.newhopevisitorscenter.org), open Sunday through Thursday
from 10am to 5pm, Friday and Saturday from 10am to 7pm.

Bucks County

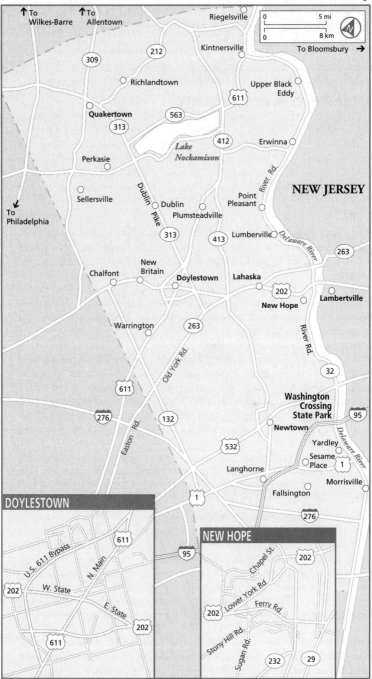

Map labels:

To Wilkes-Barre
To Allentown
Riegelsville
0 5 mi
0 8 km
To Bloomsbury
212
Kintnersville
309
Richlandtown
Upper Black Eddy
611
Quakertown
313
563
412
Erwinna
Lake Nockamixon
Perkasie
NEW JERSEY
River Rd.
Sellersville
Dublin Pike
Dublin
Point Pleasant
To Philadelphia
Plumsteadville
313
413
Lumberville
Delaware River
263
Chalfont
New Britain
Doylestown
Lahaska
202
New Hope
Lambertville
Warrington
263
River Rd.
Old York Rd.
32
611
276
132
Washington Crossing State Park
95
Easton Rd.
Newtown
Yardley
Delaware River
532
Sesame Place
1
Langhorne
Morrisville
1
Fallsington
276

DOYLESTOWN

U.S. 611 Bypass
611
N. Main
202
W. State
E. State
202
611
95

NEW HOPE

Chapel St.
202
202
Lower York Rd.
Ferry Rd.
Stony Hill Rd.
Sugan Rd.
232
29

215

Along with the specific accommodations listed below, you might want to contact the **Bucks County Bed and Breakfast Association,** P.O. Box 154, New Hope, PA 18938 (© **215/862-7154;** www.bbonline.com/pa/buckscounty). This group represents many of the top inns throughout the area, as well as those across the river in the wonderful New Jersey towns of Lambertville, Stockton, and Frenchtown. Also visit www.bedandbreakfast.com for more suggestions.

ATTRACTIONS IN BUCKS COUNTY

Fallsington   When Penn was in residence at Pennsbury Manor (see above) and wished to worship, he'd go to Fallsington, 6 miles north of his estate. This Colonial village, grouped around the Quaker meetinghouse, has been preserved virtually intact. Again, tours, given hourly, are mandatory to enter the buildings.

Tyburn Rd., Fallsington, PA. © 215/295-6567. www.bucksnet.com/hisfalls. Admission $4 adults, $2.50 seniors, $2 students 6–18. Mon–Sat 10am–4pm; Sun 1–4pm. Special free open-house days on the 2nd Sat in May and Oct. Take Pa. 13 north to Tyburn Rd. (Pa. 9), then turn right and follow the road, or south off U.S. 1 at Tyburn Rd.

Pennsbury Manor   William Penn planned and lived in this very English plantation and manor at Pennsbury Manor, along the Delaware, 24 miles north of Philadelphia on Route 32 (River Rd.). He designed a self-sustaining, pre-Georgian estate of 8,400 acres (it's now 43 acres), replete with smokehouse, icehouse, barn, herb garden, plantation office, and boathouse. The various dependencies and the manor itself were demolished but were rebuilt to the finest detail in 1939. Taking a tour, given four times daily, is mandatory if you want to see inside the buildings.

Pennsbury Manor boasts the largest collection of 17th-century antiques in Pennsylvania, spread over four floors of the house. On a sunny day, it's a treat to inspect the carefully labeled herb garden, step inside the icehouse for a cool respite, and watch the guinea fowl (more popular than chickens in the 1600s) wandering along the golden brick paths. Sundays frequently bring events such as a period Quaker wedding or a farm festival. Other special events are scheduled throughout the year. Call or check the website to see what's going on when you're visiting.

Morrisville, PA. © 215/946-0400. www.pennsburymanor.org. Admission to buildings (by guided tour only) $5 adults, $4.50 seniors, $3 children 6–12, free for children under 6. Admission to grounds alone $4.50. Tues–Sat 9am–5pm; Sun noon–5pm. Call or check the website to find out times for the (required) timed and guided tours; there are 3 or 4 daily. Take Pa. 9 (Tyburn Rd.) from U.S. 1 (intersects I-95) or U.S. 13.

Sesame Place ★★ *Kids*   The nation's only theme park based on the award-winning television show *Sesame Street* is located 30 minutes from Center City and 90 minutes from New York City. My kids and millions of others spent a day totally involved in exploring this place—climbing through three stories of sloping, swaying fun on the Nets and Climbs, crawling through tubes and tunnels amid splashing fountains and showers of spray at Mumford's Water Maze, and enjoying the daily fun-filled, interactive musical parade and celebration starring Big Bird, Elmo, Zoe, Bert and Ernie, and the rest. Kids and parents will want their swimsuits for 13 age-safe water rides including Sky Splash, the five-story water adventure in Twiddlebug Land; Rubber Duckie; Slimey's Chutes; and Big Bird's Rambling River. Changing rooms are provided. Older kids will love *Vapor Trail,* the park's roller coaster. All of the best-loved *Sesame Street* characters perform in shows at Big Bird Theater and stroll around Sesame Neighborhood for photo opportunities. Indoors, you'll find air-conditioned game rooms and attractions. Altogether, the more than 60 physical play stations and water rides are perfect for any family with 3- to 15-year-olds. Lockers, wheelchair/ECV, and stroller rentals are available.

100 Sesame Rd., Langhorne, PA. ℂ 215/752-7070. www.sesameplace.com. Admission $39 ages 3–55, $32 seniors over 55, twilight admission $20. "Elmo's Passport" offers 2 days for the price of 1 after September; 2nd-day tickets free with validated 1st-day ticket. Parking $10 per day, $13 for preferred spots. *Note:* Many hotels in the area offer discount tickets in their package rates. May to mid-June Mon–Fri 10am–5pm, Sat–Sun 10am–7pm; late June to Aug daily 9am–8pm; Sept–Oct Sat–Sun 10am–5pm. Junction of Rte. 1 and I-95.

NEW HOPE & LAMBERTVILLE

Four miles north of Washington Crossing on River Road (Pa. 32), which is punctuated by hilly, lovely farmland (as opposed to U.S. 202's factory outlets), you'll come upon New Hope, a former Colonial town turned artists' colony. Although it's somewhat commercial and heavily visited now—the weekend crowds can get fierce and parking is cramped—once you're there you'll enjoy the specialty stores, restaurants, and galleries. Lambertville, across the Delaware in New Jersey, is less crowded and more New York and sophisticated in feeling, with its beautiful antiques stores and chic restaurants.

NEW HOPE AREA ATTRACTIONS

Bucks County Playhouse   This is the center of New Hope entertainment, with a summer theater that features Broadway hits and musical revivals. It's a former gristmill with a seating capacity of almost 500.

70 S. Main St. (P.O. Box 313), New Hope, PA. ℂ 215/862-2041. www.buckscountyplayhouse.com. Tickets $19–$24. Apr–Dec: Wed–Sun evenings; Wed, Thurs, and weekend matinees.

New Hope Mule Barge   For a while in the early 1800s, canals were thought to be the ultimate transport revolution in England and the eastern United States. Coal was floated down New Hope's canal in the 1830s from mines in the Lehigh Valley, with barges pulled by mules. The barges, still pulled by mules, run from April to November and leave from New Street.

New and S. Main sts., New Hope, PA. ℂ 215/862-2842. Admission $7.50 adults, $6.75 seniors, $5.50 students, $4.75 children under 12. May 1–Oct 15 6 launchings daily; Apr and Oct 16–Nov 15 launchings on Wed and Sat–Sun.

Parry Mansion Museum   One of the loveliest old homes in town, this mansion was erected in 1784 by the elite of New Hope. The Parry family lived in this 11-room Georgian until 1966, and the rooms are decorated in different period styles ranging from 1775 (whitewash and candles) to 1900 (wallpaper and oil lamps).

Main and Ferry sts., New Hope, PA. ℂ 215/862-5652. www.parrymansion.org. Admission $5 adults, $4 seniors, $1 children under 12. Late Apr to Dec Fri–Sun 1–5pm.

Peddler's Village   Five miles south of New Hope, on Route 202, Peddler's Village is an outdoor shopping mall with an old-fashioned feeling, though most of the merchandise in over 70 specialty shops is contemporary. The village synergy kicks in with eight restaurants, an inn, and **Giggleberry Fair,** a new family entertainment corner with a restored 1922 carousel ($6.95 admission all-inclusive, or rides $1.50 each) and three-story obstacle course. Among the restaurants, **Jenny's** on Route 202 at Street Road (ℂ **215/794-4020**), offers elegant continental dining in a room decorated with brass and stained glass. The specialties of the **Cock 'n' Bull** (ℂ **215/794-4010**) include a massive buffet on Thursday, an unlimited Sunday brunch, and beef burgundy served in a loaf of bread baked in the hearth.

The 71 rooms in the **Golden Plough Inn** (ℭ 215/794-4063) include some cottages with Jacuzzis scattered throughout the village—all with private bathrooms and complimentary champagne. Rates start at $145 per night.

U.S. 202 and Rte. 263, Lahaska, PA. ℭ 215/794-4000. www.peddlersvillage.com. Most stores Mon–Thurs 10am–6pm; Fri–Sat 10am–9pm; Sun 11am–6pm. Year-round festivals and events.

OUTDOOR ACTIVITIES IN THE NEW HOPE & LAMBERTVILLE AREA

BIKING & COUNTRY WALKING   Walking or riding along the Delaware River or along the canals built for coal hauling on either side of the river can be the highlight of a summer. The following two routes are particularly convenient: The first is between Lumberville and the point, 3 miles south, where Route 263 crosses the Delaware into New Jersey. The towpath along the canal on the Pennsylvania side is charming, and Lumberville has a quaint general store.

The second route, also just south of Lumberville, follows River Road (Rte. 32) south and west to Cuttalossa Road, which winds past an alpine chalet, creeks, ponds, and grazing sheep clanking their antique Swiss bells. **Cuttalossa Inn,** Cuttalossa Road, Lumberville, PA (ℭ 215/297-5082), offers high-class cuisine in a spectacular setting.

The **Lumberville Store Bicycle Rental Co.** (Rte. 32, Lumberville, PA; ℭ 215/297-5388) has all kinds of bicycles for rent at moderate day rates. It's open daily from 8am to 5pm and has wonderful sandwiches for the road.

CANOEING & TUBING   The award for relaxing family fun goes to canoeing and tubing from **Point Pleasant Canoe and Tube,** 2 Walters Lane off Route 32, Point Pleasant, PA (ℭ 215/297-5000; www.rivercountry.net). The ride lets you drift down the Delaware from Upper Black Eddy and Riegelsville back to their headquarters 8 miles north of New Hope. The water is above 70°F (21°C) all summer, and the Delaware moves at 1½ mph, so it's really fun and very safe. Rates are $14 to $34 per person for activities ranging from tubing to kayaking.

COVERED-BRIDGE TOUR   Call ℭ 215/639-0300 for information about this self-guided free tour of the area's covered bridges.

STEAM RAILWAY TOUR   The New Hope Railroad and Ivyland Railroad **steam railway** chuffs a 45-minute loop between New Hope and Lahaska, and offers dinner and Christmas trips (ℭ 215/862-2707; www.newhoperailroad.com).

SHOPPING

Penn's Purchase Factory Outlet Stores   This pleasant faux village, straddling Route 202 between Doylestown and New Hope, contains 45 outlets for stores such as **Coach, Adidas, Etienne Aigner, Waterford Wedgwood, Jones New York,** and **Nautica.** For those immediate travel needs, there are clean restrooms, an ATM, and a Dairy Queen. You won't find too many other stores that are open on a Sunday morning around here.

Rte. 202, Lahaska, PA. ℭ 215/794-0300. www.pennspurchase.com. Mon–Fri 10am–8pm; Sat 9am–8pm; Sun 9am–6pm.

Rice's Sale & Country Market   Rice's Market is the real thing—a quality market that has been selling antiques, country goods, and crafts since 1860. Amish wares are sold in the main building, along with antiques and collectibles. Plus, more than 1,000 outdoor stalls have vendors, which can draw up to 15,000 visitors. There are indoor bathrooms and paved walkways for strollers and wheelchairs. There's an ATM on the premises. Get there early.

6326 Greenhill Rd., New Hope, PA. ℂ 215/297-5993. www.ricesmarket.com. Year-round Tues 7am–1:30pm; Mar–Dec Sat 7am–1pm. Go 1 mile north of Peddler's Village on Rte. 263, then turn left by the Victorian gazebo onto Greenhill Rd.; Rice's is 1 mile ahead on the right.

WHERE TO STAY
COUNTRY INNS

New Hope and its New Jersey neighbor across the Delaware River, Lambertville, have well-deserved reputations for their country inns and restaurants. All used to require 2-day stays and frown on children, but the economic downturn and Sesame Place's success have changed all that. The listings here only scratch the surface; other excellent choices include the romantic **Inn at Phillips Mill** in New Hope (ℂ **215/862-2984**). Two of the most luxurious inns in the area are the beautifully restored 1812 **Lambertville House** (ℂ **609/397-0200**), a European-style hotel with a clubby bar called the Left Bank, and pretty guest rooms with modern bathrooms; and the tranquil mansion rooms and very posh carriage house cottages at Stockton's **Woolverton Inn,** complete with Frette linens, fine bathrooms, and pet sheep (ℂ **609/397-0802**).

Centre Bridge Inn ℛ   Situated beside the Delaware River 3½ miles north of New Hope, the current building is the third since the early 18th century. Many of the elegant guest rooms have canopy, four-poster, or brass beds; wall-high armoires; modern private bathrooms; outside decks; and views of the river or countryside. The inn also has a pretty restaurant overlooking the river and the adjoining canal (and the mule-drawn barges coasting on it) serving lunch, dinner, and a $23 fixed-price Sunday brunch.

P.O. Box 74, Intersection of Rte. 32 and Rte. 263, New Hope, PA 18938. ℂ 215/862-2048 or 215/862-9139. www.centrebridgeinn.com. 9 units. $135–$215 weekend; less weekdays. Rates include continental breakfast. DISC, MC, V. **Amenities:** Restaurant; lounge with fireplace. *In room:* A/C, TV in 5 rooms, no phone.

Evermay on the Delaware   Thirteen miles north of New Hope, overlooking the Delaware on River Road in Erwinna, lies this gracious, rambling 1700s inn, now under the ownership of William and Danielle Moffley. Evermay once hosted the Barrymores for croquet weekends. Combining privacy with a romantic setting overlooking the Delaware, the inn, which is on the quiet and formal side, offers rooms with luxurious antique furnishings, and extensive grounds. The dining room offers a wonderful, French-influenced $68 fixed-price six-course dinner featuring local ingredients at a 7:30pm seating on Friday and Saturday, as well as on holidays; Sunday, there is a fine $45, 4-course menu, served at 5, 6, or 7pm. The restaurant is open to the public as well as guests, so reserve well in advance.

River Rd., Erwinna, PA 18920. ℂ 610/294-9100. Fax 610/294-8249. 16 units in the inn and barn, 1 carriage house suite. $145–$235 double; $275 suite. Rates include continental breakfast and 4pm tea. AE, MC, V. **Amenities:** Restaurant; lounge. *In room:* A/C, dataport, iron.

Whitehall Inn ℛ   Four miles outside New Hope is this 18th-century manor house on a former horse farm, complete with a pool. Mike and Suella Wass serve magnificent four-course breakfasts, and their "innsmanship" is nationally known, with such touches as fresh fruit bowls and a bottle of mineral water in every room.

1370 Pineville Rd., New Hope, PA 18938. ℂ 215/598-7945. 5 units. $150–$200 single or double; $220 suite. Rates include 4-course breakfast and 4pm high tea on Sat. 2-night minimum. AE, DC, DISC, MC, V. Take I-95 N to 332, exit 49, to Newtown/Yardley, keep left, make left onto 413 N. and stay straight to Pineville Rd. **Amenities:** Outdoor pool; rose garden. *In room:* A/C.

HOTELS & MOTELS

New Hope Motel in the Woods 🐕 Just a mile west of town, off Route 179, you'll find this motel tucked in a woodland setting just outside of the village. For more than 30 years it has offered modern, paneled, ground-level rooms with private bathrooms and standard motel amenities.

400 W. Bridge St., New Hope, PA 18938. ☎ **215/862-2800**. www.newhopemotelinthewoods.com. 28 units. $79–$129 double. AE, DISC, MC, V. **Amenities:** Outdoor pool. In room: A/C, TV, dataport.

Sheraton Bucks County Hotel *(Kids)* This festive, modern, 14-story hotel is right across the street from Sesame Place. The soundproof guest rooms have oversize beds and quilted fabrics, and they can put a cot in the room for kids for $10. Facilities include a health club, an indoor swimming pool and sauna, and a full-service restaurant.

400 Oxford Valley Rd., Langhorne, PA 19047. ☎ **800/325-3535** or 215/547-4100. www.starwood.com. 167 units. $139 double. Sesame Place packages in season, $129–$159 including free shuttle and free room and board for children. AE, DC, DISC, MC, V. **Amenities:** Restaurant; lounge; indoor pool; fitness facility; sauna; laundry service; dry cleaning. In room: A/C, TV w/pay movies, dataport, coffeemaker, hair dryer.

WHERE TO DINE

Esca LATIN This cool, modern spot (pronounced "Ees-ca") features low lighting, tons of sexy white votive candles to flatter the guests (and waiters), and a lively, spicy menu and a fun local crowd. The menu is Brazilian-influenced, with that country's emphasis on delicious grilled meats.

18 W. Mechanic St., New Hope, PA. ☎ **215/862-7099**. Reservations recommended. Main courses $15–$24. AE, DISC, MC, V. Tues–Sun 5–11pm.

Hamilton's Grill Room AMERICAN This insiders' spot, just across the bridge from New Hope in upscale Lambertville, is tucked away down a gravel alley by the canal, across from a wonderful bar in a former boathouse. You need to pick up your own bottle of wine (go to Welsh's Wines in the center of town), and reserve well in advance, but you'll be delighted by the cool crowd, and excellent, Mediterranean-seasoned grilled steaks or lamb eaten on a chic banquette inside, or under a beautiful white tent in the courtyard outside in summer months. The salads, small pastas, and savory fish dishes here are as good as any you'd find in Manhattan or in the countryside of Tuscany.

8 Coryell St., Lambertville, NJ. ☎ **609/397-4343**. www.hamiltonsgrillroom.com. Reservations required. Main courses $18–$30. AE, DC, DISC, MC, V. Mon–Sat 6–10pm; Sun 5–9pm.

Karla's INTERNATIONAL In the heart of New Hope, next door to the Information Center, this lively and informal restaurant, playing groovy jazz music, offers three settings: a sunlit conservatory with ceiling fans, stained glass, and plants; a gallery room with local artists' works; and a bistro with marble tabletops. The eclectic menu offers standards like Caesar salad and grilled rib-eye steak, but also spicier coconut shrimp and chicken breast with Thai ginger sauce. Lunch items are tamer.

5 W. Mechanic St., New Hope, PA. ☎ **215/862-2612**. Reservations recommended for dinner. Main courses dinner $17–$26; lunch $9–$21. AE, DC, MC, V. Sun–Thurs 11am–10pm; Fri–Sat 11am–12:30am.

Marsha Brown's CREOLE/STEAKHOUSE From the owner of Philly's Ruth's Chris steakhouse, this grandly stylish spot is set in a 125-year-old lofty stone church with gorgeous lighting through clerestory windows and lavish murals. The crowd is well-dressed and lively, with big families celebrating fun occasions, and romantic couples (both straight and gay). Expect generous plates of flavorful steakhouse classics, plus Creole-inflected dishes, courtesy of family recipes from dynamic proprietor Marsha Brown. Eggplant Ophelia is a rich casserole incorporating shrimp and crab, and crab cakes are a robust, no-filler-used classic. Meats are as well-aged and enormous as you would expect.

15 S. Main St., New Hope, PA. (C) 215/862-7044. Main courses $22–$38. AE, DC, MC, V. Mon–Sat 5–11pm; Sun 5–10pm.

Odette's Fine Country Dining INTERNATIONAL Surrounded by the river and the canal on the southern edge of town, this elegant restaurant has been an inn since 1794, and remains a gregarious spot for show tunes and upscale cabaret performances, as well as classic fare. The previous owner, Odette Myrtil, was a Ziegfeld Follies girl whose memorabilia adorns the place, and the spirited weekend cabaret blends in to the surroundings and honors Odette perfectly. The menus are seasonal and change three times a year, providing nice twists on steak, seafood, duck, and veal, and hearty dishes such as smoked pork "Porterhouse."

S. River Rd. and Rte. 32, New Hope, PA. (C) 215/862-2432. www.odettes.com. Reservations recommended. Main courses dinner $17–$29; lunch $8.50–$13. AE, DC, MC, V. Mon–Thurs 11:30am–3pm and 5–9pm; Fri–Sat 11:30am–3pm and 5–9:30pm; Sun 4–9pm; brunch Sun 10:30am–1:30pm.

DOYLESTOWN

The intersection of U.S. 202 (west of New Hope), Pa. 313 (south of Scranton), and U.S. 611 (N. Broad St. in Philadelphia) defines Doylestown, the county seat. The R5 commuter rail from Center City ends here. It's a pleasant town just to walk around, but three interesting collections invite you indoors. All were endowed by Dr. Henry Chapman Mercer (1856–1930), a collector, local archaeologist, and master of pottery techniques. Motorists should exit the Pennsylvania Turnpike at the Willow Grove Interchange (Exit 27) and follow Route 611 north to the Doylestown exit. Drive through scenic Doylestown and turn right onto Route 313 (Swamp Rd.).

DOYLESTOWN AREA ATTRACTIONS

Fonthill Museum 🍴 Everyone can call their home a castle, but eccentric Dr. Mercer could say it and mean it. The core of his castle, built from reinforced concrete in Mercer's own design in 1908, has towers, turrets, and tiles piled on beyond belief. All the rooms are different shapes, each with tiles from Mercer's own tile-making factory across the driveway, set into the floors and walls.

E. Court St., off Swamp Rd. (Rte. 313), Doylestown, PA. (C) 215/348-9461. www.buckscountyhistorical.org. Admission $8 adults, $7.50 seniors, $3.50 children. Mon–Sat 10am–5pm; Sun noon–5pm (last tour is at 4pm). Closed Thanksgiving, Christmas, and New Year's Day. Guided tours only; reservations recommended.

Mercer Museum 🍴🍴 Mercer Museum displays thousands of early American tools, vehicles, cooking pieces, looms, and even weather vanes. Mercer had the collecting bug in a big way, and you can't help being impressed with the breadth of his collection and the castle that houses it. It rivals the Shelburne, Vermont, complex for Americana—and that's 35 buildings on 100 acres! The open atrium rises five stories, suspending a Conestoga wagon, chairs, and sleighs as if they were Christmas-tree ornaments. During the summer, a log cabin, schoolhouse, and other large bits of Colonial American life are open for inspection. The museum has six hands-on stations, where children can build a log house, try on period clothes, and drive a buggy, among other activities. The old library is a functional reading room.

Pine St. at Ashland St., Doylestown, PA. (C) 215/345-0210. www.mercermuseum.org. Admission to the museum and library $7 adults, $6.50 seniors, $3.50 children 5–17, free for children under 5. Mon–Sat 10am–5pm; Sun noon–5pm; Tues 10am–9pm. Spruance Library (Bucks County history): Tues 1–9pm; Wed–Sat 10am–5pm. Closed Thanksgiving, Christmas, and New Year's Day.

Moravian Pottery and Tile Works   Down the road on Pa. 313, the Moravian Pottery and Tile Works was Dr. Mercer's next big project. If you go to the State Capitol in Harrisburg, you can see more than 400 mosaics illustrating the history of Pennsylvania—they originated here. The ceramists working at the pottery turn out tiles and mosaics available through the museum shop; prices range from $5 to $1,800.

Swamp Rd., Doylestown, PA. ✆ 215/345-6722. Admission $3.50 adults, $2 youths, $3 seniors. Daily 10am–4:45pm. Tours available every 30 min. until 4pm. Closed major holidays.

2 Exploring the Brandywine Valley

The Brandywine Valley, bridging Pennsylvania and Delaware, makes a great 1- or 2-day excursion into rolling country filled with Americana from Colonial days through the Gilded Age.

Many of the farms that kept the Revolutionary troops fed have survived to this day. There are 15 covered bridges and 100 antiques stores in Chester County alone, with miles of country roads and horse trails between them. Spring and fall are particularly colorful seasons, and don't forget Delaware's tax-free shopping.

The valley is rich in history. Without the defeat at Brandywine, Washington would never have ended up at Valley Forge, from which he emerged with a competent army. When the Du Pont de Nemours family fled post-Revolutionary France, they wound up owning powder mills on the Brandywine Creek. Every pioneer needed gunpowder and iron, and the business grew astronomically, expanding into chemicals and textiles. The Du Ponts controlled upper Delaware as a virtual fiefdom, building splendid estates and gardens. Most of these, along with the original mills, are open to visitors. On the art front, Winterthur houses the finest collection of American decorative arts ever assembled, and artists like Pyle and Wyeth left rich collections that are now on public view.

ESSENTIALS

GETTING THERE   I-95 South from Philadelphia has various exits north of Wilmington marked for specific sites, most of which are off Exit 7 to Pa. 52 North. If you have time, Pa. 100 off Pa. 52 North, linking West Chester to Wilmington, passes through picturesque pastureland, forest, and cropland. From New York, take Exit 2 off the New Jersey Turnpike onto Route 322 West over the Commodore Barry Bridge into Pennsylvania, and continue on Route 322 to Route 452; take Route 452 north 4 miles to Route 1, the main artery of the valley.

VISITOR INFORMATION   For more information, call the **Brandywine Valley Tourist Information Center,** located just outside the gates of **Longwood Gardens,** at ✆ **800/228-9933** or 610/388-2900. For motorists on I-95, Delaware maintains a visitor center just south of Wilmington, between routes 272 and 896. It operates from 8am to 8pm.

BRANDYWINE VALLEY AREA ATTRACTIONS

Brandywine Battlefield State Park   This picturesque park, 2 miles east of Chadds Ford on Route 1, has no monuments, since the British General Howe snuck north outside present Park borders to outflank Washington and eventually take Philadelphia. But Washington's and Lafayette's reconstructed headquarters mark the site, which in September 1777 saw one of the few full-army clashes between the Continentals and the British troops and mercenaries. The fields are excellent for picnicking and hiking.

The Brandywine Valley

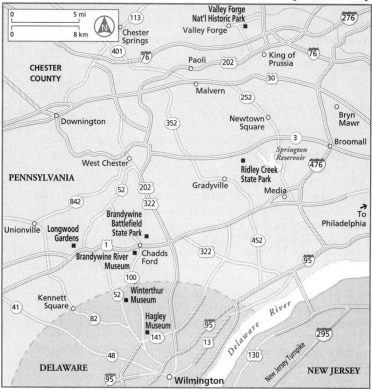

Rte. 1, east of Chadds Ford, P.O. Box 302, Chadds Ford, PA. ✆ 610/459-3342. Grounds and visitor center: Free admission. Memorial Day to Labor Day until 8pm. House tour: Admission $8.50 family, or $3.50 adults, $2.50 seniors, $1.50 children ages 6–17, free for children under 6. Tues–Sat 9am–5pm; Sun noon–5pm; last house tours at 3pm.

Brandywine River Museum   Across the road from the Brandywine Battlefield State Park, a 19th-century gristmill has been restored and joined by a dramatic spiral of brick and glass. The museum showcases American painters from the Brandywine school and other schools. A newer wing contains a gallery devoted to paintings by Andrew Wyeth. Howard Pyle, painter and illustrator of adventure tales in the late 19th century, established a school nearby; his students included N. C. Wyeth, Frank Schoonover, and Harvey Dunn. Three generations of Wyeths, including N. C., Carolyn, Andrew, and Jamie, have remained here, and the museum is particularly strong in their works. Many of the museum's exhibits display the art of book and magazine illustration at its pre-television zenith.

Rte. 1 and Rte. 100, Chadds Ford, PA. ✆ 610/388-2700. www.brandywinemuseum.org. Admission $8 adults, $5 seniors and children 6–12, free for children under 6. Daily 9:30am–4:30pm. Closed Christmas. Self-service restaurant open 11am–3pm.

Chadds Ford   This town is the site where a Native American trail (now U.S. 1) that forded the Brandywine Creek was purchased from William Penn by Francis Chadsey, an early Quaker immigrant. The present **Chadds Ford Inn,** at the junction of U.S. 1 and U.S. 100 (✆ **610/388-7361**), filled one of the village's first needs—a tavern. For small villages in the middle colonies, taverns served as mail depots, law courts, election hustings (speechmaking, voting, and other campaign-related activities), and occasionally prisons. Before the Battle of Brandywine, Washington's officers stayed at the inn; afterward, British troops slaughtered the cattle before marching on Philadelphia. There's a small shopping area next to the premises.

Hagley Museum ⭐⭐   Since the early 1800s this has been Du Pont country, and the Hagley Museum, on 235 beautiful acres, shows how and when the family got their start. It's a wonderful illustration of early American industrialism and manufacturing.

Hagley has three parts: the museum building, the reconstructed grounds, and the Upper Residence. The museum building explains the harnessing of the Brandywine River's power, which was originally used to operate flour mills. The Du Ponts, who made their first fortune in gunpowder, needed water power and willow charcoal as their raw materials, and both were just a barge ride away. E. Irénée Du Pont, the founder of the gunpowder company, lived in the Upper Residence. He had experience in France with gunpowder and supervised the delicate production process. Nonetheless, explosions happened every decade or so.

On Blacksmith Hill, part of the workers' community has been restored. A visit through the Gibbons House reveals the lifestyle of a typical family, from food to furniture. Nearby is the school the children attended, complete with lesson demonstrations. At the base of Blacksmith Hill a restored 1880s machine shop offers an exciting illustration of change in the workplace. Volunteers demonstrate how the din of power tools with whirring belts and grinding metal replaced the quiet, painstaking hand-tooling of the earlier artisans.

Jitneys traverse the powder yard, but it's just as easy to walk the part of the grounds lying between the private family roads on the Upper Residence and the Brandywine. A restored New Century Power House (1880) generates electricity here. Next to the electrical generator, a water wheel, steam engine, and water turbine show improvements in power through the decades.

The wisteria-covered Georgian residence of the Du Ponts was renovated by a member of the fourth generation, Mrs. Louis Crowninshield, who lived here until her death in 1958. Empire, Federal, and Victorian styles of furniture are highlighted in various room settings. As with all Du Pont residences, the gardens and espaliered trees are superb, and there are flowers throughout the year.

The Belin House on Blacksmith Hill offers light lunches and drinks.

P.O. Box 3630, Rte. 141, Wilmington, DE. ⓒ 302/658-2400. www.hagley.lib.de.us. Admission $11 adults, $9 seniors and students ages 14–20, $4 children 6–14, free for children under 6. Mar 15–Dec daily 9:30am–4:30pm; Jan–Mar 14 Sat–Sun 9:30am–4:30pm. Upper Eleutherian Mills Residence is open seasonally in spring and fall; last jitney leaves at 3:30pm. From Pennsylvania, take Rte. 52 to Rte. 100, go to the junction of Rte. 100 and Rte. 141, then follow directions on Rte. 141.

Longwood Gardens ⭐⭐⭐   Longwood Gardens is simply one of the world's great garden displays, and is in the midst of extensive renovations and expansions to add to its present gorgeousness. Pierre S. Du Pont devoted his life to horticulture. He bought a 19th-century arboretum and created the ultimate estate garden on 1,050 acres. You should plan at least half a day here.

The visitor center has a multimedia briefing on the gardens. Most people head to the left, toward the Main Fountain Garden, which has special water shows on Tuesday, Thursday, and Saturday evenings from June to September and fireworks shows on Friday and Saturday nights, usually preceded by hour-long garden concerts. Wrought-iron chairs and clipped trees and shrubs overlook the jets of water that rise up to 130 feet from the fountains. Near here, a topiary garden of closely pruned shrubs surrounds a 37-foot sundial.

The 4 acres of massive bronze-and-glass conservatories, renovated in 1996 and 1997, are among the finest and largest in the United States. The orangery displays are breathtaking. African violets, bonsai trees up to 400 years old, hibiscus, orchids, and tropical plants are among the specialties, but expect anything from Easter lilies to scarlet begonias. Special collections present silver desert plants, plants of the Mediterranean, and roses, among types of plants and flowers. The plants are exhibited only at their peak and are constantly replaced from the extensive growing houses.

A parquet-floor ballroom was added later, connected to the greenhouses, along with a 10,000-pipe organ, a magnificent instrument played during the year (although it's under renovation right now).

Ahead and to the right of the visitor center, more gardens and fountains await, along with the Longwood Heritage Exhibit inside the Peirce–Du Pont House, the founder's residence. This exhibit illustrates the history of the property with artifacts from 2,000-year-old Native American spear points to Du Pont family movies. The restaurant offers cafeteria-style dining year-round and full-service dining from mid-April to December, with surprisingly good meals.

Rte. 1, Kennett Square, PA. 30 miles west of Philadelphia and just west of the junction with Pa. 52. 𝓒 610/388-1000. www.longwoodgardens.org. Admission $14 for adults ($15 at Christmastime, $10 Tues), $6 for ages 16–20, $2 for ages 6–15, free for children under 6. Apr–Oct daily 9am–6pm (conservatories 10am–6pm); Nov–Mar daily 9am–5pm. The grounds and conservatories are frequently open late for special events and holiday displays.

Winterthur Museum, Garden and Library ★★★   The later home of the Du Ponts now provides the setting for America's best collection of native decorative arts. Henry Francis Du Pont, a great-grandson of E. I. Du Pont, was a connoisseur of European antiques. But when he turned his attention to a simple Pennsylvania Dutch chest in 1923, he realized no one had explored how American pieces are related to European crafts or how the concepts of beauty and taste differed on the two continents. Du Pont first collected American furniture, then decorative objects, then the interior woodwork of entire homes built between 1640 and 1840. Finally, he added to his home more than 200 rooms for the display of his collection. Because the museum started out as a private home, the rooms have a unique richness and intimacy.

In 1992, Winterthur opened the Galleries, a new building adjacent to the existing period rooms. On the first floor, the exhibition *Perspectives on the Decorative Arts in Early America* focuses on the social, practical, and other functions of objects in everyday life. The second floor features three areas displaying various aspects of American craftsmanship, with changing exhibitions. The Main Museum, which offers in-depth guided tours, displays the bulk of the collection and includes complete interiors from every eastern seaboard colony. Special landmarks include the famous Montmorenci Stair Hall, two Shaker Rooms, fine examples of Pennsylvania Dutch decorative art, and the Du Pont dining room. The Campbell Soup Tureen collection, with 125 items currently on display, is housed in the Dorrance Gallery, between the museum and the research building.

In the spring, the extensive Winterthur Garden explodes into an abundance of cherry and crabapple blossoms, rhododendrons, Virginia bluebells, and azaleas. The lush, carefully planned garden is well worth viewing any season. At Christmastime, the house is ornately decorated in period style. Garden tram rides through the grounds are available when weather permits. There are two superb gift shops selling a selection of licensed reproductions, gifts, books, jewelry, and plants. The Visitor Pavilion Restaurant cooks breakfast, lunch, brunch, and tea to order and seats 350; the Cappuccino Cafe next to the museum offers lighter fare.

6 miles northwest of Wilmington, DE, on Rte. 52, Winterthur, DE. ℂ 800/448-3883 or 302/888-4600. www.winterthur.org. Admission options include: **Garden and Galleries Pass** (includes the Galleries, the Dorrance Gallery, a self-guided garden walk, and the garden tram) $15 adults, $13 seniors and students, $5 children 2–11; **Focus Tours** (a selection of conservation or specialized "connoisseur" tours for ages 8 and up) $30. Reservations required. Tues–Sun 10am–5pm; Sun noon–5pm. Closed on major holidays.

WHERE TO STAY

Brandywine River Hotel 🍴   Built in 1988 and with a recently renovated lobby, this hotel, with a facade of brick and cedar shingle, blends into a hillside steps away from the Chadds Ford Inn. Several rooms have working fireplaces and Jacuzzis. The lobby has a huge open stone fireplace and friendly service, and guest rooms are decorated with Queen Anne cherrywood furnishings, brass fixtures, chintz fabrics, and local paintings. Breakfast is served in an attractive hospitality room with a fireplace.

Rte. 1 and Rte. 100, P.O. Box 1058, Chadds Ford, PA 19317-1058. ℂ 610/388-1200. Fax 610/388-1200, ext. 301. www.brandywineriverhotel.com. 41 units. From $99 double; $159–$210 suite; frequent specials. Rates include full continental breakfast and afternoon tea. Children under 12 stay free in parent's room. AE, DC, DISC, MC, V. **Amenities:** Fitness room. *In room:* A/C, TV, dataport, fridge, coffeemaker, hair dryer.

Fairville Inn 🍴🍴   With an 1857 main house and exquisitely comfortable lodgings (think matelassé coverlets and oversize canopied beds) in a carriage house and springhouse, this inn perfectly combines antiques-filled loveliness with modern amenities, like great bathrooms and satellite TV. It's set on a pretty stretch of Route 52, several minutes from the Brandywine River Museum, and offers excellent breakfasts and afternoon cheese and crackers. With 15 rooms, and children under age 15 generally not welcome, you'll have privacy in an intimate setting (especially in that wonderful carriage house).

506 Kennett Pike (Rte. 52), Chadds Ford, PA 19317. ℂ 877/285-7772 or 610/388-5900. 15 units. $150–$250 double. AE, DISC, MC, V. No children under 15. *In room:* A/C, satellite TV, hair dryers, iron and ironing board.

Hamanassett 🍴   Built in 1856, this inn 4 miles from downtown Chadds Ford is newly owned by Ashley and Glenn Mon, and its 7 acres and historic buildings have been updated and refreshed. There is a garden (with horses in the meadow) and billiard room. All rooms are beautifully furnished with family antiques and have just been repainted and redecorated; the first floor has a conservatory, 2,000-book and 500-video library, and a magnificent foyer stairway. Breakfast is opulent with candlelight; afternoon tea and evening coffee are available.

725 Darlington Rd., Chester Heights, PA 19317. ℂ/fax 610/459-3000. www.hamanassett.com. 7 units, all with private bathroom, and a carriage house that is pet- and child-friendly. $140–$400 double. DISC, MC, V. No smoking. **Amenities:** Game room. *In room:* A/C, cable TV/VCR (video library on premises), access to fridge with complimentary beverages, coffeemaker, hair dryer, iron and ironing board, access to microwave.

WHERE TO DINE

Chadds Ford Inn CONTINENTAL   For Wyeth fans or Revolutionary War buffs, this is extremely sacred ground, since it's got reproductions of Wyeth art (the originals, now across the street at the museum, were reputedly bartered for meals) amid tin lanterns and candlesticks that have been in use since the 1730s. Under excellent management by the Brandywine Heritage Group, which also owns convivial Buckley's Tavern on Route 53, the menu is classic, with staples of meats and seafood. The wine list is substantial and varied.

Rte. 1 and Rte. 100, Chadds Ford, PA. ✆ **610/388-7361.** Main courses dinner $12–$25; lunch $8–$13. AE, MC, V. Mon–Fri 11:30am–2:30pm; Sat 11:30am–4pm; Mon–Thurs 5:30–9:30pm; Fri–Sat 5–10pm; Sun 2:30–9pm.

Dilworthtown Inn CONTINENTAL   Another old inn, this 1758 tavern saw the last phase of the Battle of Brandywine (specifically, the British victory). It has as cozy a mood and decor as you'll find this side of the Revolutionary War, with a roaring fireplace that you could stand up in and candlelit tables amid thick plaster walls. The restaurant, which also hosts popular cooking classes, is very fine, with an excellent local mushroom tart, escargots Provençal, smoked breast of duck, and filet of beef au poivre. The wine cellar is one of the most extensive and admired in the Philadelphia region.

1390 Old Wilmington Pike, West Chester, PA. ✆ **610/399-1390.** www.dilworthtowninn.com. Reservations recommended. Jacket preferred. Main courses $22–$34. AE, DC, DISC, MC, V. Mon–Fri 5:30–9:30pm; Sat 5–9:30; Sun 3–8:30pm.

12

Lancaster County:
The Amish Country

Fifty miles west of Philadelphia is a quietly beautiful region of rolling hills, winding creeks, neatly cultivated farms, covered bridges, and towns with picturesque names like Paradise and Bird-in-Hand. This is the gorgeous Amish Country, also known as Pennsylvania Dutch Country, an area of 7,100 square miles centered in Lancaster County, which is an easy day trip or overnight excursion from Center City Philadelphia. Made even more famous in the Harrison Ford film *Witness,* the Pennsylvania Dutch Amish, Mennonites, and Brethren (see "Meet the Amish," below, for an explanation of the differences) represent 70,000 of Lancaster County's 475,000 residents. It's a small group that quietly continues to live an agrarian life centered around religious worship and family cohesiveness.

The preservation of the world of the Pennsylvania Dutch (derived from the word *"Deutsch,"* meaning German, as the community is of mostly German descent) evokes feelings of curiosity, nostalgia, amazement, and respect. The Pennsylvania Dutch, who speak a German dialect in their homes but are fluent in English, are a rare yardstick for us to measure the distance that our own "outside" world has come over the last 2 centuries. It is important to note that the Pennsylvania Dutch do not always greet the curiosity that many visitors feel towards their world with enthusiasm.

Pennsylvania Dutch Country has many special qualities that attract visitors. The area is relatively small, with good roads for motorists and bicyclists alike. There are opportunities to get to know the Mennonites and Amish on working farms that have opened their quaint doors to guests; tourism has, perhaps surprisingly, promoted continued excellence in quilt making, antiques, and farm-based crafts. There are historical sites, pretzel and chocolate factories, covered bridges, and wonderful farmer's markets, as well as modern diversions such as movie theaters, amusement parks, and great outlet mall shopping. And, of course, the family-style, smorgasbord, all-you-can-eat, or gourmet Pennsylvania Dutch restaurants are experiences in themselves.

1 Introducing the Pennsylvania Dutch Country

This area has been a major farming region since German settlers came across its limestone-rich soil and rolling hills 3 centuries ago. Lancaster County boasts the most productive nonirrigated farmland in the United States, and it's the country's fifth-largest dairy-producing county. The natural abundance of the region, the ease of getting goods to market in Philadelphia, and the strong work ethic of the area's residents have preserved major portions of the land for farming. In its day, Lancaster was a major center of commerce, culture, and politics. It was the largest inland city in the United States from 1760 to 1810, and was even a

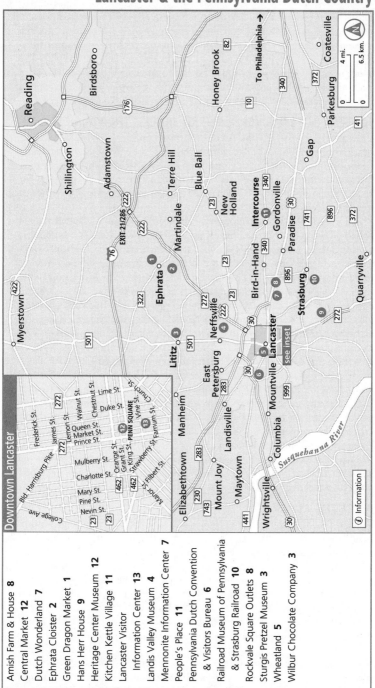

Lancaster & the Pennsylvania Dutch Country

Amish Farm & House **8**
Central Market **12**
Dutch Wonderland **7**
Ephrata Cloister **2**
Green Dragon Market **1**
Hans Herr House **9**
Heritage Center Museum **12**
Kitchen Kettle Village **11**
Lancaster Visitor
   Information Center **13**
Landis Valley Museum **4**
Mennonite Information Center **7**
People's Place **11**
Pennsylvania Dutch Convention
   & Visitors Bureau **6**
Railroad Museum of Pennsylvania
   & Strasburg Railroad **10**
Rockvale Square Outlets **8**
Sturgis Pretzel Museum **3**
Wheatland **5**
Wilbur Chocolate Company **3**

contender in the choice of the new nation's capital. The balance between factory and farm has been threatened in the past century by the development of the automobile and the construction of such major roads as the Pennsylvania Turnpike, which turned farmland into suburbs of Harrisburg and Philadelphia. The buildup of housing developments and attendant schools, services, and strip malls for an exploding population competes with the lovely, placid fields dotted with farmhouses, barns, silos, and small creeks crossed by covered bridges.

TOURIST DOLLARS VERSUS STRIP MALLS: THE AMISH TODAY

Until about 50 years ago, the Amish were not especially a "tourist attraction." But starting in the mid-1950s, with the growing presence of technology in all areas of life for the rest of the country, the Amish tenacity in maintaining their traditional customs and values made them seem both unusual and alluring. For better or worse, the Amish have spawned a major tourist industry over the last several decades.

As this process began, most people, including many Amish, saw tourism as a positive development. Money flowed into the county, and the Amish found a growing market for such goods as quilts, metalwork, crafts, and foodstuff—with customers literally appearing at their doors. But the less benign consequences of this development are becoming more and more apparent. The Amish population is about 25,000 and growing (many families have seven or more children), but as outsiders move to Lancaster County, the non-Amish population has grown to more than 450,000. Their need for affordable housing is driving up land prices and attracting strip developers. In past years when Amish families looked for land to buy for their children's farms, they turned to other, non-Amish farmers. Today, those non-Amish farmers can get better prices by selling to developers.

This means that many Amish have been forced to leave their farms and set up nonfarming businesses. The local construction business in Lancaster County includes many Amish workers who have to travel to Delaware and Maryland to work. Women who traditionally worked in the home and on the farm are increasingly running restaurants and shops or overseeing quilting and craft enterprises. Despite the injunction to remain separate from wider society, many families offer "Amish-style" dinners at their homes, and aggressively exploit the cachet that "Amish-made" gives to foods, craft objects, clothing, hex signs, and other souvenirs and products.

MEET THE AMISH

William Penn's "holy experiment" of religious tolerance, together with word of mouth about the region's fertile farmland, drew thousands of German-speaking immigrants to Pennsylvania in the early 18th century. They were lumped together as Pennsylvania "Dutch"—a corruption of *Deutsch,* which is the German word meaning German. The Mennonite sects, particularly the Amish, stayed put in Pennsylvania and became the most famous of the immigrants, but the Colonial period also saw a mixture of Scotch-Irish Presbyterians, French Protestants, English from Maryland, and Jews from Iberia settling in the region. The ethnic makeup in this part of the country has changed very little since 1796.

The religions of the Pennsylvania Dutch are part of the Anabaptist strand of the Protestant Reformation. A Christian faith that emerged during the 16th century, Anabaptists believe in the literal interpretation of the Bible, in baptism only for people adult enough to choose this rite of transformation, and in remaining separate from larger society. Menno Simons, a Catholic priest from

Holland, joined the Anabaptists in 1536 and united the various groups, who began to be called Mennonites. In 1693, Jacob Amman, a Mennonite bishop who found the Mennonite Church too tolerant of lax sinners, broke with his followers to establish the Old Order Amish church.

The three major sects in Lancaster County, the Amish, the Mennonites, and the Brethren, as well as another sect, the Schwenkfelders, share many beliefs, including those concerning baptism, nonresistance, and basic Bible doctrine. They differ in matters of dress, use or avoidance of technology, degree of literal interpretation of the Bible, and form of worship. For example, the Amish worship in services at home, while the Mennonites hold services in churches. The Amish do not proselytize, while Mennonites have a strong tradition of missionary work.

Today, the Amish live in settlements in 20 states and in Ontario, Canada. In Lancaster County, they center around Intercourse, Bird-in-Hand, and Lancaster. Mennonites are based in Terre Hill and Martindale, a few miles to the northeast. The majority of Amish people live and work on farms growing corn, wheat, tobacco (though most will not smoke it and some won't grow it), and alfalfa. But an increasing number earn their incomes at other jobs, either in crafts, in a sideline business out of the home, or in the nonfarm economy of the region. They are a trilingual people, speaking Pennsylvania Dutch (essentially a dialect of German) at home, High German at worship services (the German of Luther's Bible translation), and English with members of the larger society.

The family is the most important social unit among the Amish, and large families are the norm. Not surprisingly, the Amish population is growing—it has more than doubled since the 1980s—and more than half the Amish in Lancaster County are under the age of 18. You will see dozens of mailboxes marked with the names Zook, Stoltzfus, and Zinn—a testimony to the proliferation of extended families. The Old Testament–sounding practice of "shunning"—complete excommunication from family relations for Amish who marry outsiders or violate basic tenets—has relaxed in recent decades. Even so, about 80% of the Amish end up spending their entire lives within the community—many dying in the same house in which they were born.

Children attend school in one-room schoolhouses, built and maintained by the Amish, through the eighth grade. There are approximately 150 such schools in Lancaster County, and new ones are still being built. Amish schools teach only the basics; students have special exemptions from the standard state curriculum and are allowed to leave school at the age of 16 if they choose. There is no formal religious instruction in school; this is kept within the family.

To the visitor, the two most distinctive characteristics of the Amish are their clothing and their use of horse and buggies rather than cars. Both these features are linked to their religious beliefs. The distinctive clothing worn by about 35,000 "Plain People" in Lancaster County is meant to encourage humility and modesty as well as separation from larger society. Amish men and boys wear dark-colored suits, straight-cut coats without lapels, broadcloth trousers, suspenders, solid-colored shirts, black socks and shoes, and black or straw broad-brimmed hats. Men wait to grow beards until they are married, and do not grow mustaches. Women and girls wear modest, solid-colored dresses with long sleeves and long full skirts, covered by a cape and an apron. They never cut their hair, but gather it in a bun on the back of the head, concealed by a white prayer covering. Amish women do not wear jewelry or printed fabric. Single women in their teens and 20s wear black prayer coverings on their heads for church services. After marriage, a white covering is worn.

The Amish are reluctant to accept technology, which they believe could weaken the family structure. Their horse-drawn buggies help keep them close to home by limiting distances that can be traveled in a day. Most use no electricity or telephones. As new ideas emerge, each district congregation of about 100 families evaluates them and decides what to accept and what to reject. The fundamental criterion is that an innovation should not jeopardize the simplicity of their lives and the strength of the family unit. The 1998 arrest of two young Amish for drug trafficking, while hardly an everyday occurrence, has prompted wide re-examination of how much "outside" exposure is too much, as has 2004's UPN show "Amish in the City," in which teens from the sect explored a "Real World"–style dose of urban life and temptations. It played off the real Amish rite of passage called *rumspringa* (run wild), which allows Amish 16 year-olds to venture outside their community to see how other Americans live, so that they can decide whether or not to stay within the Pennsylvania Dutch world (the vast majority do).

There are a number of excellent books on the Amish way of life. The classic is John Hostetler's *Amish Society.* A more impassioned, ideological, New Age take is *After the Fire: The Destruction of the Lancaster County Amish* by Randy-Michael Testa. Children's books include *Growing Up Amish* by Richard Ammon, and Raymond Bial's *Amish Home,* with wonderful photographs. Since Amish do not permit photography, any film depiction is bound to be compromised; this is unfortunately the case with *Witness* (1985), in which Harrison Ford goes undercover in the region as a Philadelphia cop.

2 Essentials

The heart of Pennsylvania Dutch Country centers on wedges of land to the east and (to a lesser extent) west of Lancaster. The Susquehanna River to the west, and the Maryland border and Mason-Dixon line to the south, form the borders of the area.

GETTING THERE

Lancaster County is 57 miles and 90 minutes west of Philadelphia, directly on Route 30. From the northeast, the easiest route is to take I-95 south from New York City onto the New Jersey Turnpike, then take Exit 6 onto the Pennsylvania Turnpike (I-76), following this to Exit 266 or 286 on either side of Lancaster. You'll still be about 10 miles north of the town: From Exit 286, you'll follow Route 222 into the city; from Exit 266, Route 72. Travel time is 2¼ hours, and tolls amount to $9 from New York City. From the south, follow I-83 north for 90 minutes from Baltimore, then head east on Route 30 from York into the county. If you're in Brandywine County or Longwood Gardens, you're only minutes from Amish farms in Gap, via routes 41 and 741.

By train, Amtrak (© **800/872-7245**) takes 70 minutes from 30th Street Station in Philadelphia to the great old Lancaster station, 53 McGovern Ave. (© **717/ 291-5080**), 10 blocks from Penn Square. The adult fare is $13 to $16 one-way, and 10 trains run daily. Three Capitol Trailways buses run daily from the Greyhound Terminal at 10th and Filbert streets in Philadelphia ($16 one-way, or $32 round-trip) and take 2 hours (with a change in King of Prussia) from the Convention Center Trailways Terminal to Greyhound Bus Lines, at the train station in Lancaster (© **800/231-2222** or 717/397-4861).

VISITOR INFORMATION

Before you set out, you should get in touch with the **Pennsylvania Dutch Convention & Visitors Bureau,** 501 Greenfield Rd., Lancaster, PA 17601

(© **800/PA-DUTCH,** ext. 4, or 717/299-8901). The websites **www. padutch country.com** and **www.lancastercountypa.org** link to many attractions listed below. The office itself is off the Route 30 bypass east of Lancaster, Greenfield Road exit. They provide an excellent detailed map and visitors' guide to the region, along with answers to specific questions and help with special interests. They also have a wealth of brochures, direct telephone links to many local hotels, and a multi-image slide show, a good 14-minute overview of the county. The bureau is open June through October from 8am to 6pm (Sun 9am–6pm), and off season from 8:30am to 5pm (Sun 9am–5pm).

The **Mennonite Information Center,** 2209 Millstream Rd., Lancaster, PA 17602, near the Tanger Outlets (© **800/858-8320** or 717/299-0954; **www. mennoniteinfoctr.com**), has a lot of the same information but specializes in linking you with Mennonite guesthouses and church worship. Every half-hour they show a film featuring a Mennonite family at home on their farm, and there is a tabernacle tour given on-site They will also provide Mennonite tour guides who can accompany you to otherwise hidden farm stands or the home work-shops of local crafters and quilters—expect some gentle religious dialogue from guides. The center is open April through October, Monday through Saturday from 8am to 5pm, and Monday through Saturday from 8:30am to 4:30pm November through March.

GETTING AROUND

Lancaster County's principal artery is Route 30, which runs from Philadelphia to York and Gettysburg. But beware: Major roads like Route 30 and Route 222 at Lancaster, and Route 340 from Intercourse to Lancaster, can be crowded, especially in the summer with the onslaught of bus tours. The 25,000 horse-drawn vehicles in the county tend to stick to quieter back roads, but some high-ways cannot be avoided. Traffic is much lighter in the spring and autumn. And please be careful; the past few years have seen several horrible rear-end crashes in which tourists killed Amish families in buggies. If you're in a jam, you can reach AAA service at © **717/397-6135.**

Red Rose Transit Authority, 45 Erick Rd. (© **717/397-4246;** www.redrose transit.com), serves Lancaster County, with a base fare of $1.15 to $2.25 depending on distance. The Route no. 13 bus leaves from the Old Courthouse on Duke Street in Lancaster and goes through Bird-in-Hand and Intercourse.

ORGANIZED TOURS

An organization called the **Amish Experience,** Route 340 in Intercourse (© **717/768-3600;** www.amishexperience.com), offers guided back-road bus tours during high season at 10:30am and 2pm daily (11am only on Sun and daily from Nov–Mar), which last 2 hours and include stops at Amish farms and one-room schoolhouses. You must reserve in advance, and tickets are $22 for adults, $13 for children. The Plain and Fancy Farm Restaurant is on the same premises on Route 340 in Intercourse, as is Aaron and Jessica's Buggy Rides, and you can buy tickets at local hotels or at the farm. **Brunswick Tours** (© **717/ 397-7541**) can lead you on tours throughout Lancaster County and into Her-shey and Gettysburg. **Red Rose Excursions** (© **717/397-3175**) provides guides Monday through Saturday from 9am to 9pm to any Lancaster County location.

Your best bet for an intimate view of Amish country is an in-car tour guide. **The Mennonite Information Center** (above) has a group of friendly Mennon-ite and Amish guides on call who will ride with you in your car throughout Intercourse, Strasburg, and Bird-In-Hand, stopping in the towns or touring through the farmland. They personalize the tour to your interests—they'll make stops at Amish farms, or take you shopping for quilts or freshly made local root beer. Call ahead or stop by to book 2-hour tours priced at $36 per car.

A NOTE ON ETIQUETTE

There aren't too many settings in the world where an entire native population is a tourist attraction. Pennsylvania Dutch country is one of them, but that doesn't mean that the Amish are there as theme park characters. They are hard-working people leading busy lives. Your courtesy and respect are especially vital because their lifestyle is designed to remove them as much as possible from your fast-paced 21st-century focus.

First, *do not trespass* onto Amish farms, homesteads, or schools in session. We've listed several settings where you can visit a working farm, take a carriage ride, or even stay on a farm. Although these are not operated by the most ortho-dox Amish, you will certainly get a taste of the Amish lifestyle.

Second, if you're dealing with Pennsylvania Dutch directly, *don't even think of photographing them, and ask before taking any photographs at all.* The Amish have a strongly held belief that photographic images violate the biblical injunction against graven images and promote the sins of personal vanity and pride. Taking pictures of their land and animals is permissible; taking pictures of them is not.

Third, *watch the road.* What passes for moderate suburban speed in a car can be life-threatening in this area. Roads in Lancaster County have especially wide shoul-ders to accommodate horses, carriages, and farm tractors, and these are marked with red reflective triangles and lights at night. It's preferable, if only to better see the sights, to slow down to Amish paces. And honking disturbs the horses. If you have the time, this is superb walking and bicycling country, punctuated by farm stands for refreshment and quiet conversations with Amish families.

3 Exploring Amish Country

Amish Country's attractions are spread out over a large area in and around Lan-caster, so you'll need to plan ahead to make the best use of your time. Consider our itineraries, then note the highlights in each town.

SUGGESTED ITINERARIES

If You Have 1 Day

Start in the town of Intercourse at the **People's Place** (p. 237), where you can learn the basics of Amish life. Then head to its neighbor, **Kitchen Kettle Village** (p. 237), to shop for quilts and more in this 32-stand marketplace. Head west into Lancaster to visit the lovely estate **Wheatland** (p. 235) once home to president James Buchanan. Then drive 20 minutes northeast to the bucolic and historic **Ephrata Clois-ter** (p. 237) and, if you have time, to the **Green Dragon Market** (p. 237)

for its transactions featuring live ani-mals and local wares. To top off the day with a gourmet meal, **Doneck-ers** (p. 237) creates gourmet, French-influenced meals using local ingre-dients.

If You Have 2 Days

Follow the itinerary above for Day 1. On Day 2, head west to **Hershey, PA** (p. 239). This drive affords you a beautiful view of serene-looking farmhouses and barns where so much milk is produced by the Amish (whom you'll be passing in their modest black buggies). Once in Hershey, the kids will want to visit **Hershey's Chocolate World** for a demonstration of how the treats are made. In season, they'll enjoy the rides and animals of **Hersheypark** and **Zoo America;** you'll wander the rose garden and check out the spa at the **Hotel Hershey**.

If You Have 3 Days or more

On Days 1 and 2, follow the itinerary given above. On Day 3, spend the morning in **Adamstown** at the excellent **flea and antique markets there** (p. 241): Renninger's, Shupp's Grove, and Stoudt's Black Angus, which has an adjacent **beer garden and restaurant** (p. 249). Next, you can prepare for your re-entry into the real world by shopping at the stylish outlets of **Rockvale Square** and the **Tanger Outlet Center at Millstream** (p. 242).

LANCASTER

While Lancaster (pronounced *Lank*-uh-stir) is still the most important city in the region, it hit its peak in the Colonial era and as an early-20th-century urban beehive; this is reflected in the architecture and attractions. The basic street grid layout, copied from Philadelphia's, centers at Penn Square: the intersection of King (east-west) and Queen (north-south) streets. You won't see too many Plain People venturing into town anymore, since they can buy provisions and equipment more easily at regional stores, but they still sell at the **Central Market.** Erected just off Penn Square in 1889 but operating since the 1730s, this is the nation's oldest farmer's market, with more than 80 stalls. You can savor and select regional produce and foods, from sweet bologna and scrapple to breads, cheeses, egg noodles, shoofly pie (a concoction of molasses and sweet dough), and *schnitzel* or dried apple. The market is open Tuesday and Friday from 6am to 4:30pm and Saturday from 6am to 2pm.

Beside the Market is a **Heritage Center Museum** (© 717/299-6440) in the old City Hall, with a moderately interesting collection of Lancaster County crafts and historical artifacts; the museum also has a quilt and textile collection in a separate building. The Heritage Center is free and open Tuesday through Saturday from 10am to 5pm, Sunday noon to 5pm, closed from January to March. On the western edge of town is **Wheatland,** 1120 Marietta Ave., Rte. 23 (© 717/392-8721; www.wheatland.org), the gracious Federal mansion and 4 garden acres of the 15th U.S. president, James Buchanan. It features costumed guides and is open April through October, daily from 10am to 4pm; open November on weekends only, and in December on certain days from noon to 4pm (call for hours). Admission is $6.50 for adults, $5.50 for seniors, $3.50 for students, and $1.75 for children 6 to 12.

Tips Amish Country on Two Wheels

Cycling enthusiasts in Lancaster County tend to rely on two great resources for both bike gear and bike route suggestions:

- The store **Green Mountain Cyclery**, 285 S. Reading Rd., Ephrata, PA 17522 (© 717/859-2422; www.greenmountaincyclery.com) attracts everyone from serious riders to casual cyclists.
- The website **www.lancasterbikeclub.org** is a resource for routes that range from 7 miles (around the town of Lancaster and through Buchanan Park) to serious, 50-mile-plus rides into the hills.

Tips **The Bridges of Lancaster County**

Forget about the Midwest and Clint Eastwood—Pennsylvania is the birth-place of the covered bridge, with some 1,500 built between the 1820s and 1900. Today, 219 bridges remain, mostly on small country roads, and you can actually drive (slowly!) through most of them. Lancaster County has the largest concentration, with 28, including one on the way to Par-adise, a small village east of Lancaster City. Bridges were covered to pro-tect the trusses from the weather. Does kissing inside one bring good luck? Well, they're protected from rain, and their one-lane width means a certain amount of privacy—not to mention those evocative wooden planks. The Lancaster County Visitors Bureau map indicates all covered bridge locations; call ℂ **800/723-8824** or visit **www.800padutch.com/ covbrdg.html** for more information.

Of the 28 county bridges, the following three are interesting and relatively easy to get to:

• **Hunsecker Bridge:** This is the largest covered bridge in the county, built in 1975 to replace the original, which was washed away in Hur-ricane Agnes. From Lancaster, drive 5 miles north on Route 272. After you pass Landis Valley Farm Museum, turn right on Hunsecker Road and drive 2 miles.

• **Paradise/Leaman Place Bridge:** This bridge is in the midst of Amish cornfields and farms. An oversize truck put it out of commission in the 1980s, but it has been restored. Drive north 1 mile on Belmont Road from Route 30, just east of the center of Paradise.

• **Kauffman's Distillery Bridge:** Drive west on Route 772 from Man-heim, and make a left onto West Sunhill Road. The bridge will be in front of you, along with horses grazing nearby.

Five miles south of town near Willow Street rests the 1719 **Hans Herr House,** 1849 Hans Herr Dr., off Route 222 (ℂ **717/464-4438;** www.hansherr.org), the oldest building in the county. Now owned by the Lancaster Mennonite Historical Society, it's been restored and furnished to illustrate early Mennonite life, with a historic orchard and outdoor exhibit of agricultural tools. You can visit from April to November, Monday through Saturday from 9am to 4pm, and December brings evening candlelight tours by appointment; admission is $5 for adults, including a tour, and $1.50 for children 7 to 12.

The eastern side of town peters into a welter of faux Amish attractions and amusements like Dutch Wonderland and Running Pump Mini-Golf, fast-food restaurants, and outlet stores on Route 30 near where Route 340 splits to the north toward Intercourse. The **Amish Farm and House,** 2395 Lincoln Hwy. (ℂ **717/394-6185;** www.amishfarmandhouse.com), offers guided tours of a 10-room Amish house, with live animals and exhibits including a water wheel outside. A Dutch Food Pavilion provides local treats. It's open June through Sep-tember daily from 8:30am to 6pm; November through March from 8:30am to 4pm; and from 8:30am to 5pm other months. Admission is $6.95 for adults and $4.25 for children 5 to 11, seniors $6.25.

INTERCOURSE

Intercourse's suggestive name refers to the intersection of two old highways, the King's Highway (now Rte. 340 or Old Philadelphia Pike) and Newport Road (now Rte. 772). The Conestoga wagons invented a few miles south—these are unusually broad and deep wagons that became famous for transporting home-steaders all the way west to the Pacific coast—were used on the King's Highway.

The town, in the midst of the wedge of country east of Lancaster, is now the center of Amish life in the county. There are about as many commercial attrac-tions, which range from the schlocky to good quality, as there are places of gen-uine interest along Route 340. One thing not to miss is the **People's Place,** 3513 Old Philadelphia Pike (© **717/768-7171;** www.thepeoplesplace.com), a book-shop and gallery. Of the commercial developments, try **Kitchen Kettle Village,** also on the Old Philadelphia Pike, Route 340 (© **800/732-3538** or 717/768-8261; www.kitchenkettle.com). You'll find 32 stores selling quilts, crafts, and homemade edibles, from decoys to fudge, grouped around Pat and Bob Burn-ley's 1954 jam and relish kitchen. Their Lapp Family Farms ice-cream store, with 20 all-natural flavors, is much more convenient than the original farm stand near New Holland.

EPHRATA

Ephrata, near Exit 21 off I-76 northeast of Lancaster, combines a historic 18th-century Moravian religious site with a pleasant country landscape and the area's largest farmer's market and auction center. **Ephrata Cloister,** 633 W. Main St. (© **717/733-6600;** www.ephratacloister.org), near the junction of routes 272 and 322, housed one of America's earliest communal societies, which was known for its *fraktur*—an ornate, medieval German lettering you'll see on inscribed pottery and official documents. Ten austere wooden 18th-century buildings (put together without nails) remain in a grassy park setting. The cloister is open Monday through Saturday from 9am to 5pm and Sunday from noon to 5pm (closed Mon Jan–Feb); admission is $7 for adults, $6.50 for seniors, and $5 for children 6 to 17.

The main street of Ephrata is pleasant for strolling and features an old rail car on the place where the train line used to run. **Doneckers** (see below) has expanded from a single inn north of town into a farmer's market, gourmet restaurant, and shopping complex. On North State Street, 4 miles north of town, is the wonder-ful **Green Dragon Market & Auction** (© **717/738-1117**), open Friday from 9am to 9pm. Two auction houses make up the heart of Green Dragon—one for antiques and bric-a-brac, one for farm animals. You'll see goats and cows changing hands in the most elemental way, and children are allowed total petting access in the process. Summer brings fresh corn, fruit, and melons. A flea market and arcade have sprung up around the auctions, with plenty of cotton candy, clams on the half shell, and fresh corn.

LITITZ

Founded in 1756, this town, 6 miles north of Lancaster on Route 501, is one of the state's most charming. The cottage facades along East Main Street (Rte. 772) haven't changed much in the past 2 centuries. One of the most interesting sights is the **Linden Hall Academy,** founded in 1794 as the first school for girls in the United States. There are several Revolutionary War–era churches and buildings on the grounds of the school. Lititz was once known as "the Pretzel Town," and across the street from Linden Hall is the **Julius Sturgis Pretzel House,** 219 E.

> **Fun Fact Some facts about Pennsylvania Dutch Country**
> - The Pennsylvania Dutch Country hosts three to four million visitors a year.
> - Lancaster was the nation's capital for a day, when Congress fled from Philadelphia on September 27, 1777.
> - In-line skating is considered an acceptable form of transportation among the Amish.

Main St. (© 717/626-4354). Founded in 1861, it's the oldest such bakery in the country. At the conclusion of the 20-minute guided tours you can try your hand at rolling, twisting, and sprinkling the dough with coarse salt. Tours are given Monday through Saturday from 9:30am to 4:30pm (Dec–Apr open Sat only) for $2.

At the junction of Route 501 and Main Street is **Wilbur Chocolate Company's Candy Americana Museum & Store,** 48 N. Broad St. (© 717/626-3249; www.wilburbuds.com). Famous for its "Wilbur buds" (Hershey Kiss–style bite-size chocolates in milk and dark varieties), the factory offers a look at the process and history of chocolate-making, with samples, plus a store selling cooking or gift chocolate in a turn-of-the-20th-century atmosphere. Next door is the **Lititz Springs Park,** with a lovely duck-filled brook flowing from the 1756 spring, in addition to fields, playgrounds, and the historic **General Sutter Inn** (call © 717/626-2115 or visit www.generalsutterinn.com for lodging reservations at the inn).

STRASBURG

This little town, named by French Huguenots, is located southeast of Lancaster on Route 896 and is a paradise for rail buffs. Until the invention of the auto, railroads were the major mode of fast transport, and Pennsylvania was a leader in building and servicing thousands of engines. The **Strasburg Rail Road** (© 717/687-7522; www.strasburgrailroad.com), winds over 9 miles of preserved track from Strasburg to Paradise and back, as it has since 1832; wooden coaches and a Victorian parlor car are pulled by an iron steam locomotive. The railroad head is on Route 741 east of town and is open from April to October daily, and on weekends only from November to March. The fare is $9.50 to $16 for adults and $4.75 to $11 for children ages 3 to 11, depending on whether you go coach, dining car, or deluxe; toddlers are $2 to $6. Other attractions include the **Railroad Museum of Pennsylvania** (© 717/687-8628), displaying dozens of stationary engines right across from the Strasburg Rail Road; the **National Toy Train Museum** (© 717/687-8976), on Paradise Lane off Route 741, with five huge push-button operating layouts; and **Choo Choo Barn–Traintown USA** (© 717/687-7911; www.choochoobarn.com), a 1,700-square-foot miniature Amish Country landscape filled with animated trains and figures, which enact activities such as parades and circuses. It's linked up with the inevitable authorized Thomas Trackside Station store.

4 Especially for Kids

With the exception of beaches, Pennsylvania Dutch Country has everything for families, including rainy-day entertainment. In addition to the suggestions below, try the above-mentioned **Julius Sturgis Pretzel House** in Lititz, **People's Place** in Intercourse, and the various **railroad attractions** in Strasburg.

BUGGY RIDES

Driving for a couple of miles along a country lane in a horse-drawn carriage not only sounds irresistible but fits right in with the speed of Amish life. **Ed's Buggy Rides** (② 717/687-0360), on Route 896, 1½ miles south of Route 30 in Strasburg, has 3-mile rides leaving from the Red Caboose Motel ($8 for adults, and $4 for children), open daily from 9am till dusk.

DUTCH WONDERLAND

Dutch Wonderland (② 717/291-1888; www.dutchwonderland.com), that ersatz castle you see heading east on 2249 Lincoln Hwy. (Rte. 30) out of Lancaster, is the headquarters for a 44-acre amusement park with gardens and entertainment such as storytelling. There's a moderately wild roller coaster and a road rally, but most of the 30 rides are perfect for young families. Unlimited rides cost $26 for adults, $22 for children 3 to 5, $20 for seniors, $13 for ages 70-plus, $15 for everyone in fall and winter. The park is open from May to mid-October, with peak hours of 10am to 7pm daily during high season and weekends only in the spring and fall. In late fall (usually Thanksgiving through Christmas), there is a Winter Wonderland opening of limited rides and other holiday attractions each weekend (weekends include Fri).

BALLOON TOURS

Amish country is spectacular from the air, with its rural landscapes and generally clear weather. It's undeniably pricey at $169 per person for a 1-hour flight, but the **U.S. Hot Air Balloon Team** (② 800/763-5987 or 717/299-2274; www.balloonflights.com) lifts off for the first and last 2-hour stretches of daylight. The local departure pad is at Lancaster Host Resort, near the intersection of routes 30 and 896.

HERSHEY

Hershey is technically outside the county, 30 minutes northwest of Lancaster on Route 422, but the assembly of rides, amusements, and natural scenery in a storybook setting makes the sweetest town on earth worth the trip. Milton Hershey set up his town at the turn of the 20th century to reflect his business and philanthropy, and it is a magical spot for children (and for adults, since there is excellent golf and a wonderful spa here at the luxe Hotel Hershey). Start with the website (www.hersheypa.com) or in person with **Hershey's Chocolate World,** Park Boulevard (② 717/534-4900), a free tour that takes you from cacao beans to wrapped samples.

Hersheypark is a huge, just-renovated theme park at the junction of routes 743 and 422 (② 800/HERSHEY or 717/534-3090), with more than 50 rides and attractions including water rides, 11 roller coasters (including the brand-new Turbulence, a free-fall, 150-foot-high tower coaster, in 2005), five theaters with music, and 20 kiddie rides. The park also includes the 11-acre **ZooAmerica,** with more than 200 animals native to this continent. Hersheypark is open from mid-May to September (on weekends only in late Sept), and all summer until 10pm Monday through Thursday, and until 11pm Friday through Sunday. ZooAmerica is open year-round except for Thanksgiving, Christmas, and New Year's Day. Admission to everything at Hersheypark is $38 for adults (defined as ages 9–54), $22 for children 3 to 8 (free for kids 2 and under) and seniors 55 to 69, and $16 for seniors over 69.

The logical place to stay is the **Hershey Lodge,** West Chocolate Avenue and University Drive (② 717/534-8600), with miniature golf, tennis courts, and its own movie theater. And if you're tempted to sneak away without the kids, Hershey does have superb gardens, 72 holes of championship golf, and the palace-like **Hotel Hershey** (© 717/533-2176) up the mountain, which offers a luxurious spa with creative skin and massage services incorporating cocoa (a natural exfoliant and moisturizer).

LANDIS VALLEY MUSEUM

Following Oregon Pike (Rte. 272) north from Lancaster for 5 miles, you'll come to **Landis Valley Museum,** 2451 Kissel Hill Rd. (© **717/569-0401;** www.landis valleymuseum.org), a large outdoor museum of Pennsylvania German culture, folk traditions, decorative arts, and language. George and Henry Landis established a small museum here to exhibit family heirlooms in the 1920s; when the state acquired it in the 1950s it mushroomed into a 21-building "living arts" complex. The costumed practitioners—clock makers and clergymen, tavern keepers and tinsmiths, storekeepers, teachers, printers, weavers, and farmers—are experts in their fields and are generous with samples, which are also for sale in the shop. The museum is open Monday through Saturday from 9am to 5pm and Sunday from noon to 5pm; admission is $9 for adults, $7 for seniors, and $6 for children 6 to 17.

5 Shopping

There are many reasons to keep your credit card handy in Lancaster County. Quilts and other craft products unique to the area are sold in dozens of small stores and out of individual farms. The thrifty Pennsylvania Dutch have been keeping old furniture and objects in their barns and attics for 300 years, so antiquing is plentiful here. Fine pieces tend to migrate toward New Hope and Bucks County for resale, where you compete directly with dealers at the many fairs and shows. If antiques aren't your bag, a dozen outlet centers provide name-brand items at discounts of 30% to 70% along Route 30 east of Lancaster and in central Reading.

QUILTS

Quilts occupy a special place in Lancaster County life. Quilting is a time for fun and socializing, but it also affords an opportunity for young girls to learn the values and expectations of Amish life from their elders. German immigrant women started the tradition of reworking strips of used fabric into an ever-expanding series of pleasant, folkloric designs. Popular designs include "Wedding Ring," interlocking sets of four circles; the eight-pointed *Lone Star* radiating out with bursts of colors; "Sunshine and Shadow," virtuoso displays of diamonded color; and herringbone "Log Cabin" squares with multicolored strips. More contemporary quilters have added free-form picture designs to these traditional patterns.

The process is laborious and technically astounding—involving choosing, cutting, and affixing thousands of pieces of fabric, then filling in the design with intricate needlework patterns on the white "ground" that holds the layers of the quilt together. Interestingly, though all quilts require a great deal of sewing by hand, the Amish have used sewing machines since their introduction in the 1800s for the backing of the quilt. Within towns and communities, a sort of "assembly line" often exists from farmhouse to farmhouse, in which one woman might be very skilled at cutting fabric, another at piecing, another at batting or backing the finished quilt top.

Expect to pay $500 or more for a good-quality quilt, and $25 and up for pot holders, bags, and throw pillows.

The **People's Place** in Intercourse, 3513 Old Philadelphia Pike, is a good place to start looking for quilts; their Old Country Store (© 717/768-7171) has a knowledgeable sales staff and excellent inventory. The **Quilt Shop at Miller's,** located at the famed smorgasbord on Route 30 1 mile east of Route 896 (© 717/687-8480, ext. 49), has hundreds of handmade examples from local artisans, and is open daily. Emma Witmer's mother was one of the first women to hang out a shingle to sell quilts 30 years ago, and she continues the business with more than 100 patterns at **Witmer Quilt Shop,** 1070 W. Main St. in New Holland (© 717/656-9526). The shop is open from 8am to 6pm Tuesday through Thursday and Saturday, and until 8pm Monday and Friday.

Most of the county's back roads will have simple signs indicating places where quilts are sold; selections tend to be more limited but prices are slightly lower. Rosa Stoltzfus operates **Hand Made Quilts** at 102 N. Ronks Rd. in Ronks (no telephone) out of a room in her Amish home in the middle of cornfields. **Hannah Stoltzfoos** has a similar selection on 216 Witmer Rd. (© 717/392-4254), just south of Route 340 near Smoketown.

OTHER CRAFTS

Amish and Mennonites have created their own baskets, dolls, furniture, pillows, toys, wall hangings, and hex designs for centuries, and tourism has led to a healthy growth in their production. Much of this output is channeled into the stores lining Route 340 in Intercourse and Bird-in-Hand, such as the Amish-owned **Quilts and Fabric Shack,** 3021 Old Philadelphia Pike (© 717/768-0338), and **Dutchland Quilt Patch,** 4361 Old Philadelphia Pike (© 717/768-3981). The **Weathervane Shop** at Landis Valley Museum (see "Especially for Kids," above) has a fine collection produced by their own craftspeople, from tin and pottery to caned chairs. On the contemporary side, no one works harder than the **Artworks at Doneckers,** 100 N. State St., Ephrata (© 717/738-9503), which combines crafts with designer clothing and contemporary needs.

ANTIQUES

Two miles east of Exit 286 off I-76, Route 272 in Adamstown, just before it crosses into Berks County to the northeast, is the undisputed local center of Sunday fairs, with six or seven competitors within 5 miles. The largest are **Stoudt's Black Angus Antique Mall,** with more than 350 permanent dealers, and **Renninger's Antique and Collectors Market,** with 370 dealers; **Shupp's Grove** is smaller and mostly outdoors. At Renninger's, check out stall 52½A for Tiffany glass, 89 for children's clothes, or 32A for antique linens and hooked rugs.

FARMER'S MARKETS

Most farmer's markets in Lancaster County today are shedlike buildings with stalls at which local farmers, butchers, and bakers vend their fruits and vegetables, eggs and cheese, baked goods and pastries, and meat products like turkey sausage and scrapple. Since farmers can only afford to get away once or twice a week (to sell at Germantown and at Reading Terminal in Philadelphia, for example), the more commercial markets supplement the local goods with gourmet stalls selling everything from deerskin to candy and souvenirs. And the low-ceilinged, air-conditioned spaces you'll find at the commercial markets lack the flavor of, say, **Central Market** in Lancaster (p. 235), with its swirling fans and 1860 tiles and hitching posts, or Friday at **Green Dragon Market & Auction** (p. 237), on North State Street in Ephrata.

A notable contemporary market is the **Bird-in-Hand Farmers Market** at Route 340 and Maple Avenue (© **717/393-9674**). It's open from 8:30am to 5:30pm Friday and Saturday year-round, as well as Wednesday and Thursday during the summer. They have homemade ice cream and are linked to the Good 'n' Plenty Restaurant nearby. **Root's Country Market and Auction** (no phone), just south of Manheim on Route 72, is a very complete market on Tuesday.

Among the treats at the dozens of roadside stands that you'll pass, try the homemade root beer, breads, and pies at **Countryside Stand,** on Stumptown Road. Take a right turn from Route 772 heading west out of Intercourse and follow Stumptown for ½ mile. **Fisher's Produce,** on Route 741 between Strasburg and Gap, sells delicious baked goods along with fresh corn and melons in the summer.

OUTLET CENTERS

With over 120 stores, **Rockvale Square Outlets,** Route 30 East at the intersection with Route 896 (© **717/293-9595;** www.rockvalesquareoutlets.com), is Lancaster's largest outlet mall, and includes a hotel and six restaurants on its grounds. Jones New York, Nike, Izod, Jockey, London Fog, and Bass Shoes are represented, with Oneida, Lenox, Farberware, and Pfaltzgraff for housewares. Hours are Monday through Saturday from 9:30am to 9pm, Sunday from 10am to 6pm. I prefer the newer **Tanger Outlet Center at Millstream,** 2200 Lincoln Hwy. East, (© **717/392-7260;** www.tangeroutlet.com), for shops like Banana Republic, Gap, Polo Ralph Lauren, Reebok, J. Crew, Guess?, and Brooks Brothers. It's slightly closer to Lancaster and more compact. The complex also includes a 125-seat bakery and deli run by Miller's, of Miller's Smorgasbord fame. Tanger is open Monday through Saturday from 9am to 9pm, and Sunday from 10am to 6pm.

Home Furnishings Outlet Mall, at the junction of Exit 298 off the Pennsylvania Turnpike and Route 23 in Morgantown (© **610/286-2000**), has more than 50 stores, including Natuzzi Leather. A Holiday Inn with indoor recreation for guests rounds out the premises. It's open Monday through Saturday from 10am to 9pm and Sunday from noon to 5pm.

I don't have the space or the adjectives to fully describe the self-described "Outlet Capital of the World" in **Reading,** built out of former textile mills along the Schuylkill. Some six million shoppers are drawn here annually to 260 separate outlet centers. It's 30 minutes from Lancaster or 75 from Philadelphia, via I-76 to I-176 north to Route 422. The two largest destinations are **VF Factory Outlet Complex,** just west of the city in Wyomissing, and **Reading Outlet Center,** a multistory rehab in the heart of the city.

6 Where to Stay

From campsites, to bedrooms in working Amish farmhouses, to exquisite inns and luxury conference resorts, you'll find a wide variety of places to stay in Lancaster County. The higher the price level, the more advance notice is recommended; this also goes for some farms that only have two or three rooms. Good websites to check include: www.amishcountryinns.com and www.afarmstay.com.

HOTELS & RESORTS

Best Western Eden Resort Inn and Suites ✪   The amenities of this just-renovated hotel are incongruous with the region that surrounds it; that is, the hotel provides comforts you'd almost forgotten about, including plush, if bland, rooms (request poolside), coffeemakers, and a tropically landscaped atrium and pool. If you want a respite from the minimalist style of Amish life, this is a great, very casual place to hang out.

222 Eden Rd., Rte. 30 and Rte. 272, Lancaster, PA 17601. (C) **800/528-1234** or 717/569-6444. Fax 717/569-4208. www.edenresort.com. 276 units. From $99 double; from $140 suite. Up to 2 children under age 18 stay free in parent's room. 10% AAA/AARP discount. Some packages include breakfast. AE, DC, DISC, MC, V. Free parking. **Amenities:** 2 restaurants; lounge; indoor and outdoor pool; tennis and basketball courts; health club; Jacuzzi; business center; laundry service; dry cleaning; shuffleboard. *In room:* A/C, cable TV w/pay movies, dataport, kitchenette (Club Suites only), fridge, coffeemaker, hair dryer.

The Inns at Doneckers ⚓

Bill Donecker started building his customer service empire on Ephrata's north side in the early 1960s—now Doneckers comprises lodgings, dining, and sophisticated stores featuring gifts, accessories, fashions, and collectibles. He's since added the fine Restaurant at Doneckers serving all meals (see "Where to Dine," below), the Artworks loft spaces for contemporary artists to work in and market their crafts, the Farmer's Market (a store that sells jams and other edibles), and four inns, and he spices things up with frequent events and festivals. Of the upscale and lovely (and surprisingly affordable) accommodations, the 1777 House, built by a clock-maker member of Ephrata Cloister, is the most stately and distinguished. All rooms have hand stenciling, and local antiques and objects, and each site has a parlor with TV and library. The staff is outstanding.

322 N. State St. (near junction of Rte. 322 and Rte. 222), Ephrata, PA 17522. (C) **717/738-9502.** Fax 717/738-9554. www.doneckers.com. 40 units in 4 houses. From $65–$99 double; $150–$175 suite. Rates include full buffet breakfast. AE, DC, DISC, MC, V. Free parking. **Amenities:** Restaurant; shopping complex. *In room:* A/C, TV, Jacuzzi (in suites only).

Leola Village Inn and Suites

This year-old, lovely hotel and restaurant has 21st-century comforts built into a group of antique buildings and barns (the lobby was once an 1830s tobacco barn), in a cozy setting just 4 miles outside Lancaster. Those who like their country with plenty of comforts will appreciate the attractive decor of the 57 roomy guest rooms and suites, with their beige-and-green color scheme, down comforters, TVs, and antiques and antique reproduction furniture. Breakfast is included, with quiche, muffins, and fruit on the buffet, and there is a fitness center and the posh Mazzi's restaurant on-site—this sophisticated spot offers everything from seared scallops and Chilean sea bass to a casual fontina-topped gourmet pizza. There are several crafts shops and a beauty salon and spa on premises.

38 Deborah Dr., Rte. 23, Leola, PA 17540. (C) **717/656-7002** or 877/669-5094. www.leolavillage.com. 57 units, with 6 suites and cottages. $140–$209 double. Rates include full breakfast. AE, DISC, MC, V. **Amenities:** Restaurant; lounge; fitness center; spa; antiques and crafts shops; salon; billiards room. *In room:* TV w/cable and DVD player, kitchenette, coffeemaker, hair dryer, iron and ironing board, Jacuzzi (in some suites).

Willow Valley Family Resort

This Mennonite-owned resort (no drinking or smoking is permitted on premises) started out as a farm stand in 1943 and now combines a very complete set of modern comforts on 90 acres—a 9-hole golf course, lighted tennis courts, and indoor and outdoor pools—with local touches such as a bakery specializing in apple dumplings and fresh-baked pies (shoofly, among others). A skylit atrium is home to two smorgasbords and a restaurant. Free bus tours of the Amish country are offered Monday through Saturday.

2416 Willow St. Pike (3 miles south of Lancaster on Rte. 222), Lancaster, PA 17602. (C) **800/444-1714** or 717/464-2711. www.willowvalley.com. 352 units. From $89 double, $105 with breakfast included. Dinner smorgasbord and other special packages available. Children under 12 stay free in parent's room. AE, DC, MC, V. Free parking. **Amenities:** Restaurant; 2 indoor pools and an outdoor pool; 9-hole golf course; lighted tennis and basketball courts; fitness center; sauna; duck pond with gazebo; children's playground room. *In room:* A/C, TV, VCRs in premium rooms, fridge, coffeemaker, hair dryer, iron.

INNS

Cameron Estate Inn and Restaurant ⊛ The wide front porch alone is reason to visit this romantic, rambling 1805 mansion on 15 green acres, with lovely antiques-filled rooms that range in style from grand, French-toile–canopied suites to pale, serene hideaways under the eaves on the third floor. All rooms have their own bathrooms, and many have wood-burning fireplaces. Breakfast is included. The inn's restaurant serves indulgent, updated classics such as seafood Wellington, stuffed pork tenderloin, and pan-seared tuna with risotto.

1855 Mansion Lane, Mount Joy, PA 17552. © 717/492-0111. www.cameronestateinn.com. 18 units. $119–$289. **Amenities:** Restaurant; lounge. *In room:* Telephone with dataport.

General Sutter Inn ⊛ The General Sutter has operated continuously since 1764 at the charming intersection of routes 501 and 772. The inn boasts such niceties as verandas overlooking a fountain, and marble-topped tables. Most of the rooms occupy the original building (wings have been added), and are decorated in Victorian style with folk art touches. There is a coffee shop for breakfast, lunch, and a notable Sunday brunch; the dining room offers a solid continental gourmet menu.

14 E. Main St. (junction of Rte. 501 and Rte. 772), Lititz, PA 17543. © 717/626-2115. Fax 717/626-0992. www.generalsutterinn.com. 19 units. $63–$105 double; $150 suite. Additional guests $10. Rates include full breakfast. AE, DISC, MC, V. Free parking. **Amenities:** 2 restaurants; lounge. *In room:* A/C, TV, dataport.

Netherlands Inn and Spa ⊛ This attractive country inn, formerly the Historic Strasburg Inn, is set on 58 acres, and is completely surrounded by Amish farms. It has a brand-new spa on-site, with 102 units; it still feels like an inn, but it has a good-size pool, a fitness center, and the Bistro, a fine-dining restaurant. Rooms are Colonial-themed, with poster beds, handmade floral wreaths, and handsome chair rails. A full breakfast is served in the Strasburg Ballroom.

1 Historic Dr., Strasburg, PA 17579. © 717/687-7691. www.historicstrasburginn.com. 102 units. $109 double; $129–$169 suite. Frequent packages and AARP discount. Rates include full breakfast. AE, DC, DISC, MC, V. Free parking. **Amenities:** Restaurant; tavern; heated outdoor pool; exercise room; spa; Jacuzzi; sauna; children's playground; concierge; laundry service; dry cleaning. *In room:* A/C, cable TV/VCR or DVD, dataport, coffeemaker, hair dryer, iron.

BED & BREAKFASTS

Alden House ⊛ This 1850 brick Victorian house owned by Bob and Shirley McCarthy is at the center of the town's historic district. There are private bathrooms in all rooms. Two suites can be accessed either through the house or via an outdoor spiral staircase to the second-floor porch. The morning brings a full breakfast with waffles or cinnamon-chip pancakes served in the dining room or overlooking the charming gardens outside. The inn is nonsmoking.

62 E. Main St. (Rte. 772), Lititz, PA 17543. © 800/584-0753 or 717/627-3363. www.aldenhouse.com. 5 units. $95–$125 double and suite. Rates include full breakfast. MC, V. Free parking. *In room:* A/C, TV/VCR, dataport.

Churchtown Inn Bed and Breakfast This completely restored 1735 stone inn, written up in the *New York Times* in May 2002, has evening cocktail hours in the Victorian parlor, and an opulent breakfast is served in a glassed-in porch overlooking the garden. Guest rooms all have private bathrooms, and innkeepers Diane and Michael Franco have a standing arrangement for dinners with nearby Mennonite or Amish families if you wish it. The Cornwall iron forge nearby, still functioning as a working historic site, supplied Revolutionary War troops with cannonballs and musket shot.

Main St. (Rte. 23), Churchtown, PA 17555. © **800/637-4446** or 717/445-7794. Fax 717/445-0962. www. churchtowninn.com. 8 units. $85–$145 double. Rates include full breakfast. 2-night weekend minimum. MC, V. Free parking. Children under 16 not accepted. *In room:* A/C, TV and VCR, CD player.

Historic Smithton Inn   This inn, near Ephrata Cloister, is a pre–Revolution-ary War stagecoach stop. Dorothy Graybill, the owner, painstakingly decorates each room with canopy feather beds and collector-quality quilts, working fire-places, sitting areas, and leather upholstered chairs. Triple-pane windows for quiet, magazines, and fresh flowers are typical thoughtful touches; the grounds have lovely gardens and a gazebo. A full breakfast and snacks are served. Smok-ing is not permitted.

900 W. Main St., Ephrata, PA 17522. © **717/733-6094**. www.historicsmithtoninn.com. 8 units. $85–$160 double. Rates include full breakfast. Children welcome by prior arrangement, $20 extra ages 2–12; $35 ages 13 and up. 2-night minimum on holiday weekends. MC, V. Free parking. **Amenities:** Golf nearby. *In room:* A/C, fridge, hair dryer available, iron available, Jacuzzi (in some rooms), fireplace.

MOTELS

Best Western Revere Inn and Suites ⭐   Eight miles east of Lancaster, the original inn is built off a historic 1740 post house now used as a restaurant and lounge. A main building built in 1999 houses 65 oversize rooms and suites (but ask for a room in the attractive ca. 1790 restored farmhouse). Room amenities include coffeemakers, hair dryers, and refrigerators, as well as fireplaces and Jacuzzis in suites. It's close to the outlet malls and has both indoor and outdoor pools.

3063 Lincoln Hwy. (Rte. 30), Paradise, PA 17562. © **800/429-7383** or 717/687-7683. Fax 717/687-6141. www.revereinn.com. 95 units. $69–$169 double. Rates include continental breakfast. Children under 12 stay free in parent's room. AE, MC, V. Free parking. **Amenities:** Restaurant; lounge; 1 indoor and 1 outdoor pool; exercise room; Jacuzzi; coin-op laundry. *In room:* A/C, TV, dataport, fridge, coffeemaker, hair dryer, iron.

Bird-in-Hand Family Inn & Restaurant   This motel's location puts you directly in the heart of Amish country. I prefer the back building, with rooms off an indoor hallway, to the front building's motel setup. The hotel restaurant serves meals buffet style or from the menu, and is a popular stop for tours. Grandma Smucker's Bakery offers wet-bottom shoofly pie and apple dumplings.

Rte. 340, Bird-in-Hand, PA 17505. © **800/537-2535**. Fax 717/768-1117. www.bird-in-hand.com/familyinn. 125 units. From $49–$110 double. Packages available. Children under 16 stay free in parent's room. AE, DISC, MC, V. Free parking. **Amenities:** Restaurant; 1 indoor and 1 outdoor pool; 2 lighted tennis courts; minigolf; game room; coin-op laundry service; playground; free 2-hr. bus tour of country roads. *In room:* A/C, TV, data-port, fridge, coffeemaker, hair dryer.

Country Inn of Lancaster ⭐   Thomas Dommel's inn is very convenient to Lancaster, just east of the Route 30 bypass. More to the point, its back building overlooks beautiful Amish farmland, the decor is unusually charming, and the amenities—elevators for all second-floor guests and a large heated pool, open from 9am to 9pm—are impeccably maintained. Most furnishings are handmade locally, from Amish quilts to branch wreaths, and all rooms have porches or bal-conies with wooden rocking chairs. The complex includes two buildings, each with several complimentary breakfast stations, an adjoining restaurant (you can get discount coupons for any meal there), and an extensive gift shop.

2133 Lincoln Hwy. E. (Rte. 30), Lancaster, PA 17602. © **717/393-3413**. Fax 717/393-2889. www.countryinn oflancaster.com. 125 units. From $79 double. Rates include continental breakfast. Packages available. Children under 12 stay free in parent's room. AE, DISC, MC, V. Free parking. **Amenities:** Restaurant; indoor/outdoor pool; Jacuzzi; 24-hr. coffee and juice. *In room:* A/C, TV.

Harvest Drive Family Motel & Restaurant Farmland was converted to create this family-owned motel, and it's surrounded by corn and alfalfa fields on a quiet back road next to the family farm. The motel building has rooms with one to three double beds and pleasant but utilitarian decor. The simple restaurant features Dutch home cooking all day, and there's a gift shop in the barn.

Box 498, Intercourse, PA 17534. ✆ **800/233-0176** or 717/768-7186. Fax 717/768-4513. www.harvestdrive. com. 50 units. $46–$112 double. 2-night minimum on holiday weekends. Children under 18 stay free in parent's room. AE, DISC, MC, V. Free parking. Take Clearview Rd. south off Rte. 340 just west of Intercourse, then bear right to 3370 Harvest Dr. **Amenities:** Restaurant; children's playground. *In room:* A/C, TV, dataport.

Mill Stream Country Inn Owned by the Bird-in-Hand Corporation, this lodge has three floors of simple rooms. The rear rooms are away from the road and overlook a stream. The restaurant serves breakfast and lunch (no alcohol).

Rte. 896 (between Rte. 30 and Rte. 340), Smoketown, PA 17576. ✆ **800/355-1143** or 717/299-0931. www. bird-in-hand.com/millstream. 52 units. From $79 double. 2-night minimum on weekends. Children under 16 stay free in parent's room. AE, DISC, MC, V. Free parking. **Amenities:** Outdoor pool; golf course nearby. *In room:* AC, TV, hair dryer, iron.

FARM VACATION BED & BREAKFASTS

What better way to get the flavor of Amish life than by staying with a farm family? The **Pennsylvania Dutch Country Convention & Visitors Bureau** (✆ **800/ PA-DUTCH;** www.padutchcountry.com) has a complete listing of about 40 working farms that take guests. Reservations are recommended since most offer only three to five rooms. Expect simple lodgings, hall bathrooms, and filling, family-style breakfasts, all at less than motel rates. Dinners with the family are sometimes offered at an additional charge. You'll be able to chat with the women in the family (the men start and end their days with the sun) and get suggestions on local routes, walks, and crafts producers. One tip: Stay away from dairy and poultry farms if you have a sensitive nose!

Green Acres Farm Wayne and Yvonne Miller can sleep 26 people in this 150-year-old farmhouse, with private bathrooms in all rooms. It's a corn and soybean farm but also offers hay wagon rides, farm pets, a playhouse, and swings and major-league trampoline for kids. All rooms have one double or queen-size bed plus bunk beds. There's no smoking, but you're allowed to bring your own alcohol.

1382 Pinkerton Rd., Mount Joy, PA 17552. ✆ 717/653-4028. Fax 717/653-2840. www.thegreenacresfarm. com. 7 units. $95 double. Additional child $5. Rates include family-style breakfast served at 8am. In summer, reservations are recommended. MC, V. Pinkerton Rd. is south of Rte. 772 just west of Mt. Joy's town center. You'll wind past Groff's Farm Resort and a creek before you get to the farm. *In room:* A/C.

Rayba Acres Farm Ray and Reba Ranck offer clean, quiet rooms on a working fifth-generation dairy farm. (You're welcome to try milking and wander the grounds.) Rooms have private bathrooms and TVs, and are in motel-like units. A common room has a microwave and refrigerator. There's complimentary coffee in your room, but no smoking. Outside features a pretty pergola and gardens.

183 Black Horse Rd., Paradise, PA 17562. ✆ 717/687-6729. Fax 717/687-8386. www.raybaacres.com. 6 units, all with private bathroom. $70–$80 double. DISC, MC, V. From Paradise center, south from Rte. 30 onto Black Horse, follow 2 miles. *In room:* A/C, TV, coffeemaker.

7 Where to Dine

While Ben Franklin would probably be staggered at the size of a modern Pennsylvania Dutch meal or smorgasbord, he'd recognize everything in it—you'll still find the same baked goods, meat and poultry, and fruits and vegetables that have been offered here since Colonial times. The Amish way of life calls for substantial, wholesome, long-cooking dishes, rich in butter and cream. Don't look for crunchy vegetables—if they're not creamed, they're marinated or thoroughly boiled. The baked goods are renowned, and even the main courses tend to the sweet. Shoofly pie, a concoction of molasses and sweet dough (hence its attraction to flies), is probably the most famous. Decor tends to take a back seat to large quantities of food at low prices.

Included here are the most representative family style and smorgasbord dining spots, as well as restaurants that update local ingredients and traditions. Family style means that you'll be part of a group of 10 or 12, ushered to long tables and brought heaping platters of food, course after course. At a smorgasbord, you construct your own plate at central food stations, with unlimited refills. Prices are fixed per person at both.

And when looking for a meal, don't neglect the signs along the road, or "Community Event" listings in the Thursday "Weekend" section of the *Lancaster New Era,* for church or firehouse pancake breakfasts, corn roasts, or barbecue or game suppers. These generally charge a minimal amount for all the food you can eat and all the iced tea or soda you can drink; and they're great chances to meet the locals. You can also catch annual festivals, such as the rhubarb fair in Intercourse and the Sertoma Club's enormous chicken barbecues at Long's Park in Lancaster, both in May. The Dutch Food and Folk Fair is held in Bird-in-Hand each June. If you'd like a more traditional restaurant experience, downtown Lancaster has restaurants ranging from sushi bars to pizza spots to fine dining; visit www.lancasterpa.net for the dozens of choices here.

FAMILY STYLE/SMORGASBORD

Good 'N' Plenty Restaurant PENNSYLVANIA DUTCH They've added the 500-seat Dutch Room to the original 110-seat farmhouse here. The location is very convenient, and tables seat 10 to 12. Expect waits at peak dining hours: I wish they wouldn't wait for a "full 12" before seating anybody at a table and filling it with platters. You can purchase baked goods and other gift items.

Rte. 896, ½ mile south of its intersection with Rte. 340 and north of intersection with Rte. 30, Smoketown. © 717/394-7111. Reservations not accepted. Adults $17, children $8.50 for ages 4–12, free for children under 4; tax included. MC, V. Mon–Sat 11:30am–8pm.

Miller's Smorgasbord PENNSYLVANIA DUTCH/SMORGASBORD In 1929, Anna Miller prepared chicken and waffles for truckers while Enos Miller repaired their vehicles. For millions since then, Miller's has been the definitive, if increasingly pricey, Pennsylvania Dutch smorgasbord. Homemade chicken corn soup, slow-roasted carved beef, turkey, and ham, chicken potpies, and a rich apple pie are just the tip of the iceberg. The breakfast smorgasbord, offered only on Sunday, has made-to-order eggs and omelets, along with local sausage and pastries. The health-conscious diner will find plenty of choices here too.

Rte. 30 at Ronks Rd., 5 miles east of Lancaster and 1 mile east of Rte. 896. © 800/669-3568 or 717/687-6621. Reservations accepted. Dinner $22 adults, $6.95 for children 4–9, $9.95 for children 10–12; breakfast $12 adults, $6.95 for children 4–12; tax included. AE, DISC, MC, V. Mon–Sat noon–8pm; Sun 8am–8pm.

Plain & Fancy Farm Restaurant PENNSYLVANIA DUTCH This 45-year-old family style restaurant started out as a barn, as you can see by the posts that still support the front dining room. A back addition gives it a capacity of 300. They are less intent on filling full tables and more quick with service here. The fried chicken is crisp and flavorful. The newly renovated complex now includes a village of crafts shops and a bakery. Smoking is not permitted.

David Walbert's "Damp Bottom Shoofly Pie" Recipe

"There are two types of shoofly pie, wet bottom and dry or damp bottom. Both feature a molasses custard with a crumb topping; the only difference is the consistency of the molasses filling. The drier versions can be eaten by hand and (as was once common, for breakfast) dunked in coffee. The wetter versions require a fork.

"The origins of this pie are a mystery, though it seems to have been common at least as early as the late 1800s. The **Dutch Haven** (2857A Lincoln Hwy. E. on US Rte. 30; ✆ **717/687-0111**), a Lancaster restaurant and gift shop, made shoofly pie a symbol of the Pennsylvania Dutch Country when it began serving pies to tourists and shipping them by mail order in the 1950s. The Dutch Haven's shoofly pie is distinctly gooey, and (unfortunately, I think) that is the version that has since become most popular. Even less traditional is their practice of topping it with whipped cream. While I don't make a habit of standing on tradition, sweeter and heavier are not always better.

"This recipe makes a 'damp bottom' pie. It is good for dessert, of course, and also try dunking a leftover piece in coffee the next morning for breakfast."

Crumbs:
¾ cup flour
½ tsp. cinnamon
⅛ tsp. nutmeg
⅛ tsp. ground cloves
½ cup brown sugar
½ tsp. salt
2 tablespoons shortening

Rte. 340, 7 miles east of Lancaster, Bird-in-Hand, PA. ✆ 717/768-4400. Reservations recommended. $17 adults, $7.95 children 4–11; tax included. AE, DISC, MC, V. Noon–8pm year-round.

Shady Maple *(Value* SMORGASBORD   This is somewhat north of most of the attractions, but it does an enormous business, with waits of up to 30 minutes on Saturday for one of the 600 seats. Tourist buses have their own entrance and seating. The Pennsylvania Dutch buffet is a mind-boggling 140-feet long, with 46 salads, 14 vegetables, 8 meats, 8 breads, 27 desserts, and a make-your-own-sundae station. Breakfast includes everything you've ever imagined eating at that hour. There's a touristy gift shop and a fast-food version (why bother?) downstairs. The weekday dinner price of $14.81 includes tax, tip, and all non-alcoholic beverages (Tues is seafood night at $19.94). Smoking is not permitted.

Rte. 23, East Earl, PA (1 mile east of Blue Ball, at intersection with Rte. 897). ✆ 717/354-8222. Reservations not accepted. Dinner $15–$20; breakfast $8; lunch $10. Children 4–10 pay half-price; 10% discount for seniors. AE, DC, DISC, MC, V. Mon–Sat 5am–8pm.

MORE DINING CHOICES

The Amish Barn Restaurant *(Finds* PENNSYLVANIA DUTCH   This isn't one of the massive smorgasbord spots, but a more low-key restaurant where the authentic Amish specialties include chicken pot pie, pork and sauerkraut, and ham

Liquid:
½ tsp. baking soda
¾ boiling water
½ cup molasses (not blackstrap)
1 egg

Other:
Dough for a single pie crust
9-inch pie plate
3 mixing bowls

1. Heat the oven to 400°F. In a mixing bowl, dissolve the baking soda in the boiling water. Stir in the molasses and let cool to room temperature while you mix the dry ingredients.
2. In a second bowl, whisk together the flour, cinnamon, nutmeg, cloves, brown sugar, and salt. Add the shortening and combine with your fingertips to make crumbs.
3. Beat the egg in a third bowl. Pour in the molasses mixture and combine well. Pour the mixture into a prepared 9-inch pie shell. Scatter the crumbs evenly on top.
4. Bake for 10 to 15 minutes or until the crust just begins to brown. Reduce the oven temperature to 325°F and bake until firm (another 30 min. or so).

–David Walbert, Pennsylvania Dutch by birth, is a writer and historian living in Durham, North Carolina. He publishes
The New Agrarian *at www.newagrarian.com.*

loaf, all served in generous family-style portions. You can also order steak and seafood here. Breakfast is a heaping spread of eggs, hot cakes, home fries, ham, and scrapple (a local breakfast meat, like a flat sausage made with cornmeal).

3029 Old Philadelphia Pike, Rte. 340, 5 miles east of Rte. 30, Bird-in-Hand, PA. ✆ **717/768-8886.** Dinner $10–$18; breakfast $7; lunch $3–$8. No credit cards. Call to confirm changing hours. Daily June–Sept 8am–9pm; Oct–May 8am–7pm. Closed Jan–Mar Mon–Wed.

The Restaurant at Doneckers CONTINENTAL   Chef Greg Gables presides over this haute-cuisine menu. Prices are steep for the area, but quality is comparable to a Center City treat, though service is spottier. The menu features lobster ravioli or grilled Dover sole in a citrus butter sauce, and mixes classic French dishes with contemporary American standards like infused oils, lighter ingredients, and healthier cooking. If you're in the mood for creamy sauces, though, they'll be more than happy to indulge you. Desserts are baked on the premises daily. For lighter fare, there's a bistro-style menu offered from 4 to 10pm. The wine list is extensive.

333 N. State St., Ephrata, PA. ✆ **717/738-9501.** Reservations recommended. Main courses $20–$30. AE, DC, DISC, MC, V. Mon–Sat 11am–10pm.

Stoudt's Black Angus Restaurant & Brew Pub STEAKHOUSE/BREW PUB
Stoudt's Golden Lager, Pilsner, and other German-style varieties are brewed here

---

Tips   Dining With the Amish

For a more intimate dining experience, try dining at an Amish home. You'll get a taste of some delicious Amish home-cooking for a very low price, and will have some lively and informative conversation. Unfortunately, many of these homes like to maintain a modest business and asked us not to list their contact information. Try contacting the **Pennsylvania Dutch Convention & Visitors Bureau,** 501 Greenfield Rd., Lancaster, PA 17601 (© **800/PA-DUTCH,** ext. 4, or 717/299-8901) or ask a tour guide or a local business owner for suggestions. We won't give details, but we recommend the home of Emanuel and Katie Fisher.

---

and make a perfect conclusion to a visit to the famed Sunday antiques market next door. The family has added a steakhouse specializing in aged prime beef, a clam and oyster bar, and an agreeable pub with Pennsylvania Dutch ham and chicken dishes alongside burgers, wursts, soups, and salads. The restaurant has a 1928 Packard in the lobby, and the pub offers country dancing Friday and Saturday. The complex also includes a medieval German-style village of shops and homes.

Rte. 272, 1 mile north of Exit 21 from I-76, Adamstown, PA. © **717/484-4385.** Reservations recommended. Main courses $17–$35; brewpub $6.95–$12. AE, DC, MC, V. Mon–Thurs 4:30–10pm; Fri–Sat noon–10pm; Sun 11:30am–8pm.

Appendix:
Philadelphia in Depth

Philadelphia in 2005 boasts two new major sports arenas to the south of Center City; a gleaming downtown with a wonderful performing arts district; a thriving restaurant and lounge scene; affordable hotel packages (even at luxury properties); and a revitalized cultural life.

1 History 101: The Philadelphia Story

Although Philadelphia may conjure up thoughts of William Penn and the Revolutionary period in the minds of most Americans, it was in fact a tiny group of Swedish settlers that first established a foothold here in the 1640s. Where does William Penn fit in? Well, his father had been an admiral and a courtier under Charles II of England. The king was in debt to Admiral Penn, and the younger Penn asked to collect the debt through a land grant on the west bank of the Delaware River, a grant that would eventually be named Pennsylvania, or "Penn's forest." Penn's Quaker religion, his anti-Anglicanism, and his contempt for authority had landed him in prison, and the chance for him to set up a Quaker utopia in the New World was too good to pass up. Since Swedish farmers owned most of the lower Delaware frontage, he settled upriver, where the Schuylkill met the Delaware, and named the settlement Philadelphia—City of Brotherly Love.

COLONIAL PHILADELPHIA When Philadelphia celebrated its 300th anniversary in 1982, Penn's original city plan still adequately described the Center City, down to the public parks and the site for City Hall. Penn, who had learned the dangers of narrow streets and semidetached wooden buildings from London's terrible 1666 fire, laid out the city along broad avenues and city blocks arranged in a grid. As he intended to treat Native Americans and fellow settlers equally, he planned no city walls or neighborhood borders. Front Street, naturally, faced the Delaware, as it still does, and parallel streets were numbered up to 24th Street and the Schuylkill. Streets running east to west were named after trees and plants (although Sassafras became Race St., for the horse-and-buggy contests run along it). To attract prospective investors, Penn promised bonus land grants in the "Liberties" (outlying countryside) to anyone who bought a city lot; he took one of the largest for himself, now Pennsbury Manor (26 miles north of town). The Colonies were in the business of attracting settlers in those days, and Penn found that he had to wear a variety of hats—those of financier, politician, religious leader, salesman, and manufacturer.

Homes and public buildings filled in the map slowly. The Colonial row houses of Society Hill and Elfreth's Alley (continuously inhabited since the 1690s) near the Delaware docks were the earliest homes. Thomas Jefferson, when he wrote the Declaration of Independence in 1776 almost a century later, could still say of his boardinghouse, on 7th and Market, that it was away from the city's noise and dirt!

Around 1800, the city spread west to Broad Street. Philadelphia grew along the river and not west as Penn had planned. Southwark, to the south, and the

Northern Liberties, to the north, housed the less affluent, including many sailors. These were Philadelphia's first slums—unpaved, without public services, filled with taverns set up in unofficial alleys, and populated by those without enough property or money to satisfy voting requirements.

Although Philadelphia was founded after Boston and New York, manufacturing, financial services, excellent docking facilities, and fine Pennsylvania farm produce soon propelled it into the first city of the Colonies. It was the largest English-speaking city in the British Empire after London. Colonial Philadelphia was a thriving city in virtually every way, boasting public hospitals and streetlights, cultural institutions and newspapers, stately Georgian architecture, imported tea and cloth, and, above all, commerce. The "triangle trade" shipping route between England, the Caribbean, and Philadelphia yielded estimated profits of 700% on each leg.

One man who will always be linked with Philadelphia is the multitalented, insatiably curious Benjamin Franklin. Inventor, printer, statesman, scientist, and diplomat, Franklin was an all-around genius. It sometimes seems that his influence appears in every aspect of the city worth exploring! Colonial homes were protected by his fire-insurance company; the post office at 3rd and Market streets became his grandson's printing shop; and the Free Library of Philadelphia, the University of Pennsylvania, Pennsylvania Hospital at 8th and Spruce streets, and the American Philosophical Society all came into being thanks to Franklin's inspiration.

FROM REVOLUTION TO CIVIL WAR   Like most important Philadelphians, Franklin considered himself a loyal British subject until well into the 1770s, though he and the other colonists were increasingly subject to what they considered capricious English policy. Colonists here weren't as radical as those in New England, but tremendous political debate erupted after Lexington and Concord and the meeting of the First and Second Continental Congresses. Moderates—wealthy citizens with friends and relatives in England—held out as long as they could. But with the April 1776 decision in Independence Hall to consider drafting a declaration of independence, revolutionary fervor gained a momentum that would become unstoppable.

"These are the times that try men's souls," wrote Thomas Paine, and they certainly were for Philadelphians, who had much to lose in a war with Britain. Thomas Jefferson and John Adams talked over the situation with George Washington, Robert Morris, and other delegates at City Tavern by night and at Carpenter's Hall and Independence Hall by day. On July 2, the general congress passed their declaration; on July 8, it was read to a crowd of 8,000, who tumultuously approved.

Your visit to Independence National Historical Park will fill you in on the Revolution's effect on the City of Brotherly Love. Of the major Colonial cities, Philadelphia had the fewest defenses. The war came to the city itself because British troops occupied patriot homes during the harsh winter of 1777 to 1778. Woodford, a country mansion in what is now Fairmount Park, was hosting Tory balls while Washington's troops drilled and shivered at Valley Forge. Washington's attempt to crack the British line at Germantown ended in a confused retreat. The city later greatly benefited from the British departure and the Peace of Paris (1783), which ended the war.

Problems with the new federal government brought a Constitutional Convention to Philadelphia in 1787. This body crafted the Constitution that the United States still follows. In the years between the ratification of the Constitution and

A Portrait of the Philadelphians

The first European settlers in Philadelphia, arriving in the 1640s, were from Sweden. (You can see models of the two ships that brought them over in Gloria Dei Church.) Unusual tolerance, epitomized by the Quakers, helped lead to two separate strains of immigration during the first centuries of the city's history. One was made up of large European families drawn to the new world by the promise of cheap farmland—English, Scottish, Sephardic Jews, and Germans (*Deutsch* in German—hence the term *Pennsylvania Dutch*). The other group included thousands of London-based craftsmen, servants, and sailors, including London-based French Huguenots. German immigrants specialized in linen and wool weaving and ironwork, French Huguenots in fine silver, and all immigrants from all ethnic groups farmed and built ships.

In general the quality of life was high, despite a disastrous 1793 yellow fever epidemic. Franklin's legacy flourished. The resources of the Library Company became available to the public, and both men and women received "modern" educations—that is, more emphasis on accounting and less on classics. The 1834 Free School Act established a democratic public school system. Private academies, such as Germantown Friends School and Friends Select, are still going strong today. Culture flourished—the Walnut Street Theater, founded in 1809, is the oldest American theater still in constant use, and the Musical Fund Hall at 808 Locust St. (now apartments) hosted operas, symphony orchestras, and chamber ensembles. The 1805 Pennsylvania Academy of Fine Arts, now at Broad and Cherry streets, taught such painters as Washington Allston and the younger Peales. Charles Willson Peale, the eccentric patriarch, set up the first American museum in the Long Hall of Independence Hall; its exhibits included a portrait gallery and the first lifelike arrangements of full-size stuffed animals.

The 19th century saw the arrival of English commoners fleeing the industrialization of their countryside in the 1820s, Irish escaping from the 1840s potato famine, and waves of Germans and central Europeans seeking peace and stability during the 1870s. From the 1880s to the 1920s, Russians and Jews from eastern Europe, Italians, and free blacks from the American South all migrated in record numbers to the city. In recent years, Asian and Hispanic immigrants have filled in the gap left by the suburban exodus of earlier groups, creating a more multicultural Philadelphia than ever before.

the Civil War, the city prospered. For 10 of these years, 1790 to 1800, the U.S. government operated here while the District of Columbia was still marshland. George Washington lived in an executive mansion where the Liberty Bell is now; the Supreme Court met in Old City Hall; Congress met in Congress Hall; and everybody met at City Tavern for balls and festivals.

After the capital moved to Washington, Philadelphia retained the federal charter to mint money, build ships, and produce weapons. The city's shipyards, ironworks and locomotive works fueled the transportation revolution that made

America's growth possible. Philadelphia vied with Baltimore and New York City for transport routes to agricultural production inland. New York eventually won out as a shipper, thanks to its natural harbor and the Erie Canal. Philadelphia, however, was the hands-down winner in becoming America's premier manufacturing city, and it ranked even with New York in finance. During the Civil War, Philadelphia's manufacturers weren't above supplying both Yankees and Confederates with guns and rail equipment. Fortunately for Philadelphians, the Southern offensive met with bloody defeat at Gettysburg before reaching the city. With the end of the Civil War in 1865, port activity rebounded, as Southern cotton was spun and shipped from city textile looms.

Philadelphia became the natural site for the first world's fair held on American soil: the Centennial Exposition. It's hard to imagine the excitement that filled Fairmount Park, with 200 pavilions and displays. There's a scale model in Memorial Hall, one of the few surviving structures in the park; it gives a good idea of how seriously the United States took this show of power and prestige. University City in West Philadelphia saw the establishment of campuses for Drexel University and the University of Pennsylvania, and public transport lines connected all the neighborhoods of the city.

INTO THE 21ST CENTURY   Philadelphia's 20th century was checkered, but the city entered the 21st century with great optimism. Philadelphians are extremely proud of their two brand-new sports arenas: the delightful, open-air Phillies baseball stadium Citizens Bank Park, and Lincoln Financial Field, the stunning modern home of Eagles NFL football. The Kimmel Center for the Performing Arts, just a few years old, continues to astonish with its sound quality and steel-and-glass beauty, and the National Constitution Center and the gleaming new home of the Liberty Bell have added new life to the historic district downtown, which buzzes with visitors from all over the world. Many of the problems that plague urban centers throughout America—homelessness, drugs, crime, and inadequate resources for public services—are receding in Philadelphia, with the number of homeless in Center City down from nearly 1,000 10 years ago to about 150 in 2004. Philadelphia's marketing efforts and inventive hotel and tourism packages have raised the number of visitors per year to nearly 23 million people flocking to the city and the surrounding countryside, and 10 million of them stayed overnight.

If you go to the top of the freshly restored City Hall and look around, you'll see a panorama of factories, the old Navy Yard, warehouses, and docks. The places are virtually all turned to other uses, or about to be redeveloped as office buildings, retail, or condominiums. But you'll also see block after block of row houses built a century ago by new immigrants, whose more successful descendants have left for greener pastures. In terms of urban homeowners—an area in which Philadelphia led the world for decades—many successful citizens have left the city for more pleasant suburban areas, although the urban-renewal projects at Society Hill, the boom period of expansion along the northeast and Parkway, and the establishment of Independence National Historical Park have combated the migration somewhat. Although port and petroleum-refining operations bolstered the city's position as an industrial center until the 1980s, manufacturing in general has moved out of the city and the region. Half of the city's workforce was once employed in manufacturing. This figure has shrunk to 9% today. As industry moves out, the city is developing its service businesses to replace the revenue, and specifically aim at tourist business.

The opening of the $522-million Pennsylvania Convention Center in 1993, only minutes from both historic and business districts, was a tremendous boon for the city. The hundreds of conventions, millions of visitors, and billions of dollars projected in revenues from the center over the next decade are crucial, after some lean years, to keep the restaurants, hotels, sights, and entertainment that we recommend afloat. Most convention managers have found the labor costs and operational frustrations at the Convention Center a turnoff for future business, so change is necessary although not assured.

Pennsylvania Convention Center dollars also tie into greater safety and great infrastructure improvements, with lots of repaving, new lighting, and curb cuts along lower Market Street, Columbus Boulevard and the waterfront, and the Italian Market. A dark blue "Direction Philadelphia" signage program that's clear and coherent can guide you on and off a reconstructed expressway system, now connecting I-95 and I-76 (along the two rivers), with plenty of easy entrances and exits. The burgeoning airport, now a US Airways hub, has undergone a $1-billion capital improvement, with the new international Terminal A West, a state-of-the-art shopping mall, and new runways. The nation's second-busiest Amtrak stop, 30th Street Station, has completed a $100-million restoration, with a new bakery, charcuterie, and rejuvenated shops. Hot areas in town have radiated out from the city core. The Northern Liberties district, north of already-red-hot Old City, is becoming the cool place for 20-somethings to live, sip espresso, dine at bistros, and dance late into the night.

Corporate headquarters punctuate the northwest quadrant of Center City, and conventions throng Market Street east of City Hall. Major corporate headquarters in Philadelphia now include SmithKline Beecham (pharmaceuticals); Aramark (food and hospitality); Advanta (financial services); and CIGNA (insurance). With all those universities to train entrepreneurs and scientists, plenty of Internet and biogenetic firms are sprouting with local financing.

But tourism and hospitality are even more critical for revenue replacement, as evidenced by the coordination of public and private efforts in Center City under recent mayors Ed Rendell and John Street. The city looks ahead with a keen sense that visitors are the key to a vibrant urban core.

2 A Historic Document

Few experiences can conjure up the spirit of Old Philadelphia like sitting at a bench in Independence Square and reading the Declaration of Independence. If you have kids, ask them to read it aloud with you.

Many consider the Declaration of Independence the most important of all American documents, even more important than the United States Constitution. Before our founding fathers could establish a separate government, this document gave them the right to do so, and freed them from ties to Britain.

In the hot summer of 1776, Thomas Jefferson rented a room in the bricklayer Jacob Graff's house on the outskirts of town, intent on finding a quiet space to write. (See "Declaration House [Graff House]," on p. 139.) It's said that Jefferson slept in a small bed and often complained about the horseflies from the stable across the street as he alternately wrote and studied Virginia's constitution and other documents. He was also known to have a large tab at the nearby City Tavern during this time. But 3 weeks later, he presented his Declaration to the delegates of the Second Continental Congress, who debated, modified, and eventually ratified it on July 4, 1776.

Much of the theory behind the first half of the document is rooted in the theory of "natural rights," also argued by John Locke and Jean Jacques Rousseau, among others. The second half outlines the delegates' grievances against the "absolute Tyranny" of George III. The final paragraph formally declares the Colonies' independence.

This version of the text uses the punctuation of the original document, as reported by the Independence Hall Association (IHA). For more information about the Declaration, including its signers and rough drafts, visit **www.ushistory. org/declaration**.

THE DECLARATION OF INDEPENDENCE
IN CONGRESS, JULY 4, 1776
The unanimous Declaration of the thirteen united States of America

When in the Course of human events it becomes necessary for one people to dissolve the political bands which have connected them with another and to assume among the powers of the earth, the separate and equal station to which the Laws of Nature and of Nature's God entitle them, a decent respect to the opinions of mankind requires that they should declare the causes which impel them to the separation.

We hold these truths to be self-evident, that all men are created equal, that they are endowed by their Creator with certain unalienable Rights, that among these are Life, Liberty and the pursuit of Happiness.—That to secure these rights, Governments are instituted among Men, deriving their just powers from the consent of the governed; that whenever any Form of Government becomes destructive of these ends, it is the Right of the People to alter or to abolish it, and to institute new Government, laying its foundation on such principles and organizing its powers in such form, as to them shall seem most likely to effect their Safety and Happiness. Prudence, indeed, will dictate that Governments long established should not be changed for light and transient causes; and accordingly all experience hath shewn that mankind are more disposed to suffer, while evils are sufferable than to right themselves by abolishing the forms to which they are accustomed. But when a long train of abuses and usurpations, pursuing invariably the same Object evinces a design to reduce them under absolute Despotism, it is their right, it is their duty, to throw off such Government, and to provide new Guards for their future security.—Such has been the patient sufferance of these Colonies; and such is now the necessity which constrains them to alter their former Systems of Government. The history of the present King of Great Britain is a history of repeated injuries and usurpations, all having in direct object the establishment of an absolute Tyranny over these States. To prove this, let Facts be submitted to a candid world.

He has refuted his Assent to Laws, the most wholesome and necessary for the public good.

He has forbidden his Governors to pass Laws of immediate and pressing importance, unless suspended in their operation till his Assent should be obtained; and when so suspended, he has utterly neglected to attend to them.

He has refused to pass other Laws for the accommodation of large districts of people, unless those people would relinquish the right of Representation in the Legislature, a right inestimable to them and formidable to tyrants only.

He has called together legislative bodies at places unusual, uncomfortable, and distant from the depository of their Public Records, for the sole purpose of fatiguing them into compliance with his measures.

He has dissolved Representative Houses repeatedly, for opposing with manly firmness his invasions on the rights of the people.

He has refused for a long time, after such dissolutions, to cause others to be elected, whereby the Legislative Powers, incapable of Annihilation, have returned to the People at large for their exercise; the State remaining in the mean time exposed to all the dangers of invasion from without, and convulsions within.

He has endeavoured to prevent the population of these States; for that purpose obstructing the Laws for Naturalization of Foreigners; refusing to pass others to encourage their migrations hither, and raising the conditions of new Appropriations of Lands.

He has obstructed the Administration of Justice by refusing his Assent to Laws for establishing Judiciary Powers.

He has made Judges dependent on his Will alone for the tenure of their offices, and the amount and payment of their salaries.

He has erected a multitude of New Offices, and sent hither swarms of Officers to harass our people and eat out their substance.

He has kept among us, in times of peace, Standing Armies without the Consent of our legislatures.

He has affected to render the Military independent of and superior to the Civil Power.

He has combined with others to subject us to a jurisdiction foreign to our constitution, and unacknowledged by our laws; giving his Assent to their Acts of pretended Legislation:

For quartering large bodies of armed troops among us:

For protecting them, by a mock Trial from punishment for any Murders which they should commit on the Inhabitants of these States:

For cutting off our Trade with all parts of the world:

For imposing Taxes on us without our Consent:

For depriving us in many cases, of the benefit of Trial by Jury:

For transporting us beyond Seas to be tried for pretended offences:

For abolishing the free System of English Laws in a neighbouring Province, establishing therein an Arbitrary government, and enlarging its Boundaries so as to render it at once an example and fit instrument for introducing the same absolute rule into these Colonies:

For taking away our Charters, abolishing our most valuable Laws and altering fundamentally the Forms of our Governments:

For suspending our own Legislatures, and declaring themselves invested with power to legislate for us in all cases whatsoever.

He has abdicated Government here, by declaring us out of his Protection and waging War against us.

He has plundered our seas, ravaged our Coasts burnt our towns, and destroyed the lives of our people.

He is at this time transporting large Armies of foreign Mercenaries to compleat the works of death, desolation, and tyranny, already begun with circumstances of Cruelty & Perfidy scarcely parallelled in the most barbarous ages, and totally unworthy the Head of a civilized nation.

He has constrained our fellow Citizens taken Captive on the high Seas to bear Arms against their Country, to become the executioners of their friends and Brethren, or to fall themselves by their Hands.

He has excited domestic insurrections amongst us, and has endeavoured to bring on the inhabitants of our frontiers, the merciless Indian Savages whose known rule of warfare, is an undistinguished destruction of all ages, sexes and conditions.

In every stage of these Oppressions We have Petitioned for Redress in the most humble terms: Our repeated Petitions have been answered only by repeated injury.

A Prince, whose character is thus marked by every act which may define a Tyrant, is unfit to be the ruler of a free people.

Nor have We been wanting in attentions to our British brethren. We have warned them from time to time of attempts by their legislature to extend an unwarrantable jurisdiction over us. We have reminded them of the circumstances of our emigration and settlement here. We have appealed to their native justice and magnanimity, and we have conjured them by the ties of our common kindred. to disavow these usurpations, which would inevitably interrupt our connections and correspondence. They too have been deaf to the voice of justice and of consanguinity. We must, therefore, acquiesce in the necessity, which denounces our Separation, and hold them, as we hold the rest of mankind, Enemies in War, in Peace Friends.

We, therefore, the Representatives of the United States of America, in General Congress, Assembled, appealing to the Supreme Judge of the world for the rectitude of our intentions, do, in the Name, and by Authority of the good People of these Colonies, solemnly publish and declare, That these United Colonies are, and of Right ought to be Free and Independent States, that they are Absolved from all Allegiance to the British Crown, and that all political connection between them and the State of Great Britain, is and ought to be totally dissolved; and that as Free and Independent States, they have full Power to levy War, conclude Peace contract Alliances, establish Commerce, and to do all other Acts and Things which Independent States may of right do.—And for the support of this Declaration, with a firm reliance on the protection of Divine Providence, we mutually pledge to each other our Lives, our Fortunes and our sacred Honor.

Index

See also Accommodations and Restaurant indexes, below.

RESTAURANTS

A Guide for Every Type of Traveler

FROMMER'S® COMPLETE GUIDES

For independent leisure or business travelers who value complete coverage, candid advice, and lots of choices in all price ranges.

These are the most complete, up-to-date guides you can buy. Count on Frommer's for exact prices, savvy trip planning, sightseeing advice, dozens of detailed maps, and candid reviews of hotels and restaurants in every price range. All Complete Guides offer special icons to point you to great finds, excellent values, and more. Every hotel, restaurant, and attraction is rated from zero to three stars to help you make the best choices.

UNOFFICIAL GUIDES

For honeymooners, families, business travelers, and anyone else who values no-nonsense, *Consumer Reports*–style advice.

Unofficial Guides are ideal for those who want to know the pros and cons of the places they are visiting and make informed decisions. The guides rank and rate every hotel, restaurant, and attraction, with evaluations based on reader surveys and critiques compiled by a team of unbiased inspectors.

FROMMER'S® IRREVERENT GUIDES

For experienced, sophisticated travelers looking for a fresh, candid perspective on a destination.

This unique series is perfect for anyone who wants a cutting-edge perspective on the hottest destinations. Covering all major cities around the globe, these guides are unabashedly honest and down-right hilarious. Decked out with a retro-savvy feel, each book features new photos, maps, and neighborhood references.

FROMMER'S® WITH KIDS GUIDES

For families traveling with children ages 2 to 14.

Here are the ultimate guides for a successful family vacation. Written by parents, they're packed with information on museums, outdoor activities, attractions, great drives and strolls, incredible parks, the liveliest places to stay and eat, and more.

Visit Frommers.com

WILEY
Now you know.

A Guide for Every Type of Traveler

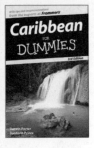

FOR DUMMIES® TRAVEL GUIDES

For curious, independent travelers.

The ultimate user-friendly trip planners, combining the broad appeal and time-tested features of the For Dummies guides with Frommer's accurate, up-to-date information and travel expertise. Written in a personal, conversational voice, For Dummies Travel Guides put the fun back into travel planning. They offer savvy, focused content on destinations and popular types of travel, with current and extensive coverage of hotels, restaurants, and attractions.

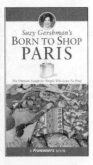

SUZY GERSHMAN'S BORN TO SHOP GUIDES

For avid shoppers seeking the best places to shop worldwide.

These savvy, opinionated guides, all personally researched and written by shopping guru Suzy Gershman, provide detailed descriptions of shopping neighborhoods, listings of conveniently located hotels and restaurants, easy-to-follow shopping tours, accurate maps, size conversion charts, and practical information about shipping, customs, VAT laws, and bargaining. The handy pocket size makes it easy to carry them in your purse while you shop 'til you drop.

FROMMER'S® $-A-DAY GUIDES

For independent travelers who want the very best for their money without sacrificing comfort or style.

The renowned series of guides that gave Frommer's its start is the only budget travel series for grown-ups—travelers with limited funds who still want to travel in comfort and style. The $-a-Day Guides are for travelers who want the very best values, but who also want to eat well and stay in comfortable hotels with modern amenities. Each guide is tailored to a specific daily budget and is filled with money-saving advice and detailed maps, plus comprehensive information on sightseeing, shopping, nightlife, and outdoor activities.

FROMMER'S® PORTABLE GUIDES

For short-term travelers who insist on value and a lightweight guide, including weekenders and convention-goers.

Frommer's inexpensive, pocket-sized Portable Guides offer travelers the very best of each destination so that they can make the best use of their limited time. The guides include all the detailed information and insider advice for which Frommer's is famous, but in a more concise, easy-to-carry format.

Visit Frommers.com

WILEY

Now you know.

Frommer's Complete Guides

Frommer's
Southeast Asia
With Coverage of the Best Temples and Beaches

The only guide independent travelers need to make smart choices, avoid rip-offs, get the most for their money, and travel like a pro.

Frommer's Alaska
Frommer's Alaska Cruises & Ports of Call
Frommer's Amsterdam
Frommer's Argentina & Chile
Frommer's Arizona
Frommer's Atlanta
Frommer's Australia
Frommer's Austria
Frommer's Bahamas
Frommer's Barcelona, Madrid & Seville
Frommer's Beijing
Frommer's Belgium, Holland & Luxembourg
Frommer's Bermuda
Frommer's Boston
Frommer's Brazil
Frommer's British Columbia & the Canadian Rockies
Frommer's Brussels & Bruges with Ghent & Antwerp
Frommer's Budapest & the Best of Hungary
Frommer's California
Frommer's Canada
Frommer's Cancun, Cozumel & the Yucatan
Frommer's Cape Cod, Nantucket & Martha's Vineyard
Frommer's Caribbean
Frommer's Caribbean Cruises & Ports of Call
Frommer's Caribbean Ports of Call
Frommer's Carolinas & Georgia
Frommer's Chicago
Frommer's China
Frommer's Colorado
Frommer's Costa Rica
Frommer's Cuba

Frommer's Denmark
Frommer's Denver, Boulder & Colorado Springs
Frommer's England
Frommer's Europe
Frommer's European Cruises & Ports of Call
Frommer's Florence, Tuscany & Umbria
Frommer's Florida
Frommer's France
Frommer's Germany
Frommer's Great Britain
Frommer's Greece
Frommer's Greek Islands
Frommer's Hawaii
Frommer's Hong Kong
Frommer's Honolulu, Waikiki & Oahu
Frommer's Ireland
Frommer's Israel
Frommer's Italy
Frommer's Jamaica
Frommer's Japan
Frommer's Las Vegas
Frommer's London
Frommer's Los Angeles with Disneyland® & Palm Springs
Frommer's Maryland & Delaware
Frommer's Maui
Frommer's Mexico
Frommer's Montana & Wyoming
Frommer's Montreal & Quebec City
Frommer's Munich & the Bavarian Alps
Frommer's Nashville & Memphis
Frommer's Nepal
Frommer's New England
Frommer's Newfoundland & Labrador
Frommer's New Mexico
Frommer's New Orleans
Frommer's New York City
Frommer's New Zealand
Frommer's Northern Italy
Frommer's Norway
Frommer's Nova Scotia, New Brunswick & Prince Edward Island
Frommer's Oregon

Frommer's Ottawa
Frommer's Paris
Frommer's Peru
Frommer's Philadelphia & the Amish Country
Frommer's Portugal
Frommer's Prague & the Best of the Czech Republic
Frommer's Provence & the Riviera
Frommer's Puerto Rico
Frommer's Rome
Frommer's San Antonio & Austin
Frommer's San Diego
Frommer's San Francisco
Frommer's Santa Fe, Taos & Albuquerque
Frommer's Scandinavia
Frommer's Scotland
Frommer's Seattle
Frommer's Shanghai
Frommer's Sicily
Frommer's Singapore & Malaysia
Frommer's South Africa
Frommer's South America
Frommer's Southeast Asia
Frommer's South Florida
Frommer's South Pacific
Frommer's Spain
Frommer's Sweden
Frommer's Switzerland
Frommer's Texas
Frommer's Thailand
Frommer's Tokyo
Frommer's Toronto
Frommer's Turkey
Frommer's USA
Frommer's Utah
Frommer's Vancouver & Victoria
Frommer's Vermont, New Hampshire & Maine
Frommer's Vienna & the Danube Valley
Frommer's Virginia
Frommer's Virgin Islands
Frommer's Walt Disney World® & Orlando
Frommer's Washington, D.C.
Frommer's Washington State

Frommer's

WILEY

Available at bookstores everywhere.

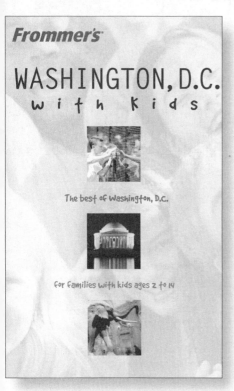

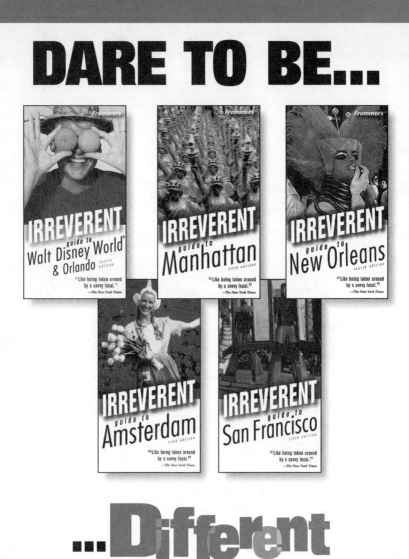

FROMMER'S® COMPLETE TRAVEL GUIDES

Alaska
Alaska Cruises & Ports of Call
American Southwest
Amsterdam
Argentina & Chile
Arizona
Atlanta
Australia
Austria
Bahamas
Barcelona, Madrid & Seville
Beijing
Belgium, Holland & Luxembourg
Bermuda
Boston
Brazil
British Columbia & the Canadian
  Rockies
Brussels & Bruges
Budapest & the Best of Hungary
Calgary
California
Canada
Cancún, Cozumel & the Yucatán
Cape Cod, Nantucket & Martha's
  Vineyard
Caribbean
Caribbean Ports of Call
Carolinas & Georgia
Chicago
China
Colorado
Costa Rica
Cruises & Ports of Call
Cuba
Denmark
Denver, Boulder & Colorado
  Springs
England
Europe
Europe by Rail
European Cruises & Ports of Call

Florence, Tuscany & Umbria
Florida
France
Germany
Great Britain
Greece
Greek Islands
Halifax
Hawaii
Hong Kong
Honolulu, Waikiki & Oahu
India
Ireland
Italy
Jamaica
Japan
Kauai
Las Vegas
London
Los Angeles
Maryland & Delaware
Maui
Mexico
Montana & Wyoming
Montréal & Québec City
Munich & the Bavarian Alps
Nashville & Memphis
New England
Newfoundland & Labrador
New Mexico
New Orleans
New York City
New York State
New Zealand
Northern Italy
Norway
Nova Scotia, New Brunswick &
  Prince Edward Island
Oregon
Ottawa
Paris
Peru

Philadelphia & the Amish
  Country
Portugal
Prague & the Best of the Czech
  Republic
Provence & the Riviera
Puerto Rico
Rome
San Antonio & Austin
San Diego
San Francisco
Santa Fe, Taos & Albuquerque
Scandinavia
Scotland
Seattle
Shanghai
Sicily
Singapore & Malaysia
South Africa
South America
South Florida
South Pacific
Southeast Asia
Spain
Sweden
Switzerland
Texas
Thailand
Tokyo
Toronto
Turkey
USA
Utah
Vancouver & Victoria
Vermont, New Hampshire &
  Maine
Vienna & the Danube Valley
Virgin Islands
Virginia
Walt Disney World® & Orlando
Washington, D.C.
Washington State

FROMMER'S® DOLLAR-A-DAY GUIDES

Australia from $50 a Day
California from $70 a Day
England from $75 a Day
Europe from $85 a Day
Florida from $70 a Day
Hawaii from $80 a Day

Ireland from $80 a Day
Italy from $70 a Day
London from $90 a Day
New York City from $90 a Day
Paris from $90 a Day
San Francisco from $70 a Day

Washington, D.C. from $80 a
  Day
Portable London from $90 a Day
Portable New York City from $90
  a Day
Portable Paris from $90 a Day

FROMMER'S® PORTABLE GUIDES

Acapulco, Ixtapa & Zihuatanejo
Amsterdam
Aruba
Australia's Great Barrier Reef
Bahamas
Berlin
Big Island of Hawaii
Boston
California Wine Country
Cancún
Cayman Islands
Charleston
Chicago
Disneyland®
Dominican Republic
Dublin

Florence
Frankfurt
Hong Kong
Las Vegas
Las Vegas for Non-Gamblers
London
Los Angeles
Los Cabos & Baja
Maine Coast
Maui
Miami
Nantucket & Martha's Vineyard
New Orleans
New York City
Paris

Phoenix & Scottsdale
Portland
Puerto Rico
Puerto Vallarta, Manzanillo &
  Guadalajara
Rio de Janeiro
San Diego
San Francisco
Savannah
Vancouver
Vancouver Island
Venice
Virgin Islands
Washington, D.C.
Whistler

FROMMER'S® NATIONAL PARK GUIDES

Algonquin Provincial Park
Banff & Jasper
Family Vacations in the National
  Parks

Grand Canyon
National Parks of the American
  West
Rocky Mountain

Yellowstone & Grand Teton
Yosemite & Sequoia/Kings
  Canyon
Zion & Bryce Canyon

FROMMER'S® MEMORABLE WALKS

Chicago
London

New York
Paris

San Francisco

FROMMER'S® WITH KIDS GUIDES

Chicago
Las Vegas
New York City

Ottawa
San Francisco
Toronto

Vancouver
Walt Disney World® & Orlando
Washington, D.C.

SUZY GERSHMAN'S BORN TO SHOP GUIDES

Born to Shop: France
Born to Shop: Hong Kong,
  Shanghai & Beijing

Born to Shop: Italy
Born to Shop: London

Born to Shop: New York
Born to Shop: Paris

FROMMER'S® IRREVERENT GUIDES

Amsterdam
Boston
Chicago
Las Vegas
London

Los Angeles
Manhattan
New Orleans
Paris
Rome

San Francisco
Seattle & Portland
Vancouver
Walt Disney World®
Washington, D.C.

FROMMER'S® BEST-LOVED DRIVING TOURS

Austria
Britain
California
France

Germany
Ireland
Italy
New England

Northern Italy
Scotland
Spain
Tuscany & Umbria

THE UNOFFICIAL GUIDES®

Beyond Disney
California with Kids
Central Italy
Chicago
Cruises
Disneyland®
England
Florida
Florida with Kids
Inside Disney

Hawaii
Las Vegas
London
Maui
Mexico's Best Beach Resorts
Mini Las Vegas
Mini Mickey
New Orleans
New York City
Paris

San Francisco
Skiing & Snowboarding in the
  West
South Florida including Miami &
  the Keys
Walt Disney World®
Walt Disney World® for
  Grown-ups
Walt Disney World® with Kids
Washington, D.C.

SPECIAL-INTEREST TITLES

Athens Past & Present
Cities Ranked & Rated
Frommer's Best Day Trips from London
Frommer's Best RV & Tent Campgrounds
  in the U.S.A.
Frommer's Caribbean Hideaways
Frommer's China: The 50 Most Memorable Trips
Frommer's Exploring America by RV
Frommer's Gay & Lesbian Europe
Frommer's NYC Free & Dirt Cheap

Frommer's Road Atlas Europe
Frommer's Road Atlas France
Frommer's Road Atlas Ireland
Frommer's Wonderful Weekends from
  New York City
The New York Times' Guide to Unforgettable
  Weekends
Retirement Places Rated
Rome Past & Present

Travel Tip: He who finds the best hotel deal has more to spend on facials involving knobbly vegetables.

Hello, the Roaming Gnome here. I've been nabbed from the garden and taken round the world. The people who took me are so terribly clever. They find the best offerings on Travelocity. For very little cha-ching. And that means I get to be pampered and exfoliated till I'm pink as a bunny's doodah.

travelocity®

1-888-TRAVELOCITY / travelocity.com / America Online Keyword: Travel

Travel Tip: Make sure there's customer service for any change of plans — involving friendly natives, for example.

One can plan and plan, but if you don't book with the right people you can't seize le moment and canoodle with the poodle named Pansy. I, for one, am all for fraternizing with the locals. Better yet, if I need to extend my stay and my gnome nappers are willing, it can all be arranged through the 800 number at, oh look, how convenient, the lovely company coat of arms.

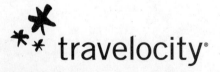